03615

The Independent Study Catalog

NUCEA's Guide to Independent Study Through Correspondence Instruction 1983-1985

JOAN H. HUNTER, Editor

The Guide Committee of the Division of Independent Study, NUCEA

Robert W. Batchellor, University of Illinois; Chair
Hugh Harris, University of Oklahoma
Norma Harwood, Graduate School, USDA
C. K. Lee, Mississippi State University
Clair Woodward, Indiana State University
Roger G. Young, University of Missouri

Division of Independent Study, Administrative Committee Officers

Richard Moffitt, Ohio University; Chair
Norman Lowenthal, University of North Carolina; Chair-Elect
Kathryn R. Allen, University of Texas; Secretary
Deborah Nelson, University of Minnesota; Immediate Past Chair

Administrative Committee

Robert W. Batchellor, University of Illinois
Nancy Colyer, University of Kansas
Frank DiSilvestro, Indiana University
Charles W. Hartsell, University of Tennessee
Lawrence J. Keller, Indiana University
Harold Markowitz, University of Florida
Monty McMahon, University of Nebraska
Deborah Nelson, University of Minnesota
John Strain, Texas Tech University
Roger G. Young, University of Missouri

A Peterson's Guides Publication for the National University Continuing Education Association

Published by Peterson's Guides for the National University Continuing Education Association.

Additional copies of this book may be ordered prepaid ($5.95 plus $1.25 postage/handling) from: NUCEA Book Order Department, Peterson's Guides, P.O. Box 2123, Princeton, New Jersey 08540.

Cover design: Janice Conklin
Printed in the United States of America.

ISBN 0-87866-180-8
ISSN 0733-6020

10 9 8 7 6 5 4 3 2 1

The membership of the National University Continuing Education Association (NUCEA) consists of universities, colleges, and related organizations and their professional staffs who are dedicated to lifelong learning and public service. Through continuing education programs, NUCEA members make their institutional and community resources available to youth and adults, individuals and groups, volunteer organizations, government units, and private industry. They are devoted to the enrichment of living by making continuing education available—and attractive—to individuals in every segment of the population.

For other Peterson's publications of interest, please see the annotated book list at the back of this volume.

CONTENTS

In parentheses following each institution's name is each division of instruction offered by the institution for courses listed in this Guide, as follows: E = Elementary, H = High School, C = College, G = Graduate, NC = Noncredit.

Contents

Correspondence study is individual instruction by mail. It is flexible, convenient, and personalized. Students can enroll at any time, study at home, and set their own pace. Work is done on a one-to-one basis with faculty experts who design the instructional materials, guide course study, and prepare specific responses to the submitted work.

Correspondence study helps a wide range of people meet their educational needs and objectives. Individuals who are unable to come to the classroom, or who prefer to study at their own pace, can earn credit toward a degree or toward a professional certificate. Adults with work and family responsibilities can gain new job skills and learn about new subjects for personal enrichment or satisfaction. With an increased choice of courses, students can:

- Solve campus scheduling problems
- Meet prerequisites
- Gain advanced standing
- Explore new subjects
- Study while away from campus
- Accelerate their programs

Credit courses are offered for every academic level from elementary school (including preschool) through graduate work, although the emphasis is on high school and undergraduate courses.

Noncredit courses and courses offered for certification purposes are also available from most NUCEA institutions.

Additional study opportunities for off-campus students include telecourses, courses by newspaper, group study, credit by examination, and external degree programs. (See the section on "Special Study Opportunities," page 6.)

Correspondence study is demanding. Since the printed word and written exchanges are the principal learning media, it is essential that students have reasonably strong reading and writing skills. While the flexibility of correspondence study is one of its distinct advantages, it is also one of its greatest hazards. Many people who enroll in correspondence courses do not finish them. Being on their own, unsupported by the discipline of the traditional classroom, correspondence students *must* have the initiative and self-reliance to develop good study habits, work independently, and establish and maintain a regular schedule of study.

In general, students who complete correspondence courses feel that they have learned as much as—if not more than—they would have in a traditional course, but they often feel that the experience has been more rigorous. Those who are able to take responsibility for their own education find correspondence study rewarding and satisfying. Anyone contemplating enrollment in correspondence study should give careful consideration to both the advantages and drawbacks of the correspondence study method before enrolling.

Accreditation

Members of the National University Continuing Education Association (NUCEA) are primarily degree-granting institutions of higher education accredited by one of the six regional accrediting associations that hold membership in the Council on Postsecondary Accreditation (COPA) or, with the approval of the Board of Directors, by any other accrediting agency that holds membership in COPA. In addition, member institutions must have substantial programs in continuing education.

Approximately 300 colleges and universities in the United States currently have met the requirements for membership in NUCEA. Of these, over 70 have established correspondence courses which are included in the accreditation of the institution offering the courses. Some high school courses are approved by state educational agencies.

Two NUCEA members in this book are not degree-granting institutions and, therefore, are not accredited by one of the six regional accrediting associations. The Graduate School, USDA, is a non-degree-granting institution that offers a continuing education program for working adults. Its courses are designed to meet the specific needs of federal employees, but most are applicable to the private sector as well. The Home Study Institute is the extension division for the Association of Seventh-day Adventist Colleges and Universities in North America. These schools are accredited by their regional accrediting associations. The Home Study Institute is accredited by the National Home Study Council.

In addition, Canada does not have a system of regional accreditation; rather, qualified degree-granting institutions are chartered by their respective provincial governments—the nearest Canadian equivalent to U.S. accreditation. The two Canadian universities in this book, Athabasca University and Memorial University of Newfoundland, have such charters.

The six U.S. regional accrediting associations that hold membership in COPA are the New England Association of Schools and Colleges, the Middle States Association of Colleges and Schools, the North Central Association of Colleges and Schools, the Northwest Association of Schools and Colleges, the Southern Association of Colleges and Schools, and the Western Association of Schools and Colleges. The National Home Study Council, which also holds membership in COPA, is the specialized accrediting body for institutions and organizations that have been established primarily to offer programs for home study.

Admission

In general, correspondence study courses listed in this Guide are open to all individuals, regardless of age or previous educational experience. Applications are usually accepted without entrance examinations or proof of prior educational experience. However, some institutions may impose certain requirements before they will accept correspondence study credit, and some courses or programs may require previous study or experience. *Students should determine the requirements of the resident institution or of the particular program for which they intend to earn credit before enrolling in a correspondence study course.* An institution's catalog will list both general admission requirements and prerequisites for individual courses.

Enrollment, Registration Forms, and Catalogs

Usually, to enroll in a correspondence course, the student simply fills in the registration form provided by the institution and sends a check or money order to cover tuition and fees, as listed in the catalog.

After reviewing the course names shown in this Guide, prospective students may obtain registration forms and catalogs, providing descriptions of the courses, from all NUCEA member institutions listed in this Guide. In addition, some institutions offer detailed information about individual courses, such as a course outline, which will be sent upon request. To obtain these materials, the contact name and address or telephone number shown at the top of each institution's entry in the "Institutions and Correspondence Courses Offered" section should be used.

Time Requirements

Courses are not tied to an academic year. Students can enroll at their convenience and work at their own pace. An enrollment is valid for a certain period, often for twelve months, and most institutions provide for extensions of time. Some institutions, however, do have regulations prohibiting rapid completion of a course to ensure the validity of the learning experience and to enable the instructor to respond to the student's work before the final examination. (Such regulations are listed in the institutional catalog.) Within these broad limits, students determine the time it will take to complete their program of study.

The Mechanics of Correspondence Study

While each institution has somewhat different policies and procedures, correspondence study generally follows the pattern outlined below.

1. **Study Materials.** A study guide that includes a list of required textbooks and materials, supplementary information, specific learning assignments, and all other details neces-

sary for successful completion of the course is sent to a student as soon as the enrollment process is complete. (Details of the enrollment procedures are contained in the institutional catalog.)

2. **Textbooks.** The required textbooks and other course materials may be obtained in a number of ways, depending upon the procedures of the particular institution. They are either ordered at the time of enrollment and sent at the same time as the study guide, ordered from a designated bookstore after the receipt of the study guide, or obtained from local sources. Audiovisual aids, if any, are usually sent with the study guide, and charges for these are indicated in the catalogs of the individual institutions.

3. **Study Assignments.** The study guide divides the course into segments, usually called "lessons" or "assignments." Each lesson directs certain study activities, such as readings, self-check exercises, occasional field trips, interviews, and any other activities that are appropriate to the subject area of the course. These are done in preparation for the successful completion of the next step.

4. **Assignments for Evaluation.** After the study activities in each lesson are completed, a written assignment is submitted for evaluation. This varies widely from course to course, and sometimes even within the same course. A written assignment may consist of prescribed objective or essay questions, a report, a paper, or any other example of written work. In some instances, the student has the opportunity to submit a cassette, answering questions or performing orally.

These assignments are evaluated and returned as soon as possible. The instructor expresses a judgment of the quality of the assignment, most often with descriptive comments and a grade.

5. **Examinations.** Credit courses usually require one or two examinations that must be taken under the supervision of an authorized proctor. Generally, students are able to arrange for supervision of the examination at an institution near their home. In some cases, noncredit courses also require final examinations. Examination forms are sent directly to the proctor, and the completed examination is returned to the institution by the proctor after it has been administered to the student. Specific details are given in the catalog or the study guide of the enrolling institution.

6. **Records and Transcripts.** A record of a completed correspondence course is maintained by each institution. For credit courses, the student's grade is recorded, and transcripts of the credit earned may be requested from the institution. Generally, a small charge is assessed for each transcript. For noncredit and certificate courses, some institutions award a certificate of completion or Continuing Education Units (CEUs).

Credit

Limits of Correspondence Study Credit. Students who wish to apply credit earned through correspondence study to a college degree or a high school diploma should consult the resident institution **before enrolling in a correspondence study course.** Most institutions have limitations on the number and kinds of correspondence study credits that they will accept.

Some accredited colleges and universities offer a college degree or high school diploma mainly or entirely by correspondence. Students interested in external degree or diploma programs should contact the institution of their choice and inquire if such a program is available.

College Credit. Academic credit is measured in semester or quarter hours. The equivalent value of semester and quarter hours is as follows:

1⅓ semester hours	=	2 quarter hours
2 semester hours	=	3 quarter hours
2⅔ semester hours	=	4 quarter hours
3 semester hours	=	4½ quarter hours
3⅓ semester hours	=	5 quarter hours

Grades and Transcripts for College Courses. Each institution follows its regular grading policies in evaluating the work of independent students. When a course is completed, a grade report is sent to the student, the grade is recorded at the institution, and a transcript will be sent to any address designated by the student in a written request. Most institutions charge for additional transcripts.

Transfer of Credit. Credit earned in correspondence study courses taken from a regionally accredited institution is normally transferable from one institution to another; however, since policies and degree requirements vary among universities and colleges, students are urged to consult appropriate officials of the institution from which they expect to receive a degree to ascertain whether credit is transferable. If course work is taken from an institution that is not regionally accredited, the transferability of the course work for credit to another institution may be more difficult.

High School Credit. Most institutions offering credit for high school courses tailor their credit units to coincide with the method most common in the state system they serve. Generally, courses are offered for one-half unit of credit (equal to one semester of course work in a regular classroom) or for one-quarter credit, depending on the state system.

High schools that offer a diploma by correspondence award credit on a semester basis of one-half unit of credit per course. Prior approval of correspondence work should be obtained from the resident high school to ensure acceptance of the credit.

Enrollment in Credit Courses on a Noncredit Basis. Most NUCEA member universities and colleges accept enrollments in credit courses on a noncredit basis and take special interest in students who are studying for personal satisfaction without regard to credit.

The Continuing Education Unit or CEU. The Continuing Education Unit (CEU) is used to recognize and measure achievement in noncredit courses. The CEU is defined as 10 contact hours of participation in an organized continuing education experience under responsible sponsorship, capable direction, and qualified instruction. Individuals interested in receiving CEUs for noncredit courses listed in this Guide should request information from the institutions offering the courses.

Financial Considerations

The costs associated with taking a correspondence course vary from course to course and from one college or university to another. Each institution sets its own pricing structure, based upon the expenses associated with a course and the institution's overall fee policies.

In general, a person can expect direct charges for tuition, textbooks, and other necessary course materials, and sometimes for postage and handling fees.

Tuition. Tuition for college and university credit courses is most often figured on the basis of a set amount per credit hour, regardless of whether the institution uses the semester or quarter unit of measurement. (Example: Accounting 101 offered for 3 credits at $30 per credit requires a tuition of $90, to be sent with the registration: $3 \times \$30 = \$90$.)

Tuition for noncredit and high school courses is usually stated as a flat fee for the course rather than in terms of a set amount per credit hour. For such courses, no computation is needed in completing a registration form.

Tuition rates for credit courses at NUCEA member institutions currently range from a low of $20 to a high of $60 per credit unit. Rates for high school and noncredit courses also vary widely and change frequently. Before enrolling, any interested person should check the catalog of the individual institution for current rates.

Textbooks. In most cases, the cost of textbooks is not included in the cost of the course, and students must purchase their own books. The catalog of the enrolling institution or the study guide that is mailed to a student who enrolls will indicate exactly how the texts can be obtained and the exact or approximate cost. The cost can vary widely, depending upon the number and kinds of texts. In a few instances, the study guide is also the text.

Course Materials. Course materials always include a study guide, which is usually provided as part of the initial cost. In addition, workbooks, procedure manuals, kits, audiotapes, phonograph records, filmstrips or slides, photographs, or various other audiovisual aids may be required, in which case the cost is borne by the student. Although these items are sometimes quite expensive, they often cost only a few dollars. In some cases, the material is loaned to the student, who pays a deposit that is partially refunded when the material is returned. Details about costs for course materials will be listed in the institution's catalog or in the study guide.

Postage. In all cases, students bear the cost for postage on items that they mail. Some institutions levy a postage fee for items mailed to their students, such as course materials and returned assignments. Rates for domestic postage are not high, but rates for postage to foreign countries can be a major expense, with total foreign postage for course materials and returned assignments being as much as $50. When possible, students going to foreign countries should enroll before they leave the United States, taking their textbooks and course materials with them in order to avoid both postage and tariff expenses. An institution's catalog will identify policies and costs for foreign enrollments.

Handling and Special Fees. Some institutions charge a handling fee to help them defray the cost for processing materials and registration. The fee range is from $2 to $15. In addition, rental fees, usually small, are sometimes charged for special course materials.

Payment Plans. Most institutions require at the time of registration full payment of all charges due. The preferred method of payment is a check or money order. In a few instances, textbooks are paid for separately. Some institutions accept credit cards, and a few have some form of partial or deferred payment plan, but the number of institutions that offer these options is small. It is necessary to examine the catalog or bulletin of the institution to determine its payment policies.

Financial Aid

Financial aid is not as readily available for correspondence study students as it is for traditional classroom students. However, the sources listed below can occasionally provide some financial aid, and students who require aid should explore all applicable possibilities.

Employers. Many employers provide educational benefits to their employees. These are generally administered through the personnel or benefits department of the organization.

Unions. Unions have been negotiating educational benefits into many of their contracts. The union's business manager would be the person to provide information.

Veterans' and Military Benefits. All of the federal veterans' assistance acts have had provisions for financial assistance for college and university correspondence study, usually under the term independent study. The amount and type of assistance varies, and it is best to check with a local Veterans Administration office for specific details.

Active-duty military personnel have two specific options available to them for financial assistance. The first is "in-service" VA benefits. Under specified conditions, a person on active duty may be eligible for financial assistance under the Veterans' Readjustment Benefits Act of 1966, as amended, or under the Post–Vietnam Era Veterans' Educational Assistance Program (Public Law 94-502, as amended). The second is "tuition assistance," which comes from the military person's respective service. In either case, the Educational Service Officer of the base, post, or ship can provide information.

In addition to the federal government's VA tuition assistance plans, some states have educational benefits for veterans. Questions and inquiries should be directed to the state veterans or military affairs offices.

Vocational Rehabilitation. Nearly all states provide financial benefits for the education of persons with some form of handicap. A number of states include correspondence study in the forms of education allowable for benefits. Any inquiries should be directed to a state's department of vocational rehabilitation.

Institutional Aid. A small number of colleges and universities have a limited amount of financial aid available for correspondence study. Guide users should carefully examine the catalogs of the institutions for financial aid information or consult the office of financial aid.

Special Study Opportunities

While the focus of this Guide is on correspondence courses, other related opportunities are frequently offered by independent study programs. To obtain details, you will need to contact an institution's independent study office.

Some institutions use periodic or regular **television** or **radio** broadcasts to supplement independent study instruction. Courses having **newspaper components** are also occasionally offered. These courses are generally limited both by time of offering and by geographical area. Some correspondence courses also use **audiocassette tape recordings, laboratory kits,** and **computer programs** as instructional tools.

Such opportunities as **credit by examination, tutorial study,** and **directed study** are also available at some institutions. Credit by examination allows students to receive degree credit for successful scores on the various tests of the College-Level Examination Program (CLEP) or on institutionally administered tests. Tutorial study makes it possible for students to arrange for correspondence instruction in courses not otherwise offered by the correspondence method. Directed study allows the student to substitute special projects or submissions for the assignments usually required in a course. Some correspondence courses include **optional class meetings.** Others lend themselves well to **group study** projects for the benefit of friends or associates who wish to study the same subject. In some instances such projects may include visits with the instructor or other experts. These variations of the traditional correspondence format are especially helpful for students with special needs.

In many states correspondence courses serve as a way of meeting requirements for **professional certification** or recertification. Teachers constitute one major group that has benefited in this way, though persons in other professions should also determine if correspondence study might allow them to complete requirements in their fields. Some institutions offer entire **series of correspondence courses** in specific subject areas, sometimes in relation to vocational or professional requirements. Often a certificate of completion is awarded to individuals who complete the full series.

Related in concept to correspondence courses are **external degree programs,** which are now offered by numerous colleges and universities in the United States. These flexible programs make it possible for students to complete all degree requirements with little or no attendance on campus. Correspondence courses are one of several ways that requirements toward external degrees may be met.

Special Advice and Counseling

As a prospective nontraditional student in correspondence study, you face three major questions that institutions have helped traditional students answer but to which you must find the answers yourself: (1) Why am I taking this course? (2) What options are available to me for taking this course? (3) How do I study?

Anyone contemplating independent study should determine the answers to these questions before enrolling in a correspondence course. In some instances, the correspondence study offices of the colleges and universities can answer a few questions, particularly in reference to their own institution. However, it is best to get official information from the admissions office, the academic department in which you wish to take a course, or the counseling service of the college or university. In addition, it is vitally important that you seek formal counseling and advice from the institution's counseling service, particularly when college or high school credit is involved. Very few of the correspondence study offices have the personnel to answer questions or to advise you, and in many cases they are not authorized to do so.

The section below offers you help in finding answers to the three basic questions.

Question 1. Why am I taking this course?

If the course is for college or high school credit, you must ask:
  a. Will any college or high school accept the course credit and apply it toward my graduation?
  b. How many credits by correspondence will be accepted toward graduation?
  c. Will my institution accept credit for correspondence work transferred from another institution?
  d. Will credits earned by correspondence be accepted in my area of concentration?

If the course is being taken for certification and not for degree purposes, you should ask:
  a. What are the certification requirements?
  b. Will the course be acceptable to the certifying agency?
  c. How many credits can be earned or how much work can be done by correspondence?

Question 2. What options are available to me for taking this course?

Some institutions offer optional ways of taking their courses or of earning degree credit. For these, you should ask:
  a. Is the pass-fail option acceptable to my college or certifying agency?
  b. Is credit by examination acceptable?
  c. Is credit for experiential learning available and acceptable?
  d. Are the external degree programs that some institutions offer by correspondence acceptable to other colleges, employers, and certifying agencies?

Question 3. How do I study?

Since successful correspondence study requires really good study habits, you should take the time to evaluate your own approach to studying before you enroll. Assess your study habits and decide, with as much objectivity as possible, how well you think you can study on your own.

Schedule. It is extremely important to set aside a regularly scheduled time for study. If you have not been involved in academic pursuits recently, you may find that your career, family, hobbies, or social and civic commitments leave little time for studying. In order to make room for study in your schedule, you may have to sacrifice other activities. To help you decide how to do this, keep a record for a week or two of how you spend your time, and see what you are willing to give up. Since you won't have the built-in pacing of classes and preestablished deadlines set by instructors, you may find it hard to make progress unless you set up a definite study schedule.

Try to schedule this study for a time when you will be mentally fresh and able to devote at least one hour to your work. Think of the hour as "reserved time," but don't get discouraged if you can't always keep the schedule. After all, one of the advantages of correspondence study is its flexibility. Just keep in mind that regularly scheduled study is the ideal, and make it your goal. If you miss too many study periods, revise your schedule.

Where to Study. You'll find it easier to focus on your work if you arrange an appropriate environment for study. You will need a place that is quiet and free from reminders of other responsibilities. You might consider a public library if your home does not offer a suitable place.

Reading Skills. The abilities to read with comprehension and to retain what you read are necessary for real learning to take place, especially in correspondence study. These skills can be developed by concentrating on what you read and by taking frequent pauses to organize and review the material in your mind. At the end of a study session, you should review everything you have read, making special notes of important points learned in that session.

Writing Skill. Writing is also an essential skill. Written assignments provide the main channel of communication between you and your instructor. In your written assignments, you collect and synthesize what you've learned, demonstrating to your instructor that you are progressing according to plan. An elementary skill in writing is prerequisite to taking a correspondence course, but it is also a skill that is developed further in most courses.

In preparing written assignments, you must pay careful attention to instructions and be sure you understand what is being asked. Are you willing to work at preparing a good answer? You may need to develop a brief outline of your responses or draft your answer and check it over before preparing a final copy. Organization, grammar, and writing style are important in most correspondence study courses. If your skills in these areas need improvement, you may need to do extra work in a writing handbook.

If you do not understand some point, inquiries can be made only by mail. Responses to your instructor's comments on your lessons, requests for clarification of comments, and all other exchanges between you and your instructor will take time. This written interaction with your instructor can be very rewarding, but you must be willing to take the initiative, and you must have a great deal of patience in order to make it worthwhile.

Completing a correspondence course is not always easy. It requires a great deal of self-discipline and work. However, the benefits you derive can also be great. In addition to the mastery of subject matter, the study skills you develop should help you to undertake other difficult educational tasks with more confidence.

Division of Independent Study, NUCEA

The Division of Independent Study is one of five divisions within the Council on Continuing Education Delivery Systems of the National University Continuing Education Association (NUCEA). Over 70 of the Association's 300 or so members offer correspondence study programs, and the Division of Independent Study provides the professional base for the various staff members of these programs.

The purpose of the Division of Independent Study is to provide a means of developing guidelines for programs of high quality and to offer professional training for staff members. The division also acts to promote the concept of correspondence study, encourage research, and offer a forum for the exchange of information.

The Independent Study Catalog: NUCEA's Guide to Independent Study Through Correspondence Instruction is one of the major projects of the division. The intent of this book is to offer a composite picture of the college- and university-based correspondence study opportunities that are currently available through 72 of the NUCEA member institutions. The Guide provides in convenient form the title and course number, sponsoring department, credit value, and level of instruction of each correspondence course.

The National University Continuing Education Association is the premier association concerned with the postsecondary continuing education movement in the United States. It currently has a membership of approximately 300 colleges, universities, and other educational institutions, all of which have a commitment to the part-time student.

The purposes of the Association are:

1. To provide a means by which institutions may cooperate to advance the concept of lifelong, continuing education
2. To encourage institutions to communicate and cooperate
3. To provide leadership in research and professional judgment
4. To maintain liaison with other agencies and organizations
5. To publish journals, newsletters, and educational materials
6. To provide information as a representative of university extension interests

The Independent Study Catalog: NUCEA's Guide to Independent Study Through Correspondence Instruction is just that, a "guide" to colleges and universities providing correspondence instruction and to the courses offered by those institutions. There are three ways of using the Guide:

Finding Courses

1. **Finding Courses from a Particular Institution.** If you have already decided to study at a particular institution listed in this book, simply find the institution's page number in the Contents, turn to its page in the "Institutions and Correspondence Courses Offered" section, and review the courses offered.

   Course names are grouped together on an institution's page by academic or subject-matter area. To the right of each course name is the department offering the course, the number of the course, the number of credits earned by its successful completion, and the level of instruction.

2. **Finding Courses Through the Index.** To locate a course in a particular category, turn to the Index. Listed there alphabetically are broad subject-matter areas, representing major academic disciplines, with more specific areas grouped under them in two levels of subordination. The name of an area is followed by the **code number of each institution** offering one or more courses in that area, plus a **code letter for each kind of course** the institution offers in that area (E = Elementary, H = High School, C = College, G = Graduate, N = Noncredit; see the following section entitled "Kinds of Courses"). Institutional code numbers and their corresponding institutional names are listed numerically and alphabetically both in the Contents and on the pages in the "Institutions and Correspondence Courses Offered" section of this book.

   After finding a subject-matter area of interest in the Index, make a note of its **NCES number** (to left of area name) and the code number of each institution offering a course in that area. Identify the institution and page number in the Contents, and turn to the institution's page. Or turn directly to its page in the "Institutions and Correspondence Courses Offered" section, where the code numbers and corresponding institutional names are listed numerically and alphabetically at the beginning of institutional entries and—in dictionary fashion—at the top of pages.

   To find the specific course name(s) on an institution's page, run down the numerical listing of NCES numbers (first column) until you find the one that corresponds to the subject-matter area of interest. You will find the name of each course offered by the institution in that category, the department offering it, the number of the course, the number of credits earned by its successful completion, and the level of instruction. The abbreviations used for department names are explained on page 11.

3. **Finding a Specific Subject-Matter Area.** If you have difficulty locating a subject-matter area in the Index, refer to the Alphabetical Listing of Subject-Matter Areas, which precedes the Index. Then turn to the Index and follow the instructions above.

This Guide does not and cannot provide all of the information needed to actually enroll in a course. To do that, the prospective student must use the address at the top of an institution's entry to request a copy of the correspondence study catalog and specific information about enrolling. Some institutions offer detailed information about individual courses, such as an outline of the course, which will be sent upon request.

In general, course selection should follow an assessment of the purpose for which the course is needed: (1) for credit to apply toward a degree or diploma; (2) for personal development, without regard to credit; or (3) for certification in a professional program.

Students who expect to apply credit earned through correspondence study to a degree or a diploma should contact the resident institution for counseling and advice in order to ensure that the credit will be accepted. (See the sections on "Credit," page 3, and "Special Advice and Counseling," page 6.)

Kinds of Courses

Five kinds of correspondence study courses are listed in this Guide:

1. **Elementary School Courses.** One institution (Home Study Institute) offers correspondence courses for preschool through grade eight.

2. **High School Courses.** Courses covering virtually every area of high school study are offered by NUCEA member institutions. A few institutions offer high school diplomas by correspondence, but in most cases correspondence credit is accepted by the local high school, which issues the diploma. Students should have approval from the diploma-granting institution before enrolling in a correspondence study course.

3. **College Courses.** A great variety of courses offering undergraduate credit are provided.

4. **Graduate Courses.** Only a few institutions offer courses for graduate credit only, although some offer courses that are applicable toward credit at either the upper-division collegiate **or** graduate level. Some institutions will not accept correspondence study courses as credit toward a graduate degree.

5. **Noncredit Courses.** Courses designed to meet the job-related, professional, cultural, or personal needs of individuals who do not desire credit are offered by most NUCEA institutions. In addition, most courses that are offered for credit can **also** be taken on a noncredit basis.

In addition to offering single courses, some institutions offer complete programs of courses to meet certification, vocational, or professional needs. Students should consult an institution's catalog to obtain specific information.

In general, vocational courses are not listed in the Guide. Individuals who are interested in this type of study can secure information about such courses from institutions that are members of the National Home Study Council. The NHSC is the accrediting association for private, proprietary correspondence schools and publishes the **Directory of Accredited Home Study Schools.** A copy of this directory can be obtained from the National Home Study Council, 1601 Eighteenth Street, N.W., Washington, D.C. 20009.

Course Information and Abbreviations

All information in the section entitled "Institutions and Correspondence Courses Offered" has been supplied by the institutions themselves in response to a 1982 NUCEA survey. If any part of the usual data does not appear with a course listing, it was not supplied by the college or university, and students are advised to write directly to the institution for further information.

NCES Code Numbers. The first number appearing on a line with the name of a course in an institution's entry is the National Center for Education Statistics (NCES) number, as determined by the institution offering the course. This number derives from the taxonomy, or system of numerical classification, of educational subject matter prepared by the National Center for Education Statistics. This taxonomy is also used as a basis for the alphabetical listing of subject-matter areas and the subject-matter index in the Guide, although only those portions of it that relate to courses in this book are shown. Those who are interested in reviewing the complete taxonomy, including definitions of individual subject-matter areas, should write for a copy of the handbook, **A Classification of Educational Subject Matter,** for sale by the Superintendent of Documents, U.S. Government Printing Office, Washington, D.C. 20402; Stock Number 017-080-01876-4.

Course Names and Numbers. Wherever possible, course names have been written in full, with the name of the department offering the course and the course number appearing to the right. However, because of space limitations, it has been necessary to abbreviate long course names. If there is any question about the specific content of a course, students should write directly to the institution offering the course, referring to the department and course number.

Credit Code. The credits earned by successful completion of courses listed in this Guide are indicated by the number of credits followed, usually, by S or Q to indicate the specific number of semester or quarter credit hours. (Example: 2S = 2 semester hours.) One or more of the following codes may also be used:

TN = tenth unit
QT = quarter unit
TH = third unit
HF = half unit
2T = two-thirds unit
TQ = three-quarters unit
1U = one unit
NC = noncredit
VC = credit varies

Level of Instruction. The level of instruction for each course listed in this Guide is indicated by one of the following codes:

L = Lower-division collegiate
U = Upper-division collegiate
B = Upper-division collegiate **or** graduate
G = Graduate
V = Vocational certificate
D = Developmental or remedial
H = High school
E = Elementary

Department Name Abbreviations. The name of the department offering a course has usually been abbreviated and is shown to the right of the course name, although the names of some departments are written in full (e.g., Art = Art). In some instances, the same abbreviation may be used for the name of two different departments (e.g., Fin = Finance **or** Finnish), but the title of the course should make the correct department name clear. The following list defines abbreviations appearing in this Guide:

A&S	Anthropology and Sociology
AAM	Academy of Adventist Ministers
Acc, Acct, Acctg, Acta	Accounting
ACS	Agronomic Crop Sciences, American Cultural Studies
AdmSt	Administrative Studies
AdSci	Administrative Science
ADT	Automotive Diesel Technology
Adv	Advertising
AE	Aerospace Engineering, Architectural Engineering
AEB	Agriculture, Economics, and Business
Aero	Aerospace
AfAmS	Afro-American Studies
AFHE	Administration, Foundations, and Higher Education
AG, AmGvt	American Government
Agcr, Agri	Agriculture
AgEc, AgEcn, AgEco, AgrEc	Agricultural Economics
AgEd	Agricultural Education
Agro	Agronomy
AgSci	Agricultural Science
AH, AmH, AmHis	American History
AJ	Administration of Justice

Alg	Algebra
AmCul	American Culture
AmL	American Literature
AmS, AmSt	American Studies
AnHis	Ancient History
AnSci	Animal Sciences
Ant, Anth, Anthr, Anthy	Anthropology
AOM	Administrative Office Management
Arab	Arabic
ArAEg	Aerospace and Aeronautical Engineering
Arch	Architecture
Archy	Archaeology
ArHis, Art H	Art History
ArPlg	Architecture and Planning
ArsIn	Arson Investigation
As St	Asian Studies
Ast, Astro	Astronomy
Atmo, AtmSc, AtS	Atmospheric Sciences
ATS	Advanced Texas Studies
Avi	Aviation
BA, BAdm, BuAd, BusAd	Business Administration
Bact	Bacteriology
BC, BuC, BuCom	Business Communications
BCEd	Business Career and Education
BDEOA	Business-Distributive Education and Office Administration
B Ecn, BusEc	Business and Economics
Bio, Biol	Biology
Bioch	Biochemistry
Bk, Bkp	Bookkeeping
BL, B Law, BuL, BuLaw, BusL, BusLw	Business Law
BlgIn	Building Inspection
B Log	Business Logistics
BlS	Black Studies
Bmet	Biometeorology
BOA	Business Office Administration
BOE	Business and Office Education
Bot	Botany
Brdcs	Broadcasting
BTWr	Business and Technical Writing
Bus, Buss	Business
BusEc	Business Economics
BusEd	Business Education
BusHS	Business, high school level
BVEd	Business and Vocational Education
C&I, CI, CrIns, CuIns	Curriculum and Instruction
CCJ	Corrections and Criminal Justice
C E, ChmEg	Chemical Engineering
CE	Consumer Economics
CEd, CntEd, ConEd	Continuing Education
CEE	Civil and Environmental Engineering
CET	Civil Engineering Technology
ChD	Child Development
ChEd	Child Education
Chem	Chemistry
ChFam	Child and Family Studies
Chi	Chinese, Chinese Studies
Cit, Citz	Citizenship
Civ	Civics
CivEg, CivEn	Civil Engineering
CJ, CJus, CJust, Cr, CrJ, Crm J, CrmJ	Criminal Justice
Clas, Class, Clsx	Classics
ClCiv	Classical Civilization

C Lit, CmLit, ComLi	Comparative Literature
ClLL	Classical Languages and Literature
ClP	Clinical Psychology
ClTx, CTe	Clothing and Textiles
CmDis, Com D, ComD	Communicative Disorders
CmpSc	Computer Science
COAS	College of Arts and Sciences
ComEg	Computer Engineering
Comm	Commerce
CommS, ComS	Communication Studies
Comms, Commu	Communications
CP	Career Planning
CPo	Comparative Politics
CpScM	Computer Science and Mathematics
Crim	Criminology
CRK	Clerical Record Keeping
CrW	Creative Writing
CSLP	Civil Service License Preparation
Curr	Curriculum
DA	Dental Assisting
Dan	Danish
Dem	Democracy
DeP	Developmental Psychology
Des, Dsgn	Design
DesT	Design Technology
DGTS	Division of General and Technology Studies
DisEd	Distributive Education
DLT	Dental Laboratory Technology
DP	Data Processing
Dr, DrEd, DriEd	Driver Education
DRad	Dental Radiology
DySc	Dairy Science
EAsLL	East Asian Languages and Literature
Econ	Economics
EconM	Economics and Mathematics
EdAd	Educational Administration
EdF	Educational Foundations
EdFA	Educational Foundations and Administration
EdFM	Educational Foundations and Media
EdP, EdPsy	Educational Psychology
EdPSF	Educational Psychology and Social Foundations
EdRes	Educational Research
Educ	Education
E E, EEg	Electrical Engineering
EED	Education: Emotional Disorders
E G	Engineering Graphics
Eg, Engr	Engineering
EH, EngHS	English, high school level
EIn	Engineering: Industrial
ElEd, Elem	Elementary Education
ElIns	Electrical Inspection
EMech, EngrM, EnMec	Engineering Mechanics
Eng, Engl	English
EngAS	Engineering and Applied Science
EngLL	English Language and Literature
EngrT	Engineering Technology
EngSc, EnSci	Engineering Science
EnSt	Environmental Studies
Entm, Ento, Entom	Entomology
EntSc	Entomological Science
EnvD	Environmental Design
EnvSB	Environmental Study Board
EnvSc	Environmental Science
EPA	Educational Policies and Administration

EPR	Educational Psychology and Research
ErSci, ESci	Earth Science
ESI	Engineering Systems: Industrial
ESLR	Educational Systems and Learning Resources
EuH	European History
EVI	Education: Visually Impaired
ExtEd	Extension Education
FA, FnArt	Fine Arts
Famil	Family
FamSc	Family Science
FdAcg	Fundamentals of Accounting
FdNut, FN	Food and Nutrition
Fin, Finan	Finance
Fin, Finn	Finnish
FinL	Finance Law
FL, F Lan, ForLa, ForLg, FornL	Foreign Languages
FLHS	Family and Local History Studies
Flklr, Folk	Folklore
FMHCS	Family Management and Housing and Consumer Science
FmTng	Fireman Training
FNIM	Food, Nutrition, and Institution Management
FOM	Fundamentals of Mathematics
For	Forestry
ForES	Forestry and Environmental Studies
ForLL	Foreign Languages and Literature
For M	Forestry Management
Fors	Forensics
FoS	Food Studies
FPro	Fire Protection
Fr, Frech, Fren, Frnch	French
FrC	Fruit Culture
FrEng	Freshman English
FRM	Family Resource Management
FrSci	Fire Science
FSc	Food Science
FScN, FSN	Food Science and Nutrition
FSHA	Food Service and Housing Administration
FSoS	Family Social Science
FSS	Food Services for Supervisors
FueEg	Fuels Engineering
GB, GBu, GenBs	General Business
GBio	General Biology
GC	General College
GED	General Educational Development
GeGe	Geography/Geology
Gen	Genetics
Genea	Genealogy
GenEg, GEngr	General Engineering
GenS, GenSt, GStd	General Studies
Geo, Geog	Geography
Geo, Geom	Geometry
Geol, Gly	Geology
GeoSc	Geological Science
Geosc	Geosciences
Ger, Germ, GL, Grmn	German
Geron	Gerontology
GIBM	Growth in Basic Mathematics
GInt	Government and International Studies
GnKno	General Knowledge
GnMth	General Mathematics
Gov, Govmt, Govt	Government
Graph	Graphic Arts (Design)
GrBks	Great Books

Greek, Grk	Greek
GRP	Graded Reading Program
GS	General Science
GSS	General Social Science
Guid, Guida	Guidance
H, Hea, Heal, Hlth, Hth	Health
H&FL	Home and Family Living
H&R	Hobbies and Recreation
H&S	Health and Safety
HDFL	Human Development and Family Life
HE, HEd, HEdu, HelEd, HlEd	Health Education
Heb	Hebrew
H Ec, HEco, HmEc, HomeE	Home Economics
HeS, HSci	Health Sciences
HFS	Housing and Food Service
HFT	Hospitality, Food, Tourism
His, Hist, Histo	History
HLang	High School Languages
HM	Home Management
HMath	High School Mathematics
HNFSM	Human Nutrition and Food Service Management
HoA	Hotel Administration
HOM	History of Mathematics
HomLv	Home Living
Hort	Horticulture
HPER, HPRe	Health, Physical Education, and Recreation
HPSc	History and Philosophy of Science
HRP	Health, Recreation, and Physical Education
HS	Home Study
HsHCA	Hospital and Health Care Administration
HSMgt	Health Systems Management
HSSci	High School Science
HSSSt	High School Social Studies
HuDev	Human Development
Hum, Hums	Humanities
HuN	Human Nutrition
IA	Introductory Algebra
ID	Interior Design
ID, IDS, Int	Interdisciplinary Studies
I E, IndEg, InEg	Industrial Engineering
I Ed, IndEd, InEd	Industrial Education
IEOR	Industrial Engineering/Operations Research
IFS	Individual and Family Studies
IM	Instructional Media
InArt, IndA	Industrial Arts
InCo	Interpersonal Communication
InDec	Interior Decoration
IndTc	Industrial Technology
Ins	Insurance
InSci	Instructional Science
IntBu	International Business
IntEn	Interior Environment
IntRe	International Relations
IR	Industrial Relations
Irr	Irrigation
IS	Individual Study
ISCS	Intermediate Science Curriculum Study
Ital	Italian
Jap, Jpn	Japanese
JMC	Journalism and Mass Communications
Jou, Journ, Jrnl	Journalism
JrEng	Junior English

JusAd	Justice Administration
Just	Justice
LA&S	Liberal Arts and Sciences
LabSt, LS	Labor Studies
LAEP	Landscape Architecture and Environmental Planning
LAm, LAS	Latin American Studies
Lang	Languages
LanHS	Languages, high school level
Law	Law, preparation for
LEA	Law Enforcement Administration
LegS	Legal Studies
LeiSt	Leisure Studies
LET	Law Enforcement Technology
LfSci	Life Sciences
LibSc	Library Sciences
LibSt	Liberal Studies
Ling	Linguistics
LiS	Literary Studies
Lit	Literature
LMT	Library Media Technology
MAF	Marriage and Family
Man, Mgmt	Management
ManSc	Management Science
Mar, Mktg	Marketing
Mat, Math, Ms	Mathematics
MatHS	Mathematics, high school level
MCE	Mathematics and Consumer Economics
MComm	Mass Communications
M E, ME	Mechanical Engineering
MEAS	Mathematics, Engineering, and Applied Sciences
Mech	Mechanics
Met, Meteo	Meteorology
MgtFn	Management/Finance
Micro	Microbiology
Milit	Military Sciences
Misc	Miscellaneous Studies
MLang	Modern Languages
Multi	Multidisciplinary Studies
Musc	Music
Museo	Museology
MWPE	Men/Women Physical Education
NatrS	Natural Sciences
NELL	Near Eastern Languages and Literature
NF	Nutrition and Foods
NFS	Nutrition and Food Science
Nor	Norwegian
Nrsng, Nurs	Nursing
Nutr	Nutrition
NutSc	Nutritional Sciences
OAd, OffAd	Office Administration
Ocean	Oceanography
OR	Outdoor Recreation
OrStu	Oriental Studies
PA, PAd	Police Administration
PCD	Principles of Curriculum Design
PCG	Psychology, Counseling and Guidance
PEdu, Ph Ed, PhyEd	Physical Education
PerDv	Personal Development
Persi	Persian
Pharm	Pharmacology
Phi, Phil, Philos	Philosophy

Photo	Photography
Ph Sc, PhSc, PhySc, PS	Physical Sciences
Phys	Physics
PIAD	Problems in American Democracy
Pl Ed	Paralegal Education
PlS, PlSci	Plant Sciences
PlSc, Pol, PolS, PolSc, PolSi, PoSci, PS, PSci	Political Science
Plsh	Polish
P N G	Petroleum and Natural Gas
Polic	Police Science
Port	Portuguese
P Path, PPath	Plant Pathology
PPe	Psychology of Personality
PrArt	Practical Arts
PreS	Preschool
PrPM	Procurement and Property Management
PSS	Plant and Soil Science
Psy, Psych	Psychology
PTher	Physical Therapy
PuAdm, PubAd	Public Administration
PubHl	Public Health
PuR	Public Relations
QBA	Quantitative Business Analysis
QM	Quantitative Methods
R&TC	Research and Training Center in Mental Retardation
RadTV	Radio/Television
R E, RE, RlEs	Real Estate
Read	Reading
Rec	Recreation
RecEd	Recreation Education
Rehab	Rehabilitation Studies
Rel, Relig, Rel S, Rlgn, Rl St	Religion (Religious Studies)
Res	Resources
Rhet	Rhetoric
RHIM	Restaurant, Hotel, and Institutional Management
RngSc	Range Science
Rom	Romance Languages
RS	Reading and Study Skills
Rus	Russian
RuSoc	Rural Sociology
Scand	Scandinavian Languages
ScEd	Science Education
Sci, Scien	Science
SDA, SpDrA	Speech and Dramatic Arts
SEAS	Southeast Asian Studies
SecEd	Secondary Education
Secr, SecTr	Secretarial Training
S Ed	Safety Education
Sfty	Safety
Shhnd, Shthd	Shorthand
SHS	Speech and Hearing Sciences
Slav	Slavic Languages and Literature
Soc, Soci, Socio	Sociology
SocHS	Social Studies, high school level
SocS, SoS, So Sc, SoSci	Social Science
SocSt, SoStu, SS, S St	Social Studies
SocW, SocWk, SoW. SoWk	Social Work
SoEng	Sophomore English
SoJu	Society and Justice
SoP	Social Psychology
SOP	Secretarial Office Procedure

SoWel	Social Welfare
Sp	Speech and Theater
Span	Spanish
Spch, Speec	Speech
SpCHR	Speech Communications and Human Relations
SPEA	School of Public and Environmental Affairs
SpEd	Special Education
SrEng	Senior English
SST	Security Safety Technology
Sta, Stat	Statistics
StSki, StSkl	Study Skills
Sur	Surveying
Swed	Swedish
TAM	Theoretical and Applied Mechanics
TchPr	Teacher Preparation
Tech	Technology
TEd	Teacher Education
ThArt	Theater Arts
Theo	Theology
Thy	Therapy
Trans	Transportation
Trg	Trigonometry
TV	Television
Type, Typg	Typewriting
UC	University College
UnStu	University Studies
UrPl	Urban Planning
VetSc	Veterinary Sciences
VisAr	Visual Arts
VocT, VoTec	Vocational and Technical Education, Vocational Technology
VTIE	Vocational, Trade, and Industrial Education
WCiv	Western Civilization
WGS	World Geography Studies
Wildl, WlfSc	Wildlife Science
WmSt, Wom S, WomSt	Women's Studies
Writ, Writi	Writing
WshMg	Watershed Management
YthLd	Youth Leadership
Zoo, Zool, Zoolo	Zoology

① ADAMS STATE COLLEGE

Mr. Donald F. Eden
Director of Extension
Extension Division
Adams State College
Alamosa, Colorado 81102
Phone: (303) 589-7671

Gifted high school students are permitted to enroll in undergraduate courses for credit. Overseas enrollment accepted for college courses.

NCES No.	Course Title	Dept.	Course No.	Credits	Level
	College courses				
060799	Programming in BASIC	Math	110	3S	L
070516	Math for elem teachers	Math	108A	3S	L
070516	Math for elem teachers	Math	108B	3S	L
160301	Arithmetic	Math	103	3S	L
160302	Algebra	Math	104	3S	L
160406	Differential equations	Math	327	3S	U
161201	Math for business majors	Math	206A	3S	L
161201	Math for business majors	Math	206B	3S	L

② ARIZONA STATE UNIVERSITY

Dr. Obadiah S. Harris
Assistant Dean
University Continuing Education
Arizona State University
ASB 110
Tempe, Arizona 85287
Phone: (602) 965-6563

Only in exceptional cases are gifted high school students permitted to enroll in undergraduate courses for credit. Overseas enrollment accepted for college courses.

NCES No.	Course Title	Dept.	Course No.	Credits	Level
	College courses				
040101	Elementary accounting	Acc	AC211	3S	L
040101	Elementary accounting	Acc	AC212	3S	L
040601	Business communications	Bus	AD233	3S	L
040604	Business report writing	Bus	AD431	3S	U
040904	Principles of management	Mgmt	MG301	3S	U
0499	Elmnts of bus enterprise	Bus	AD101	3S	L
0499	Business law	Bus	AD305	3S	U
0499	Business law	Bus	AD306	3S	U
051199	Urban communication	Commu	CO494	3S	U
051199	Intercultural communicats	Commu	CO363	3S	U
051199	Crisis communication	Com	CO478	3S	U
051199	Death and dying	Commu	CO494	3S	U
051199	Woman and communications	Commu	CO494	3S	U
051199	Communication and aging	Commu	CO479	3S	U
051199	Medical communication	Commu	CO494	3S	U
051299	Nonverbal communication	Commu	CO330	3S	U
051299	Sktch skls for spch clncn	SHS	CD294	1S	L
070302	Comm behav in elem school	Educ	CO415	3S	U
070303	Prin & curr of sec schls	Educ	SE311	3S	U
070520	Educational psychology	Educ	ED310	3S	U
070520	St: principles of beh mod	EdP	ED494	3S	U
070610	Reading in content areas	Educ	RD467	2S	U
070610	Practicum rdg in content	Educ	RD480	1S	U
070806	Mental retardation	Educ	SP312	3S	U
070811	Nature of stuttering	SHS	494	3S	U
0799	Exploration of education	Educ	ED111	3S	L
0799	History of American educ	Educ	SP411	3S	U
100313	Human nutrition	HmEc	FO141	3S	L
100602	Family relationships	HmEc	FA331	3S	U
120299	Books for children	LiS	LI494	3S	U
1210	Elementary French	Frnch	FR101	4S	L
1210	Elementary French	Frnch	FR102	4S	L
1210	Intermediate French	Frnch	FR201	4S	L
1210	Intermediate French	Frnch	FR202	4S	L
121007	French literature	Frnch	FR321	3S	U
121007	French literature	Frnch	FR322	3S	U
1225	Elementary Spanish	Span	SP101	4S	L
1225	Elementary Spanish	Span	SP102	4S	L
1225	Intermediate Spanish	Span	SP201	4S	L
1225	Intermediate Spanish	Span	SP202	4S	L

NCES No.	Course Title	Dept.	Course No.	Credits	Level
160302	Intermediate algebra	Math	MA106	3S	L
160302	College algebra	Math	MA117	3S	L
160302	Math for soc life mgmt	Mat	MA141	2S	L
160602	Plane trigonometry	Math	MA118	3S	L
2099	Intro to psychology	Psych	PG100	3S	L
2099	Prsnlty thry and research	Psych	PG315	3S	U
2099	Abnormal psychology	PGS	PG466	3S	U
220201	Principles of economics	Econ	EC201	3S	L
220201	Principles of economics	Econ	EC202	3S	L
220423	Japan	His	HI477	3S	U
220423	Japan	His	HI478	3S	U
220423	Asian civilizations	His	HI305	3S	U
220423	Asian civilizations	His	HI306	3S	U
220426	Hitler—man and legend	Hist	HI434	3S	U
220432	United States history	Hist	HI103	3S	L
220432	United States history	Hist	HI104	3S	L
220432	American urban history	Hist	HI419	3S	U
220432	American urban history	Hist	HI420	3S	U
220432	The West in 20th century	His	HI369	3S	U
220432	The American Southwest	His	HI425	3S	U
220433	Western civilization	Hist	HI102	3S	L
220453	Modern American cltrl his	Hist	HI304	3S	U
220453	Contemporary America	Hist	HI411	3S	U
220501	American national govt	PolSc	PO300	3S	U
220501	Az constitution and govt	PolSc	PO311	2S	U
220602	The criminal justice syst	CrJ	CR100	3S	L
220602	The police function	CrJ	CR306	3S	U
220602	Criminal justice theory	CrJ	CR402	3S	U
220605	Courtship and marriage	Socio	SO305	3S	U
220699	Intro to sociology	Socio	SO101	3S	L
220699	Socio of deviant behavior	Socio	SO340	3S	U

③ ARKANSAS STATE UNIVERSITY

Ms. Doris H. Cruce
Correspondence Coordinator
Correspondence Division
Arkansas State University
Center for Continuing Education
P.O. Box 2260
State University, Arkansas 72467
Phone: (501) 972-3052

Gifted high school students are permitted to enroll in undergraduate courses for credit. Overseas enrollment accepted for college courses. High school students must have a letter of approval from their principal. The time limit for a correspondence course is no more than six months or no less than three weeks. A person can, however, take out an extension for three months at an extra cost of $8.

NCES No.	Course Title	Dept.	Course No.	Credits	Level
	College courses				
030402	Fundamentals of theater	Drama	12283	3S	L
030402	History of the theater I	Drama	42263	3S	U
030402	History of the theater II	Drama	42313	3S	U
040101	Principles of acctg I	Acctg	20003	3S	L
040101	Principles of acctg II	Acctg	20013	3S	L
040601	Business communications	Bus	25063	3S	L
040904	Office mgmt and control	Mgmt	45043	3S	U
041106	Supervisory management	Mgmt	21613	3S	L
050399	Motion picture appreciatn	Commu	32283	3S	U
0509	Principles of pub relatns	Jrnl	30003	3S	U
061104	Intro to computer DP	DP	24823	3S	L
070201	History of education	Educ	31543	3S	U
070302	Lit for the elem school	Educ	20023	3S	
070302	Foundations of education	ElEd	10003		L
120302	Lit, philo, & religion I	EngLL	20003	3S	L
120302	Lit, philo, & religion II	EngLL	20013	3S	L
120305	Freshman English I	Engl	10003	3S	L
120305	Freshman English II	Engl	10013	3S	L
150303	Biological science	Bio	10003	3S	L
150307	Genetics	Bio	33103	3S	U
150899	Physical science	PhySc	10203	3S	L
160301	Basic mathematics	Math	10103	3S	L
160301	Mod math for elem tchrs I	Math	20113	3S	L
160302	College algebra	Math	14023	3S	L
190502	Health and safety	PhyEd	23513	3S	L
200102	History of psychology	Psych	32513	3S	U
200504	Child psychology	Psych	32533	3S	U

NCES No.	Course Title	Dept.	Course No.	Credits	Level
200504	Adolescent psychology	Psych	32543	3S	U
200599	Personal and social psych	Psych	22513	3S	L
200702	Social psychology	Psych	32523	3S	U
200804	Educational psychology	Psych	32553	3S	U
210304	Intro to law enforcement	LET	10023	3S	L
220201	Principles of economics I	Econ	20313	3S	L
220201	Principles of econ II	Econ	20323	3S	L
220306	World regional geography	Geog	32603	3S	U
220306	Geog of US and Canada	Geog	32613	3S	U
220428	History of Arkansas	Hist	21783	3S	L
220432	The United States to 1876	Hist	21763	3S	L
220432	The US since 1876	Hist	21773	3S	L
220433	World civ to 1660	Hist	12013	3S	L
220433	World civ since 1660	Hist	12023	3S	L
220501	United States government	PolSc	22313	3S	L
220606	Principles of sociology	Socio	22913	3S	L
220613	Social problems	Socio	22923	3S	L

(4) ATHABASCA UNIVERSITY

15015 123rd Avenue
Edmonton, Alberta T5V 1G9, Canada
Phone: (403) 452-3466

Enrollment on a noncredit basis accepted in all credit courses. Only in exceptional cases are gifted high school students permitted to enroll in undergraduate courses for credit. Enrollment from outside Canada not accepted. Athabasca specializes in undergraduate programs through distance education involving a variety of media. It serves adults who cannot or do not wish to attend a conventional university.

NCES No.	Course Title	Dept.	Course No.	Credits	Level
	College courses				
030399	Hist pop music 1: 1900-40	LibSt	285	3	L
030399	Hist pop music 2: 1940-70	LibSt	286	3	L
040108	Intro financial acctg	AdmSt	253	3	L
040108	Intermediate finan acctg	AdmSt	353	3	U
040111	Intro managerial acctg	AdmSt	254	3	L
040301	Intro to financial mgmt	AdmSt	370	3	U
040903	Commu & problem solving	AdmSt	377	3	U
040904	Administrative principles	AdmSt	232	3	L
040999	Motivation and management	AdmSt	319	6	U
041001	Intro to marketing	AdmSt	398	3	U
0411	Intro personnel mgmt	AdmSt	386	3	U
051103	Intro interpersonal commu	AdmSt	229	3	L
051103	Prac interpersonal commu	AdmSt	329	3	U
051103	Interpersonal commu, mgmt	AdmSt	243	3	L
060199	Computer science in admin	LibSt	245	3	L
0699	Computers in perspective	LibSt	205	6	L
0699	Science projects	LibSt	314	3	U
070509	Prin tchng/lrng hlth prof	LibSt	382	3	U
120201	Comp lit & great authors	LibSt	339	6	U
120201	Comp Canadian literature	LibSt	350	6	U
120299	Images of man in mod lit	LibSt	301	3	U
120299	Shakespeare 1	LibSt	324	3	U
120299	Trends in mod Brit drama	LibSt	332	3	U
120299	Lit of Canadian West	LibSt	337	6	U
120299	Joyce & Dostoevsky	LibSt	356	3	U
120299	Plays of Ibsen & Shaw	LibSt	392	3	U
120299	Nineteenth-cen Engl novel	LibSt	395	6	U
120299	Shakespeare 2	LibSt	396	3	U
120299	Twentienth-cen Engl novel	LibSt	397	6	U
120307	Literary forms & technol	LibSt	210	6	L
120307	Intro to Canadian lit	LibSt	302	6	U
120310	Writing skills	LibSt	255	3	L
1210	Ensemble: Fr for beginner	LibSt	103	6	L
1210	Sur le vif: 1st-yr French	LibSt	242	6	L
1210	Allez France: 2nd-yr Fren	LibSt	361	6	U
1210	Français pour tous	LibSt	312	3	U
121005	Vocabulary expansion	LibSt	375	3	U
121007	Intro à la lit Can-fran	LibSt	374	6	U
121007	Intro à la lit frança	LibSt	393	6	U
121010	Composition française	LibSt	401	3	U
1302	Commercial law	AdmSt	369	3	U
150304	World ecology	LibSt	201	6	L

NCES No.	Course Title	Dept.	Course No.	Credits	Level
150324	Le corps humain (Fr)	LibSt	104	3	L
150326	Human genetics	LibSt	341	3	U
150399	Human sexuality	LibSt	378	3	U
150401	Chemical principles	LibSt	209	6	L
150408	Organic chemistry	LibSt	320	3	U
1505	Understanding the earth	LibSt	231	6	L
150599	Our physical resources	LibSt	313	3	U
1599	Science projects	LibSt	314	3	U
1603	Algebra & analytic geom	LibSt	101	3	L
160401	Calculus	LibSt	212	6	L
160406	Ordinary diff equations	LibSt	376	3	U
160602	Trigonometry	LibSt	102	3	L
1608	Intro to statistics	LibSt	215	3	L
161101	Business mathematics	LibSt	244	3	L
161199	Undrstndng res in nursing	LibSt	325	3	U
1699	Science projects	LibSt	314	3	U
180405	East meets West	LibSt	360	3	U
2001	Intro psychology	LibSt	206	6	L
200406	Learning	LibSt	387	3	U
200504	Intro child development	LibSt	228	3	L
200504	Social psych/adult devmt	LibSt	381	3	U
200504	Psych de l'enfant (Fr)	LibSt	257	3	L
210199	Canadian public admin	AdmSt	390	3	U
2201	Intro human diversity	LibSt	207	6	L
220199	Contemporary native issue	LibSt	326	3	U
220199	Anthropology & the city	LibSt	394	3	U
220201	Macroeconomics	LibSt	246	3	L
220201	Microeconomics	LibSt	247	3	L
220301	Intro to human geography	LibSt	262	3	L
220305	Intro to physical geog	LibSt	261	3	L
220399	Man & environment	LibSt	317	6	U
220406	Marx to Freud	LibSt	306	6	U
220406	Wstrn thought bet wars	LibSt	310	6	U
220406	From Sumer to Athens	LibSt	248	3	L
220406	Rome & early Christianity	LibSt	249	3	L
220407	Era of world wars	LibSt	264	3	L
220425	Canadian his: 1500-1867	LibSt	224	3	L
220425	Canadian his: 1867-presnt	LibSt	225	3	L
220425	Hist of Canadian West	LibSt	338	6	U
220426	Revolutionary Europe	LibSt	263	3	L
220426	Intro to Renaissance	LibSt	300	3	U
2205	Power, control & lib dem	LibSt	214	3	L
220599	Intro Canadian govt & pol	LibSt	260	3	L
2206	Intro sociology	LibSt	208	6	L
2206	Sociological perspective	LibSt	315	6	U
220605	Family in world perspec	LibSt	384	3	U
220605	Sociology of the family	LibSt	316	3	U
220610	Sociology of deviance	LibSt	365	3	U
220614	Canadian urban developmnt	LibSt	303	6	U
220699	Sex roles	LibSt	349	3	U
220699	Technology and change	LibSt	259	3	L
2299	Intro human communities	LibSt	202	6	L
2299	Making sense of society	LibSt	226	6	L
2299	Res methods in social sci	LibSt	366	3	U

(5) AUBURN UNIVERSITY

Ms. Becky S. Dunning
Program Director
Independent Study, Office of Continuing Education
Auburn University
100 Mell Hall
Auburn, Alabama 36849
Phone: (205) 826-5100

Enrollment on a noncredit basis accepted in all credit courses. Gifted high school students are permitted to enroll in undergraduate courses for credit. Overseas enrollment accepted. Gifted high school students who wish to enroll must have the recommendation of their school's principal.

NCES No.	Course Title	Dept.	Course No.	Credits	Level
	College courses				
040601	Written business commu	Engl	EH415	3Q	U
040604	Bus & prof report writing	Engl	EH315	3Q	U
050402	Technical writing	Engl	EH304	3Q	U
0701	Development of voc ed	VEd	441	5Q	U
0706	Org of inst in Vo-Tech ed	VEd	474	5Q	U
070601	Prog & tchng in voc agr	VEd	414	5Q	U

NCES No.	Course Title	Dept.	Course No.	Credits	Level
0708	Probls in tchg dis adults	VEd	491	5Q	U
0799	Learning res in voc ed	VEd	456	5Q	U
100313	Nutrition and man	NF	112	5Q	L
120307	Literature in English	Engl	EH253	5Q	L
120307	The short story	EngLL	EH325	5Q	U
120307	Survey of American lit I	EngLL	EH357	5Q	U
120307	Survey of American lit II	EngLL	EH358	5Q	U
190104	Hist & principles of PE	HSci	201	3Q	U
1905	Health science	HSci	195	2Q	L
1905	School & community health	HSci	296	3Q	L
190704	Recreation leadership	HSci	386	3Q	U
190799	Principles of recreation	HSci	282	3Q	L
200901	Industrial psychology	Psych	PG561	5Q	U
2099	Psychology	Psych	PG011	5Q	L
220201	Principles of economics	Econ	EC201	5Q	L
220301	Cultural geog of the world	Geog	GY405	5Q	U
220302	Economic geography	Geog	GY302	5Q	U
220399	Principles of geography	Geog	GY102	5Q	L
220426	European hist 1500-1815	Hist	207	5Q	L
220427	History of Latin America	Hist	HY300	5Q	U
220428	History of Alabama	Hist	HY381	5Q	U
220432	Hist of the US to 1865	Hist	HY201	5Q	L
220432	Am syst & Jacksonian dem	Hist	HY403	5Q	U
220432	Hist of the US since 1865	Hist	202	5Q	L
220499	History of the West	Hist	HY371	5Q	U
220501	American government	PolSc	209	5Q	L
220511	American st & local govt	PolSc	PO210	5Q	L
220601	Community organization	Socio	SY362	5Q	U
220602	Criminology	Socio	SY302	5Q	U
220608	Rural social organization	Socio	SY461	5Q	U
220613	Social problems	Socio	SY202	5Q	L
220699	Introduction to sociology	Socio	SY201	5Q	L
220699	Minority groups	Socio	SY304	5Q	U

Noncredit courses

NCES No.	Course Title	Dept.	Course No.	Credits	Level
100702	Dietetic asst indep study	NF	DA	NC	L
100702	Dietetic asst supp pract	NF	DASP	NC	L

⑥ **BRIGHAM YOUNG UNIVERSITY**

Mr. Richard Eddy
Department Chairman
Independent Study
Brigham Young University
206 Harmon Continuing Education Building
Provo, Utah 84602
Phone: (801) 378-2868

Enrollment on a noncredit basis accepted in all credit courses. Gifted high school students are permitted to enroll in undergraduate courses for credit. The institution accepts overseas enrollment for high school, college, and noncredit courses.

NCES No.	Course Title	Dept.	Course No.	Credits	Level
	High school courses				
020103	Inter design & decoration	HomLv	6	HF	H
030302	Beginning piano Pt 1	Music	1	HF	H
030302	Beginning piano Pt 2	Music	2	HF	H
030302	Beginning guitar Pt 1	Music	3	HF	H
030302	Beginning guitar Pt 2	Music	4	HF	H
030403	Intro to the theater	EngLL	47	HF	H
040104	Bookkeeping 1 Pt 1	Bus	2	HF	H
040104	Bookkeeping 1 Pt 2	Bus	3	HF	H
040114	Understanding 1981 taxes	Bus	6	HF	H
040199	Business law Pt 1	Bus	11	HF	H
040199	Business law Pt 2	Bus	12	HF	H
040205	Shorthand: Gregg Pt 1	Bus	8	HF	H
040205	Shorthand: Gregg Pt 2	Bus	9	HF	H
040207	Beginning typing Pt 1	Bus	4	HF	H
040207	Beginning typing Pt 2	Bus	5	HF	H
0403	Finance and credit	Bus	35	HF	H
040502	Starting your own busnss	Bus	29	HF	H
040502	Ldg and supv in busnss	Bus	32	HF	H
040999	Work experience	Bus	1	HF	H
041001	Merchandising	Bus	17	HF	H
041001	Gen merchandise retailing	Bus	38	HF	H
041003	Creative selling	Bus	20	HF	H
041003	Basic salesmanship	Bus	19	HF	H
041099	Wholesaling & phys distri	Bus	18	HF	H

NCES No.	Course Title	Dept.	Course No.	Credits	Level
041099	Petroleum marketing	Bus	39	HF	H
0411	Survival today	SoSci	23	HF	H
0413	Real estate	Bus	40	HF	H
0501	Advertising services	Bus	33	HF	H
050101	Advertising	Bus	21	HF	H
050102	Display and promotion	Bus	22	HF	H
050199	Communications in mrktng	Bus	23	HF	H
050499	Man & mass media Pt 1	EngLL	36	HF	H
050499	Man & mass media Pt 2	EngLL	37	HF	H
0509	Psych & hum rel in mrktng	Bus	27	HF	H
051107	Intro to pub speaking 1	EngLL	45	HF	H
0799	Eff study & adjst to coll	SoSci	25	HF	H
090101	General health	HSci	1	HF	H
090272	Home nursing Pt 1	HomLv	14	HF	H
090403	The drug scene	Sci	5	HF	H
1001	Fashion merchandising	Bus	34	HF	H
100103	Clothing selection & care	HomLv	4	QT	H
100104	Basic clothg constr Pt 1	HomLv	1	HF	H
100104	Basic clothg constr Pt 2	HomLv	2	HF	H
1003	Food marketing	Bus	36	HF	H
100309	Food services	Bus	37	HF	H
100311	Food and your future	HomLv	5	HF	H
100401	Practical decision making	SoSci	22	HF	H
100601	Child development Pt 1	HomLv	7	HF	H
100601	Child development Pt 2	HomLv	8	HF	H
100601	Child development Pt 3	HomLv	9	HF	H
100602	Personal development	HomLv	3	QT	H
100699	Preprg fr resp parenthood	HomLv	16	HF	H
110411	Radio electronics	IndEd	3	HF	H
110413	Auto fundamentals Pt 1	IndEd	7	HF	H
110413	Auto fundamentals Pt 2	IndEd	8	HF	H
110503	Keys to drawing accuracy	Art	3	HF	H
110504	General photography	Sci	18	HF	H
110599	General art Pt 1	Art	1	HF	H
110599	General art Pt 2	Art	2	HF	H
120303	Semantics word power	EngLL	38	HF	H
120303	Principles of debate	EngLL	49	HF	H
120305	9th grade English Pt 1	EngLL	1	HF	F
120305	9th grade English Pt 2	EngLL	2	HF	H
120305	Business English	EngLL	9	HF	H
120305	Basic spelling skills	EngLL	42	HF	H
120305	English usage Pt 1	EngLL	53	HF	H
120305	English usage Pt 2	EngLL	54	HF	H
120306	Speed-reading	EngLL	57	HF	H
120307	Preserving individualism	EngLL	11	QT	H
120307	The year 2100	EngLL	18	QT	H
120307	Self-esteem	EngLL	12	QT	H
120307	Bible as literature	EngLL	22	HF	H
120308	12th grade English Pt 2	EngLL	8	HF	H
120308	Remedial develpt reading	EngLL	26	HF	H
120308	Recreational reading	EngLL	27	QT	H
120308	Reading for main idea	EngLL	29	QT	H
120308	Reading comp for ind stu	EngLL	23	HF	L
120308	Critical reading Pt 1	EngLL	24	HF	H
120310	10th grade English Pt 1	EngLL	3	HF	H
120310	10th grade English Pt 2	EngLL	4	HF	H
120310	11th grade English Pt 1	EngLL	5	HF	H
120310	11th grade English Pt 2	EngLL	6	HF	H
120310	12th grade English Pt 1	EngLL	7	HF	H
120310	Comp expo writing	EngLL	31	HF	H
120310	Comp narr description	EngLL	32	HF	H
120310	Creative writing	EngLL	33	HF	H
120310	College writing Pt 1	EngLL	34	HF	H
120310	Editing & proofreading	EngLL	43	HF	H
120399	Vocabulary building	EngLL	44	HF	H
120705	Beginng Chinese Mandarin	ForLg	7	HF	H
121105	German Pt 1	ForLg	1	HF	H
121105	German Pt 2	ForLg	2	HF	H
122505	Spanish Pt 1	ForLg	3	HF	H
122505	Spanish Pt 2	ForLg	4	HF	H
150301	Biology Pt 1	Sci	1	HF	H
150301	Biology Pt 2	Sci	2	HF	H
150301	Life science Pt 1	Sci	52	HF	H
150301	Life science Pt 2	Sci	53	HF	H
150304	Ecology Pt 1	Sci	3	HF	H
150304	Ecology Pt 2	Sci	4	HF	H
150401	Chemistry Pt 1	Sci	16	HF	H
150401	Chemistry Pt 2	Sci	17	HF	H
150799	Nonmath physics Pt 1	Sci	9	HF	H
150799	Nonmath physics Pt 2	Sci	10	HF	H
150799	Elements of psychology	SoSci	31	QT	H

NCES No.	Course Title	Dept.	Course No.	Credits	Level
150899	Earth science Pt 1	Sci	57	HF	H
150899	Earth science Pt 2	Sci	58	HF	H
1509	Earth & space sci Pt 1	Sci	13	HF	H
1509	Earth & space sci Pt 2	Sci	14	HF	H
160301	Remedial arithmetic Pt 1	Math	1	HF	H
160301	Remedial arithmetic Pt 2	Math	2	HF	H
160302	1st course algebra Pt 1	Math	5	HF	H
160302	1st course algebra Pt 2	Math	6	HF	H
160302	2nd course algebra Pt 1	Math	7	HF	H
160302	2nd course algebra Pt 2	Math	8	HF	H
160399	Computerized rem math 1	Math	13	HF	H
160399	Computerized rem math 2	Math	14	HF	H
160601	Plane geometry Pt 1	Math	9	HF	H
160601	Plane geometry Pt 2	Math	10	HF	H
160602	Trigonometry Pt 1	Math	11	HF	H
160602	Trigonometry Pt 2	Math	12	HF	H
161101	Mathematics in marketing	Bus	26	HF	H
161201	Bus & consumer math Pt 1	Math	3	HF	H
161201	Bus & consumer math Pt 2	Math	4	HF	H
161201	Consumer mathematics	Math	54	HF	H
190102	Fitness for living	PhyEd	3	HF	H
190102	Jogging	PhyEd	7	HF	H
190103	Tennis	PhyEd	4	HF	H
190103	Bowling	PhyEd	5	HF	H
190404	Social dance	PhyEd	11	HF	H
190404	Beg Latin American dance	PhyEd	12	HF	H
200199	Elements psychology Pt 2	SoSci	32	QT	H
200499	Undstdg & improvg memory	SoSci	26	HF	H
200502	Educ & career planning	SoSci	20	HF	H
200799	Dating–romance & reason	SoSci	16	HF	H
200799	Engmt & wedg–rom & reason	SoSci	17	HF	H
2099	Project self-discovery	SoSci	39	HF	H
220201	Economic problems	SoSci	19	HF	H
220306	World geography	SoSci	29	HF	H
220432	US history–foreign policy	SoSci	5	QT	H
220432	US history–government	SoSci	6	QT	H
220432	American government Pt 1	SoSci	12	HF	H
220432	American government Pt 2	SoSci	13	HF	H
220432	US history Pt 1	SoSci	51	HF	H
220432	US history Pt 2	SoSci	52	HF	H
220432	US hist: liberty/soc chng	SoSci	1	HF	H
220432	US hist: Amer chrt/ec	SoSci	2	HF	H
220433	World hist–modern era	SoSci	7	QT	H
220433	World hist: Europe/Asia	SoSci	8	HF	H
220433	World hist: Ltn Am/Mid Ea	SoSci	9	HF	H
220499	How to climb yr fam tree	SoSci	21	HF	H
220499	Current events	SoSci	38	HF	H
220502	Citizenship	SocSci	53	HF	H
220601	Sociology 1	SoSci	27	HF	H
220615	Sociology 2	SoSci	28	HF	H

College courses

NCES No.	Course Title	Dept.	Course No.	Credits	Level
010101	Real estate appraisal	AgrEc	425	3S	U
010103	Farm & ranch management	AgrEc	325	3S	U
010406	Beef cattle production	AnSci	335	3S	U
010602	Heredity	Bio	276	3S	L
010602	Heredity	Zool	276	3S	L
020101	Sur of art & architecture	ArHis	212	3S	L
020103	Interior design	Desgn	102	3S	L
020103	Historical furnishings	Desgn	326	3S	U
020103	Hist comt furshng architc	Desgn	327	3S	U
030301	Group performance instruc	Music	105R	2S	L
030403	Intro to the theatre	ThArt	115	3S	L
030403	Playwriting	ThArt	378R	3S	U
030502	19th century European art	ArHis	309	3S	U
030603	Contemporary art	Art	314	3S	U
0399	Intro to the humanities	Hum	101	3S	L
040108	Elementary accounting	Acctg	201	3S	L
040108	Elementary accounting	Acctg	202	3S	L
040108	Mathematics of business	Acctg	232A	1 1/2S	L
040108	Mathematics of business	Acctg	232B	1 1/2S	L
040109	Intro to commercial law	Acctg	242	3S	L
040201	Intro to admin management	Bus	305	3S	U
040205	Shorthand 1	Bus	111	4S	L
040207	Production typewriting	Bus	203	3S	L
040311	Financial management	Bus	301	3S	U
040601	Business communications	Bus	320	3S	U

NCES No.	Course Title	Dept.	Course No.	Credits	Level
041004	Marketing management	Bus	341	3S	U
050605	Magazine writing	Commu	427	3S	U
050608	News writing	Commu	211	3S	L
0509	Public relations	Commu	335	3S	U
051102	Analysis of communication	Commu	100	3S	L
051107	Public speaking	Commu	102	3S	L
051107	Argumentation	Comms	202	3S	U
0701	Improving your teaching	InSci	514R7	1S	U
070199	Youth agencies & organiza	YthLd	344	2S	U
070199	Yth mtgs, activts & con	YthLd	371	2S	U
070199	Cub Scout leadership	YthLd	372R1	2S	U
070199	Boy Scout leadership	YthLd	372R2	2S	U
070199	Explorer leadership	YthLd	372R3	2S	U
070199	Techniques of outdoor adv	YthLd	378	2S	U
070299	The professional teacher	SecEd	37665	1S	U
070299	The professional teacher	EdAd	452	1S	U
070301	Early chil learn experien	ElEd	514R9	2S	U
070309	Adult education	EdAd	500	2S	U
070309	Community education	EdAd	604	2S	U
070401	5 stps to effctv tutoring	InSci	51420	2S	U
070402	Creativity in the classrm	SecEd	37611	1S	U
070402	Improv student behavior	SecEd	37634	1S	U
070402	Form useful instruc objec	SecEd	37645	1S	U
070402	Questions that turn stdts	SecEd	37646	1S	U
070402	Intro to test & appraisal	EdPsy	501	3S	U
070404	Working with pict & displ	InSci	51456	1S	U
070404	Projected images multi co	InSci	51457	1S	U
070404	Using other instru techni	InSci	51458	1S	U
070512	Children's literature	ElEd	340	2S	U
070512	Apply stru tutor mod rdg	InSci	51422	2S	U
070512	Apply struc tutor adv rdg	InSci	51424	2S	U
070512	Tutor model rdg sec educ	InSci	51432	2S	U
070512	Screen stud mat read plac	ElEd	51510	3S	U
070512	Shakespeare	Engl	282	3S	L
070512	Intro to English language	Engl	320	3S	U
070512	Am lit 1914 to mid-centry	Engl	363	3S	U
070516	Apply struc mod bsc math	InSci	51425	2S	U
070516	Metric measurements	ElEd	514R8	1S	U
070516	Metric measurements	SecEd	514R8	1S	U
070522	Geography for teachers	SecEd	51444	3S	U
070599	Equity in education	EdPsy	51416	2S	U
070602	Life plan & decision makg	CarEd	115	2S	L
070602	Career exploration	CarEd	116	1S	U
070611	Struc tut tchg Eng 2d lan	InSci	51431	2S	U
070613	Org adm driver safety ed	HSci	444	2S	U
070699	Individ curriculum projec	ElEd	51415	TH	U
070699	Individ curriculum projec	SecEd	51415	TH	U
070701	How to eliminate self-def	EdPsy	514R1	1S	U
070701	Resolving studt hostility	EdPsy	514R5	2S	U
070701	Obtaining stu coop class	EdPsy	51443	1S	U
070701	Counsel guidance services	EdPsy	545	2S	U
070703	Teaching career education	SecEd	51518	1S	U
070803	Educ of exceptional child	EdPsy	205	3S	L
070803	Behav mod tech tchr exce	EdPsy	51450	2S	U
070806	Educ severely mntly retrd	EdPsy	519	2S	U
070899	Implem public law ed hand	EdPsy	51451	1S	U
070902	Community relationships	YthLd	332	3S	U
071001	Help stud learn by inquir	SecEd	37647	1S	U
071101	Simulation and games	SecEd	37656	HF	U
071103	Evaluating stud learning	SecEd	37635	1S	U
07119	Measuring student effect	SecEd	37620	1S	U
071201	Selecting effective instr	SecEd	37660	1S	U
080704	Eng mech/mech of material	CivEn	203	3S	L
080707	Elem structural theory	CivEn	321	3S	U
0810	Intro to engineering grph	Tech	111	3S	L
081104	Vector mechanics/statics	CivEn	104	3S	L
081104	Eng mechanics/dynamics	CivEn	204	3S	L
090272	Family health management	Nurs	288	2S	L
090403	Drug use and abuse	HSci	460	2S	U
090504	First aid & safety instr	HSci	121	2S	L
090504	School hlth for ele tchrs	HSci	361	3S	U
090504	School hlth for sec tchrs	HSci	362	2S	U
090702	Consumer health	HSci	370	2S	U
090702	Community health	HSci	451	2S	U
090799	Safety education	HSci	325	2S	U
090902	Personal health	HSci	129	1S	L
090902	Personal health	HSci	130	2S	L
100101	General textiles	ClTx	260	3S	L
100104	Flat pattern designing	ClTx	145	1S	L
100206	Personal finance	Bus	200	2S	L

NCES No.	Course Title	Dept.	Course No.	Credits	Level
100206	Persnl/fam financial mgt	FamSc	241	3S	L
100299	Money mgt & consumer skls	FamSc	240	2S	L
100302	Essentials of nutrition	FSN	115	2S	L
100399	Special problems food sci	FSN	494R	VC	U
100402	Mgt for indiv & families	FamSc	220	2S	L
100601	Child development	FamSc	210	3S	L
100601	Prncpls of child guidance	FamSc	312	2S	U
100602	The LDS family	FamSc	261	2S	L
100602	Topics in child dev fam	FamSc	595R	VC	U
100699	Achvg success in marriage	FamSc	360	3S	U
100699	Psychology of parenting	Psych	222	3S	L
110104	Basic electricity	InArt	101	3S	L
120305	Vocabulary building	Engl	225	2S	L
120305	Study in Engl grammars	Engl	321	3S	U
120305	Modern American usage	Engl	322	3S	U
120307	Fundmntls of literature	Engl	251	3S	L
120307	Vital themes in Amer lit	Engl	260	3S	L
120307	Masterpieces of Engl lit	Engl	270	3S	U
120307	The English novel	Engl	333	3S	U
120307	The 19th-century Amer nov	Engl	335	3S	U
120307	The 20th-century Amer nov	Engl	336	3S	U
120307	Modern poetry	Engl	366	2S	U
120307	Engl lit from 1780-1832	Engl	374	3S	U
120307	Lit for adolescents	Engl	420	2S	U
120307	Intro to French lit	Frnch	301	3S	U
120307	Frnch lit Mid Ages-16th c	Frnch	441	3S	U
120307	Frnch lit 17th & 18th cen	Frnch	442	3S	U
120307	Bible as literature	Engl	350	3S	U
120307	The short story	Engl	359	3S	U
120308	College reading	Engl	114	2S	L
120308	Wrtg for chldrn & adolesc	Engl	217	2S	L
120308	Coll developmental readng	GenSt	1211	2S	L
120308	Rdg skls for law students	GenSt	1212	2S	L
120310	Writing laboratory	Engl	113	2S	L
120310	Creative writing	Engl	218	3S	L
120310	Writing personal history	Engl	220	2S	L
120310	Writing about literature	Engl	252	3S	L
120310	Critical & interprtv wrtg	Engl	312	3S	U
120310	Exposition & report wrtg	Engl	315	3S	U
120310	Technical writing	Engl	316	3S	U
120310	Writing of fiction	Engl	318R	3S	U
120310	Writing of poetry	Engl	319R	3S	U
120399	Study habits	GenSt	111	VC	L
121005	Interm French read & conv	Frnch	201	4S	L
121105	Second-year German	Ger	201	4S	L
121105	Third-yr Ger grammar-comp	Ger	321	3S	U
121107	Intermediate German readg	Ger	301	3S	U
121107	German lit in 18th cent	Ger	442	3S	U
121341	First-yr biblical Hebrew	Heb	131	4S	L
1225	Inter Span read & convers	Span	201	4S	L
122505	Third-yr Span gram & comp	Span	321	3S	U
122505	Third-yr Span gram & comp	Span	322	3S	U
122505	Introductory Spanish	Span	100A	2S	L
122507	Intro to Spanish lit	Span	339	3S	U
122507	Survey of Spanish lit	Span	441	3S	U
122507	Survey of Hispanic Am lit	Span	451	3S	U
130101	Intro to justice admin	JusAd	101	3S	U
130101	Law enforcement admin	JusAd	102	3S	L
130103	Evidence	JusAd	301	3S	U
130199	Investigation	JusAd	302	3S	U
130402	Crmnl justice procedure	JusAd	304	3S	U
130403	Adm of juvenile justice	JusAd	305	3S	U
130503	Indus & retail security	JusAd	303	3S	U
150302	Principles of biology	Bio	100	3S	L
150304	Environmental biology	Bio	250	3S	L
150304	Conservation of nat rescs	Bio	400	2S	U
150304	Environmental biology	Zool	250	3S	L
150311	General microbiology	Micro	321	3S	U
150329	Ichthyology	Zool	443	2S	U
150399	Hist & philos of biology	Zool	321	2S	U
150399	Plant kingdom	Bio	105	3S	L
150401	Elementary coll chemistry	Chem	100	3S	L
150504	Life of the past	Geol	103	3S	L
150599	Intro to geology	Geol	101	3S	L
150599	Landforms & their origin	Geol	306	3S	U
150799	Fundamentals of physics	Phys	100	3S	L
160101	Math & the humanities	Math	307	3S	U
160102	History of mathematics	Math	300	3S	U
160199	Review of basic math	Math	100D	2S	L
160205	Combinatorics	Math	110D	HF	L
160301	Concepts of mathematics	Math	306	3S	U
160301	Basic concepts of math	Math	305	4S	U
160302	Beginning algebra	Math	100B	2S	L
160302	Intermediate algebra	Math	100E	2S	L
160302	Review of fundamentals	Math	100F	1S	L
160302	Foundations of algebra	Math	301	3S	U
160306	Matrices/linear equations	Math	110C	HF	L
160306	Linear programming	Math	110E	HF	L
160399	Polynomial/rational fndtl	Math	110A	1S	L
160399	Exponential/logarith fndt	Math	110B	HF	L
160406	Intro ordinary diffent eq	Math	434	3S	U
160412	Intro to calculus	Math	119	4S	L
160499	Technical mathematics	Math	121	3S	U
160602	Trigonometry	Math	111A	2S	L
160603	Analytic geometry	Math	111B	HF	L
160603	Analytic geom-calculus 1	Math	112	4S	L
160603	Analytic geom-calculus 2	Math	113	4S	L
160603	Analyt geom-calculus 3	Math	214	3S	L
160604	Modern geometry	Math	451	3S	U
160699	Survey of geometry	Math	302	3S	U
160706	Elementary probability	Stat	341	3S	U
160801	Prin of statistics 1	Stat	221	3S	L
160801	Prin of statistics 2	Stat	222	4S	L
160801	Prin of statistics 3	Stat	223	1S	L
160802	Applied social statistics	Socio	205	3S	L
180504	Logic and language	Philo	205	3S	L
181202	The New Testament	Relig	211	2S	L
181202	The New Testament	Relig	212	2S	L
181202	The Old Testament	Relig	301	2S	U
181202	The Old Testament	Relig	302	2S	U
181202	The doctrine & covenants	Relig	324	2S	U
181299	Intro to Book of Mormon	Relig	121	2S	L
181299	Intro to Book of Mormon	Relig	122	2S	L
181299	The doctrine & covenants	Relig	325	2S	U
181299	The pearl of great price	Relig	327	2S	U
181299	Writings of Isaiah	Relig	304	2S	U
181603	Gospel in prin & practice	Relig	231	2S	L
181603	Gospel in prin & practice	Relig	232	2S	L
181603	Intro to genealogy	Relig	261	2S	L
181603	Teach of the living proph	Relig	333	2S	U
181603	LDS chrch hist after 1846	Relig	342	2S	U
181603	LDS church hist to 1846	Relig	341	2S	U
181603	Apply gosp prin in youth	Relig	365	2S	U
181603	Special studies in relig	Relig	392R	1S	U
181603	Spec topics in chur hist	Relig	540R	3S	U
181603	Interntl LDS Church hist	Relig	343	2S	U
181603	Genealogy of LDS family	Relig	362	2S	U
181608	Sharing the Gospel	Relig	130	2S	L
190102	Fitness for living	PhyEd	177	HF	L
190102	Jogging	PhyEd	179	HF	L
190102	Intermediate swimming	PhyEd	161	HF	L
190108	Principles of PE	PhyEd	330	3S	U
190108	Mgt of athletic intra pro	PhyEd	414	3S	U
190311	Football: fundmtl coaching	PhyEd	371	2S	U
190311	Basketball: fndtl coaching	PhyEd	372	2S	U
190401	Ballroom dance: Amer begin	PhyEd	180	HF	L
190401	Ballroom dance: Latin Amer	PhyEd	189	HF	L
200104	General psychology	Psych	111	3S	L
200199	Independent reading	Psych	495R	1S	U
200199	Psychology statistics	Psych	301	3S	U
2003	Environmental psychology	Psych	359	3S	U
200504	Child psychology	Psych	320	3S	U
200504	Adolescent psychology	Psych	321	3S	U
200504	Adult psychology	Psych	322	3S	U
200505	Personal & social adjust	Psych	240	3S	L
200507	Exceptional children	Psych	346	3S	U
200508	Psychology of sex roles	Psych	225	3S	L
200599	Emotional cont/self-consl	EdPsy	514R2	1S	U
200702	Interprsnl growth group	Psych	357	3S	U
200702	Interprsnl growth group	Socio	357	3S	U
200703	Organizational psychology	Psych	330	3S	U
200799	Intro to social psychol	Psych	350	3S	U
200799	Intro sociology	Socio	111	3S	L

NCES No.	Course Title	Dept.	Course No.	Credits	Level
200804	The community educ philos	RecEd	585	2S	U
210101	Intro public admin	PolSc	330	3S	U
210202	Sanitation public health	Micro	311	2S	U
210404	Intr to field of soc work	SocWk	360	3S	U
220206	Econmy, society & pub pol	Econ	110	3S	L
220213	Macroecon for bus decisns	Econ	301	3S	U
220216	Microecon for bus decisns	Econ	300	3S	U
220302	Economic geography	Geog	231	3S	L
220303	Geography & world affairs	Geog	120	3S	L
220306	North America	Geog	450	3S	U
220399	Intro to geography	Geog	101	3S	L
220399	Travel & tourism patterns	Geog	250	3S	L
220399	Tour operation	Geog	352	3S	L
220424	England	Hist	335	3S	U
220424	British resch Eng/Wales 16	Hist	393R1	3S	U
220424	Brtsh resch Scotlnd/Ireld	Hist	393R3	3S	U
220426	France	Hist	332	3S	U
220426	Danish research	Hist	395R1	3S	U
220426	Norwegian research	Hist	395R2	3S	U
220426	Swedish research	Hist	395R3	3S	U
220428	Utah	Hist	366	3S	U
220431	USSR & Eastern Europe	Hist	331	3S	U
220432	The United States	Hist	120	3S	L
220432	The United States	Hist	121	3S	L
220432	California	Hist	365	2S	U
220432	American heritage	SocSc	100	3S	L
220432	Intro to genealogy	FLHS	261	2S	L
220432	North American research 1	FLHS	280R	3S	L
220432	Northeast US and Canada	Hist	391R1	3S	U
220432	Southern states	Hist	391R2	3S	U
220432	Middle states	Hist	391R3	3S	U
220432	Seminar and spec problems	FLHS	400R	2S	U
220433	World civilization 1	Hist	110	3S	L
220433	World civilization 2	Hist	111	3S	L
220499	Directed readings	Hist	498R	3S	U
220499	Cultural hist of the US	Hist	390R1	3S	U
220499	Cultural hist Scotld/Irel	Hist	390R2	3S	U
220499	Paleography/English	Hist	400R1	2S	U
220501	Amer govt and politics	PolSc	110	3S	L
220509	Moral foundations of poli	PolSc	302	3S	U
220511	State-local govt politics	PolSc	311	3S	U
220604	Juvenile delinquency	Socio	383	3S	U
220605	Family relationships	Socio	361	3S	U
220607	Intro to social psycholog	Socio	350	3S	U
220613	Soc aspects of mental hlt	Socio	389	3S	U
220613	Soc services for sr citiz	Socio	390R1	1S	U
220699	Mthds of rsch in sociolog	Socio	300	3S	U
220699	Stress & coping behavior	Socio	390R3	1S	U

Noncredit courses

NCES No.	Course Title	Dept.	Course No.	Credits	Level
040902	Way to become success mgr	Bus	70	NC	
050604	Journalism for correspond	Writi	71	NC	
070701	Elim self-defeatg behavr	Famil	70	NC	
090302	Slim chnce in a fat world	Hlth	70	NC	
100401	Practical decision making	PerDv	70	NC	
100601	Early child lrng exp home	Famil	74	NC	
100604	Building your vocabulary	PerDv	72	NC	
100604	Help yourself: self-improv	PerDv	74	NC	
100604	Handle conflict at home	PerDv	75	NC	
110599	Keys to drawing accuracy	Cultu	72	NC	
120299	Child creative writing	Writi	70	NC	
120310	Remedial spelling	GenSt	15R1	NC	D
120310	Remedial grammar	GenSt	15R2	NC	D
181608	Missionary prep for cples	Relig	70	NC	
200599	Spirit roots human relats	Famil	71	NC	
220424	British rsch 1: survey	Genea	73-1	NC	
220424	British rsch 1: Brit Pt 1	Genea	73-2	NC	
220424	Brit rsch 2: Scot rsch 1	Genea	74-1	NC	
220424	Brit rsch 2: Irish rsch 1	Genea	74-3	NC	
220432	N Am rsch 1: get new facts	Genea	71-1	NC	
220432	N Am rsch 1: get new facts	Genea	71-2	NC	
220432	N Am rsch 2: NE states Can	Genea	72-1	NC	
220432	N Am rsch 2: sthrn states	Genea	72-2	NC	
220432	N Am rsch 2: midwest sts	Genea	72-3	NC	
220605	Paired unity succes marri	Famil	80	NC	

⑦ CALIFORNIA STATE UNIVERSITY, SACRAMENTO

Mr. Kenneth D. Kerri
Professor of Civil Engineering
Department of Civil Engineering
California State University, Sacramento
6000 J Street
Sacramento, California 95819
Phone: (916) 454-6142

Enrollment on a noncredit basis accepted in some credit courses. Gifted high school students are permitted to enroll in undergraduate courses for credit. Overseas enrollment accepted for college and noncredit courses.

NCES No.	Course Title	Dept.	Course No.	Credits	Level
	College courses				
081304	Op/mgt wastewater coll sy	CivEg	X11	6S	L
081304	Oper wastewater treatment	CivEg	X12A	6S	L
081304	Oper wastewater treatment	CivEg	X12B	6S	L
081304	Oper wastewater treatment	CivEg	X12C	6S	L

⑧ CENTRAL MICHIGAN UNIVERSITY

Ms. Ann Marie N. Bridges
Coordinator, Office of Independent Study
Continuing Education and Community Services
Central Michigan University
Rowe Hall 127N
Mount Pleasant, Michigan 48859
Phone: (517) 774-3715 Ext. 213

Only in exceptional cases are gifted high school students permitted to enroll in undergraduate courses for credit. Overseas enrollment accepted for college courses.

NCES No.	Course Title	Dept.	Course No.	Credits	Level
	College courses				
030402	History of drama/theater	EngLL	386	3S	L
030402	History of drama/theater	EngLL	387	3S	L
030499	Hist of drama & theater	SDA	386	3S	L
030499	Hist of drama & theater	SDA	387	3S	L
030599	Understanding art	Art	125	2S	L
040101	Financial accounting	Acctg	201	4S	L
040111	Managerial accounting	Acctg	221	3S	L
040114	Survey of taxation	Acctg	215	3S	L
050699	Journalism: special study	Jrnl	497	VC	
051103	Persuasion	SDA	365	3S	L
051108	Communication theory	SDA	251	3S	L
051108	Hist of communication thy	SDA	558	3S	L
060801	Assembly language program	CmpSc	210	3S	L
070201	Intro to education admin	Educ	560	3S	L
070299	Intro to school law	Educ	566	3S	L
070299	Workshop in educa admin	Educ	592	VC	
070309	Prin of community educ	Educ	567	3S	L
070516	Arithmetic in elem school	Educ	320	2S	L
071103	Measurement & evaluation	Educ	570	3S	L
100601	Readings: child developt	HmEc	500	3S	L
100602	Readings in the family	HmEc	513	3S	L
120101	Contrastive appl linguist	ForLL	510	3S	L
120307	English literature	EngLL	235	3S	L
120307	English literature	EngLL	236	3S	L
120307	American literature	EngLL	251	3S	L
120307	American literature	EngLL	252	3S	L
120307	Shakespeare	EngLL	349	3S	L
121005	Intermediate French	ForLL	201	4S	L
121005	Intermediate French	ForLL	202	4S	L
121007	French literature	ForLL	303	3S	L
121007	French literature	ForLL	304	3S	L
121008	French lit: 17th century	ForLL	404	3S	L
121008	French lit: 19th century	ForLL	407	3S	L
121008	French lit: 20th century	ForLL	409	3S	L
121009	Advanced language skills	ForLL	332	3S	L
121009	French diction	ForLL	370	3S	L
121010	French composition	ForLL	212	2S	L
121099	French for travelers	ForLL	321	3S	L
121099	French for travelers	ForLL	322	3S	L
121099	French independent study	ForLL	597	VC	L
121105	Elementary German	ForLL	101	4S	L
121105	Intermediate German	ForLL	202	4S	L

NCES No.	Course Title	Dept.	Course No.	Credits	Level
122508	Spanish lit to 18th cent	ForLL	304	3S	L
1299	Masterpieces: ancient lit	EngLL	261	3S	L
1299	Masterpieces: Europ lit	EngLL	262	3S	L
150304	Ecology	Bio	340	3S	L
150306	Evolution	Bio	301	3S	L
150311	Topics in microbiology	Bio	397	3S	L
150316	Nature study	Bio	229	3S	L
150399	Conserva of nat resources	Bio	240	3S	L
150399	Human animal	Bio	328	3S	L
150399	Human ecology	Bio	338	3S	L
150799	Physics for poets	Phys	100	3S	L
150799	Materials for teachg phys	Phys	303	1S	L
150899	Phys sci for elem grades	Phys	351	3S	L
160102	Hist of elementary math	Math	253	2S	L
160102	History of mathematics	Math	573	3S	L
160199	Fundamntls of mathematics	Math	201	3S	L
160499	Theory of equations	Math	420	3S	L
160602	Plane trigonometry	Math	106	3S	L
160801	Intro to statistics	Math	282	3S	L
161101	Mathematics for business	Math	116	3S	L
161101	Mathematics for business	Math	216	3S	L
161101	Mathematics of finance	Math	214	4S	L
190104	Foundations of phys ed	PhyEd	106	2S	L
190104	Hist of phys ed & sports	PhyEd	515	3S	L
190107	Phys ed curriculum	PhyEd	316	2S	L
190405	History of dance	PhyEd	530	3S	L
190502	Community health	HEd	317	3S	L
190505	Environmental health	HEd	252	3S	L
190509	Personal health	HEd	106	3S	L
190599	Safety education	HEd	209	2S	L
190701	Playgrounds/community ctr	Rec	402	3S	L
190701	Admin of recreation parks	Rec	505	3S	L
190703	Camp counseling	Rec	220	3S	L
200599	Mental retardation	Psych	260	3S	L
200699	Intro to psych statistics	Psych	311	3S	L
220102	Cultural anthropology	Socio	170	3S	L
220106	Physical anthropology	Socio	171	3S	L
220199	Human evolution	Socio	347	3S	L
220201	Principles of economics 1	Econ	201	3S	L
220201	Principles of economics 2	Econ	202	3S	L
220301	Cultures of the world	Geog	121	3S	L
220399	Weather	Geog	201	4S	L
220424	History of England	Hist	350	3S	L
220424	History of England	Hist	351	3S	L
220425	History of Canada	Hist	334	3S	L
220428	Michigan history	Hist	332	3S	L
220429	Near East to Alexander	Hist	236	3S	L
220432	Westward movement in Amer	Hist	322	3S	L
220432	United States to 1865	Hist	211	3S	L
220499	Western civilization	Hist	101	3S	L
220499	Western civilization	Hist	102	3S	L
220501	Intro: Am govt & politics	PolSc	201	3S	L
220501	Amer legislative process	PolSc	320	3S	L
220503	Comparative politics: Euro	PolSc	240	3S	L
220599	Intro to political sci	PolSc	100	3S	L
220602	Criminology	Socio	421	3S	L
220604	Juvenile delinquency	Socio	222	3S	L
220605	The family	Socio	411	3S	L
220606	Introductory sociology	Socio	100	3S	L
220607	Social psychology	Socio	201	3S	L
220613	Social problems	Socio	221	3S	L
220699	Intro to human sexuality	Socio	213	3S	L
220699	Educational sociology	Socio	311	3S	L
220699	Socio of health/illness	Socio	312	3S	L
220699	Religion in society	Socio	319	3S	L
220699	Minorities	Socio	323	3S	L

⑨ **COLORADO STATE UNIVERSITY**

Ms. Susan E. Benson
Coordinator
Division of Continuing Education
Colorado State University
Loveland Satellite Center
Loveland, Colorado 80537
Phone: (303) 669-1701

Enrollment on a noncredit basis accepted in some credit courses. Gifted high school students are permitted to enroll in undergraduate courses for credit. Overseas enrollment accepted. Students wishing to drop courses must inform the Division in writing within forty days of registration. Tuition minus a $10 administrative fee is refunded when study materials are returned. Courses at the 400 level may be accepted for graduate credit.

NCES No.	Course Title	Dept.	Course No.	Credits	Level
	College courses				
010407	Basic nutrition for pets	AnSci	AN322	2S	U
010603	Ind study/pesticides	Agri	A495	3S	U
011299	Hunter educ for instructr	For	FW355	2S	U
020199	Ecology & env issues	Fores	NR130	3S	L
070309	Independent study	Educ	AD495	VC	B
070899	Educational psychology	Educ	ED355	3S	U
070899	Exceptionality in hum rel	Educ	ED428	3S	U
0709	Evaluation of achievement	Educ	ED452	2S	B
100313	Nutrition & preschool chl	HmEc	FN160	2S	L
100401	Decision making: pers/fam	HmEc	HC330	3S	U
100601	Infancy & early childhood	HmEc	HD211	3S	L
100601	Play behavior	HmEc	HD430	2S	B
100601	Creative exper for childr	HmEc	HD217	3S	L
100602	Ind & family development	HmEc	HD101	3S	L
100699	Practicum I	HmEc	HD286	2S	L
100699	Adm of human dvlpmt ctrs	HmEc	HD438	3S	B
120103	Study of language	Engl	E320	3S	U
120299	Western American lit	Engl	E179	3S	L
120399	Composition analysis	Engl	E402	3S	B
220431	Imperial Russia	Hist	HY440	3S	B
220599	US foreign policy	PolSc	PO435	3S	B
	Graduate courses				
050602	Seminar: grantsmanship	InArt	IS692	3S	G
070309	Adult education	Educ	AD520	3S	G
070699	Seminar: curr multicultr	Educ	ED693	3S	G
070899	Educ exceptional student	Educ	ED528	2S	G
	Noncredit courses				
010407	Basic nutrition for pets	AnSci	CE521	NC	
010603	Pesticides: how & why	Agri	CE102	NC	
070309	Program development	Educ	3107	NC	
070309	Administration	Educ	3108	NC	
070309	Adult development	Educ	3109	NC	
070309	Adult basic education	Educ	3111	NC	
070309	Adult learner	Educ	3112	NC	
070309	Adult teaching	Educ	3113	NC	
0804	Emissions control	InArt	CE860	NC	
080999	Fund of electrical systms	EngAS	3205	NC	
100313	Food preservation	HmEc	3804	NC	

⑩ **EASTERN KENTUCKY UNIVERSITY**

Mr. Kenneth D. Tunnell
Dean, Continuing Education
Division of Continuing Education
Eastern Kentucky University
217 Perkins Building
Richmond, Kentucky 40475-0951
Phone: (606) 622-2001

Enrollment on a noncredit basis accepted in all credit courses. Gifted high school students are permitted to enroll in undergraduate courses for credit. Overseas enrollment accepted for high school and college courses. High school students who wish to enroll must have the approval of their school's principal or superintendent.

NCES No.	Course Title	Dept.	Course No.	Credits	Level
	High school courses				
120305	English grammar	Engl	11	HF	H
120305	English grammar	Engl	12	HF	H
120307	American literature	Engl	11A	HF	H
120307	American literature	Engl	11B	HF	H
120307	British literature	Engl	12A	HF	H
120307	British literature	Engl	12B	HF	H
190502	Personal/community health	Hea	1	HF	H
220201	Economics	Econ	12	HF	H
220399	World geography	Geog	10A	HF	H
220399	World geography	Geog	10B	HF	H
220432	American history	Hist	11A	HF	H
220432	American history	Hist	11B	HF	H
220433	World history	Hist	10A	HF	H

NCES No.	Course Title	Dept.	Course No.	Credits	Level
220433	World history	Hist	10B	HF	H
220501	Government	Gov	12	HF	H
220502	Civics	Civ	9	HF	H
220606	Sociology	Socio	12	HF	H
	College courses				
030302	Enjoyment of music	Music	271	3S	L
040299	Introduction to business	OAd	101	3S	L
040299	Business communications	OAd	301	3S	U
041001	Marketing	Mktg	300	3S	U
050199	Advertising	Mktg	320	3S	U
120201	Survey of world lit 1	Engl	211	3S	L
120201	Survey of world lit 2	Engl	212	3S	L
120305	English composition 1	Engl	101	3S	L
120305	English composition 2	Engl	102	3S	L
120307	American literature 1	Engl	350	3S	U
150399	Economic plants	Bio	300	3S	U
160199	Understanding arithmetic	Math	201	3S	L
160302	Introductory algebra	Math	105	3S	L
160302	College algebra	Math	107	3S	L
160602	Trigonometry	Math	108	3S	L
190502	Personal/community health	Hea	281	2S	L
190511	Safety and first aid	Hea	202	2S	L
200199	Psychology as a social sc	Psych	202	3S	L
200501	Abnormal psychology	Psych	308	3S	U
2103	Police administration	PAd	101	3S	L
220201	Principles of economics 1	Econ	230	3S	L
220201	Principles of economics 2	Econ	231	3S	L
220302	Economic geography 1	Geog	330	3S	U
220302	Economic geography 2	Geog	331	3S	U
220308	Urban geography	Geog	421	3S	U
220399	Cons, technol & env probl	Geog	402	3S	U
220405	History of science	Sci	310	3S	U
220432	American civiliz to 1877	Hist	202	3S	L
220432	American civ since 1877	Hist	203	3S	L
220433	Preindustrial world civ	GSS	246	3S	L
220433	Industrialism in wrld civ	GSS	247	3S	L
220499	South in American history	Hist	406	3S	U
220499	Kentucky history	Hist	516	3S	U
220501	Intro to American govt	PolSc	101	3S	L
220511	Amer state & local govt	PolSc	230	3S	L
220599	Government of Kentucky	PolSc	332	3S	U

⑪ EASTERN MICHIGAN UNIVERSITY

Dr. Arthur McCafferty
Director of Credit Programs
Eastern Michigan University
323 Goodison Hall
Ypsilanti, Michigan 48197
Phone: (313) 487-0407

Enrollment on a noncredit basis accepted in some credit courses. Only in exceptional cases are gifted high school students permitted to enroll in undergraduate courses for credit. Overseas enrollment accepted for high school and college courses.

NCES No.	Course Title	Dept.	Course No.	Credits	Level
	College courses				
0999	Health educ: elementary	HEd	320	2S	L
120305	Modern English syntax	Engl	302	3S	L
120307	Shakespeare	EngLL	210	3S	L
120307	Shakespeare	EngLL	305	3S	L
120310	Intermediate college comp	Engl		3S	L
120310	Expository writing	Engl	325	3S	L
1509	Earth science	ESci	108	4S	L
180999	World religions	Hist	110	1S	L
2099	General psychology	Psych	101	3S	L
220511	Michigan government	Gov	113	3S	L
220699	Introduction to sociology	Socio	105	3S	L

⑫ EAST TENNESSEE STATE UNIVERSITY

Dr. M. T. Morgan
Professor and Chairman
Department of Environmental Health
East Tennessee State University
P.O. Box 22960A
Johnson City, Tennessee 37614
Phone: (615) 929-4268

Enrollment on a noncredit basis accepted in some credit courses. Gifted high school students are permitted to enroll in undergraduate courses for credit. Overseas enrollment accepted for college courses.

NCES No.	Course Title	Dept.	Course No.	Credits	Level
	College courses				
090799	Environtl sanitation surv	818	4917	3S	B
090799	Institutional health	818	4927	2S	B
090799	Insect & rodent control	818	4937	2S	B
090799	Water-quality control	818	4947	2S	B
090799	Food-borne-disease contrl	818	4957	2S	B
090799	Environtl prog evaluation	818	4967	2S	B
090799	Environtl health law	818	4977	2S	B

⑬ GRADUATE SCHOOL, USDA

Ms. Norma L. Harwood
Head, Correspondence Study Programs
Graduate School, USDA
600 Maryland Avenue, S.W., Room 133
Washington, District of Columbia 20024
Phone: (202) 447-7123

Only in exceptional cases are gifted high school students permitted to enroll in undergraduate courses for credit. Overseas enrollment accepted. Courses are designed to meet the specific needs of federal employees, but most are applicable to the private sector as well. The Graduate School, USDA, is not a regionally accredited college or university, does not grant degrees, and has never sought that authority. Students who wish to transfer Graduate School, USDA, courses for credit to another college or university should consult the college or university before registration. The U.S. Office of Personnel Management accepts the credits of the school, for examination and qualification purposes, on the same basis as those from accredited colleges and universities.

NCES No.	Course Title	Dept.	Course No.	Credits	Level
	College courses				
010702	Soil surveys and uses	Agri	101	3Q	L
040101	Prin of accounting I	Acctg	101	4Q	L
040101	Prin of accounting II	Acctg	102	4Q	L
040101	Intermediate acctg I	Acctg	201	4Q	L
040101	Intermediate acctg II	Acctg	202	4Q	L
040101	Prin of accounting III	Acct	103	4Q	L
040105	Fed budgetary procedure I	Acctg	120	3Q	L
040105	Fed budget procedure II	Acctg	121	3Q	L
040106	Cost accounting I	Acctg	250	2Q	L
040106	Cost accounting II	Acctg	251	2Q	L
040106	Cost accounting III	Acctg	252	2Q	L
040109	REA accounting—electric	Acctg	211	4Q	L
040109	REA accounting—telephone	Acctg	212	4Q	L
040109	Federal govt acctg I	Acctg	260	3Q	L
040109	Federal govt acctg II	Acctg	261	3Q	L
040114	Fed income taxes I	Acctg	420	4Q	U
040114	Fed income taxes II	Acctg	421	4Q	U
040502	Estab-operating small bus	Mgmt	223	3Q	L
041106	Modern supervisory prac	Mgmt	201	3Q	L
041106	Success-oriented supervis	Mgmt	202	4Q	L
041199	Federal personnel proc	Mgmt	130	3Q	L
0508	Principles of editing	Commu	140	4Q	L
0508	Intermediate editing	Commu	230	3Q	L
0508	Printing, layout & design	Commu	270	3Q	L
0508	Basic indexing	Commu	360	3Q	U
0508	Applied indexing	Commu	361	4Q	U
0508	Publishing managment	Commu	375	3Q	U
060404	Microcomputers	CmpSc	226	3Q	
060799	Intro computer programmng	CmpSc	102	3Q	L
061104	Concepts of data processg	CmpSc	101	3Q	L
080799	Storm-water management	CivEg	401	4Q	U
080903	Basic electronics	EEg	201	4Q	L

NCES No.	Course Title	Dept.	Course No.	Credits	Level
080907	Basic electricity	EEg	101	3Q	L
080907	Elec trans and dist	EEg	202	3Q	L
080907	Electrical wiring	EEg	203	3Q	L
081104	Hydraulics I: hydrostatic	EngAS	204	3Q	L
081104	Hydralics II	EngAS	205	3Q	L
100604	Individualized retirement	Socio	100	3Q	L
120310	Better letters	Engl	101	1Q	L
120310	Writing for govt & bus	Engl	102	3Q	L
120310	Report writing	Engl	201	3Q	L
120310	Regulations writing	Engl	350	3Q	U
120399	Intro to speech writing	Engl	103	3Q	L
130101	Admin law and procedure	Law	310	3Q	U
130402	Criminal evidence—proc	Law	135	3Q	L
130702	Buiness associations	Law	320	3Q	U
130799	Business law	Law	120	3Q	L
131599	Intro law for paralegals	Law	110	3Q	L
1401	Intro to library tech	LibSc	110	3Q	L
140199	Prin of lib organization	LibSc	230	3Q	L
140401	Cataloging and classif I	LibSc	120	3Q	L
140402	Cataloging & classif II	LibSc	220	3Q	L
140701	Use of archives & manusct	LibSc	211	3Q	L
140703	Intro to bibliographies	LibSc	225	3Q	L
140709	Library media services	LibSc	210	4Q	L
140799	Legal literature	LibSc	255	3Q	L
140804	Basic ref service & tools	LibSc	245	3Q	L
150202	Dynamic meteorology I	Meteo	161	4Q	L
150202	Dynamic meteorology II	Meteo	162	4Q	L
160302	College algebra I	Math	201	3Q	L
160302	College algebra II	Math	202	3Q	L
160401	Calculus I	Math	210	4Q	L
160401	Calculus II	Math	211	4Q	L
160602	Trigonometry	Math	103	3Q	L
160603	Analytic geometry	Math	105	3Q	L
160802	Elements of statistics	Stat	301	3Q	U
160802	Adv agricultural statist	Stat	401	6Q	U
161199	Basic mathematics	Math	101	3Q	L
2101	Fed procurement/contract	PrPM	108	3Q	L
2101	Fed procurement/ procedure	PrPM	121	3Q	L
2101	Fed supply schedule	PrPM	170	2Q	L
2101	Proposal evaluation	PrPM	211	3Q	L
2101	Contracting for services	PrPM	213	3Q	L
2101	Gov construction contract	PrPM	225	2Q	L
2101	R & D contracting	PrPM	235	3Q	L
2101	ADP procurement	PrPM	303	3Q	U
2101	Gov contract law	PrPM	310	3Q	U
2101	Cost and price analysis	PrPM	370	3Q	U
2101	Contract administration	PrPM	376	3Q	U
2101	Contracting for small bus	PrPM	425	1Q	U
2101	Fed cont default & repro	PrPM	426	2Q	U
2101	Intro property management	PrPM	107	3Q	L
2101	Inventory management	PrPM	109	2Q	L
2101	Equip & facilities mgmt	PrPM	110	3Q	L
2101	Fed property proc	PrPM	120	3Q	L
2101	Gov leasing proc	PrPM	212	3Q	L
2101	Grants management	PrPM	375	3Q	U
220201	Prin of economics I	Econ	110	3Q	L
220201	Prin of economics II	Econ	111	3Q	L
220201	Prin of economics III	Econ	112	3Q	L

Graduate courses

NCES No.	Course Title	Dept.	Course No.	Credits	Level
040901	Zero-base budgeting	Mgmt	550	3Q	B
080703	Hydrology I	CivEg	501	4Q	B
080703	Hydrology II	CivEg	502	4Q	B
120310	Effectve writing—profess	Engl	501	4Q	B
131502	Legal research	Law	550	3Q	B
140199	Library tech readings	LibSc	599	3Q	B
160809	Sample survey methods	Stat	501	4Q	B
161107	Stat meth in biol & agric	Stat	502	3Q	B

Noncredit courses

NCES No.	Course Title	Dept.	Course No.	Credits	Level
0409	Work objectives	Mgmt	001	NC	D
120305	Refresher English I	Engl	001	NC	D
120305	Refresher English II	Engl	002	NC	D
161201	Everyday mathematics	Math	011	NC	D

⑭ **HOME STUDY INSTITUTE**

Dr. D. W. Holbrook
President
Home Study Institute
6940 Carroll Avenue
Takoma Park, Maryland 20912
Phone: (202) 722-6572

Enrollment on a noncredit basis accepted in some credit courses. Gifted high school students are permitted to enroll in undergraduate courses for credit. Overseas enrollment accepted. Home Study Institute offers preschool, elementary, secondary, college, and continuing education courses from a Christian perspective. Lessons are generally returned to students within two days.

HSI is the recognized extension division in correspondence studies for Seventh-Day Adventist colleges and universities in North America, all of which are regionally accredited. HSI is also accredited by the National Home Study Council—the accrediting body for private correspondence schools.

NCES No.	Course Title	Dept.	Course No.	Credits	Level
Elementary school courses					
040207	Elementary typing	ETypg	6		E
040207	Elementary typing	ETypg	7		E
040207	Elementary typing	ETypg	8		E
09	Science health 1st sem	EHlth	71		E
09	Science health 2nd sem	EHlth	72		E
09	Science health 1st sem	EHlth	81		E
09	Science health 2nd sem	EHlth	82		E
120399	Language 1st sem	EEngl	71		E
120399	Language 2nd sem	EEngl	72		E
120399	Language 1st sem	EEngl	81		E
120399	Language 2nd sem	EEngl	82		E
161199	Mathematics 1st sem	EMath	71		E
161199	Mathematics 2nd sem	EMath	72		E
161199	Mathematics 1st sem	EMath	81		E
161199	Mathematics 2nd sem	EMath	82		E
1899	Bible 1st sem	ERlgn	71		E
1899	Bible 2nd sem	ERlgn	72		E
1899	Bible 1st sem	ERlgn	81		E
1899	Bible 2nd sem	ERlgn	82		E
2299	Social studies 1st sem	EHist	71		E
2299	Social studies 2nd sem	EHist	72		E
2299	United States history 1s	EHist	81		E
2299	United States history 2s	EHist	82		E
High school courses					
010399	Agriculture	SAgrc	3	HF	H
040102	Bookkpng & acctg 1st sem	SActg	3	HF	H
040102	Bookkpng & acctg 2nd sem	SActg	4	HF	H
040207	Typing 1st sem	STypg	7	HF	H
040207	Typing 2nd sem	STypg	8	HF	H
100104	Beg clothing construction	SHmEc	16	HF	H
100702	Foods	SHmEc	17	HF	H
100799	Home planning	SHmEc	18	HF	H
120299	Adventist literature	SEngl	13	HF	H
120305	English I 1st sem	SEngl	1	HF	H
120305	English I 2nd sem	SEngl	2	HF	H
120305	English II 1st sem	SEngl	3	HF	H
120305	English II 2nd sem	SEngl	4	HF	H
120307	American lit 1st sem	SEngl	9	HF	H
120307	American lit 2nd sem	SEngl	10	HF	H
120307	English lit 1st sem	SEngl	11	HF	H
120307	English lit 2nd sem	SEngl	12	HF	H
120399	Selected Amer writings	SEngl	7	HF	H
120399	Structure of writing	SEngl	8	HF	H
1210	French I 1st sem	SFren	1	HF	H
1210	French I 2nd sem	SFren	2	HF	H
1210	French II 1st sem	SFren	3	HF	H
1210	French II 2nd sem	SFren	4	HF	H
1211	German I 1st sem	SGrmn	5	HF	H
1211	German I 2nd sem	SGrmn	6	HF	H
1211	German II 1st sem	SGrmn	7	HF	H
1211	German II 2nd sem	SGrmn	8	HF	H
1225	Spanish I 1st sem	SSpan	13	HF	H
1225	Spanish I 2nd sem	SSpan	14	HF	H
1225	Spanish II 1st sem	SSpan	15	HF	H
1225	Spanish II 2nd sem	SSpan	16	HF	H
1503	Biology 1st sem	SBiol	5	HF	H
1503	Biology 2nd sem	SBiol	6	HF	H
1504	Chemistry 1st sem	SChem	7	HF	H

NCES No.	Course Title	Dept.	Course No.	Credits	Level
1504	Chemistry 2nd sem	SChem	8	HF	H
160302	Algebra I 1st sem	SMath	5	HF	H
160302	Algebra I 2nd sem	SMath	6	HF	H
160302	Algebra II	SMath	11	1U	H
160604	Basic geometry 1st sem	SMath	7	HF	H
160604	Basic geometry 2nd sem	SMath	8	HF	H
160604	Modern geometry 1st sem	SMath	9	HF	H
160604	Modern geometry 2nd sem	SMath	10	HF	H
161202	Consumer math 1st sem	SMath	3	HF	H
161202	Consumer math 2nd sem	SMath	4	HF	H
1899	Breakthru w God 1st sem	SRlgn	1	HF	H
1899	Breakthru w God 2nd sem	SRlgn	2	HF	H
1899	God's church 1st sem	SRlgn	5	HF	H
1899	God's church 2nd sem	SRlgn	6	HF	H
1899	God's Word	SRlgn	9	HF	H
1899	God's Word	SRlgn	10	HF	H
1899	God's world	SRlgn	13	HF	H
1899	God's world	SRlgn	14	HF	H
190515	Health	SHlth	15	HF	H
220432	American hist 1st sem	SHist	7	HF	H
220432	American hist 2nd sem	SHist	8	HF	H
220433	World history 1st sem	SHist	3	HF	H
220433	World history 2nd sem	SHist	4	HF	H
220501	American govt 1st sem	SHist	9	HF	H
220501	American govt 2nd sem	SHist	10	HF	H
	College courses				
030302	Music appreciation	Musc	204	3S	L
040101	Prin of acctg 1st sem	Acct	101	3S	L
040101	Prin of acctg 2nd sem	Acct	102	3S	L
040207	Typing 1st sem	Secr	105	2S	L
040207	Typing 2nd sem	Secr	106	2S	L
051109	Speech	Spch	101	3S	L
070299	Admin of the elem school	Educ	350	3S	U
070599	Teaching the social stu	Educ	340	3S	U
070599	The teaching of reading	Educ	354	3S	U
070699	Meth of teaching elem sch	Educ	202	3S	L
070699	Meth of teaching sec sch	Educ	203	3S	L
071103	Evaluation in teaching	Educ	360	3S	U
100313	Nutrition	HmEc	300	3S	U
100601	Adolescent growth and dev	Psyc	344	3S	U
100601	Child development	Psyc	242	3S	L
100601	Exploring early childhood	Psyc	254	2S	L
120299	American lit 1st sem	Engl	221	2S	L
120299	American lit 2nd sem	Engl	222	2S	L
120307	English lit 1st sem	Engl	241	2S	L
120307	English lit 2nd sem	Engl	242	2S	L
120310	Freshman comp 1st sem	Engl	101	3S	L
120310	Freshman comp 2nd sem	Engl	102	3S	L
1210	French I 1st sem	Fren	101	2S	L
1210	French I 2nd sem	Fren	102	2S	L
1210	French II 1st sem	Fren	103	2S	L
1210	French II 2nd sem	Fren	104	2S	L
1210	Intermed French 1st sem	Fren	201	3S	L
1210	Intermed French 2nd sem	Fren	202	3S	L
1211	German I 1st sem	Grmn	101	2S	L
1211	German I 2nd sem	Grmn	102	2S	L
1211	German II 1st sem	Grmn	103	2S	L
1211	German II 2nd sem	Grmn	104	2S	L
1211	Intermed German 1st sem	Grmn	201	3S	L
1211	Intermed German 2nd sem	Grmn	202	3S	L
1212	Beginning Greek 1st sem	Grek	201	4S	L
1212	Beginning Greek 2nd sem	Grek	202	4S	L
1212	Intermed Greek 1st sem	Grek	311	3S	U
1212	Intermed Greek 2nd sem	Grek	312	3S	U
1225	Spanish I 1st sem	Span	101	2S	L
1225	Spanish I 2nd sem	Span	102	2S	L
1225	Spanish II 1st sem	Span	103	2S	L
1225	Spanish II 2nd sem	Span	104	2S	L
1225	Intermed Spanish 1st sem	Span	251	3S	L
1225	Intermed Spanish 2nd sem	Span	252	3S	L
150199	Astronomy	Phys	241	3S	L
1505	Geology	Geol	254	3S	L
1509	Scientfc stdy of creation	Biol	311	2S	U
160302	Algebra	Math	121	3S	L
160602	Trigonometry	Math	122	3S	L
161199	Foundations of math	Math	130	3S	L
161299	Math in the elem school	Educ	355	3S	U
180999	Bible doctrines 1st sem	Rlgn	321	2S	U
180999	Bible doctrines 2nd sem	Rlgn	322	2S	U
180999	World religions	Rlgn	300	2S	U
181406	Life & tchngs of Jesus 1s	Rlgn	201	2S	L

NCES No.	Course Title	Dept.	Course No.	Credits	Level
181406	Life & tchngs of Jesus 2s	Rlgn	202	2S	L
1899	Bible survey 1st sem	Rlgn	101	2S	L
1899	Bible survey 2nd sem	Rlgn	102	2S	L
1899	Corinthian Epistles	Rlgn	340	2S	U
1899	Daniel	Rlgn	311	2S	U
1899	Old Testmt prophets— early	Rlgn	335	3S	U
1899	Old Testmt prophets—later	Rlgn	336	3S	U
1899	Philos of Adventist educ	Educ	210	3S	L
1899	Prophetic guidance	Rlgn	360	2S	U
1899	Revelation	Rlgn	312	2S	U
1899	Science & Chrstian belief	Rlgn	314	1S	U
190515	Health & religion	Rlgn	260	3S	L
190599	Health principles	Hlth	100	2S	L
200406	Psychology of learning	Psyc	365	3S	U
2099	General psychology	Psyc	120	3S	L
220101	Archy of the Middle East	Rlgn	330	3S	U
220299	Macroeconomics	Econ	331	3S	U
220299	Microeconomics	Econ	332	3S	U
220303	Geography 1st sem	Geog	351	2S	U
220303	Geography 2nd sem	Geog	352	2S	U
220426	Eur since Waterloo sem 1	Hist	451	3S	U
220426	Eur since Waterloo sem 2	Hist	452	3S	U
220432	US history 1st sem	Hist	201	3S	L
220432	US history 2nd sem	Hist	202	3S	L
220499	Church history 1st sem	Hist	311	3S	U
220499	Church history 2nd sem	Hist	312	3S	U
220499	Hist of civiliz 1st sem	Hist	101	3S	L
220499	Hist of civiliz 2nd sem	Hist	102	3S	L
220501	Govt in the United States	Hist	203	3S	L
220506	Asian backgrounds	Hist	305	2S	U
220699	Sociology	Soci	204	3S	L
	Noncredit courses				
1899	Work of the Bible instruc	CEd		1U	
1899	Work of the church elder	CEd		1U	
1899	Literature evangelism	CEd		2U	

(15) INDIANA STATE UNIVERSITY

Dr. Clair D. Woodward
Director, Independent Study
AC 209
Indiana State University
Terre Haute, Indiana 47809
Phone: (812) 232-6311 Ext. 5567

Enrollment on a noncredit basis accepted in all credit courses. Gifted high school students are permitted to enroll in undergraduate courses for credit. Overseas enrollment accepted for college and noncredit courses. ISU pays return postage on lessons. Enrollment active for one year. If study is terminated within one month, ISU refunds full tuition less $10; within one to three months, half tuition less $10.

The two noncredit courses, entitled Basic Management and Supervision (course numbers BSBM 1 and 2), are widely used by hospitals, nursing homes, government agencies, and similar institutions in training supervisory personnel on the job. Materials will be sent on approval upon request.

NCES No.	Course Title	Dept.	Course No.	Credits	Level
	College courses				
030499	Intro to the theatre	Spch	174	3S	L
0399	Arts in civilization	Art	151	3S	L
040601	Business communications	BDEOA	330	3S	U
040604	Business report writing	BDEOA	336	2S	U
040604	Business report writing	BDEOA	336	3S	U
040708	Risk and insurance	MgtFn	340	3S	U
041308	Real estate II	MgtFn	346	3S	U
050608	Newswriting	Jrnl	116	3S	L
051001	Survey of broadcasting	Spch	218	3S	L
051004	Writing for brdcst media	Spch	290	3S	L
051110	Voice and diction	Spch	201	3S	L
070102	Philosophy of education	GrEd	406	3S	U
070402	Elem school classrm mgt	ElEd	444	2S	U
070499	Jr high–middle sch curric	SecEd	460	3S	U
070899	Foundations of spec educ	SpEd	162	3S	L
071102	Tests & msrmt & clsrm mgt	ElEd	459	3S	U
100206	Personal finance mgmt	MgtFn	108	2S	L

Indiana State University

NCES No.	Course Title	Dept.	Course No.	Credits	Level
120305	Grammars of English	Engl	310	3S	U
120307	Intro to literature	Engl	130	2S	L
120307	Intro to literature	Engl	130	3S	L
120307	Intro to the short story	Engl	231	2S	L
120307	Lit for younger children	Engl	280	3S	L
120307	The Bible as literature	Engl	334	3S	U
120310	Intro to fiction writing	Engl	220	3S	L
120310	Expository writing	Engl	305	2S	U
120310	Expository wrtng–technicl	Engl	305T	2S	U
150199	General astronomy	Astro	470	3S	U
160299	Basic elementary math I	Math	104	3S	L
160302	Intermediate algebra	Math	111	4S	L
160399	College algebra & trig	Math	115	3S	L
160399	Basic elementary math III	Math	304	3S	U
160801	Principles of statistics	Math	241	3S	L
161101	Math of finance	Math	212	3S	L
161199	Fundamentals & applicatns	Math	201	3S	L
190104	Hist & principles of PE	MWPE	201	2S	L
190109	Org & admin of phys educ	MWPE	441	3S	U
190504	Adv first aid & emer care	H&S	211	2S	L
190509	Personal health science	H&S	111	2S	L
190511	Intro to general safety	H&S	323	3S	U
190599	Traffic & transp safety	H&S	325	3S	U
190599	Ath trng & emer first aid	MWPE	292	3S	L
200199	General psychology	Psych	101	3S	L
200501	Abnormal psychology	Psy	368	3S	U
200504	Developmental psychology	EdPsy	221	3S	L
200509	Psy of personality & adjt	EdPsy	426	3S	U
200799	Intro to social psycholgy	Socio	240	3S	L
200804	Educational psychology	EdPsy	322	3S	U
200804	Adolescent psychology	EdPsy	422	3S	U
210499	Intro to soc wlfr/soc wrk	SocWk	290	3S	L
210499	Child welfare services	SocWk	392	2S	L
220301	Political geography	Geog	432	3S	U
220301	Global geography	Geog	330	3S	U
220302	Intro to economic geog	Geog	213	3S	L
220305	Man's physical environmnt	Geog	111	3S	L
220305	Intro to earth & sky sci	Geog	113	3S	L
220308	Urban geography	Geog	431	3S	U
220399	Conservation of nat resrs	Geog	433	3S	U
220432	The US since 1865	Hist	202	3S	L
220433	Studies in world civlztn	Hist	101	3S	L
220433	Studies in world civlztn	Hist	102	3S	L
220602	Criminology	Crim	200	3S	L
220602	Correctional institutions	Crim	430	3S	U
220602	Criminal investigations	Crim	435	3S	U
220605	Courtship & marriage	Socio	260	3S	L
220605	Sociology of the family	Socio	460	3S	U
220606	Principles of sociology	Socio	120	3S	L
220610	Dynam of crim & dev behav	Crim	427	3S	U
Noncredit courses					
040299	Basic mgmt & supervision	CntEd	BSBM1	NC	
040299	Basic mgmt & supervision	CntEd	BSBM2	NC	

⑯ INDIANA UNIVERSITY

Mr. Frank DiSilvestro
Associate Director for Extended Studies for Independent Study
Independent Study Program
Indiana University
Owen Hall 001
Bloomington, Indiana 47405
Phone: (812) 335-3693

Enrollment on a noncredit basis accepted in all credit courses. Gifted high school students are permitted to enroll in undergraduate courses for credit. Overseas enrollment accepted. Persons wishing information about the External Degree Program should contact Dr. Louis Holtzclaw, External Degree Program, Room A109, 1201 East 38th Street, Indianapolis, Indiana 46205.

NCES No.	Course Title	Dept.	Course No.	Credits	Level
High school courses					
010599	Horticulture 1st sem	Scien	21H	HF	H
010599	Horticulture 2nd sem	Scien	22H	HF	H
030302	Music history & lit	Music	01M	HF	H
030501	Basic draw & storytelling	Art	05D	HF	H
030502	Art history	Art	01H	HF	H
030502	Creative vision	Art	31T	HF	H
040104	Elem bookkeeping 1st sem	BusEd	21B	HF	H
040104	Elem bookkeeping 2nd sem	BusEd	22B	HF	H
040104	Adv bkkpg & acctg 1st sem	BusEd	51B	HF	H
040205	Shorthand 1st sem	BusEd	31S	HF	H
040206	Secretarial practices	BusEd	31P	HF	H
040207	Typewriting 1st sem	BusEd	21T	HF	H
040207	Typewriting 2nd sem	BusEd	22T	HF	H
0404	Data processing	BusEd	31D	HF	H
040601	Business English	BusEd	31E	HF	H
0499	Gen bus 1st sem	BusEd	11G	HF	H
0499	Gen bus 2nd sem	BusEd	12G	HF	H
0499	Retail merchandising	DisEd	31M	HF	H
0499	Salesmanship	DisEd	31S	HF	H
050699	Journalism	Engl	01J	HF	H
0599	Mass media	Engl	01M	HF	H
080102	Fundmntls of aeronautics	Multi	01A	HF	H
090403	Legal & illegal drugs	Hlth	05A	HF	H
090903	Pers & prof health care	Hlth	12H	HF	H
090999	Health & safety education	Hlth	11B	HF	H
100101	Textiles	HmEc	21T	HF	H
100202	Consumer education	HmEc	41C	HF	H
100299	Voc info–career planning	Multi	01V	HF	H
100313	Foods and nutrition	HmEc	11N	HF	H
100402	Family management	HmEc	02F	HF	H
100599	Housing	HmEc	41H	HF	H
100601	Child development	HmEc	31C	HF	H
100699	Pers adj/marr/fam living	HmEc	01F	HF	H
110503	Mech drawing 1st sem	IndA	11M	HF	H
110503	Mech drawing 2nd sem	IndA	12M	HF	H
110503	Architectural drawing	IndA	21A	HF	H
120304	Etymology	Engl	01V	HF	H
120304	Introduction to semantics	Engl	91V	QT	H
120305	Eng grammar & comp review	Engl	51R	HF	H
120307	Freshman English 1st sem	Engl	11E	HF	H
120307	Freshman English 2nd sem	Engl	12E	HF	H
120307	Sophomore English 1st sem	Engl	21E	HF	H
120307	Sophomore English 2nd sem	Engl	22E	HF	H
120307	American lit 1st sem	Engl	31L	HF	H
120307	American lit 2nd sem	Engl	32L	HF	H
120307	Women writers	Engl	33L	HF	H
120307	Contemporary prose	Engl	42C	HF	H
120307	Eng lit 1st sem	Engl	41L	HF	H
120307	Eng lit 2nd sem	Engl	42L	HF	H
120307	Four American novels	Engl	73L	QT	H
120307	Children's literature	Engl	81K	QT	H
120307	The short story	Engl	81L	QT	H
120307	Literature of the future	Engl	82L	QT	H
120307	Mythology	Engl	83L	QT	H
120307	Roots: Amer's early lit	Engl	91L	QT	H
120307	Mysteries	Engl	84L	QT	H
120307	The Bible and literature	Engl	51B	HF	H
120308	Developmental reading	Engl	01R	HF	H
120310	Senior-year composition	Engl	41W	HF	H
120310	Intro to creative writing	Engl	51W	HF	H
120310	Basic composition	Engl	81W	QT	H
120310	Advanced composition	Engl	91W	QT	H
120310	Creative writing: poetry	Engl	52W	HF	H
120399	Vocabulary improvement	Engl	81V	QT	H
120399	How to study in college	Engl	91S	QT	H
1210	First-yr French 1st sem	Fren	11F	HF	H
1210	First-yr French 2nd sem	Fren	12F	HF	H
1210	Second-yr French 1st sem	Fren	21F	HF	H
1210	Second-yr French 2nd sem	Fren	22F	HF	H
1211	First-yr German 1st sem	Ger	11G	HF	H
1211	First-yr German 2nd sem	Ger	12G	HF	H
1211	Second-yr German 1st sem	Ger	21G	HF	H
1211	Second-yr German 2nd sem	Ger	22G	HF	H
121641	First-yr Latin 1st sem	Latin	11L	HF	H
121641	First-yr Latin 2nd sem	Latin	12L	HF	H
121641	Second-yr Latin 1st sem	Latin	21L	HF	H
121641	Second-yr Latin 2nd sem	Latin	22L	HF	H
1225	First-yr Spanish 1st sem	Span	11S	HF	H
1225	First-yr Spanish 2nd sem	Span	12S	HF	H

NCES No.	Course Title	Dept.	Course No.	Credits	Level
1225	Second-yr Spanish 1st sem	Span	21S	HF	H
1225	Second-yr Spanish 2nd sem	Span	22S	HF	H
130799	Business law	BusEd	31L	HF	H
1499	Library & research skills	Engl	23L	HF	H
150399	General biology 1st sem	Scien	21B	HF	H
150399	General biology 2nd sem	Scien	22B	HF	H
150799	Physics 1st sem	Scien	41P	HF	H
150799	Physics 2nd sem	Scien	42P	HF	H
150899	Physical science 1st sem	Scien	11P	HF	H
150899	Physical science 2nd sem	Scien	12P	HF	H
1509	Earth science 1st sem	Scien	11E	HF	H
1509	Earth science 2nd sem	Scien	12E	HF	H
160199	General math 1st sem	Math	11M	HF	H
160199	General math 2nd sem	Math	12M	HF	H
160302	Algebra 1st sem	Math	11A	HF	H
160302	Algebra 2nd sem	Math	12A	HF	H
160302	Advanced algebra I	Math	21A	HF	H
160302	Advanced algebra II	Math	22A	HF	H
160401	Calculus 1st sem	Math	41C	HF	H
160601	Plane geometry 1st sem	Math	21G	HF	H
160601	Plane geometry 2nd sem	Math	22G	HF	H
160602	Trigonometry	Math	41T	HF	H
161201	Business mathematics	Math	11B	HF	H
161202	Consumer mathematics	Math	03C	HF	H
200199	Psychology	SocSt	01P	HF	H
220201	Economics	SocSt	41E	HF	H
220399	World geography 1st sem	SocSt	21G	HF	H
220399	World geography 2nd sem	SocSt	22G	HF	H
220432	American history 1st sem	SocSt	31A	HF	H
220432	American history 2nd sem	SocSt	32A	HF	H
220433	World history 1st sem	SocSt	11W	HF	H
220433	World history 2nd sem	SocSt	12W	HF	H
220501	United States govt I	SocSt	41G	HF	H
220501	US govt II—current probs	SocSt	42G	HF	H
220699	Sociology	SocSt	01S	HF	H
220699	Males & females in Am soc	SocSt	51S	HF	H
2299	Environmental studies	Multi	31E	HF	H
2299	Intro to social studies	SocSt	11X	HF	H

College courses

NCES No.	Course Title	Dept.	Course No.	Credits	Level
030399	Appreciation of music I	Music	M174	3S	L
030399	Rudiments of music	Music	T109	4S	L
030401	Drama: play, perform, prc	Thtr	T490A		U
030501	Textiles	HmEc	H203	3S	L
030502	Intro to African art	FnArt	A250	3S	L
040101	Intro to accounting I	Bus	A201	3S	L
040101	Intro to accounting II	Bus	A202	3S	L
040106	Cost accounting	Bus	A325	3S	U
040109	Prins of hospital acctg	Bus	A203	3S	L
040109	Intermed hospital acctg	Bus	A233	3S	L
040109	Hosp budget & cost analys	Bus	A333	3S	U
040109	Fund accounting	Bus	A335	3S	U
040114	Intro to taxation	Bus	A328	3S	U
040114	Advanced income tax	Bus	A339	3S	U
040199	Intermediate acctg theory	Bus	A211	3S	L
040199	Intermediate acctg probs	Bus	A212	2S	L
040199	Adv financial acctg I	Bus	A322	3S	U
040199	Prof aspects of acctg	Bus	A434	3S	U
040299	Administrative systems	Bus	C300	3S	U
040299	Administrative policy	Bus	J401	3S	U
040302	Personal finance	Bus	F260	3S	L
040304	Mgt comm banks & finan inst	Bus	F466	3S	U
040306	Investment	Bus	F420	3S	U
040312	Bus enterprise & pub pol	Bus	G406	3S	U
040601	Business communications	Bus	C204	3S	L
040708	Prin of risk & insurance	Bus	N300	3S	U
0408	Internat'l business admin	Bus	D300	3S	U
0408	Environ anal for int bus	bus	D419	3S	U
040902	Retail management	Bus	M419	3S	U
040903	Org behav & leadership	Bus.	Z300	3S	U
040903	Org behav & ldrship-hosp	Bus	Z300H	3S	U
040904	Financial management	bus	F301	3S	U
041001	Intro to marketing	Bus	M300	3S	U
041303	Prins of real estate	Bus	R300	3S	U
0499	Business admin: intro	Bus	W100	3S	L
0499	Job search techniques	Bus	X425	1S	U
0499	Basic career development	COAS	Q294	1S	L
0499	Career decision making	COAS	Q394	1S	U
0499	Principles of urban econ	Bus	G330	3S	U
050605	Writing for publication	Jrnl	J327	3S	U

NCES No.	Course Title	Dept.	Course No.	Credits	Level
051103	Interpersonal communicatn	Speec	S122	2S	L
051107	Public speaking	Speec	S121	2S	L
0599	Intro to mass communicats	Jrnl	C200	3S	L
0599	Citizen and the news	Jrnl	C300	3S	U
060103	Computers & their applica	Educ	F400	1S	U
060103	Computers & their applica	Educ	F400	2S	U
060103	Computers & their applica	Educ	F400	3S	U
060599	Data processing fundmntls	DGTS	K100	3S	L
060799	Intr to computer programg	CmpSc	C201	4S	L
070401	Math in elementary school	Educ	E343	3S	U
070401	Prins of secondary educ	Educ	S485	3S	U
070401	Prins: jr hi & mid sch ed	Educ	S486	3S	U
070404	Man & environ: instr meth	Educ	Q400	3S	U
070503	Self-instruction in art	Educ	M135	1S	L
070503	Self-instruction in art	Educ	M135	2S	L
070503	Self-instruction in art	Educ	M135	3S	L
070503	Self-instruction in art	Educ	M135	4S	L
070503	Self-instruction in art	Educ	M135	5S	L
070503	Art expers—elem teacher	Educ	M333	2S	U
070516	Math for elem teachers 1	Math	T101	3S	L
070516	Math for elem teachers 2	Math	T102	3S	L
070516	Math for elem teachers 3	Math	T103	3S	L
070899	Intr to exceptional child	Educ	K205	3S	L
090118	Basic pharmacology	Nurs	B219	3S	L
090255	Dynamics of nursing I	Nurs	J355	3S	U
090255	Dynamics of nursing II	Nurs	J356	3S	U
090255	Dynamics of nursing III	Nurs	J357	3S	U
090255	Dynamics of nursing IV	Nurs	J358	3S	U
090999	Greek/Latin—med terminol	Clas	C209	2S	L
100999	Marriage & family interac	HmEc	H258	3S	L
110699	Prins of transportation	Bus	T300	3S	U
120199	Intro to study of lang	Ling	L103	3S	L
120201	Introduction to film	CmLit	C190	3S	L
120201	Mod lit & other arts: intr	CmLit	C255	2S	L
120204	Literary interpretation	Engl	L202	3S	L
120204	Crit stdy: Eng lit to 1700	Engl	L211	3S	L
120204	Cr stdy Eng lit snce 1700	Engl	L212	3S	L
120305	Intro to the English lang	Engl	G205	3S	L
120307	Classical mythology	Clas	C205	2S	L
120307	Introduction to drama	Engl	L203	3S	L
120307	Intr: novel & short story	Engl	L204	3S	L
120307	Introduction to poetry	Engl	L205	3S	L
120307	Women and literature	Engl	L207	3S	L
120307	Intro to Shakespeare	Engl	L220	3S	L
120307	Late Shakespeare plays	Engl	L314	3S	U
120307	Am novel: Cooper—Dreiser	Engl	L355	3S	U
120307	American drama	Engl	L363	3S	U
120307	Mod drama: continental	Engl	L365	3S	U
120307	Children's literature	Engl	L390	3S	U
120308	Reading/learning techs 1	Educ	X150	1S	D
120308	Reading/learning techs 3	Educ	X152	1S	D
120308	Read/learn techs 3: human	Educ	X152A	1S	D
120308	Read/learn tech 3: soc sc	Educ	X152B	1S	D
120308	Read/learn techs 3: scien	Educ	X152C	1S	D
120308	Literary masterpieces I	Engl	L213	3S	L
120308	Literary masterpieces II	Engl	L214	3S	L
120308	Amer lit since 1914	Engl	L354	32	U
120308	Native American lit	Engl	L364	3S	U
120309	Effective oral communicat	Speec	S124	3S	L
120309	Bus & prof speaking	Speec	S223	3S	L
120309	Freedom of speech	Speec	S339	3S	U
120310	Elementary composition	Engl	W131	3S	L
120310	Creative writing	Engl	W203	3S	L
120310	Prof writing skills	Engl	W231	3S	L
120310	Advanced expository writg	Engl	W350	3S	U
120310	Creative writing: poetry	Engl	W203A	3S	L
120310	Creative writing: prose	Engl	W203B	3S	L
120310	Creative wrtg: poet/prose	Engl	W203C	3S	L
120310	Intro creative writing	Engl	W103	3S	L
120399	Intr: wrtg & lit study I	Engl	L141	4S	L
120399	Intr: wrtg & lit study II	Engl	L142	4S	L
120399	Intr wrtg & lit: murder	Engl	L141A	4S	L
121499	Elementary Italian I	Ital	M100	4S	L
121499	Elementary Italian II	Ital	M150	4S	L
121641	Elementary Latin I	Clas	L100	4S	L
121641	Elementary Latin II	Clas	L150	4S	L
122508	2nd yr Spanish reading I	Span	S216	3S	L
122508	2nd yr Spanish reading II	Span	S266	3S	L
122599	Elementary Spanish I	Span	S110	4S	L
122599	Elementary Spanish II	Span	S150	4S	L
130299	Leg environment of bus	Bus	L201	3S	L

NCES No.	Course Title	Dept.	Course No.	Credits	Level
130299	Commercial law II	Bus	L303	3S	U
131099	Labor law	LabSt	L201	3S	L
150102	The solar system	Astro	A100	3S	L
150103	Stellar astronomy	Astro	A105	3S	L
150199	Introduction to astronomy	Astro	A110	3S	L
150399	Contemporary biology	Bio	N100	3S	L
150599	Earth sci: matls/process	Geol	G103	3S	L
150799	Physics in modern world I	Phys	P101	4S	L
150799	Energy	Phys	P110	2S	L
150799	Energy and technology	Phys	P120	3S	L
160199	Excursions into math	Math	M110	3S	D
160203	Finite mathematics	Math	M118	3S	L
160302	Basic algebra	Math	M014	4S	D
160399	Pre-calculus mathematics	Math	M125	3S	L
160401	Brief surv of calculus I	Math	M119	3S	L
160602	Trigonometric functions	Math	M126	2S	L
160603	Analyt geom & calc I	Math	M215	5S	L
160603	Analyt geom & calc II	Math	M216	5S	L
160899	Statistical techniques	Psych	K300	3S	U
180399	Elementary ethics	Philo	P140	3S	L
180401	Ancient Greek philosophy	Philo	P201	3S	L
1808	Intro to philosophy	Philo	P100	3S	L
181104	Intro to relig in West	Relig	R152	3S	L
1899	Philosophy of woman	Philo	P282	3S	L
190106	Issues phys ed: admin etc	HPER	P444	3S	U
190502	Health probs in community	HPER	H366	3S	U
190508	Nutritional ecology	HmEc	H220	3S	L
190509	Personal health	HPER	H363	3S	U
190513	Organiz of health educ	HPER	H464	2S	U
190703	Recreation and leisure	HPER	R160	3S	L
200199	Introd psychology I	Psych	P101	3S	L
200199	Introd psychology II	Psych	P102	3S	L
200501	Abnormal psychology	Psych	P324	3S	U
200508	Psy: childhood & adolesc	Psych	P316	3S	U
200509	Psychology of personality	Psych	P319	3S	U
200799	Social psychology	Psych	P320	3S	U
200804	Psych measurement–schools	Educ	P407	3S	U
210199	Personnel mgt in pub sect	SPEA	Y373	3S	U
210199	Public administration	SPEA	Y366	3S	U
210199	Policy in state govt	SPEA	V445	3S	U
210199	Cont issues in public aff	SPEA	V450	3S	U
210199	Personnel supervision	DGTS	J101	3S	L
210399	Fndtns criminal investig	Fors	P320	3S	U
210399	Amer juvenile justice sys	Fors	P475	3S	U
220101	Human origins & prehist	Anthr	A105	3S	L
220102	Intro to cultures/Africa	Anthr	E310	3S	U
220102	Culture and society	Anthr	E105	3S	L
220201	Intro to microeconomics	Econ	E103	3S	L
220201	Intro to macroeconomics	Econ	E104	3S	L
220206	Public finance: survey	Econ	E360	3S	U
220213	Intro to managerial econ	Bus	G300	3S	U
220301	Intro to human geography	Geog	G110	3S	L
220305	Phys systems–environment	Geog	G107	3S	L
220306	World regional geography	Geog	G201	3S	L
220399	Environmental conservatn	Geog	G315	3S	U
220399	Meteorology & phys clima	Geog	G304	3S	U
220406	Mod Am soc & intel hist	Hist	A317	3S	U
220420	History of Africa II	Hist	E432	3S	U
220421	American colonial hist I	Hist	A301	3S	U
220423	Mod East Asian civiliz	Hist	H207	3S	L
220426	Europe in 20th century I	Hist	B361	3S	U
220426	Europe in 20th century II	Hist	B362	3S	U
220426	French Rev & Napoleon	Hist	B356	3S	U
220426	Europe: Renaissance/Napol	Hist	H103	3S	L
220426	Europe: Napoleon/present	Hist	H104	3S	L
220427	Lat-Am culture & civiliz	Hist	H211	3S	L
220432	American history I	Hist	H105	3S	L
220432	American history II	Hist	H106	3S	L
220433	World in 20th century I	Hist	H101	3S	L
220450	Ancient Greek culture	Clas	C101	3S	L
220450	Roman culture	Clas	C102	3S	L
220451	Hist backgrd–contemp prob	Hist	H111	3S	L
220472	Women in American life	Hist	H225	3S	L
220499	The American West	Hist	A318	3S	U
220499	History of Indiana	Hist	A333	2S	U
220499	American military history	Hist	H220	3S	L
220499	American labor history	LabSt	L101	3S	L

NCES No.	Course Title	Dept.	Course No.	Credits	Level
220507	Pol parties & int groups	Pol	Y301	3S	U
220509	Intro to Amer politics	Pol	Y103	3S	L
220510	Intro to political theory	Pol	Y105	3S	L
220599	Labor & political system	LabSt	L203	3S	L
220599	Union org & govt	LabSt	L270	3S	L
220599	Women & the law	Pol	Y200	3S	L
220599	Black politics	Pol	Y220	3S	L
220599	Intro to world politics	Pol	Y109	3S	L
220601	The community	Soc	S309	3S	U
220603	Population & human ecol	Soc	S305	3S	U
220605	Sociology of the family	Soc	S316	3S	U
220606	Soc analysis of society	Soc	S100	3S	L
220606	Principles of sociology	Soc	S161	3S	L
220606	Social theory	Soc	S340	3S	U
220610	Deviant bhvr/soc control	Soc	S320	3S	U
220612	Social change	Soc	S215	3S	L
220612	Social organization	Soc	S210	3S	L
220613	Social problems	Soc	S163	3S	L
220699	Society & the individual	Soc	S230	3S	L
220699	Sociology of religion	Soc	S313	3S	U
220699	Sociology of work	Soc	S315	3S	U
220699	Social stratification	Soc	S317	3S	U
220699	Sociology of sex roles	Soc	S338	3S	U
220699	Sociology of law	Soc	S424	3S	U
2299	Introduction to folklore	Flklr	F101	3S	L
2299	Intro to Amer folklore	Flklr	F220	3S	L
2299	Technology & Western civ	HPSc	X210	3S	L U
2299	Intro to philos of sci	HPSc	X303	3S	U
2299	Int to scientific reason	HPSc	X200	3S	L

Graduate courses

NCES No.	Course Title	Dept.	Course No.	Credits	Level
060103	Computers & their applica	Educ	F500	1S	G
060103	Computers & their applica	Educ	F500	2S	G
060103	Computers & their applica	Educ	F500	3S	G

Noncredit courses

NCES No.	Course Title	Dept.	Course No.	Credits	Level
010504	Horticulture	H&R	1	NC	
040206	Secretarial procedures	Bus	3	NC	
040206	Real estate secretary	RE	2	NC	
040306	Securities & investing	PF	1	NC	
040699	Business English	Bus	2	NC	
050699	Labor journalism	LS	1	NC	
070703	Employ search strat: pers	CP	4	NC	
070703	Employ search strat: jobs	CP	5	NC	
100299	Vocational information	CP	1	NC	
100603	Plan soc rec/older adults	CP	3	NC	
100699	Preparation for retiremnt	CP	2	NC	
120305	Eng grammar & comp review	RS	3	NC	
120308	Techs for reading & study	RS	1	NC	
120399	Vocabulary improvement	RS	2	NC	
120399	Understndg/improvg memory	RS	4	NC	
130799	Business law	Bus	1	NC	
160199	Overcoming math anxiety	GIBM	3	NC	
160399	Arithmetic for algebra I	GIBM	1	NC	
160399	Arithmetic for algebra II	GIBM	2	NC	
1899	Intro to meditation	RelS	1	NC	
1999	Intro to collectibles	H&R	2	NC	
1999	Finding your roots	H&R	3	NC	
220502	English & government	Cit	1	NC	
220502	Our Constitution & govt	Cit	2	NC	

(17) LOUISIANA STATE UNIVERSITY

Mr. Don Hammons
Director
Independent Study by Correspondence
Louisiana State University
Baton Rouge, Louisiana 70803
Phone: (504) 388-3171

Enrollment on a noncredit basis accepted in all credit courses. Gifted high school students are permitted to enroll in undergraduate courses for credit. Overseas enrollment accepted. High school students must meet university guidelines.

NCES No.	Course Title	Dept.	Course No.	Credits	Level
	High school courses				
030599	Art	Art	121	HF	H
030599	Art	Art	122	HF	H

NCES No.	Course Title	Dept.	Course No.	Credits	Level
040104	Bookkeeping	Bus	231	HF	H
040104	Bookkeeping	Bus	232	HF	H
040205	Shorthand	Bus	221	HF	H
040205	Shorthand	Bus	222	HF	H
040207	Typewriting	Bus	211	HF	H
040207	Typewriting	Bus	212	HF	H
040299	Clerical practice	Bus	241	HF	H
041299	Data processing	Bus	251	HF	H
0499	General business	Bus	201	HF	H
0499	General business	Bus	202	HF	H
0810	Drafting technology	InArt	161	HF	H
100202	Consumer education	HmEc	153	HF	H
100312	Nutrition education	HmEc	155	HF	H
100699	Home and family	HmEc	151	HF	H
120399	English I	Engl	311	HF	H
120399	English I	Engl	312	HF	H
120399	English II	Engl	321	HF	H
120399	English II	Engl	322	HF	H
120399	English III	Engl	331	HF	H
120399	English III	Engl	332	HF	H
120399	English IV	Engl	341	HF	H
120399	English IV	Engl	342	HF	H
120399	Business English	Engl	351	HF	H
121099	French	Frnch	141	HF	H
121099	French	Frnch	142	HF	H
122505	Spanish	Span	145	HF	H
122505	Spanish	Span	146	HF	H
1503	Biology	Biol	511	HF	H
1503	Biology	Biol	512	HF	H
150899	General science	Sci	501	HF	H
150899	General science	Sci	502	HF	H
160301	Mathematics I	Math	401	HF	H
160301	Mathematics I	Math	402	HF	H
160301	Mathematics II	Math	441	HF	H
160301	Mathematics II		442	HF	H
160302	Algebra I	Math	411	HF	H
160302	Algebra I	Math	412	HF	H
160302	Algebra II	Math	431	HF	H
160302	Algebra II	Math	432	HF	H
160602	Trigonometry	Math	451	HF	H
161201	Business math	Math	421	HF	H
161201	Business math	Math	422	HF	H
161202	Consumer mathematics	Math	461	HF	H
161202	Consumer mathematics	Math	462	HF	H
190599	Health	HEd	131	HF	H
190599	Health	HEd	132	HF	H
220299	Free enterprise	SoSci	661	HF	H
220399	World geography	SoSci	601	HF	H
220399	World geography	SoSci	602	HF	H
220432	American history	SoSci		HF	H
220433	World history	SoSci	621	HF	H
220501	American government	SoSci		HF	H
220611	Sociology	SoSci		HF	H
220612	Sociology	SoSci		HF	H
2299	Civics	SoSci	611	HF	H
2299	Civics	SoSci	612	HF	H

College courses

NCES No.	Course Title	Dept.	Course No.	Credits	Level
010199	Coop in agriculture	Agri	4020C	3S	U
010406	Elements of dairying	DySc	1048C	3S	L
020902	Home planning	ID	3721C	3S	U
030399	Music appreciation	Music	1751C	3S	L
030399	Music appreciation	Music	1752C	3S	L
030399	Music history	Music	4451C	3S	U
030399	Music history	Music	4452C	3S	U
030499	Introduction to theater	Spch	1020C	3S	L
030499	Argumentation & debate	Spch	2063C	3S	L
030499	Stage costuming	Spch	4122C	3S	U
040101	Intro financial acctg	Acctg	2001C	3S	L
040101	Intermediate acctg Pt I	Acctg	2021C	3S	L
040101	Intermediate acctg Pt II	Acctg	3021C	3S	U
040101	Advanced acctg	Acctg	3022C	3S	U
040103	Auditing	Acctg	3222C	3S	U
040106	Cost analysis & control	Acctg	3121C	3S	U
040111	Intro managerial acctg	Acctg	2101C	3S	L
040114	Income-tax acctg	Acctg	3221C	3S	U
040201	Office management	OAdm	3400C	3S	U
040203	Records management	BAdm	3200C	3S	U
040205	Beginning shorthand	OAdm	2100C	3S	L
040207	Beginning typewriting	OAdm	2000C	3S	L
040207	Intermediate typing	OAdm	2001C	3S	L
040207	Advanced typing	OAdm	3000C	3S	U
040301	Basic business finance	Fin	3715C	3S	L
040308	Money and banking	Econ	3500C	3S	L
040399	Business law	Fin	3201C	3S	U
040399	Commercial transactions	Fin	3202C	3S	U
040399	Principles of real estate	Fin	3351C	3S	U
040601	Business communication/	BAdm	2071C	3S	L
040705	Life and health insurance	Fin	3441C	3S	U
040709	Property & liability ins	Fin	3442C	3S	U
040709	Risk and insurance	Fin	3440C	3S	U
040901	Mgmt prin & policies	Mgmt	3159C	3S	U
040901	Bus policies & problems	Mgmt	3190C	3S	U
040903	Human behavior in orgn	Mgmt	4164C	3S	U
040999	Business communication	Mgmt	2071C	3S	L
040999	Operations & info systems	Mgmt	3115C	3S	U
040999	Collective bargaining	Mktg	3127C	3S	U
041001	Prins of marketing	Mktg	3401C	3S	U
041004	Sales management	Mktg	4423C	3S	U
041004	Retailing management	Mktg	4431C	3S	U
041004	Marketing management	Mktg	4451C	3S	U
041099	Consumer anal & behavior	Mktg	3411C	3S	U
041099	Marketing research	Mktg	3413C	3S	U
041099	Mkt comm selling & advtg	Mktg	4421C	3S	U
041107	Personnel–human resources	Mgmt	4167C	3S	U
041299	Operations & info systems	QM	3115C	3S	U
0499	Intro to business	Bus	1001C	3S	L
060701	FORTRAN programming	CmpSc	1240C	3S	L
060701	COBOL programming	CmpSc	1270C	3S	L
070199	Intro to study of educ	Educ	2000C	3S	L
070514	School libraries	Educ	3553C	3S	U
070599	Books & AV for children	Educ	3551C	3S	U
070801	Char of excep children	Educ	3700C	3S	U
070806	Intro to mentally retardd	Educ	3750C	3S	U
071199	Evaluation of instruction	Educ	3200C	2S	U
0810	Engineering graphics	Engr	1001C	2S	L
0810	Machine drawing	Engr	2162C	2S	L
081104	Dynamics	ME	3133C	3S	U
100103	Clothing and human behavr	HmEc	1030C	3S	L
100312	Intro to human nutrition	HmEc	1010C	3S	L
100602	Changing home & family	HmEc	1050C	3S	L
1199	Intro to voc education	VTIE	2070C	3S	L
120305	English grammar	Engl	2210C	3S	L
120307	English lit to 1798	Engl	2020C	3S	L
120307	Engl lit 1798-pres	Engl	2022C	3S	L
120310	English composition	Engl	1001C	3S	L
120310	English composition	Engl	1002C	3S	L
120310	Advanced composition	Engl	2001C	3S	L
120310	Technical writing	Engl	2002C	3S	L
120399	Intro to fiction	Engl	2025C	3S	L
120399	Intro to drama & poetry	Engl	2027C	3S	L
120399	Major American writers	Engl	2070C	3S	L
121008	Elementary French	Frnch	1001C	5S	L
121008	Intermediate French	Frnch	2051C	5S	L
121008	Intermediate French	Frnch	2053C	3S	L
121108	Intermediate German	Ger	2053C	3S	L
121109	Elementary German	Ger	1001C	5S	L
121109	Intermediate German	Ger	2051C	5S	L
121608	Elementary Latin	Latin	1001C	5S	L
121608	Intermediate Latin	Latin	2051C	5S	L
121608	Vergil	Latin	2055C	3S	L
122508	Elementary Spanish	Span	1001C	5S	L
122508	Intermediate Spanish	Span	2051C	5S	L
122508	Intermediate Spanish	Span	2053C	3S	L
122508	Readings in Spanish lit	Span	2055C	3S	L
150103	Stellar astronomy	Astro	1102C	3S	L
150199	The solar system	Astro	1101C	3S	L
1503	Human physiology	Biol	2160C	3S	L
150399	General biology	Bio	1001C	3S	L
150399	General biology	Bio	1002C	3S	L
150599	Geology	Geol	1001C	3S	L
150799	General physics	Phys	2001C	3S	L
150799	General physics	Phys	2002C	3S	L
150899	Physical science	PhSc	1001C	3S	L
150899	Physical science	PhSc	1002C	3S	L
160302	Algebra	Math	1021C	3S	L
160302	Algebra and applications	Math	1015C	3S	L
160302	Linear algebra	Math	2085C	3S	L

NCES No.	Course Title	Dept.	Course No.	Credits	Level
160305	Introductory coll math I	Math	1009C	3S	L
160305	Introductory coll math II	Math	1010C	3S	L
160401	Analyt geom & calculus II	Math	1452C	5S	L
160401	Multidimensional calculus	Math	2057C	3S	L
160602	Plane trigonometry	Math	1022C	3S	L
160603	Analyt geom & calculus I	Math	1450C	5S	L
160801	Statistcl methods/models	QM	2000C	3S	L
160802	Intro to business science	QM	2001C	3S	L
160802	Statistical analysis	QM	3001C	3S	U
160803	Foun for operations resch	QM	3002C	3S	U
161103	Calculus with bus & econ	Math	1431C	3S	L
161103	Finite math—bus & econ	Math	1435C	3S	L
180301	Intro to philosophy	Philo	1011C	3S	L
180502	Elementary logic	Philo	1021C	3S	L
180502	Intro to logic theory	Philo	2010C	3S	L
190502	Personal & comm health	HPRe	1600C	2S	L
190511	Occupational safety	InEd	2051C	3S	L
190512	Human sexuality	HPRe	2600C	3S	L
190599	School health program	HPRe	4600C	3S	U
190599	Community safety educ	HPRe	4602C	3S	U
200199	Intro to psychology	Psych	2000C	3S	L
200505	Psychology of adjustment	Psych	2004C	3S	L
200599	Child psychology	Psych	2076C	3S	L
200599	Adolescent psychology	Psych	2078C	3S	L
200804	Educational psychology	Psych	2060C	3S	L
210304	Intro to law enforcement	CJ	1107C	3S	L
210304	Police process	CJ	2131C	3S	L
210304	Judicial process	CJ	2132C	3S	L
210304	Correctional process	CJ	2133C	3S	L
210304	Public & comm relations	CJ	3152C	3S	U
210304	Criminal investigation	CJ	4133C	3S	U
220102	Culture growth	Anthr	1003C	3S	L
220199	General anthropology	Anthr	1001C	3S	L
220201	Econ prins & problems	Econ	2010C	3S	L
220201	Econ prins & problems	Econ	2020C	3S	L
220201	Economic principles	Econ	2030C	3S	L
220209	Dev of econ system in US	Econ	1010C	3S	L
220211	Labor economics	Econ	4210C	3S	U
220212	Economics of consumption	Econ	3310C	3S	U
220299	Macroecon anal & policy	Econ	2035C	3S	L
220299	Econ of govt regulation	Econ	4440C	3S	U
220301	Human geography	Geog	1001C	3S	L
220301	Human geography	Geog	1003C	3S	L
220406	History of Western civ	Hist	1001C	3S	L
220406	History of Western civ	Hist	1003C	3S	L
220421	Colonial Amer 1607-1763	Hist	4051C	3S	U
220421	The American Revolution	Hist	4052C	3S	U
220424	English history	Hist	2012C	3S	L
220424	English history	Hist	2011C	3S	L
220426	Mod European history	Hist	2021C	3S	L
220426	Mod European history	Hist	2022C	3S	L
220428	History of Louisiana	Hist	2071C	3S	L
220432	American history	Hist	2055C	3S	L
220432	American history	Hist	2057C	3S	L
220432	Recent American history	Hist	4059C	3S	U
220432	Recent American history	Hist	4060C	3S	U
220432	The antebellum South	Hist	4071C	3S	U
220432	The new South	Hist	4072C	3S	U
220501	American government	PolSc	2051C	3S	L
220503	Intro to comparative pol	PolSc	2053C	3S	L
220507	Pol parties in the US	PolSc	4031C	3S	U
220602	Criminology	Socio	4461C	3S	U
220602	Criminology	SocW	3007C	3S	U
220605	Marriage and family relat	Socio	2505C	3S	L
220608	Rural sociology	Socio	2351C	3S	L
220613	Current social problems	Socio	2501C	3S	L
220699	Introductory sociology	Socio	2001C	3S	L

NCES No.	Course Title	Dept.	Course No.	Credits	Level
Noncredit courses					
040101	Basic accounting	Acct	0000	NC	V
120310	English composition	Engl	0001C	NC	L
150704	Electricity–alt current	InArt	0002	NC	V
150704	Electricity–dir current	InArt	0001	NC	V
160301	Refresher math	Math	0000	NC	D
160301	Arithmetic for college	Math	0002C	NC	D
160302	Intro to college algebra	Math	0004C	NC	D
160302	Intro to college algebra	Math	0005C	NC	D
210302	Firefighter I	FmTng	I	NC	V
210302	Firefighter II	FmTng	II	NC	V
210302	Firefighter III	FmTng	III	NC	V
210302	Fire service inspector I	FmTng	0000	NC	V

(18) **LOYOLA UNIVERSITY OF CHICAGO**

Dr. Ruth E. McGugan
Director
Correspondence Study Division
Loyola University of Chicago
Lewis Towers 510
820 North Michigan Avenue
Chicago, Illinois 60611
Phone: (312) 670-3018

Enrollment on a noncredit basis accepted in all credit courses. Only in exceptional cases are gifted high school students permitted to enroll in undergraduate courses for credit. Overseas enrollment accepted for college courses. Fourteen new courses are available as departmental offerings, including communication, nursing, finance, and management. Loyola is also the only Roman Catholic university that offers theology courses by correspondence.

NCES No.	Course Title	Dept.	Course No.	Credits	Level
	College courses				
030402	Dram struc & theat proc I	ThArt	203	3S	L
030499	Hist of the theater I	ThArt	256	3S	L
030499	Hist of the theater II	ThArt	257	3S	L
040101	Intro to accounting I	Acctg	201	3S	L
040101	Intro to accounting II	Acctg	202	3S	L
040101	Intermed accounting I	Acctg	303	3S	U
040101	Intermed accounting II	Acctg	304	3S	U
040106	Cost accounting	Acctg	231	3S	L
040302	Financ couns & pers finan	Finc	339	3S	U
040904	Theory of orgnztn & mgmt	Mgmt	316	3S	U
0599	Intro to mass communicatn	Commu	270	3S	L
070102	Hist of Western education	Foun	310	3S	U
070102	Philosophy of education	Foun	320	3S	U
070102	Hist of Amer education	Foun	344	3S	U
070103	Sociology of education	Foun	327	3S	U
070199	Psychology of adolescence	Foun	337	3S	U
070199	Psychology of personality	Foun	338	3S	U
070199	Statistical methods	Foun	380	3S	U
070404	Techn teachg/secondry sch	Curr	M13	3S	U
070512	Children's literature	Curr	206	3S	L
070512	Teachg bgn readg lang arts	Curr	M11	3S	U
070512	Mat pro tchg rd lang arts	Curr	M51	3S	U
070512	Teachg readg in sec schls	Curr	M55	3S	U
070516	Teachg metric sys/ele sch	Curr	305	3S	U
070516	Maters & methods in arith	Curr	M40	3S	U
070516	Math for teachers I	Curr	104	3S	L
070516	Math for teachers II	Curr	105	3S	L
090601	Nursing management	Nurs	320	3S	U
120202	Introduction to poetry	Engl	271	3S	L
120202	Introduction to drama	Engl	272	3S	L
120202	Introduction to fiction	Engl	273	3S	L
120299	Maj Amer wri 1607-1900	Engl	293	3S	L
120299	English lit to 1485	Engl	320	3S	U
120299	English lit 1485-1660	Engl	325	3S	U
120299	Romantic period 1798-1837	Engl	335	3S	U
120299	Classical mythology	Clas	271	3S	L
120299	Classical epics	Clas	272	3S	L
120299	Classical theatre	Clas	273	3S	L
120299	Studies in detective fict	EngLL	285	3S	L
120299	Chaucer	EngLL	322	3S	U
120310	College English I	Engl	101	3S	L
120310	College English II	Engl	201	3S	L
120310	Creative writing	Engl	315	3S	U
120310	Fundamentals of writing	Engl	098	2S	D
1210	Elemen French I	Frnch	101	3S	
1210	Intermed French I	Frnch	111	3S	
1210	Intermed French II	Frnch	112	3S	
1211	Elemen German I	Ger	101	3S	
1211	Elemen German II	Ger	102	3S	
1211	Intermed German I	Ger	111	3S	
1211	Intermed German II	Ger	112	3S	
121241	Elementary Greek I	Greek	131	3S	L
121241	Elementary Greek II	Greek	132	3S	L
121243	Intro New Testament Greek	Greek	267	3S	L
1214	Elemen Italian I	Ital	101	3S	L
1214	Elemen Italian II	Ital	102	3S	L
1214	Intermed Italian I	Ital	111	3S	L
1214	Intermed Italian II	Ital	112	3S	L
121641	Elementary Latin I	Latin	131	3S	L

NCES No.	Course Title	Dept.	Course No.	Credits	Level
121641	Elementary Latin II	Latin	132	3S	L
1225	Elemen Spanish I	Span	101	3S	L
1225	Elemen Spanish II	Span	102	3S	L
1225	Intermed Spanish I	Span	111	3S	L
1225	Intermed Spanish II	Span	112	3S	L
1225	Adv Spanish composition	Span	202	3S	L
1225	Survey of Spanish lit I	Span	209	3S	L
1225	Survey of Spanish lit II	Span	210	3S	L
1225	Spanish gram for tchrs I	Span	306	3S	U
122504	Modern Span-Amer literatr	Span	322	3S	U
130499	Issues in crim justice	CrmJ	325	3S	U
130499	Criminal justice system	CrmJ	131	3S	L
130599	Business and government	LegS	315	3S	U
130701	American legal system	LegS	250	3S	L
130799	Law and business organizs	LegS	351	3S	U
130799	Law and specialized relat	LegS	352	3S	U
130999	Real estate princ pract	LegS	255	3S	L
140101	Catalg & clsfn of lib mtl	LibSc	202	3S	L
140199	Intro to library methods	LibSc	201	3S	L
140306	Public library service	LibSc	208	3S	L
140399	Institution libraries	LibSc	209	3S	L
140408	Sel acqu of libr material	LibSc	204	3S	L
140799	Reference work	LibSc	205	3S	L
160302	Intermediate algebra	Math	100	3S	L
160602	Plane trigonometry	Math	101	3S	L
160899	Fundmntls of statistics	Math	107	3S	L
180302	Action and values: ethics	Philo	281	3S	L
180499	Gen hist of philosophy	Philo	200	3S	L
180599	Knowl & reality: logic	Philo	274	3S	L
180603	Knowl & reality: religion	Philo	271	3S	L
180607	Philosophy of man	Philo	120	3S	L
180902	Theology of St. Paul	Theo	306	3S	U
180902	The Orthodox Christn trad	Theo	279	3S	L
180999	Religions of the world	Theo	322	3S	U
181099	Protestnt churches in US	Theo	353	3S	U
181199	Christian marriage	Theo	293	3S	L
181201	Old Testament	Theo	100	3S	L
181202	New Testament	Theo	270	3S	L
181202	Intro New Testament Greek	Theo	307	3S	L
181301	Eastern religions	Theo	281	3S	L
181399	Church in crisis	Theo	367	3S	U
181399	The Orthodox Christn trad	Theo	279	3S	L
181401	God in the modern world	Theo	332	3S	U
181405	Theo of the Sacraments	Theo	278	3S	L
181406	Jesus Christ	Theo	287	3S	L
200101	General psychology	Psych	101	3S	L
200202	Comparative psychology	Psych	301	3S	U
200406	Learning and behavior	Psych	251	3S	L
200501	Abnormal psychology	Psych	331	3S	U
200504	Developmental psychology	Psych	273	3S	L
200509	Psychology of personality	Psych	338	3S	U
200599	Psychology of adolescence	Psych	348	3S	U
200799	Social psychology	Psych	275	3S	L
210404	Field of social work	SoWk	200	3S	L
210404	Child welfare	SoWk	205	3S	L
220201	Princp of economics I	Econ	201	3S	L
220201	Princp of economics II	Econ	202	3S	L
220201	Microeconomics	Econ	303	3S	U
220205	Macroeconomics	Econ	304	3S	U
220213	Economics of labor	Econ	360	3S	U
220426	Ev Wst ideas/inst to 1648	Hist	101	3S	L
220426	Evol W ideas/ins snc 1648	Hist	102	3S	L
220429	History of Mediter world	Hist	205	3S	L
220432	The US to 1865	Hist	251	3S	L
220432	The US since 1865	Hist	252	3S	L
220499	Era of Fren Rev Napoleon	Hist	316	3S	U
220499	History of Amer education	Hist	388	3S	U
220501	American politics	PolSc	101	3S	L
220511	State govt and politics	PolSc	221	3S	L
220599	The legislative process	PolSc	210	3S	L
220601	Community	Socio	235	3S	L
220602	Pattns of crim activity	Socio	212	3S	L
220605	The family	Socio	240	3S	L
220606	The sociological perspect	Socio	101	3S	L
220613	Issues in Amer society	Socio	120	3S	L

⑲ MASSACHUSETTS DEPARTMENT OF EDUCATION

Ms. Ellen H. Maddocks
Supervisor of Correspondence Instruction
Bureau of Student, Community, and Adult Services
Massachusetts Department of Education
1385 Hancock Street
Quincy, Massachusetts 02169
Phone: (617) 770-7582

Enrollment on a noncredit basis accepted in all credit courses. No overseas enrollment accepted.

NCES No.	Course Title	Dept.	Course No.	Credits	Level
	High school courses				
040104	Bookkeeping	Acctg	BUS1	1U	H
040207	Typewriting	Bus	BUS2	HF	H
040502	Small-business mgt	Bus	BUS4	HF	H
0804	Automotive engines	EngAS	AUT1	HF	H
0804	Automotive chassis	EngAS	AUT2	HF	H
090901	Modern health	HSci	SCI2	1U	H
100202	Consumer economics	Econ	SS10	HF	H
100299	Practical economics	Econ	SS9	HF	H
100503	Interior design	Graph	ART2	1U	H
110503	Basic drawing techniques	Graph	ART1	HF	H
120305	English for everyone	EngLL	ENG2	1U	H
120307	Bible backg for Engl lit	EngLL	ENG9	HF	H
120308	Improving your reading	EngLL	ENG10	1U	H
120399	English IX	EngLL	ENG3	1U	H
120399	English X	EngLL	ENG4	1U	H
120399	English XI: general	EngLL	ENG6	1U	H
120399	English XI: college prep	EngLL	ENG5	1U	H
120399	English XII: general	EngLL	ENG8	1U	H
120399	English XII: college prep	EngLL	ENG7	1U	H
1210	French I	Frnch	LAN3	1U	H
1210	French II	Frnch	LAN4	1U	H
121641	Latin I	CILL	LAN1	1U	H
121641	Latin II	CILL	LAN2	1U	H
1225	Spanish I	Span	LAN7	1U	H
1225	Spanish II	Span	LAN8	1U	H
130799	Business law	Bus	BUS3	HF	H
1503	General biology	Bio	SCI1	1U	H
150401	Chemistry	Chem	SCI4	1U	H
160302	Elementary algebra	Math	MATH5	1U	H
160302	Intermediate algebra	Math	MATH6	1U	H
160601	Geometry	Math	MATH7	1U	H
161201	Business mathematics	Bus	MATH3	1U	H
161299	General mathematics	Math	MATH4	1U	H
200102	General psychology	Psych	SS8	1U	H
220432	Amer history coll prep	Hist	SS5	1U	H
220432	American history general	Hist	SS11	1U	H
220433	World history	Hist	SS6	1U	H
220501	Problems of democracy	Hist	SS7	1U	H
	Noncredit courses				
0809	Basic electricity	EEg	EEG1	NC	D
080903	Basic electronics	EEg	EEG5	NC	D
080999	Basic television	EEg	EEG4	NC	D
080999	Transistors	EEg	EEG6	NC	D
110104	Journeyman electric prep	CSLP	CSLP4	NC	D
110405	Building custodian's prep	CSLP	CSLP2	NC	D
120309	Vocabulary building	Eng	ENG1	NC	D
120399	High school equiv prep	GED	GED1	NC	D
1318	Law and the legal system	Law	SS4	NC	D
160199	The metric system	Math	MATH2	NC	D
160301	Everyday review math	Math	MATH1	NC	D
160399	High school equiv prep	GED	GED1	NC	D
2199	Basic civil service train	CSLP	CSLP1	NC	D
220502	Prep for naturalization	Pol	CSLP6	NC	D
220506	Practical politics	PolSc	SS1	NC	D
2299	High school equiv prep	GED	GED1	NC	D

⑳ MEMORIAL UNIVERSITY OF NEWFOUNDLAND

Dr. A. H. Roberts
Dean, Part-time Credit Studies
Memorial University of Newfoundland
St. John's, Newfoundland A1B 3X8, Canada
Phone: (709) 738-8700

Overseas enrollment is not encouraged; each case is judged on an individual basis. It is difficult to service out-of-province students due to the number of assignments required and problems with the mail service for long distances. Then, too, entry and exit in these courses follow the on-campus semester timetable.

NCES No.	Course Title	Dept.	Course No.	Credits	Level
	College courses				
120307	Major writers to 1800	Engl	2000	3S	U
120307	Canadian lit to the 1930s	Engl	3150	3S	U
120307	American lit to 1880	Engl	4251	3S	U
160699	Euclidean & rel geometry	Math	3040	3S	U
180499	Contemporary issues	Philo	2802	3S	U
200199	Intro to psychology I	Psych	1000	3S	U
200199	Intro to psychology II	Psych	1001	3S	U
200401	Operant analysis of behav	Psych	2400	3S	U
200501	Abnormal behavior	Psych	3600	3S	U
200504	Human development III	Psych	2012	3S	U
200509	Personality	Psych	2200	3S	U
200599	Brain and behavior	Psych	2500	3S	U
220303	Historical geog of Nfld	Geog	3290	3S	U
220309	Introduction to geography	Geog	1000	3S	U
220399	Quantitative methods	Geog	2220	3S	U
220399	Conserva of nat resources	Geog	2320	3S	U
220399	Nfld space economy	Geog	2490	3S	U
220423	India and Southeast Asia	Hist	3550	3S	U
220499	Introduction to history	Hist	1000	3S	U
220499	N Atlantic hist to 1820	Hist	2100	3S	U
220503	Intro to comparative pol	PolSc	2300	3S	U
220606	Principles of sociology	Socio	2000	3S	U
220610	Deviance	Socio	3290	3S	U
220699	Canadian soc and culture	Socio	2240	3S	U

㉑ MISSISSIPPI STATE UNIVERSITY

Dr. C. K. Lee
Director, Independent Study Office
Continuing Education
Mississippi State University
Drawer 5247
Mississippi State, Mississippi 39762
Phone: (601) 325-3473

Enrollment on a noncredit basis accepted in some credit courses. Gifted high school students are permitted to enroll in undergraduate courses for credit. Overseas enrollment accepted.

NCES No.	Course Title	Dept.	Course No.	Credits	Level
	High school courses				
0499	General business	Buss		1U	H
070515	General science	Scien		1U	H
100699	Personal & family relatns	HmEc		HF	H
120307	English I	Eng		1U	H
120307	English II	Eng		1U	H
120307	English III	Eng		1U	H
120307	English IV	Eng		1U	H
160199	General mathematics I	Math		1U	H
160199	General mathematics II	Math		1U	H
160199	Senior math	Math		1U	H
160199	Consumer math	Math		1U	H
160302	Algebra I	Math		1U	H
160302	Algebra II	Math		1U	H
160601	Plane geometry	Math		1U	H
160601	Solid geometry	Math		HF	H
160602	Trigonometry	Math		HF	H
220199	General psychology	Psych		1U	H
220201	Economics	SoStu		HF	H
220399	World geography	SoStu		HF	H
220432	American history	SoStu		1U	H
220433	World history	SoStu		1U	H
220499	Mississippi history	SoStu		HF	H
220501	American government	SoStu		HF	H
220599	Civics	SoStu		HF	H
220599	Problems in American demo	SoStu		HF	H
220606	Sociology	SoStu		HF	H
	College courses				
011202	Game conservation & mgt	Wildl	4513	3S	U
011299	Env prob: forest water	Wildl	4143	3S	L
040101	Accounting principles I	Acctg	1413	3S	L

NCES No.	Course Title	Dept.	Course No.	Credits	Level
040101	Accounting principles II	Acctg	1423	3S	L
040106	Cost accounting	Acctg	2213	3S	L
040203	Filing records and mgmnt	Bus	2052	2S	U
040206	Secretarial procedures	Bus	3113	3S	U
040299	Office management	Bus	3133	3S	U
040301	Business finance	Bus	2223	3S	U
040308	Money and banking	Bus	2113	3S	U
041001	Principles of marketing	Mktg	2313	3S	U
041099	Retailing	Mktg	2223	3S	U
070504	Tchg of basic bus subjcts	Bus	4213	3S	U
070516	Tcng math: elem & jr high	Elem	5453	3S	U
070520	General psychology	Psych	1013	3S	L
070520	Prin of educational psych	Psych	2123	3S	U
070520	Human growth & develpmnt	Psych	1053	3S	L
070520	Psychology of adolescence	Psych	1073	3S	L
070520	Learning theories classrm	Psych		3S	U
070520	Pers adj & school child	Psych	4073	3S	U
070609	Intro vocational educ	Educ	1063	3S	L
070701	Basic course in guidance	Guid		3S	U
070705	Guid ser & mental health	Guid	4113	3S	U
070899	Work/parents of excpt ch	SpEd	5113	3S	U
070899	Tchg the disadvantaged ch	SpEd	5123	3S	U
071199	Measurement & evaluation	Psych	4313	3S	U
090114	Pro solv micro & med tech	Bio	5223	3S	U
090114	Elem microbiology	Bio	1113	3S	L
090199	Science of public health	Bio	1123	3S	L
100399	Indiv & family nutrition	HmEc	3213	3S	U
100799	Purch food & equip instit	HmEc	5293	3S	U
1210	Intermediate French	Lang	1133	3S	L
1210	Intermediate French	Lang	1143	3S	L
1225	Intermediate Spanish	Lang	1133	3S	L
1225	Intermediate Spanish	Lang	1143	3S	L
150199	Descriptive astronomy	Phys	1063	3S	L
150401	Intro to chemistry	Chem	1003	3S	L
150899	Physical science survey	Phys	1013	3S	L
150899	Physical science survey	Phys	1023	3S	L
160202	Structure real number sys	Math	1513	3S	L
160204	Informal geometry & meas	Math	1523	3S	L
160302	College algebra	Math	1153	3S	L
160399	Mathematics	Math	1053	3S	L
160401	Finite math & intro calcu	Math	1263	3S	L
160401	Calculus I	Math	1713	3S	L
160401	Calculus II	Math	1723	3S	L
160602	Trigonometry	Math	1253	3S	L
160899	Intro to business statist	Bus	1513	3S	L
180302	Intro to ethics	Philo	1123	3S	L
180302	Intro to Old Testament	Relig	1213	3S	L
180302	Intro to New Testament	Relig	1223	3S	L
180302	World religions I	Relig	2203	3S	U
180302	World religions II	Relig	2213	3S	U
181101	Intro to philosophy	Philo	1103	3S	L
190199	Prin of elem health & PE	PhyEd	3123	3S	U
190502	Community recreation	PhyEd	3362	2S	U
190502	Community hygiene	PubHI	1003	3S	L
190503	Consumer health	PhyEd	2163	3S	U
190504	Communicable disease cont	PubHI	2003	3S	U
190511	General safety methods	PhyEd	3433	3S	U
190599	Health education	PhyEd	3233	3S	U
190599	Foodborne-disease control	PubHI	2013	3S	U
190599	Vectorborne-disease contr	PubHI	2023	3S	U
190599	Waterborne-disease contr	PubHI	2033	3S	U
220201	Prin of economics I	Econ	1113	3S	L
220201	Prin of economics II	Econ	1123	3S	L
220432	Early US history	Hist	1063	3S	L
220432	Modern US history	Hist	1073	3S	L
220499	Early Western world	Hist	1013	3S	L
220499	Modern Western world	Hist	1023	3S	L
220499	Mississippi history	Hist	3333	3S	U
220501	American government	Govt	1013	3S	L
220502	Comparative government	Govt	1513	3S	U
220505	International relations	Govt	1313	3S	L
220602	Intro to criminal justice	SocWk	3103	3S	U
220604	Juvenile delinquency	SocWk	4233	3S	U
220606	Intro to sociology	Socio	1003	3S	L
220699	Current issues in correct	SocWk	4303	3S	U

㉒ MURRAY STATE UNIVERSITY

Mr. Donald E. Jones
Dean of Extended Education
Extended Education
Murray State University
Sparks Hall
Murray, Kentucky 42071
Phone: (502) 762-4159

Enrollment on a noncredit basis accepted in all credit courses. Gifted high school students are permitted to enroll in undergraduate courses for credit. The university accepts only members of the military services for overseas enrollment for college courses.

NCES No.	Course Title	Dept.	Course No.	Credits	Level
	College courses				
0104	Animal science	Agri	100	3S	L
0104	Poultry science	Agri	121	3S	L
0104	Swine science	Agri	326	3S	L
0106	Crop science	Agri	240	3S	L
0109	Introduction to forestry	Agri	269	3S	L
0401	Federal Income tax	Acctg	302	3S	L
040101	Prin of accounting I	Acctg	200	3S	L
040101	Prin of accounting II	Acctg	201	3S	L
0402	Prin of office administra	OAd	360	3S	L
040203	Records management	OAd	235	3S	L
1203	Composition I	Engl	101	3S	L
1203	Composition II	Engl	102	3S	L
1203	Introduc to literature	Engl	201	3S	L
1203	Tech writing/ind technol	Engl	225	3S	L
1307	Business law I	LST	240	3S	L
1307	Business law II	LST	540	3S	U
1603	College algebra	Math	101	4S	L
1603	Trigonometry	Math	104	3S	L
1901	Intro to phys education	PhyEd	175	3S	L
2001	General psychology	Psy	180	3S	L
2001	Educational psychology	Psy	580	3S	U
2001	Developmentanl psychology	Psy	252	3S	L
2105	Personal health	Heal	191	2S	L
2105	First aid and safety	Heal	195	2S	L
2105	School health	Heal	598	3S	U
2105	Intro to recreation	Rec	101	3S	L
2204	Modern France	Hist	411	3S	U
2204	Latin Am national period	Hist	451	3S	U
2204	Europe since 1914	Hist	503	3S	U
2204	Colonial Amer to 1689	Hist	529	3S	U
2204	Civil War and Reconstruc	Hist	534	3S	U
2204	Modern Europe	Hist	201	3S	L
2204	Amer experience to 1865	Hist	221	3S	L
2204	Amer experience snc 1865	Hist	222	3S	L
2205	American national govt	Pol	140	3S	L
2205	State and local govt	Pol	240	3S	L
2206	Introductory sociology	Socio	133	3S	L
2206	Social problems	Socio	231	3S	L
2206	The family	Socio	331	3S	L

㉓ NORTHERN MICHIGAN UNIVERSITY

Mr. Harold Salzwedel Jr.
Assistant Director
Continuing Education Credit Programs
Northern Michigan University
410 Cohodas Administrative Center
Marquette, Michigan 49855
Phone: (906) 227-2101

Enrollment on a noncredit basis accepted in all credit courses. Gifted high school students are permitted to enroll in undergraduate courses for credit. Overseas enrollment accepted for college courses. A candidate for a bachelor's degree may not present more than 16 semester hours carried by correspondence. An associate degree candidate may not present more than 8 hours by correspondence.

NCES No.	Course Title	Dept.	Course No.	Credits	Level
	College courses				
130499	Intro to criminal justice	CJust	CJ110	4S	L
130499	Police operations	CJust	CJ112	4S	L
130499	Survey of corrections	CJust	CJ120	4S	L

NCES No.	Course Title	Dept.	Course No.	Credits	Level
220432	US history to 1865	Hist	HS126	4S	L
220432	US history since 1865	Hist	HS127	4S	L
220433	Hist of Westn civ to 1500	Hist	HS101	4S	L
220433	Hist Wstn civ since 1500	Hist	HS102	4S	L

㉔ OHIO UNIVERSITY

Dr. Richard Moffitt
Director, Independent Study
Ohio University
Tupper Hall 303
Athens, Ohio 45701
Phone: (614) 594-6721

Enrollment on a noncredit basis accepted in all credit courses. Gifted high school students are permitted to enroll in undergraduate courses for credit. Overseas enrollment accepted. Students may enroll in individual courses or complete selected two- or four-year degrees through the Independent Study External Student Program. High school students must have permission from their principal or guidance counselor. Overseas enrollment excludes courses requiring slides.

NCES No.	Course Title	Dept.	Course No.	Credits	Level
	College courses				
010601	Plant biology	Bio	102	5Q	L
030302	Hist and lit of music	Music	321	3Q	U
030302	Jazz history	Music	428	3Q	U
030502	History of art	ArHis	211	3Q	U
040101	Acctg princ and proced	Acctg	303	4Q	U
040103	Analytical accounting	SST	260	3Q	L
040106	Cost accounting	Acctg	310	4Q	U
040111	Managerial accounting	Acctg	101	4Q	L
040111	Managerial accounting	Acctg	102	4Q	L
040301	Managerial finance	Fin	325	4Q	U
040502	Small-business administra	BusAd	445	4Q	U
040599	Bus and its environment	BusAd	101	4Q	L
040604	Comm behav in mod organzs	Mgmt	325	4Q	U
040903	Introd to management	Mgmt	200	4Q	L
040999	Production management	BusAd	310	4Q	U
040999	Security administration	SST	240	3Q	L
041001	Cons surv in the mktplace	Mktg	101	4Q	L
041004	Marketing principles	Mktg	301	4Q	U
041108	Occup safety and health	SST	120	3Q	L
041201	Introd to prob and stat	QM	201	4Q	L
050201	Introd to mass communica	Jrnl	105	4Q	L
050699	Supv school publications	Jrnl	484	4Q	U
051001	Introd to radio-TV	RadTV	106	4Q	L
051101	Fund of human communica	InCo	101	3Q	L
051104	Parliamentary procedure	InCo	210	2Q	L
051302	Introd to radio-TV	RadTV	106	4Q	L
0599	Intro to black media	AfAmS	119	3Q	L
060503	Inf and data systems sel	SST	230	3Q	L
070509	Personal and comm health	HPER	202	4Q	L
070512	Readings in English educ	Engl	457	5Q	U
070516	Elem topics in math	Math	120	5Q	L
070516	Elem topics in math	Math	121	5Q	L
070519	Kinesiology	HPER	302	4Q	U
070610	Children's literature	Educ	321	4Q	U
0799	Effective study skills	UC	110	2Q	L
080102	Pri pilot ground instruc	Avi	110	4Q	L
080102	Comm pilot ground instruc	Avi	310	4Q	U
080102	Instrument ground instruc	Avi	350	4Q	U
080699	Intro to chemical engrg	ChmEg	200	4Q	L
080699	Prin of engr materials	ChmEg	331	4Q	U
090704	Bio and the future of man	Zool	390	5Q	U
090705	Occup safety and health	SST	120	3Q	L
100199	Elementary textiles	HmEc	315	4Q	U
100313	Introd to nutrition	HmEc	128	4Q	L
100501	Furnishing today's home	HmEc	180	3Q	L
120201	Humanities: Great Books	Hum	107	3Q	L
120201	Humanities: Great Books	Hum	108	3Q	L
120201	Humanities: Great Books	Hum	109	3Q	L
120201	Intro to mod lit III	Engl	206	5Q	L
120201	Spanish lit in English	Span	336A	4Q	U
120201	Spanish lit in English	Span	336B	4Q	U
120202	Interpretation of fiction	Engl	201	5Q	L
120202	Interpretation of poetry	Engl	202	5Q	L
120202	Interpretation of drama	Engl	203	5Q	L

NCES No.	Course Title	Dept.	Course No.	Credits	Level
120202	Crit approach to pop lit	Engl	210	4Q	L
120202	Shakespeare—histories	Engl	301	5Q	U
120202	Shakespeare—comedies	Engl	302	5Q	U
120202	Shakespeare—tragedies	Engl	303	5Q	U
120202	Med and Ren English lit	Engl	312	5Q	U
120202	Res and neoclass Engl lit	Engl	313	5Q	U
120202	Am lit to the Civil War	Engl	321	5Q	U
120202	Am lit since the Civil Wr	Engl	322	5Q	U
120202	20th-cent Brit and Am lit	Engl	331	5Q	U
120308	Speed readg & comprehensn	UC	112	2Q	L
120310	Fundamental usage skills	Engl	150	4Q	L
120310	Lit of initiation	Engl	171A	5Q	L
120310	Man-woman: images in lit	Engl	171D	5Q	L
120310	Contemporary writg skills	Engl	172	5Q	L
120310	Advanced composition	Engl	308	5Q	U
120310	Creative writing–poetry	Engl	309A	5Q	U
120310	Creative writing–fiction	Engl	309B	5Q	U
120310	Cont writ skill/tech writ	Engl	1727	5Q	L
121105	Elementary German	Ger	111	4Q	L
121241	Beginning Greek	Greek	111	4Q	L
121241	Beginning Greek	Greek	112	4Q	L
121241	Beginning Greek	Greek	113	4Q	L
121641	Beginning Latin	Latin	111	4Q	L
121641	Beginning Latin	Latin	112	4Q	L
121641	Intermediate Latin	Latin	211	4Q	L
130299	Law of commercial transac	BusL	357	4Q	U
130399	Constit, crim & civil law	LET	120	3Q	L
130402	Criminal investigation	LET	260	3Q	L
130703	Law of mgmt process	BusL	356	4Q	U
130799	Law and society	BusL	255	4Q	L
130902	Law of prop and real est	BusL	442	4Q	U
131004	Occup safety and health	SST	120	3Q	L
131004	Fire safety and fire code	SST	201	4Q	L
140199	Intro to libr & libr tech	LMT	101	3Q	L
140199	Sup oper for public serv	LMT	102	4Q	L
150316	Principles of biology	Bot	101	5Q	L
150323	Principles of biology	Zool	101	5Q	L
150323	Introduction to zoology	Zool	150	6Q	L
150399	Nature study	Bot	133	5Q	L
150399	Bioethic prob in biol/med	Zool	384	5Q	U
150399	Biol and future of man	Zool	390	5Q	U
150399	Human biology	Zool	103	5Q	L
150401	Principles of chemistry	Chem	121	4Q	L
150401	Principles of chemistry	Chem	122	4Q	L
150408	Organic chemistry	Chem	301	3Q	U
150408	Organic chemistry	Chem	302	3Q	U
150799	Introduction to physics	Phys	201	3Q	L
150799	Introduction to physics	Phys	202	3Q	L
150799	Introduction to physics	Phys	203	3Q	L
150899	Physical world	PhySc	121	4Q	L
150899	Physical world	PhySc	122	4Q	L
160301	Basic mathematics	Math	101	4Q	L
160302	Algebra	Math	113	5Q	L
160303	Elem topics in math	Math	120	5Q	L
160303	Elem topics in math	Math	121	5Q	L
160306	Elem linear algebra	Math	211	5Q	L
160401	Intro to math	Math	115	5Q	L
160401	Intro to calculus	Math	163A	5Q	L
160401	Analytic geom and calc	Math	263A	5Q	L
160401	Analytic geom and calc	Math	263B	5Q	L
160408	Finite math	Math	250A	5Q	L
160602	Analytic trigonometry	Math	116	2Q	L
160603	Plane analytic geometry	Math	130	3Q	L
160603	Analytic geom and calc	Math	263A	5Q	L
160603	Analytic geom and calc	Math	263B	5Q	L
160605	Foundations of geometry	Math	230	5Q	L
160802	Elem stat for behav sci	Psych	121	5Q	L
180101	Philosophy of art	Philo	232	3Q	L
180302	Introduction to ethics	Philo	130	4Q	L
180302	Bioethic prob in bio/med	Zool	384	5Q	U
180401	Hist of West phil: ancient	Philo	310	5Q	U
180501	Principles of reasoning	Philo	120	4Q	L
180605	Philosophy of culture	Philo	350	5Q	U
1808	Fundamentals of philo	Philo	101	5Q	L
1808	Introduction to philo	Philo	301	3Q	U
190104	Hist and prin of phys ed	HPER	404	4Q	U
190106	Org and adm of phys ed	HPER	406	4Q	U
190299	Kinesiology	Zool	352	4Q	U
190299	Kinesiology	HPER	302	4Q	U
190302	Community recreation	HPER	449	4Q	U
190502	Personal and comm health	HPER	202	4Q	L
200199	General psychology	Psych	101	5Q	L
200199	Elem stat for behav sci	Psych	121	5Q	L
200399	Environmental psychology	Psych	335	4Q	U
200501	Abnormal psychology	Psych	332	5Q	U
200504	Studies of children	Educ	200	4Q	L
200505	Psychology of adjustment	Psych	131	4Q	L
200508	Psych of adulthood/aging	Psych	374	4Q	U
200509	Psychology of personality	Psych	333	5Q	U
200799	Social psych of justic	Psych	337	5Q	U
200804	Educational psychology	Psych	275	5Q	L
210304	Introd to law enforc tech	LET	100	3Q	L
210304	Const, crim and civil law	LET	120	3Q	L
210304	Interview & report writg	LET	130	3Q	L
210304	Criminal investigation	LET	260	3Q	L
210305	Intro to protectn service	SST	101	3Q	L
210305	Physical security systems	SST	110	3Q	L
210305	Occup safety and health	SST	120	3Q	L
210305	Fire safety and fire code	SST	201	4Q	L
210305	Loss prev in modern read	SST	210	3Q	L
210305	Anal of sec needs–survey	SST	220	3Q	L
210305	Inf and data systems sec	SST	230	3Q	L
210305	Security administration	SST	240	3Q	L
210305	Current prob in security	SST	250	3Q	L
210305	Analytical accounting	SST	260	3Q	L
210305	Spec area stud: terrorism	SST	290A	3Q	L
210305	Spec area stud: law/secur	SST	290B	3Q	L
210502	Community recreation	HPER	449	4Q	U
220201	Principles of economics	Econ	101	4Q	L
220201	Principles of economics	Econ	102	4Q	L
220205	Macroeconomics	Econ	304	4Q	U
220206	Public finance	Econ	430	4Q	U
220211	Labor economics	Econ	320	4Q	U
220213	Microeconomics	Econ	303	4Q	U
220214	International economics	Econ	340	4Q	U
220301	Elements of cultural geog	Geog	121	4Q	L
220305	Elements of physical geog	Geog	101	5Q	L
220421	American hist to 1828	Hist	211	4Q	L
220426	Western civ in mod times	Hist	101	4Q	L
220426	Western civ in mod times	Hist	103	4Q	L
220432	Hist of US 1828-1900	Hist	212	4Q	L
220432	Hist of US since 1900	Hist	213	4Q	L
220432	American hist to 1828	Hist	211	4Q	L
220470	Black comm in 20th cent	AfAmS	340	4Q	U
220499	Hist of injustice in US	AfAmS	254	5Q	L
220501	American nationl govt	PolSc	101	4Q	L
220501	Issues in Amer politics	PolSc	102	4Q	L
220606	Principles of sociology	Socio	302	5Q	U
220609	Elem research techniques	Socio	351	4Q	U

Graduate course

050699	Supv school publications	Jrnl	584	4Q	G

Noncredit course

160302	Elementary algebra	Math	011	NC	L

(25) OKLAHOMA STATE UNIVERSITY

Mr. Charles E. Feasley
Director
Independent and Correspondence Study Department
Oklahoma State University
001 Classroom Building
Stillwater, Oklahoma 74078
Phone: (405) 624-6390

Enrollment on a noncredit basis accepted in all credit courses. Overseas enrollment accepted. Master Charge accepted. All course materials to be delivered inside the United States are sent by insured, return-postage-guaranteed mail. Book service is offered through the Independent and Correspondence Study Department.

NCES No.	Course Title	Dept.	Course No.	Credits	Level
	High school courses				
040101	Accounting IA	Acctg	IA	HF	H
040101	Accounting IB	Acctg	IB	HF	H
040601	Business English	Bus	I	HF	H
070602	Salesmanship IA	Bus	IA	HF	H
070602	Salesmanship IB	Bus	IB	HF	H
120201	World lit IA	EngLL	1AW	HF	H
120201	World lit IB	EngLL	1BW	HF	H

NCES No.	Course Title	Dept.	Course No.	Credits	Level
120308	English IA	EngLL	1A	HF	H
120308	English IB	EngLL	1B	HF	H
120308	English IIA	EngLL	2A	HF	H
120308	English IIB	EngLL	2B	HF	H
120308	English IIIA	EngLL	3A	HF	H
120308	English IIIB	EngLL	3B	HF	H
120308	English IVA	EngLL	4A	HF	H
120308	English IVB	EngLL	4B	HF	H
120310	Mystery fiction	Engl	I	HF	H
120310	The short story	Engl	I	HF	H
120310	Science fiction	Engl	I	HF	H
160302	Algebra IA	Math	1AA	HF	H
160302	Algebra IB	Math	1AA	HF	H
160302	Algebra IIA	Math	2AA	HF	H
160302	Algebra IIB	Math	2BA	HF	H
160601	Plane geometry IA	Math	1AG	HF	H
160601	Plane geometry IB	Math	1BG	HF	H
180302	Technology & change		I	HF	H
220208	Consumer economics IA	SocSt	IA	HF	H
220208	Consumer economics IB	SocSt	IB	HF	H
220399	Geography IA	Geog	1A	HF	H
220399	Geography IB	Geog	1B	HF	H
220421	American history IA	Hist	1BA	HF	H
220433	World history IA	Hist	IA	HF	H
220433	World history IB	Hist	IB	HF	H
220450	Ancient & medieval hst IA	Hist	1AAN	HF	H
220450	Ancient & medieval hst IB	Hist	1BAN	HF	H
220499	Oklahoma history IA	Hist	1AO	HF	H
220499	American history IB	Hist	1BA	HF	H

College courses

NCES No.	Course Title	Dept.	Course No.	Credits	Level
010106	Internatnl programs/ag ed	Agri	4713	3S	U
010302	Intro to engr agriculture	Agri	1413	3S	L
010406	Ecology of agri animals	AnSci	3903	3S	U
010407	Livestock feeding	AnSci	2123	3S	L
010601	Problems in agronomy	Agri	4470	3S	U
010607	Intro to plant sciences	Agron	1214	4S	L
010701	Fundaments of soil scienc	Agri	2124	4S	L
010903	For environ & resources	For	3643	3S	U
020102	Prin of hort & lndscp des	Hort	1013	3S	L
030402	Intro theater in Wstn civ	ThArt	2413	3S	L
030402	Theater history I	ThArt	4453	3S	L
030402	Theater history II	ThArt	4463	3S	L
040101	Principles of accounting	Acctg	2130	3S	L
040101	Principles of accounting	Acctg	2203	3S	L
040106	Cost accounting	Acctg	3203	3S	U
040599	Small-business management	Mktg	4113	3S	U
040601	Written communication	Bus	3113	3S	U
040604	Int tech & report writing	Eng	3323	3S	U
040902	Production/operation mgmt	Mgmt	3223	3S	U
041001	Marketing	Mktg	3213	3S	U
041003	Sales management	Mktg	3513	3S	U
060802	Programming in FORTRAN	CmpSc	2113	3S	L
061199	Computer role in mod life	CmpSc	1112	2S	L
070102	Philosophy of education	Educ	3713	3S	U
070199	History of education	Educ	4123	3S	U
070309	Community education	Educ	4221	1S	U
070401	Human learng in ed psych	Educ	4223	3S	U
070403	Teaching discipline	Educ	5720	1S	U
070403	Teacher training	Educ	5740	1S	U
070404	Evaluation: elemen school	Educ	4052	2S	U
070404	Organize for individ inst	Educ	5720A	1S	U
070404	Humanize the classroom	Educ	5720B	1S	U
070511	Trade & industrial educ	Educ	3203	3S	U
070516	Math for teachers	Math	2413	3S	L
070516	Structure concepts/teach	Math	2513	3S	L
070811	Spch-lang path for tchrs	SpEd	3213	3S	U
071203	Educational media	Educ	3122		U
080603	Thermodynamics	ChmEg	2213	3S	L
080901	Digital electronics	EEg	2650	3S	L
080901	Linear integrated circuit	EEg	2050	3S	L
080903	Elements of electronics	EEg	1102	2S	L
080999	Elem of elec/electronics	EEg	1320		L
082303	Radiological safety	NucEg	3233	3S	U
082599	Intro to petrol industry	EngAS	1113	3S	L
082599	Properties of petroleum	EngAS	1234	4S	L
0899	Elementary dynamics	EngAS	2122		L
0899	Technical drawing	VisAr	1153	3S	L
090121	Radiation biology	NucEg	4050	3S	U
090504	First aid	HSci	2602	2S	L

NCES No.	Course Title	Dept.	Course No.	Credits	Level
090901	Personal & comm hlth sci	HSci	2603	3S	L
100304	Intro to nutrition	HmEc	1113	3S	L
100402	Resource mgt ind/family	HmEc	2413	3S	L
100503	Housing for cont living	HmEc	2313	3S	L
100601	Child & family developmnt	HmEc	2113	3S	L
100601	Human sexuality	HmEc	1113	3S	L
120201	The short story	Lit	3333	3S	U
120201	Shakespeare	Lit	3883	3S	U
120201	Readings in the novel	Lit	4223	3S	U
120201	Period study Am colonial	Engl	4943	3S	U
120202	Introduction to new media	Lit	2423	3S	L
120204	Intro to lit & critic wrt	EngLL	2413	3S	L
120305	English grammar	Engl	4013	3S	U
120310	Freshman composition I	Engl	1113	3S	L
120310	Freshman composition II	Engl	1323	3S	L
120310	Short fiction writing	Engl	3033	3S	U
120310	Poetry writing	Engl	3043	3S	U
130799	Business law I	Law	3213	3S	U
130799	Business law II	Law	3323	3S	U
130799	Const law & insurance	Law	3563	3S	U
140199	Intro to library science	LibSc	1011	1S	L
140307	School library administra	LibSc	3023	3S	U
140902	Children's literature	LibSc	4023	3S	U
150101	Cosmos	Astro	4010	3S	U
150103	Elementary astronomy	Astro	1104	4S	L
150202	Descriptive meteorology	Geog	2013	3S	L
150301	Biological sciences	Bio	1114	4S	L
150306	Evolution	Bio	3903	3S	U
150307	Heredity & man	Bio	3003	3S	U
150408	Organic chemistry	Chem	2344	4S	L
150599	General geology	Geol	1014	4S	L
150599	Energy & the way we live	Geol	4990	3S	U
150600	Intro to oceanography	Geog	3113	3S	U
150799	Descriptive physics	Math	1014	4S	L
160199	Metric system	Math	4910	1S	U
160301	Basic math wth calculator	Math	4910B	2S	U
160302	Intermediate algebra	Math	1213	3S	L
160302	College algebra	Math	1513	3S	L
160401	Elementary calculus	Math	2713	3S	L
160602	College algebra & trig	Math	1715	5S	L
160602	Trigonometry	Math	1613	3S	L
160606	Differential equations	Math	2613	3S	L
180302	Philos & quality of life	Philo	3300	3S	U
180599	Intro critical thinking	Philo	1313	3S	L
190799	Swimming pool management	Rec	4222	2S	U
1999	Theory of flight	Rec	1113	3S	L
200102	History of psychology	Psych	3273	3S	U
200104	Psych & human problems	Psych	2313	3S	L
200199	Intro to psychology	Psych	1113	3S	L
200599	Psych found of childhood	Psych	3113	3S	U
200599	Excep child psychology	Psych	3202	2S	U
200599	Psychology of adolescence	Psych	3213	3S	U
210302	Structural fire protectn	EngAS	2143	3S	L
210302	Fire protection mgt	EngAS	2153	3S	L
220199	North American cultures	Anthr	3823	3S	U
220215	Economics of soc issues	Econ	1113	3S	L
220301	Intro to geog behavior	Geog	1113	3S	L
220305	Physical geography	Geog	1114	4S	L
220306	Geography of Oklahoma	Geog	3653	3S	U
220399	Geog of music	Geog	4223	3S	U
220423	Modern Japan	Hist	3423	3S	U
220423	Traditional Japan	Hist	3980A	3S	U
220426	Survey of European hist	Hist	1723	3S	L
220432	American history to 1865	Hist	1483	3S	L
220432	American history since 1865	Hist	1493	3S	L
220450	Ancient Greece	Hist	3023	3S	U
220450	Ancient Rome	Hist	3033	3S	U
220499	Genealogical research	Hist	4980	3S	U
220499	Oklahoma history	Hist	2322	2S	L
220499	The Great Plains exper	Hist	3980B	3S	U
220501	American government	PolSc	1013	3S	L
220604	Juvenile delinquency	Socio	3523	3S	U
220606	Principles of sociology	Socio	1113	3S	L
220612	Social ecol & life proc	Soc	4433	3S	U
220613	Social problems	Soc	2123	3S	L
220613	Death and dying	Soc	2510	3S	L
220615	Soc of American family	Soc	3723	3S	U

Noncredit courses

NCES No.	Course Title	Dept.	Course No.	Credits	Level
020599	Earth-sheltered housing	Arch		NC	
082599	Intro to petroleum indust	EngAS	1	NC	

NCES No.	Course Title	Dept.	Course No.	Credits	Level
089900	Hydraulic calc of sprklrs	EngAS		NC	
150600	Intro to oceanography	Geog		NC	
160301	Intro hand-held calculatr	Math		NC	
220423	Modern Japan	Hist		NC	
220423	Traditional Japan	Hist		NC	
220499	The Great Plains exper	Hist		NC	

㉖ **OREGON STATE SYSTEM OF HIGHER EDUCATION**

Ms. Jeanne Dimond
Coordinator, Office of Independent Study
Continuing Education
Oregon State System of Higher Education
P.O. Box 1491
Portland, Oregon 97207
Phone: (503) 229-4865

Gifted high school students are permitted to enroll in undergraduate courses for credit. Overseas enrollment accepted. Students, including high school students, may enroll in independent study courses at any time, and there are no entrance requirements. However, some courses do have prerequisites. The enrollment period is twelve months. A six-month extension is permitted upon request and payment of the required fee. Requests for catalogs received from countries outside the United States are not filled unless postage is provided. This program does not offer an external high school diploma or an external college degree.

NCES No.	Course Title	Dept.	Course No.	Credits	Level
	High school courses				
040101	Intro to accounting	BusAd	1	HF	H
040101	Intro to accounting	BusAd	2	HF	H
040302	Personal finance I	BusAd	3	HF	H
040302	Personal finance II	BusAd	4	HF	H
040601	Business English	Engl	14	HF	H
120305	English review	Engl	1	HF	H
120305	Tenth-grade English III	Engl	3	HF	H
120305	Eleventh-grade English V	Engl	5	HF	H
120305	Twelfth-grade English VII	Engl	7	HF	H
120305	Corrective English	Engl	13	HF	H
120307	Tenth-grade English IV	Engl	4	HF	H
120307	Eleventh-grade English VI	Engl	6	HF	H
120307	Twelfth-grade Eng VIII	Engl	8	HF	H
1503	Biology I	Bio	1	HF	H
1503	Biology II	Bio	2	HF	H
1509	General science I	GS	1	HF	H
1509	General science II	GS	2	HF	H
160301	General math I	Math	1	HF	H
160301	General math II	Math	2	HF	H
160302	Elements of algebra	Math	10	HF	H
190509	Health education I	H	1	HF	H
190509	Health education II	H	2	HF	H
220201	Modern problems II	PRB	8	HF	H
220432	US history I	Hist	1	HF	H
220432	US history II	Hist	2	HF	H
220433	World history I	Hist	3	HF	H
220433	World history II	Hist	4	HF	H
2299	Modern problems I	PRB	7	HF	H
	College courses				
010406	Animal science	AnSci	121	3Q	L
010604	Crop production	ACS	211	5Q	L
010699	Weed control	ACS	418	3Q	U
020299	Housing and arch phil	Arch	178	3Q	L
030501	Basic drawing	Art	291	3Q	L
030501	Watercolor	Art	292	3Q	L
040101	Intermed finan acctg I	BusAd	317	4Q	U
040101	Intermed finan acctg II	BusAd	318	4Q	U
040103	Auditing	BusAd	427	4Q	B
040109	Acctg not-for-profit inst	BusAd	423	3Q	B
040205	Stenography	AOM	111	3Q	L
040205	Stenography	AOM	112	3Q	L
040205	Stenography	AOM	113	3Q	L
040206	Medical terminology	SST	230	3Q	L
040299	Med ofc and hos procedure	SST	240	3Q	L
041004	Retailing	Mktg	462	3Q	U
041199	Personnel management	BusAd	467	3Q	U
041303	Real estate principles	FinL	436	3Q	U

NCES No.	Course Title	Dept.	Course No.	Credits	Level
060404	Intro to microcomputers	CmpSc	410	3Q	U
060705	Intro to FORTRAN	CmpSc	133	4Q	L
060705	Intro to COBOL	CmpSc	199	4Q	L
060705	Adv FORTRAN programming	CmpSc	421	4Q	U
060806	Intro to computer systems	CmpSc	199	3Q	L U
070399	The junior high school	CI	484	3Q	U
070399	School in American life	Educ	324	3Q	U
070404	Prin of secondary teachng	CI	325	3Q	U
070404	Tchg readg in elem school	CI	335	3Q	U
070506	Calc and comp in elem sch	CmpSc	407	2Q	B
070509	Elem sch health education	HE	440	3Q	U
070509	Health instruction	HE	441	3Q	U
070610	Tchng soc stud lang arts	CI	334	5Q	U
070610	Reading in high school	Educ	469	3Q	U
070899	Psych of excep children	SpEd	462	3Q	B
071099	Measurement in education	EdPsy	424	3Q	U
0799	Social education	Educ	491	3Q	U
0804	Intern combust eng theory	ADT	101	3Q	L
0804	Fund auto electricity	ADT	121	3Q	L
080706	Highway materials	CET	229	3Q	L
0810	Graphics	Graph	115	3Q	L
120201	World literature	Engl	107	3Q	L
120201	World literature	Engl	108	3Q	L
120201	World literature	Engl	109	3Q	L
120201	Contemporary literature	Engl	384	3Q	U
120201	Contemporary literature	Engl	385	3Q	U
120307	Survey of English lit	Engl	101	3Q	L
120307	Survey of English lit	Engl	102	3Q	L
120307	Survey of English lit	Engl	103	3Q	L
120307	Shakespeare	Engl	201	3Q	L
120307	Shakespeare	Engl	202	3Q	L
120307	Shakespeare	Engl	203	3Q	L
120307	Survey of American lit	Engl	253	3Q	L
120307	American fiction	Engl	366	3Q	U
120310	English composition	Writ	121	3Q	L
120310	English composition	Writ	122	3Q	L
120310	English composition	Writ	123	3Q	L
120310	Short story writing	Writ	324	3Q	U
120310	Poetry writing	Writ	341	3Q	U
120310	Poetry writing	Writ	342	3Q	U
120399	American folklore	Engl	419	3Q	B
1210	First-year French	Rom	50	4Q	L
1210	First-year French	Rom	51	4Q	L
1210	First-year French	Rom	52	4Q	L
1211	First-year German	GL	101	4Q	L
1211	First-year German	GL	102	4Q	L
1211	First-year German	GL	103	4Q	L
130199	The courts	AJ	112	3Q	L
130402	Criminal law process	AJ	444	3Q	U
130402	Criminal law process	AJ	445	3Q	U
130402	Criminal law: defense side	AJ	451	3Q	U
150202	Intro to atmosphere	AtS	300	3Q	U
150202	Weather analysis lab	AtS	430	3Q	U
1505	General geology	Geol	101	3Q	L
1505	General geology	Geol	102	3Q	L
1505	General geology	Geol	103	3Q	L
150599	Geologic history of life	Geol	301	3Q	U
1506	Intro to oceanography	Geol	353	3Q	U
150799	General physics	Phys	201	3Q	L
150799	General physics	Phys	202	3Q	L
150799	General physics	Phys	203	3Q	L
1599	Foundations of phys sci	GS	104	3Q	L
1599	Foundations of phys sci	GS	105	3Q	L
1599	Foundations of phys sci	GS	106	3Q	L
160302	Intermediate algebra	Math	95	4Q	L
160302	College algebra	Math	101	4Q	L
160306	Intro linear algebra	Math	411	3Q	U
160401	Elements of calculus	Math	106	4Q	L
160401	Calculus	Math	200	4Q	L
160401	Calculus	Math	201	4Q	L
160602	Trigonometry	Math	102	4Q	L
181002	Intro to world religions	Relig	101	3Q	L
190509	Personal health problems	HE	250	3Q	L
200199	Psych as a social science	Psych	204	3Q	L
200199	Psych as a natural sci	Psych	205	3Q	L
200501	Abnormal psychology	Psych	480	3Q	U
200504	Developmental psychology	Psych	407	3Q	U
200599	Psychology of adolescence	Psych	412	3Q	U
200804	Human devel and education	EdPsy	321	2Q	U

NCES No.	Course Title	Dept.	Course No.	Credits	Level
200804	Human learning and educ	EdPsy	322	2Q	U
200804	Psych and problems in ed	EdPsy	323	2Q	U
220102	The American Indian	Anthr	417	3Q	U
220102	The American Indian	Anthr	418	3Q	U
220102	The American Indian	Anthr	419	3Q	U
220201	Principles of economics	Econ	213	4Q	L
220201	Principles of economics	Econ	214	4Q	L
220305	Introductory geography	Geog	105	3Q	L
220305	Introductory geography	Geog	106	3Q	L
220305	Introductory geography	Geog	107	3Q	L
220406	Hist of Western civiliz	Hist	101	3Q	L
220406	Hist of Western civiliz	Hist	102	3Q	L
220406	Hist of Western civiliz	Hist	103	3Q	L
220432	History of the US	Hist	201	3Q	L
220432	History of the US	Hist	202	3Q	L
220432	History of the US	Hist	203	3Q	L

Noncredit courses

NCES No.	Course Title	Dept.	Course No.	Credits	Level
030599	Kiln construction	Art	044	NC	
040103	Municipal auditing review	BusAd	T-71	NC	
040103	Audits state/local govt	BusAd	T-73	NC	
040109	Intro to fund accounting	BusAd	T-74	NC	
120305	Corrective English	Writ	10	NC	
160302	Elements of algebra	Math	10	NC	
220502	Prep for citizenship	PolSc	01	NC	

㉗ PENNSYLVANIA STATE UNIVERSITY

Dr. Linda Ellinger
Coordinator, Student and Instructional Services
Department of Independent Study by Correspondence
Pennsylvania State University
128 Mitchell Building
University Park, Pennsylvania 16802
Phone: (814) 865-5403

Gifted high school students are permitted to enroll in undergraduate courses for credit. Overseas enrollment accepted. College-level credit courses are available to anyone who has a high school diploma or its equivalent (GED) and who has the prerequisites necessary for enrollment in any given course.

NCES No.	Course Title	Dept.	Course No.	Credits	Level
	High school courses				
090709	Modern health	HSSci	001	HF	H
090709	Modern health	HlSci	002A	HF	H
120305	Basic English	HLang	010	HF	H
120307	Ninth-grade English	HLang	001A	HF	H
120307	Ninth-grade English	HLang	002A	HF	H
120307	Tenth-grade English	HLang	003A	HF	H
120307	Tenth-grade English	HLang	004A	HF	H
120307	Eleventh-grade English	HLang	005A	HF	H
120307	Eleventh-grade English	HLang	006A	HF	H
120307	Twelfth-grade English	HLang	007A	HF	H
120307	Twelfth-grade English	HLang	008A	HF	H
120308	Improv of reading skills	HLang	025	HF	H
120308	Improv of reading skills	HLang	026	HF	H
160302	Elementary algebra	HMath	001A	HF	H
160302	Elementary algebra	HMath	002A	HF	H
160302	Advanced algebra	HMath	005A	HF	H
160302	Advanced algebra	HMath	006A	HF	H
160302	Modern 4th-year math	HMath	017	HF	H
160302	Modern 4th-year math	HMath	018	HF	H
160302	Elementary algebra	HMath	001B	HF	H
160601	Geometry	HMath	003A	HF	H
160601	Geometry	HMath	004A	HF	H
160602	Trigonometry	HMath	007	HF	H
190699	Driver education	HDrEd	001	HF	H
220432	American history	HSSSt	005A	HF	H
220432	American history	HSSSt	006A	HF	H
220433	World history	HSSSt	003A	HF	H
220433	World history	HSSSt	004A	HF	H
	College courses				
030399	Rudiments of music	Music	8	3S	L
030402	Principles of playwriting	Thea	440	3S	U
0399	Survey of Western art	Art H	110	3S	L
0401	Intermediate accounting	Acctg	201	3S	L
040101	Intro financial acctg	Acctg	101	3S	L
040111	Managerial accounting	Acctg	102	3S	L
040301	Corporation finance	Fin	105	3S	L

NCES No.	Course Title	Dept.	Course No.	Credits	Level
040302	Personal finance	Fin	108	3S	L
040306	Security markets	Fin	204	3S	L
040311	Introduction to finance	Fin	100	3S	L
040604	Business writing	Engl	119	3S	L
040902	Problems of small bus	B A	250	3S	L
040903	Intro organizatl behavior	Mgmt	200	3S	L
041001	Marketing	Mktg	800	3S	L
041007	Physical distribution	B Log	102	3S	L
041007	Transport systems	B Log	104	3S	L
041299	Elementary bus statistics	QBA	101	3S	L
041299	Elementary bus statistics	QBA	102	3S	L
050101	Advertising and public rl	Journ	240	3S	L
060601	Intro to algorithmic proc	CmpSc	101	3S	L
070199	History of education US	EdThp	430	3S	U
070306	Vocational education	I Ed	1V	3S	L
070306	Vocational education	I Ed	1	3S	L
070708	Ed psy for prof effective	EdPsy	297	3S	L
080703	Fluid flow	C E	861	3S	L
080901	Signals and circuits I	E E	51	3S	L
080901	Signals and circuits II	E E	52	3S	L
080903	Fundamentals dc circuits	E E	801	3S	L
0810	Engineering drawing	E G	1	2S	L
0810	Intro engineering graphic	E G	10	1S	L
0810	Engrg design graphics	E G	11	1S	L
0810	Engineering design graph	E G	11	1S	L
0810	Spatial analysis	E G	12	2S	L
0810	Advan engineering drawing	E G	803	3S	L
0811	Elementary mechanics	E Mch	811	3S	L
081103	Strength & prop of metals	E Mch	813	3S	L
081104	Statics	E Mch	11	3S	L
081104	Dynamics	E Mch	12	3S	L
081104	Statics	E Mch	11	3S	L
081302	Community noise fundamtls	CmDis	297	3S	L
081302	Community noise fundamtls	CmDis	497	3S	B
081304	Water pollution control	C E	370	3S	U
081599	Industrial organ and admn	I E	315	3S	U
081999	Strength of materials	E Mch	13	3S	L
082006	Product design	M E	810	3S	L
082099	Kinematics	M E	805	3S	L
0899	Engineering orientation	Engr	2	1S	L
100302	Normal diet modifications	Nutr	800	4S	L
100313	Elementary nutrition	Nutr	150	2S	L
100399	Nutrition of the family	Nutr	351	3S	U
100601	Infancy and early childhd	IFS	329	3S	U
100701	San/hskpng hlth care facl	HFS	802	3S	L
100702	Intro to hea fac food ser	FSHA	103	3S	L
100702	Food serv delivery system	HFS	850	4S	L
100702	Food service supervision	HFS	860	4S	L
100799	Equip & util hea care fac	FSHA	320	3S	U
100799	Training and supervision	HFS	805	3S	L
100799	San hskpng/com food serv	HSF	802	3S	L
120201	Mastrpcs Wstn lit snc Ren	C Lit	2	3S	L
120202	Masterpieces Wstn lit/Ren	C Lit	1	3S	L
120305	English language analysis	Engl	100	3S	L
120307	British lit of 19th cent	Engl	122	3S	L
120307	Contemporary British lit	Engl	123	3S	L
120307	Amer lit Civ War to WWI	Engl	132	3S	L
120307	Understanding literature	Engl	101	3S	L
120310	Composition & rhetoric I	Engl	10	3S	L
120310	Composition & rhetoric II	Engl	20	3S	L
1210	Elementary French I	Fr	1	4S	L
1210	Elementary French II	Fr	2	4S	L
121099	Intermediate French	Fr	3	4S	L
1211	Basic German I	Ger	1	3S	L
1211	Basic German II	Ger	2	3S	L
1211	Intermediate German I	Ger	3	3S	L
1211	Intermediate German II	Ger	4	3S	L
121207	Greek lit translation I	Class	26	3S	L
121207	Greek lit translation II	Class	27	3S	L
121607	Latin lit Eng translation	Class	34	3S	L
122008	Elementary Russian	Rus	5	3S	L
1225	Intermediate Spanish	Span	3	4S	L
1307	Legal envir of business	B Law	243	3S	L
150201	Phys climatol for teacher	Meteo	401	3S	U
150202	Weather and man	Meteo	300	2S	U
150202	Tropical meteorology	Meteo	420	3S	U
150202	Physical meteorology	Meteo	443	3S	U
150202	Applic of stat to meteoro	Meteo	450	3S	U
150202	Intro to dynamic meteorol	Meteo	451	3S	U

NCES No.	Course Title	Dept.	Course No.	Credits	Level
150202	Intro synoptic meteorol	Meteo	411	3S	U
150299	Hydrodynamics of the atmo	Meteo	452	3S	U
150301	Man and environment	BiSci	3	3S	L
150399	Physiology	Biol	41	3S	L
150401	Chemical principles	Chem	12	3S	L
150408	Organic chemistry	Chem	34	3S	L
150706	Optic laboratory	Phys	204P	1S	L
150799	General physics	Phys	202	4S	L
150799	General physics with lab	Phys	202	4S	L
150799	General physics	Phys	203	3S	L
150799	General physics	Phys	202A	4S	L
150899	Physical science	Ph Sc	7	3S	L
160103	Insights into mathematics	Math	36	3S	L
160199	General view of math	Math	35	3S	L
160203	Finite mathematics	Math	17	3S	L
160302	Intermediate algebra	Math	4	3S	L
160302	College algebra	Math	5	3S	L
160303	Number systems	Math	200	3S	L
160306	Elementary linear algebra	Math	18	3S	L
160399	Precalculus mathematics	Math	10	3S	L
160401	Elem calc and anal geom I	Math	161	3S	L
160401	Elem calc & anal geom II	Math	162	3S	L
160401	Intermed calc with app I	Math	240	3S	L
160401	Techniques of calculus I	Math	120	3S	L
160401	Techniques of calculus II	Math	121	3S	L
160406	Differential equations	Math	250	3S	L
160602	Plane trigonometry	Math	6	3S	L
160801	Elementary statistics	Stat	200	4S	L
160899	Matrices and statistics	Math	260	3S	L
1611	Basic mathematics	Math	0	3S	L
180404	Introduction to philosphy	Phil	2	3S	L
180499	Basic problems of philos	Phil	4	3S	L
180501	Introduction to logic	Phil	1	3S	L
180502	Element of symb logic	Phil	12	3S	L
181304	Intro to religion of West	Rl St	4	3S	L
181304	Religions of the East	Rl St	3	3S	L
1899	Intro study of religion	Rl St	1	3S	L
1899	Relig in Am life & thought	Rl St	19	3S	L
190104	Hist or prin of hl ph ed	Ph Ed	58	3S	L
190107	Admn hlth/phys ed in schl	Ph Ed	491	3S	U
190108	Adapted physical educatn	Ph Ed	400	3S	U
190110	Measurmt eval in hlth/PE	Ph Ed	490	2S	U
190301	Intramural athletics	Ph Ed	489	3S	U
190308	Admin & mgmnt aquatic prg	Ph Ed	366	3S	U
190311	Meth prin of ath coaching	Ph Ed	460	3S	U
190501	Drugs in society	H Ed		1S	L
190503	Prin healthful living	H Ed	60	3S	L
190503	Consumer health	Hl Ed	57	1S	L
190504	Man and disease	H Ed	19	1S	L
190706	Leisure in human experien	Rc Pk	120	3S	L
2001	Psychology	Psy	2	3S	L
200505	Mental health	Psy	37	3S	L
220102	Cultural anthropology	Anthy	45	3S	L
220199	Introductory anthrcpology	Anthy	1	3S	L
220201	Principles of economics	Econ	14	3S	L
220204	Intro microecon anal pol	Econ	2	3S	L
220204	Intro macroecon anal pol	Econ	4	3S	L
220211	Labor economics	Econ	315	3S	U
220426	Modern Europe 1815-presnt	Hist	19	3S	L
220426	Modern Europe 1500-presnt	Hist	18	3S	L
220428	History of Pennsylvania	Hist	12	3S	L
220432	Hist of the US since 1865	Hist	21	3S	L
220432	Hist of US to 1865	Hist	20	3S	L
220450	Intro to hist of anc wrld	Hist	16	3S	L
220452	Intro hist Middle Ages	Hist	17	3S	L
220499	Hist of American worker	Hist	156	3S	L
220501	Gov and pol of Am states	Pl Sc	425	3S	U
220501	American national govmt	Pl Sc	1	3S	L
220503	Comparative pol West Eur	Pl Sc	20	3S	L
220504	Govt & poltics in mod soc	Pl Sc	3	3S	L
220511	Amer local govt & admin	Pl Sc	417	3S	U
220603	Social stratification	Soc	429	3S	U
220604	Urbanization of man	So Sc	1	3S	L
220605	Sociology of the family	Soc	30	3S	L
220606	History of social theory	Soc	422	3S	U
220606	Intro to sociology	Soc	1	3S	L

NCES No.	Course Title	Dept.	Course No.	Credits	Level
220607	Introductory social psych	Soc	3	3S	L
220614	Urban sociology	Soc	15	3S	L
2299	Urbanization of man	So Sc	1	3S	L
2299	Intro to American studies	AmSt	100	3S	L
Noncredit courses					
020101	Planned rdg & arch detail	A E	901	NC	
020101	Planned rdg & arch detail	A E	1901	NC	
030402	Theater: fund raising	Thea	5203	NC	
030402	Theater: mgt finan/facilt	Thea	5204	NC	
030402	Theater: audience dvlpt	Thea	5205	NC	
030499	Organizational structure	Thea	5202	NC	
040604	Technical writing	Engl	901	NC	
041106	Basic supervision	I E	601	NC	
041106	Advanced supervision	I E	602	NC	
0509	Dynamics volunteer progrm	H Dev	5703	NC	
080301	Buildng construct & tech	A E	5525	NC	
080903	Electronic fundamentals	E E	921	NC	
080903	Industrial electronics	E E	922	NC	
081103	Appl mech/strength of mat	E Mch	902	NC	
081103	Strength of materials	E Mch	903	NC	
081199	Elementary mechanics	E Mch	901	NC	
081302	Community noise fundamtls	CmDis	5401	NC	
082501	Petro & naturl gas explor	P N G	952	NC	
082599	Oil & gas production prac	P N G	953	NC	
090255	Thoracic aneurysms	Nurs	7567	NC	
100304	Fat chance: eating & nutr	Nutr	7385	NC	
100701	Sanitation & housekeeping	HFS	5701	NC	
110504	Intro to photography	Art	5209	NC	
161299	Use & underst of metr sys	Math	5950	NC	
190799	Beginning stamp collectng	L A	5834	NC	
190799	Begin stamp collect/adult	L A	5836	NC	
190799	Intermed stamp collect I	L A	5837	NC	

㉘ PURDUE UNIVERSITY

Mr. Gerald W. O'Brien
Director
Division of Independent Study
Purdue University
116 Stewart Center
West Lafayette, Indiana 47907
Phone: (317) 494-7231

Enrollment on a noncredit basis accepted in all credit courses. Gifted high school students are permitted to enroll in undergraduate courses for credit. Overseas enrollment is not encouraged; each case is judged on an individual basis.

NCES No.	Course Title	Dept.	Course No.	Credits	Level
Noncredit courses					
010403	Pest control technology	Entm		NC	V
090411	Pharmacy correspondence	Pharm		NC	V
090905	Central service tech trng	RHIM		NC	V
100702	Food service mgt & supv	RHIM		NC	V
100702	Food purchasing and procu	RHIM		NC	V

㉙ ROOSEVELT UNIVERSITY

Mr. Rance Conley
Coordinator, External Degree Program
College of Continuing Education
Roosevelt University
430 South Michigan Avenue
Chicago, Illinois 60605
Phone: (312) 341-3866

Enrollment on a noncredit basis accepted in all credit courses. Only in exceptional cases are gifted high school students permitted to enroll in undergraduate courses for credit. Overseas enrollment is not encouraged; each case is judged on an individual basis. In addition to the strictly correspondence program, the university has an external degree program for students in the Chicago area, offering phone contact with instructors.

NCES No.	Course Title	Dept.	Course No.	Credits	Level
	College courses				
040199	Introduction to acctg I	Acctg	101	3S	L
040199	Introduction to acctg II	Acctg	102	3S	L
220201	Principles of economics	Econ	102	3S	L
220299	Introduction to economics	Econ	101	3S	L

㉚ SAVANNAH STATE COLLEGE

Ms. Brenda D. Groover
Coordinator, Correspondence Study/Short Courses
Correspondence Study Office
Savannah State College
Joint Continuing Education Center
P.O. Box 20372
Savannah, Georgia 31404
Phone: (912) 356-2243

Overseas enrollment accepted for college courses. To register for any credit course, the prospective enrollee must be a graduate of an accredited or approved high school or must have completed successfully the General Educational Development (GED) test.

NCES No.	Course Title	Dept.	Course No.	Credits	Level
	College courses				
040308	Money, credit & banking	Bus	323	5Q	U
040314	Business finance	Bus	320	5Q	U
041299	Quantitative analysis	Bus	332	5Q	U
0499	Introduction to business	Bus	105	5Q	L
130399	Amer constitutional law	PolSc	311	5Q	U
160302	College algebra	Mat	107	5Q	U
160899	Bus & econom statistics	Bus	331	5Q	U
200599	Psych basis for hum behav	Soc	201	5Q	U
220299	Introduction to economics	Bus	200	5Q	U
220399	World & human geography	Soc	111	5Q	L
220426	US & Afro-Am snc Civ War	His	203	5Q	U
220426	His of early modrn Europe	His	331	5Q	U
220426	His of early modrn Europe	His	332	5Q	U
220432	US & Afro-Am thr Civ War	His	202	5Q	U
220433	History of Western civil	His	101	5Q	L
220433	History of Western civil	His	102	5Q	L
220501	Government	PolSc	200	5Q	U
220599	Black politics	PolSc	390	5Q	U
220599	American political proc	PolSc	405	5Q	U
220605	The family	Soc	315	5Q	U
220613	Social problems	Soc	350	5Q	U
220699	Introduction to sociology	Soc	201	5Q	U

㉛ SOUTHERN ILLINOIS UNIVERSITY AT CARBONDALE

Dr. M. J. Sullivan
Coordinator, Individualized Learning
Department of Continuing Education
Southern Illinois University at Carbondale
Washington Square C
Carbondale, Illinois 62901
Phone: (618) 536-7751

Enrollment on a noncredit basis accepted in all credit courses. Overseas enrollment accepted for college courses. All courses contain additional audiovisual components. Some utilize videotapes; others utilize audio cassettes, microfiche, or color slides. Accessibility to playback equipment should be considered before enrolling. Illinois residents may find certain courses available in local libraries or community college resource centers.

NCES No.	Course Title	Dept.	Course No.	Credits	Level
	College courses				
030501	Survey of 20th-cen art	ArHis	346	3S	U
070699	Sp-needs learner and work	VocT	464	3S	U
220305	Understanding the weather	Geog	330	3S	U
220507	Political parties	PolSc	319	3S	U
220607	Sociology of the individl	Socio	321	3S	U

㉜ TEXAS TECH UNIVERSITY

Mr. John Strain
Assistant Director of Continuing Education
Correspondence Section, Division of Continuing Education
Texas Tech University
P.O. Box 4110
Lubbock, Texas 79409
Phone: (806) 742-2352

Enrollment on a noncredit basis accepted in all credit courses. Gifted high school students are permitted to enroll in undergraduate courses for credit. Overseas enrollment accepted.

NCES No.	Course Title	Dept.	Course No.	Credits	Level
	High school courses				
010107	Gen agriculture sem 1	Agri	S1	S	H
010107	Gen agriculture sem 2	Agri	S2	S	H
040104	Bookkeeping	Acctg	S1	S	H
040599	General business	Bus	S1	S	H
040599	General business	Bus	S2	S	H
040999	Bus organization & mgmt	Mgmt	S1	S	H
040999	Bus organization & mgmt	Mgmt	S2	S	H
0499	Salesmanship	Bus	S1	S	H
0499	Salesmanship	Bus	S2	S	H
050102	Journalism I: advtg media	Jrnl	S2	S	H
050606	Journalism I: history	Jrnl	S1	S	H
050699	Journalism II	Jrnl	S1	S	H
050699	Journalism II	Jrnl	S2	S	H
100601	Child development	HmEc	S1	S	H
100699	Home & family living	HmEc	S1	S	H
100699	Home & family living	HmEc	S2	S	H
120204	Life & lit of Southwest	Engl	S1	S	H
120305	English I sem 1	Engl	S1	S	H
120305	English I sem 2	Engl	S2	S	H
120305	English II sem 1	Engl	S1	S	H
120305	English II sem 2	Engl	S2	S	H
120305	English III sem 1	Engl	S1	S	H
120305	English III sem 2	Engl	S2	S	H
120305	English IV sem 1	Engl	S1	S	H
120305	English IV sem 2	Engl	S2	S	H
130799	Business law	Bus	S1	S	H
150399	Biology I	Bio	S1	S	H
150399	Biology I	Bio	S2	S	H
150799	Physics	Phys	S1	S	H
150799	Physics	Phys	S2	S	H
150899	Physical science	Phys	S1	S	H
150899	Physical science	Phys	S2	S	H
160302	Introductory algebra	Math	S1	S	H
160302	Introductory algebra	Math	S2	S	H
160302	Introductory algebra	Math	S3	S	H
160302	Introductory algebra	Math	S4	S	H
160302	Algebra	Math	S1	S	H
160302	Algebra	Math	S2	S	H
160302	Algebra	Math	S3	S	H
160302	Algebra	Math	S4	S	H
160401	Elementary analysis	Math	S1	S	H
160601	Geometry	Math	S1	S	H
160601	Geometry	Math	S2	S	H
160602	Trigonometry	Math	S1	S	H
161202	Fundamentals of math	Math	S1	S	H
161202	Fundamentals of math	Math	S2	S	H
161202	Fundamentals of math	Math	S3	S	H
161202	Fundamentals of math	Math	S4	S	H
161202	Math of consumer econom	Math	S1	S	H
161202	Math of consumer econom	Math	S2	S	H
181202	Bible sem 1	Relig	S1	S	H
181202	Bible sem 2	Relig	S2	S	H
190509	Health education	HSci	S1	S	H
200199	Psychology	Psych	S1	S	H
220199	Anthropology	Anthr	S1	S	H
220215	Economics	Econ	S1	S	H
220299	Fund of free enterprise	Econ	S1	S	H
220428	Advanced Texas studies	Hist	S1	S	H
220432	American history	Hist	S1	S	H
220432	American history	Hist	S2	S	H
220433	World history	Hist	S1	S	H
220433	World history	Hist	S2	S	H
220501	American government	PolSc	S1	S	H
220501	American government	PolSc	S2	S	H
220699	Advanced soc sci problems	Socio	S1	S	H
220699	Sociology	Socio	S1	S	H
	College courses				
010102	Agricultural finance	Agri	232	3S	L
010103	Prin of mktg agric prod	Agri	236	3S	L
010104	The agri industry	Agri	111	1S	L
010199	Agricultural economics	Agri	131	3S	L
010402	Sheep wool mohair producn	Agri	4316	3S	U
010699	Plant & soil science	Agri	4324	3S	U
010704	Soil fertility	Agri	4335	3S	U
040101	Elementary accounting I	Acctg	2300	3S	L
040101	Elementary accounting II	Acctg	2301	3S	L

NCES No.	Course Title	Dept.	Course No.	Credits	Level
040111	Prin cost/managerial acct	Acctg	3306	3S	U
040114	Income tax accounting	Acctg	4300	3S	U
040199	Industrial acctg en	Acctg	2304	3S	L
040199	Personal finance	Acctg	2320	3S	L
040199	Corporation finance	Acctg	3320	3S	U
040304	Prin of money/bankg/credt	Acctg	3323	3S	U
040366	Investments	Bus	4324	3S	U
040707	Life & health insurance	Ins	3327	3S	U
040999	Managerial communication	Mgmt	3373	3S	U
041001	Principles of marketing	Mktg	3350	3S	U
041299	Intro business statistics	Bus	2445	4S	L
041399	Real estate fundamentals	RIEs	3332	3S	U
0499	Reprtg/interp finan data	Acctg	3302	3S	U
050199	Adv prin of public relat	Adv	331	3S	U
050606	Hist of Amer journalism	Jrnl	335	3S	U
0509	Intro to mass communicatn	Commu	130	3S	L
070103	Foundations of ed soc	Educ	4323	3S	U
070199	History & philos of educ	Educ	4314	3S	U
070610	Children's literature	Educ	4350	3S	U
070610	Teaching Engl in sec schs	Engl	4336	3S	U
100304	Food and nutrition	HmEc	1301	3S	L
100602	Courtship and marriage	HmEc	2322	3S	L
100701	Fam mgt/hsg/home	HmEc	230	3S	L
120201	Masterpieces of lit	Engl	231	3S	L
120201	Masterpieces of lit	Engl	232	3S	L
120204	Short story	Engl	331	3S	U
120204	American novel	Engl	3325	3S	U
120204	Modern American drama	Engl	4343	3S	U
120302	Hist of the Engl language	Engl	438	3S	U
120310	English: college rhetoric	Engl	131	3S	L
120310	English: college rhetoric	Engl	132	3S	L
130799	Business law I	Bus	3391	3S	U
130799	Business law II	Bus	3392	3S	U
130799	Oil & gas law	Bus	3395	3S	U
150599	Man & his earth	Geol	138	3S	L
160302	College algebra	Math	133	3S	L
160401	Intro to math analysis	Math	137	3S	L
160401	Intro to math analysis	Math	138	3S	L
160401	Analyt geom & calculus I	Math	151	5S	L
160401	Analyt geom & calculus II	Math	152	5S	L
160401	Calculus I	Math	1317	3S	L
160401	Calculus II	Math	1318	3S	L
160401	Calculus III	Math	235	3S	L
160602	Trigonometry	Math	131	3S	L
160603	Analytical geometry	Math	1316	3S	L
181202	Intro to New Testament	Relig	132	3S	L
181299	Intro to Old Testament	Relig	131	3S	L
190504	Chron dis/quality of life	HSci	221	2S	L
190509	Patterns of healthful liv	HSci	133	3S	L
190701	Progmng for leisure actvs	Rec	331	3S	U
190701	Manag urban leisure servs	Rec	438	3S	U
200102	History of psychology	Psych	4316	3S	U
200403	Human learning	Psych	4319	3S	U
200406	Psychology of learning	Psych	3317	3S	U
200501	Abnormal psychology	Psych	435	3S	U
200504	Child psychology	Psych	231	3S	L
200504	Adolescent psychology	Psych	235	3S	L
200505	Mental health	Psych	232	3S	L
200599	General psychology	Psych	130	3S	L
2099	Personality	Psych	336	3S	L
220102	Cultural anthropology	Anthr	232	3S	L
220201	Principles of economics I	Econ	231	3S	L
220201	Prin of economics II	Econ	232	3S	L
220306	Regional geog of world	Geog	2351	3S	L
220428	History of Texas	Hist	330	3S	U
220432	History of US to 1877	Hist	231	3S	L
220432	History of US since 1877	Hist	232	3S	L
220433	Western civilization I	Hist	1300	3S	L
220433	Western civilization II	Hist	1301	3S	L
220501	Amer govt organization	PolS	231	3S	L
220501	American public policy	PolS	232	3S	L
220605	Sociology of marriage	Socio	2331	3S	L
220606	Intro to sociology	Socio	2301	3S	L
220608	Rural sociology	Socio	3361	3S	U
220613	Current social problems	Socio	2320	3S	L

Noncredit course

NCES No.	Course Title	Dept.	Course No.	Credits	Level
190507	Rational self-counseling	HSci		NC	

33 UNIVERSITY OF ALABAMA

Dr. Nancy G. Williams
Director
Independent Study Department
University of Alabama
P.O. Box 2967
University, Alabama 35486
Phone: (205) 348-7642

Enrollment on a noncredit basis accepted in all credit courses. Only in exceptional cases are gifted high school students permitted to enroll in undergraduate courses for credit. Overseas enrollment accepted.

NCES No.	Course Title	Dept.	Course No.	Credits	Level
	High school courses				
040104	General business	Bus	1A	HF	H
040104	General business	Bus	1B	HF	H
090101	Modern health	HSci	1A	HF	H
090101	Modern health	HSci	16	HF	H
120307	Ninth-grade English	Engl	9A	HF	H
120307	Ninth-grade English	Engl	9B	HF	H
120307	Tenth-grade English	Engl	10A	HF	H
120307	Tenth-grade English	Engl	10B	HF	H
120307	Eleventh-grade English	Engl	11A	HF	H
120307	Eleventh-grade English	Engl	11B	HF	H
120307	Twelfth-grade English	Engl	12A	HF	H
120307	Twelfth-grade English	Engl	12B	HF	H
120307	Basic grammar review	Engl	13	HF	H
1211	Beginning German	Ger	1A	HF	H
1211	Beginning German	Ger	1B	HF	H
1211	Second-year German	Ger	2A	HF	H
1211	Second-year German	Ger	2B	HF	H
160301	General mathematics	Math	13A	HF	H
160301	General mathematics	Math	13B	HF	H
160302	Algebra I	Math	9A	HF	H
160302	Algebra I	Math	9B	HF	H
160302	Algebra II	Math	11A	HF	H
160302	Algebra II	Math	11B	HF	H
160304	Unified geometry	Math	10A	HF	H
160304	Unified geometry	Math	10B	HF	H
160602	Trigonometry	Math	12	HF	H
161202	Consumer mathematics	Math	14	HF	H
220403	Economics	Hist	12A	HF	H
220428	Alabama history	Hist	9A	HF	H
220428	Alabama history	Hist	96	HF	H
220432	American history	Hist	11A	HF	H
220432	American history	Hist	11B	HF	H
220433	World history	Hist	10A	HF	H
220433	World history	Hist	10B	HF	H
220501	Government	PolSc	12B	HF	H
	College courses				
030399	Intro to listening	Music	121C	3S	L
030399	Intro to study of music	Music	421C	3S	U
040101	Prin of accounting I	Acctg	201C	3S	L
040101	Prin of accounting II	Acctg	202C	3S	L
040104	Intermediate accounting I	Acctg	310C	3S	U
040104	Intermediate Acctg II	Acctg	311C	3S	U
040106	Cost accounting	Acctg	361C	3S	U
040109	Acctg: nonprofit organizs	Acctg	456C	3S	U
040114	Income tax procedure	Acctg	371C	3S	U
040301	Business finance	Bus	302C	3S	U
040306	Investments	Bus	414C	3S	U
040308	Money and banking	Bus	301C	3S	U
040312	Public finance	Bus	423C	3S	U
040399	Transportation	Bus	351C	3S	U
040601	Written bus communication	Bus	206C	2S	L
040604	Written bus communication	Bus	372C	2S	U
040905	Organ theory & behavior	Mgmt	300C	3S	U
041001	Marketing	Mktg	300C	3S	U
041099	Retail management	Mktg	321C	3S	U
041099	Sales management	Mktg	338C	3S	U
041099	Promotional strategy	Mktg	444C	3S	U
041099	Essen of multinatnl mktg	Mktg	455C	3S	U
041099	Marketing research	Mktg	473C	3S	U
041099	Salesmanship	Mktg	337C	3S	U
041104	Collective bargaining	Mgmt	430C	3S	U
041199	Intro human resources mgt	Mgmt	301C	3S	U
041199	Personnel management	Mgmt	310C	3S	U
041199	Management group behavior	Mgmt	320C	3S	U
041301	Real estate appraisal	Bus	432C	3S	U

NCES No.	Course Title	Dept.	Course No.	Credits	Level
041303	Principles of real estate	Bus	431C	3S	U
041306	Real estate finance	Bus	436C	3S	U
050499	Intro to mass communica	Commu	101C	3S	L
050499	Mass media law & regula	Commu	401C	3S	U
070404	Methods of teaching	Educ	383C	3S	U
070499	Devel of instruction mate	Educ	380C	3S	U
070499	Devel of voc educ in US	Educ	384C	3S	U
070499	Occupational analysis	Educ	377C	3S	U
070499	Occupational competency I	Educ	378C	3S	U
070499	Occu competency II	Educ	379C	3S	U
070799	Guidance for teachers	Educ	411C	3S	U
080699	Process calculations	ChmEg	252C	3S	L
080699	Thermodynamics calculatns	ChmEg	253C	3S	L
090699	Intro to health system	HSci	370C	3S	U
090699	Anal of health-care mgmt	HSci	371C	3S	U
100206	Personal finance	HmEc	404C	3S	U
100299	Consumer protection	HmEc	401C	3S	U
100299	Consumer behavior	CEd	313C	3S	U
100399	Nutrition: birth thru adol	HmEc	302C	3S	U
100399	Nutrition and health	HmEc	400C	3S	U
100401	Decision mkg & fam resour	HmEc	201C	3S	L
100504	Household equipment	HmEc	240C	3S	L
100601	Child devel: school age	HmEc	301C	3S	U
100601	Child devel: adolescence	HmEc	302C	3S	U
100602	Marriage and the family	HmEc	262C	3S	L
100699	Human development	HmEc	101C	3S	L
120299	Greek & Roman mythology	Clas	222C	2S	L
120307	English literature	EngLL	205C	3S	L
120307	English literature	EngLL	206C	3S	L
120307	American literature	EngLL	209C	3S	L
120307	American literature	EngLL	210C	3S	L
120307	Major American writers	EngLL	340C	3S	U
120307	Major American writers	EngLL	341C	3S	U
120307	Contemporary American lit	EngLL	345C	3S	U
120307	Southern literature	EngLL	347C	3S	U
120307	Eng Bible as literature	EngLL	363C	3S	U
120307	Shakespeare	EngLL	366C	3S	U
120307	The English novel	EngLL	387C	3S	U
120307	The modern short story	EngLL	390C	3S	U
120307	The Age of Browning	EngLL	485C	3S	U
120307	The Age of Hardy	EngLL	486C	3S	U
120307	Modern British fiction	EngLL	491C	3S	U
120310	English composition	Engl	101C	3S	L
120310	English composition	Engl	102C	3S	L
120399	American folklore	Hum	221C	3S	L
120399	Popular culture in Amer	Hum	222C	3S	L
120399	The American experience	Hum	300C	3S	U
120399	Independent study reading	Hum	421C	3S	U
1210	Intermediate French	Frnch	201C	3S	L
1210	Intermediate French	Frnch	202C	3S	L
121105	Elementary German	Ger	101C	4S	L
121105	Elementary German	Ger	102C	4S	L
121105	Intermediate German	Ger	201C	3S	L
121105	Intermediate German	Ger	202C	3S	L
121105	Intermed scientific Ger	Ger	209C	3S	L
121105	Intermed scientific Ger	Ger	210C	3S	L
121105	German for reading profic	Ger	103C	3S	L
121105	German for reading profic	Ger	104C	3S	L
121605	Elementary Latin	Latin	101C	3S	L
121605	Elementary Latin	Latin	102C	3S	L
122505	Intermediate Spanish	Span	201C	3S	L
122505	Intermediate Spanish	Span	202C	3S	L
122505	Advanced grammar & comp	Span	356C	3S	U
122507	Survey of Spanish lit	Span	371C	3S	U
122507	Survey of Spanish lit	Span	372C	3S	U
122599	Spanish civilization	Span	364C	3S	U
130499	Intro to criminal justice	Socio	200C	3S	L
130499	Intro to law enforcement	Socio	201C	3S	L
130499	Intro to corrections	Socio	202C	3S	L
130499	Criminal investigation	Socio	240C	3S	L
130499	Intro to private security	Socio	260C	3S	L
130499	Org & man con in crim jus	Socio	330C	3S	U
130499	Crime prev & control	Socio	460C	3S	U
130799	Law, business & society	Law	200C	3S	L
130999	Real & pers property law	Law	201C	3S	U
150399	Heredity	Bio	209C	3S	L
150399	Human reproduction	Bio	210C	2S	L
150399	Hum anatomy & physiology	Bio	213C	3S	L
150399	Hum anatomy & physiology	Bio	214C	3S	L
150399	History of biology	Bio	281C	2S	L
150399	Medical etymology	Bio	209C	2S	L
150799	Desc physics non-sci majr	Phys	115C	3S	L
150799	Desc physics non-sci majr	Phys	116C	3S	L
160302	College algebra	Math	109C	3S	L
160302	High school algebra	Math	001C	1U	L
160399	Intro college mathematics	Math	111C	3S	L
160399	Plane geometry	Math	002C	1U	L
160401	Calculus & analytic geom	Math	126C	4S	L
160401	Calculus	Math	227C	4S	L
160401	Introduction to calculus	Math	121C	3S	L
160403	Analytic geom & calculus	Math	125C	4S	L
160602	Analytic trigonometry	Math	115C	3S	L
160801	Statistical methods I	Stat	250C	3S	L
160801	Statistical methods II	Stat	251C	3S	L
180302	Ethics	Philo	200C	3S	L
180599	Intro to deductive logic	Philo	101C	3S	L
180799	Intro to philosophy	Philo	100C	3S	L
180902	New Testm: earlier commun	Rel	112C	3S	L
180902	New Testm: later commun	Rel	212C	3S	L
181102	Intro religious studies	Rel	100C	3S	L
190199	Phys ed in elem school	PEdu	363C	3S	U
190509	Personal health	HEd	270C	3S	L
1999	Intro health, PE & recrea	HPER	191C	2S	L
200199	Intro to psychology	Psych	101C	3S	L
200505	Psychology of adjustment	Psych	207C	3S	L
2099	Elementary statistic meth	Psych	211C	3S	L
2099	Applied psychology	Psych	228C	3S	L
210401	Soc services for delinq	PubAd	308C	3S	U
210401	Family & child welfare	PubAd	310C	3S	U
220199	General anthropology I	Anthr	101C	3S	L
220199	General anthropology II	Anthr	102C	3S	L
220201	Prin of economics I	Econ	101C	3S	L
220201	Prin of economics II	Econ	102C	3S	L
220202	Hist of economic concepts	Econ	450C	3S	U
220299	Amer economic institution	Econ	160C	3S	L
220305	Survey of physicl geogra	Geog	103C	3S	L
220306	World regional geography	Geog	105C	3S	L
220399	Geography of Anglo-Amer	Geog	243C	3S	L
220399	Geography of Europe	Geog	246C	3S	L
220408	Hist of Chris chu to 1500	Hist	235C	3S	L
220408	Hist Chris chu since 1500	Hist	236C	3S	L
220408	Religion in Amer South	Rel	221C	3S	L
220421	US hist: colonial period	Hist	220C	3S	L
220424	England to 1688	Hist	247C	3S	L
220424	England since 1688	Hist	248C	3S	L
220427	Colonial Latin American	Hist	237C	3S	L
220427	Mod Latin Amer since 1808	Hist	238C	3S	L
220428	Hist of Alabama to 1865	Hist	225C	3S	L
220428	Hist of Alabama since 1865	Hist	226C	3S	L
220431	Russia to 1894	Hist	361C	3S	U
220431	Rus & Sov Union snce 1894	Hist	362C	3S	U
220432	Wstrn movemnt in Amer his	Hist	321C	3S	U
220432	The US since 1945	Hist	318C	3S	U
220432	Western civiliz to 1648	Hist	101C	3S	L
220432	Western civ since 1648	Hist	102C	3S	L
220433	Comparative world civiliz	Hist	110C	3S	L
220453	US in twentieth century	Hist	222C	3S	L
220499	US in nineteenth century	Hist	221C	3S	L
220501	Intro to American govt	PolSc	101C	3S	L
220501	Intro to public policy	PolSc	103C	3S	L
220511	State & local government	PolSc	211C	3S	L
220599	International politics	PolSc	204C	3S	L
220599	Public administration	PolSc	206C	3S	L
220602	Criminology	Socio	301C	3S	U
220605	The family	Socio	206C	3S	L
220613	Analysis of social prob	Socio	102C	3S	L
220615	Minority peoples	Socio	215C	3S	L
220699	Intro to sociology	Socio	101C	3S	L
220699	Human relations–industry	Socio	355C	3S	U

Noncredit courses

NCES No.	Course Title	Dept.	Course No.	Credits	Level
040306	Stocks, bonds & beg inves	Bus	NC69	NC	
051102	Intercultural communicatn	Commu	NC71	NC	

NCES No.	Course Title	Dept.	Course No.	Credits	Level
120305	Vocabulary bldg for adult	Lang	NC70	NC	
220502	Citizenship	Hist	NC	NC	

(34) UNIVERSITY OF ALASKA

Dr. Margaret K. Wood
Director, Learning Resources
Correspondence Study
University of Alaska
115 Eielson Building
403 Salcha Street
Fairbanks, Alaska 99701
Phone: (907) 474-7222

Enrollment on a noncredit basis accepted in all credit courses. Gifted high school students are permitted to enroll in undergraduate courses for credit. Overseas enrollment accepted. The course entitled Alaska History for Local Historians–Bering Straits Region (Hist 250C) is available only to students who live in the Bering Straits region.

NCES No.	Course Title	Dept.	Course No.	Credits	Level
	College courses				
040101	Elementary accounting I	Acctg	101C	3S	L
040101	Elementary accounting II	Acctg	102C	3S	L
040111	Hospitality indus acctg	Hotel	202C	3S	L
040201	Hotel front office proced	Hotel	201C	3S	L
040306	Pract guide to mod invest	BA	170C	3S	L
040601	Business English	OOc	071C	1S	L
040601	Business correspondence	OOc	072C	1S	L
040603	Hotel communications	Hotel	214C	3S	L
040903	Intro to hotel-motel mgt	Hotel	103C	3S	L
041006	Hotel-motel sales promo	Hotel	205C	3S	L
041103	Hotel human relations	Hotel	204C	3S	L
041104	Hotel supervisory dvlpmnt	Hotel	220C	3S	L
041308	Real estate/property law	BA	223C	3S	L
050699	Intro to mass comm	Jrnl	101C	3S	L
051103	Fund of oral communicatn	Sph	111C	3S	L
070102	Philosophy of education	Educ	422C	3S	U
070102	Human development	Educ	312C	3S	U
070401	Comm in a cross-cult clrm	Educ	393C	3S	U
070499	Tests & measurements	Educ	332C	3S	U
070516	Math for elem teachers I	Math	205C	3S	L
070516	Math for elem teachers II	Math	206C	3S	L
070516	Teaching metrics in class	Educ	467C	2S	U
090106	Epidemiology principles	HSci	430C	3S	U
090114	Communicable disease cont	HSci	412C	3S	U
090702	Community health	HSci	410C	3S	U
090703	Environmental protection	HSci	415C	3S	U
090799	Vectorborne-disease contr	HSci	413C	3S	U
090799	Waterborne-disease contr	HSci	414C	3S	U
090799	Foodborne-disease control	HSci	416C	3S	U
100701	Supervisory housekeeping	Hotel	211C	3S	L
100702	Food & beverage managemnt	Hotel	209C	3S	L
100799	Hotel maintenance & engin	Hotel	212C	3S	L
110601	Private pilot ground schl		100C	AT	L
120103	Nature of language	Ling	101C	3S	L
120201	Masterpieces of world lit	Engl	302C	3S	U
120201	Aleut, Eskimo & Ind lit	Engl	349C	3S	U
120307	Frontier lit of Alaska	Engl	350C	3S	U
120310	Methods of written comm	Engl	111C	3S	L
120310	Intermediate exposition	Engl	211C	3S	L
121509	Elementary Japanese	Jpn	101C	3S	L
121709	Elem Inupiaq Eskimo I	Esk	111C	5S	L
121709	Elem Inupiaq Eskimo II	Esk	112C	5S	L
130701	Business law I	BA	331C	3S	U
130702	Business law II	BA	332C	3S	U
130999	Hotel-motel law	Hotel	207C	3S	U
150408	Chemistry	Chem	104C	3S	L
160199	The metric system	Math	100FC	1S	L
160301	Univ math w a calculator	Math	093	1S	L
160302	College algebra	Math	107C	3S	L
160302	Elementary algebra I	Math	075C	3S	L
160302	Elementary algebra II	Math	076C	3S	L
160602	Trigonometry	Math	108C	3S	L
200104	Intro to psychology	Psych	101C	3S	L
200504	Developmental psychology	Psych	240C	3S	L
200799	Drugs & drug dependence	Psych	370C	3S	U

NCES No.	Course Title	Dept.	Course No.	Credits	Level
210304	Intro to criminal justice	Just	110C	3S	L
210304	Intro to criminal investi	PA	110C	3S	L
210304	Criminal investigation	PA	255C	3S	L
220102	General anthropology	Anth	101C	3S	L
220199	Anth of Alaskan natives	Anth	342C	3S	U
220399	Geography of Alaska	Geog	302C	3S	U
220453	History of Western civ I	Hist	101C	3S	L
220453	History of Western civ II	Hist	102C	3S	L
220499	History of Alaska	Hist	341C	3S	U
220499	Maritime hist of Alaska	Hist	345C	3S	U
220499	Polar exploration & lit	Hist	380C	3S	U
220499	Alskn hist/Bering Straits	Hist	250C	3S	U
220511	State & local government	PolSc	211C	3S	L
220603	Population & ecology	Socio	207C	3S	L
220605	Sociology of the family	Socio	242C	3S	L
220613	Social problems	Socio	201C	3S	L
220615	American minority groups	Socio	408C	3S	U
220699	Drugs & drug dependence	Socio	370C	3S	U

(35) UNIVERSITY OF ARIZONA

Mr. Harry Norman
Assistant
Independent Study
University of Arizona
1717 East Speedway, Babcock Building
Tucson, Arizona 85719
Phone: (602) 626-5838

Enrollment on a noncredit basis accepted in all credit courses. Gifted high school students are permitted to enroll in undergraduate courses for credit. Overseas enrollment accepted.

NCES No.	Course Title	Dept.	Course No.	Credits	Level
	High school courses				
0305	Acrylic painting	Art	9-12	HF	H
0305	Beginning drawing	Art	9-12	HF	H
0305	Commercial art	Art	9-12	HF	H
040104	Elementary accounting	Acct	11A	HF	H
040104	Elementary accounting	Acct	11B	HF	H
120310	Composition	Eng	11A	HF	H
120310	Expository writing	Eng	11B	HF	H
120310	Current literature	Eng	12A	HF	H
120310	Creative writing	Eng	12B	HF	H
120310	Language and usage	Eng	9-12A	HF	H
120310	Vocabulary study	Eng	11-12	HF	H
1509	Basic earth science	Sci	10A	HF	H
1509	Basic earth science	Sci	10B	HF	H
160301	General math	Math	9A	HF	H
160301	General math	Math	9B	HF	H
160302	Elementary algebra	Math	9C	HF	H
160302	Elementary algebra	Math	9D	HF	H
160601	Plane geometry	Math	10A	HF	H
160601	Plane geometry	Math	10B	HF	H
160602	Plane trigonometry	Math	11A	HF	H
200599	Elementary psychology	SocSt	12	HF	H
220399	World geography	Geo	10A	HF	H
220399	World geography	Geo	10B	HF	H
220428	Arizona history	Hist	11-12	HF	H
220432	US history	Hist	12	HF	H
220432	US history to 1865	Hist	11A	HF	H
220432	US history from 1865	Hist	11B	HF	H
220501	American government	Govt	12	HF	H
220501	US government	Govt	11-12	HF	H
220511	Arizona government	Govt	11-12	HF	H
220606	Elementary sociology	SocSt	12	HF	H
229999	Free enterprise	SocSt	12	HF	H
	College courses				
010499	Feeds and feeding	AnSci	4134A	1U	L
010499	Feeds and feeding	AnSci	4134B	2U	L
0114	Conserv of nat resources	RNR	4135	3U	L
030399	Basic musicianship	Music	4100	3U	L
040101	Principles of accounting	Acctg	4200A	3U	L
040101	Principles of accounting	Acctg	4200B	3U	L
040203	Records management	BCEd	4379	3U	L
040399	Risk management	Fin	4453	3U	L
040601	Intro to bus commun	BCEd	4373	3U	L
041099	Creative advertising	Mrkt	4364	3U	U
041099	Public relations	Mrkt	4366	3U	U

NCES No.	Course Title	Dept.	Course No.	Credits	Level
041199	Personnel management	Mgmt	4330	3U	U
070103	Social found and adminstr	EdFA	4350	3U	U
070512	Teaching LA in elem sch	ElEd	4322	3U	U
070512	Teaching rdng in elem sch	ElEd	4323	3U	U
070516	Teaching math in elem sch	ElEd	4326	3U	U
070806	Mental retardation	SpEd	4470	3U	U
070899	Study of exceptionl child	SpEd	4403	3U	U
090403	Problems of drug abuse	Rehab	4480	3U	U
090903	Sec sch health education	Hlth	4180	3U	L
090999	International health pblm	Hlth	4433	3U	U
090999	Safety ed & accident prev	Hlth	4435	3U	U
100601	Child development	HEco	4223	3U	L
100602	Family relations	HmEc	4337	3U	U
100699	Education for marriage	HEco	4137	3U	L
120305	Modern grammar & usage	Engl	4406	3U	U
120307	Modern literature	Engl	4261	3U	L
120307	English literature	Engl	4370B	3U	U
120308	Major American writers	Engl	4265	3U	L
120308	Shakespeare	Engl	4431A	3U	L
120308	Shakespeare	Engl	4431B	3U	U
120308	American Romanticism	Engl	4482	3U	U
1210	Elementary French	Frech	4101A	2U	L
1210	Elementary French	Frech	4101B	2U	L
1210	Intermediate French	Frech	4201A	2U	L
1210	Intermediate French	Frech	4201B	2U	L
121010	Intermediate French	Frech	4201B	27	L
1211	Elementary German	Ger	4101A	2U	L
1211	Elementary German	Ger	4101B	2U	L
1211	Intermediate German	Ger	4201A	2U	L
1225	Elementary Spanish	Span	4101A	2U	L
1225	Second-semester Spanish	Span	4101B	2U	L
1225	Third-semester Spanish	Span	4201A	2U	L
1225	Fourth-semester Spanish	Span	4201B	2U	L
1225	Commercial & tech Spanish	Span	4371A	2U	U
1225	Commercial & tech Spanish	Span	4371B	2U	U
1299	Literature of India	OrStu	4444A	3U	U
1299	Literature of India	OrStu	4444B	3U	U
150102	Essentials of astronomy	Astro	4100	3U	L
150202	Intro meteorology/climate	Atmo	4171	3U	L
150316	Plants useful to man	GBio	4412	2U	U
150321	General plant pathology	PPath	4205	3U	L
1505	Intro to geology	GeoSc	4101A	3U	L
1505	Intro to geology	GeoSc	4101B	3U	L
1599	Insects and man	Ento	4151	3U	L
160302	Intermediate algebra	Math	4116	3U	L
160302	College algebra	Math	4117	3U	L
160401	Calculus	Math	4125A	3U	L
160401	Calculus	Math	4125B	3U	L
160401	Vector calculus	Math	4223A	2U	L
160401	Vector calculus	Math	4223B	2U	L
160401	Elements of calculus	Math	4123	3U	L
160602	Trigonometry	Math	4118	2U	L
160899	Intro to statistics	Math	4160	3U	L
160999	Finite mathematics	Math	4119	3U	L
161199	Survey of math thought	Math	4101A	2U	L
161199	Survey of math thought	Math	4101B	2U	L
161199	Mod elem mathematics	Math	4105A	3U	L
161199	Modern elem mathematics	Math	4105B	3U	L
180499	Intro to philosophy	Phil	4111	3U	L
180502	Intro to logic	Phil	4112	3U	L
180799	Intro to moral & soc phil	Phil	4113	3U	L
190513	Elem sch health education	Hlth	4181	2U	L
200504	Elementary psychology	Psych	4100A	3U	L
200504	Elementary psychology	Psych	4100B	3U	L
200599	Child development	EdPsy	4301	3U	U
200599	Adolescent development	EdPsy	4302	3U	U
200805	Learning in the schools	EdPsy	4310	3U	U
2099	Intro to psych statistics	Psych	4245	3U	L
220199	Intro to anthropology	Anthr	4100A	3U	L
220199	Intro to anthropology	Anthr	4100B	3U	L
220199	Native peoples of the SW	Anthr	4205B	2U	L
220199	Intro to Asian civiliz	Anthr	4170A	3U	L
220199	Intro to Asian civiliz	Anthr	4170B	3U	L
220199	Cultural anthropology	Anthr	4200	3U	L
220199	Native peoples of the SW	Anthr	4205A	3U	L
220201	Principles of economics	Econ	4201A	3U	L
220201	Principles of economics	Econ	4201B	3U	L
220204	Money and banking	Econ	4330	3U	U
220423	Oriental humanities	OrStu	4140A	3U	L

NCES No.	Course Title	Dept.	Course No.	Credits	Level
220423	Intro to Asian civiliz	OrStu	4170A	3U	L
220423	Intro to Asian civiliz	OrStu	4170B	3U	L
220423	Modern Chinese history	OrStu	4476A	3U	U
220423	Modern Chinese history	OrStu	4476B	3U	U
220423	Intro to Asian civiliz	Hist	4170A	3U	L
220423	Intro to Asian civiliz	Hist	4170B	3U	L
220423	Intro to Asian civiliz	OrStu	4170B	3U	L
220424	History of England	Hist	4117A	3U	L
220424	History of England	Hist	4117B	3U	L
220426	French Revolut & Napoleon	Hist	4420	3U	U
220432	Intro to hist of Wstn wld	Hist	4101A	3U	L
220432	Intro to hist of Wstn wld	Hist	4101B	3U	L
220432	Hist of the United States	Hist	4130A	3U	L
220432	Hist of the United States	Hist	4130B	3U	L
220432	US: 1945 to present	Hist	4440	3U	U
220432	History of Am foreign rel	Hist	4449B	3U	U
220470	American ethnic history	Hist	4452	3U	U
220499	History of China	Hist	43756	3U	U
220499	Modern Chinese history	Hist	4476A	3U	U
220499	Modern Chinese history	Hist	4476B	3U	U
220501	Am national government	PolSc	4102	3U	L
220505	Intro to internatl relat	PolSc	4150	3U	L
220511	Am state & local govt	PolSc	4103	3U	L
220511	Arizona government	PolSc	4214B	1U	L
220599	Nat & state constitutions	PolSc	4110	3U	L
220599	Soviet foreign policy	PolSc	4451	3U	U
220601	Intro to sociology	Soc	4100	3U	L
220602	Criminology	Soc	4342	3U	U
220603	World population	Soc	4289	3U	U
220604	Juvenile delinquency	Soc	4341	3U	U
220613	American social problems	Soc	4201	3U	L
220614	Minority rel & urban soc	Soc	4160	3U	L
220699	Sociology of the family	Soc	4321	3U	U
2299	Intro to black studies	BIS	4220	3U	L
	Noncredit courses				
0305	Acrylic painting	Art	80-17	NC	V
0305	Beginning drawing	Art	80-18	NC	V
0305	Commercial art	Art	80-20	NC	V
040601	Devel power/negot skill	BCEd	80-6	NC	V
040999	Time mgmt for pers growth	Mgmt	80-15	NC	V
041106	Supervision	Bus	80-13	NC	V
0506	Beginning journalism	Engl	80-19	NC	V
1006	Leadership	HmEc	80-9	NC	V
100604	Deal w complaint, critcsm	HmEc	80-7	NC	V
100604	Problem analysis	HmEc	80-11	NC	V
100604	Positive thoughts	HmEc	80-21	NC	V
100699	Working women	HmEc	80-16	NC	V
120308	The short story	EngLL	80-5	NC	V
120310	Creative writing	EngLL	80-3	NC	V

㊱ UNIVERSITY OF ARKANSAS

Mr. William E. Manning
Director, Department of Independent Study
Center for Continuing Education
University of Arkansas
2 University Center
Fayetteville, Arkansas 72701
Phone: (501) 575-3647

Gifted high school students are permitted to enroll in undergraduate courses for credit. Overseas enrollment is not encouraged; each case is judged on an individual basis. The department offers an external high school diploma. It does not offer an external college degree.

NCES No.	Course Title	Dept.	Course No.	Credits	Level
	High school courses				
040104	Accounting	Acctg	11A	HF	H
040104	Accounting	Acctg	11B	HF	H
040201	Secretarial office proced	SOP	11A	HF	H
040201	Secretarial office proced	SOP	11B	HF	H
040203	Records management	AdSci	NL	HF	H
040205	Shorthand	Shhnd	12A	HF	H
040205	Shorthand	Shhnd	12B	HF	H
040207	Typing	Type	11A	HF	H
040207	Typing	Type	11B	HF	H
040601	Business communications	Engl	1	HF	H

NCES No.	Course Title	Dept.	Course No.	Credits	Level
040601	Business communications	Engl	2	HF	H
0810	Industrial arts drafting	InArt	12A	HF	H
0810	Industrial arts drafting	InArt	12B	HF	H
120201	World literature	Engl	1	HF	H
120201	World literature	Engl	2	HF	H
120305	Grammar	Engl	11	HF	H
120305	Grammar	Engl	12	HF	H
120305	Remedial language arts	Engl	1	HF	H
120305	Advanced language arts	Engl	1	HF	H
120307	Literature	Engl	11	HF	H
120307	Literature	Engl	12	HF	H
120308	Vocab improv and read dev	Engl	1	HF	H
120399	Grammar and literature	Engl	9A	HF	H
120399	Grammar and literature	Engl	9B	HF	H
120399	Grammar and literature	Engl	10A	HF	H
120399	Grammar and literature	Engl	10B	HF	H
120399	Grammar and literature	Engl	11A	HF	H
120399	Grammar and literature	Engl	11B	HF	H
120399	Grammar and literature	Engl	12A	HF	H
120399	Grammar and literature	Engl	12B	HF	H
121605	Latin	FornL	9A	HF	H
121605	Latin	FornL	9B	HF	H
121605	Latin	FornL	10A	HF	H
121605	Latin	FornL	10B	HF	H
122505	Spanish	FornL	9A	HF	H
122505	Spanish	FornL	9B	HF	H
1299	Introduction to mythology	Engl	1	HF	H
150399	Biology	Sci	10A	HF	H
150399	Biology	Sci	10B	HF	H
160301	Remedial arithmetic	Math	I	HF	H
160301	Remedial arithmetic	Math	II	HF	H
160302	Algebra	Math	9A	HF	H
160302	Algebra	Math	9B	HF	H
160302	Advanced algebra	Math	11A	HF	H
160302	Advanced algebra	Math	11B	HF	H
161101	Business mathematics	Math	I	HF	H
161101	Business mathematics	Math	II	HF	H
161199	Vocational mathematics	Math	I	HF	H
161199	Vocational mathematics	Math	II	HF	H
190509	Physiology and hygiene	Sci	11A	HF	H
190509	Physiology and hygiene	Sci	11B	HF	H
220201	Economics	SocSt	12	HF	H
220302	Commercial geography	SocSt	9A	HF	H
220302	Commercial geography	SocSt	9B	HF	H
220306	United States geography	SocSt	10A	HF	H
220306	United States geography	SocSt	10B	HF	H
220432	United States history	SocSt	11A	HF	H
220432	United States history	SocSt	11B	HF	H
220433	World history	SocSt	10A	HF	H
220433	World history	SocSt	10B	HF	H
220501	American government	SocSt	12A	HF	H
220501	American government	SocSt	12B	HF	H
220502	Civics	SocSt	9A	HF	H
220502	Civics	SocSt	9B	HF	H

College courses

NCES No.	Course Title	Dept.	Course No.	Credits	Level
0101	Agricultural economics	Agri	2103	3S	L
010404	Principles of genetics	AnSci	3123	3S	U
010699	Plant geography	Bot	3513	3S	U
0114	Conservation of nat resou	Geog	3003	3S	U
030402	Intro to dramatic art	SpDrA	2223	3S	L
030499	Origins of modern theater	SpDrA	5753	3S	U
040101	Principles of acctg I	Acctg	2013	3S	L
040101	Principles of acctg II	Acctg	2023	3S	L
040601	Business communications	Mgmt	2323	3S	L
040904	Intro to management	Mgmt	1033	3S	L
051104	Parliamentary procedure	SpDrA	2351	1S	L
051303	Writing for television	SpDrA	4833	3S	U
070401	Intro to childhood educ	ElEd	1103	3S	L
070401	Principles of sec educ	SecEd	4033	3S	U
070401	Prin & meth in middle sch	SecEd	4043	3S	U
070403	Tech of tchng in sec sch	SecEd	4133	3S	U
070404	Teaching science	ElEd	3303	3S	U
070499	Meth & mat sch & comm rec	Rec	3813	3S	U
070511	Drafting	VocEd	1603	3S	L
070511	Electricity	VocEd	1643	3S	L
070511	Industrial design I	VocEd	3603	3S	U
070512	Children's literature	ElEd	2273	3S	L
070512	Creatv writg for children	ElEd	3733	3S	U
070512	Reading & other lang arts	ElEd	3333	3S	U

NCES No.	Course Title	Dept.	Course No.	Credits	Level
070516	Teaching math	ElEd	4413	3S	U
070516	Teaching math	SecEd	4223	3S	U
070519	Meth & mats phy ed el sch	PhyEd	3373	3S	U
070522	Teaching of social stud	SecEd	4232	2S	U
071103	Diagnostic & eval techs	ElEd	4023	3S	U
071103	Secon tests & measurement	SecEd	4723	3S	U
081102	Mechanics of fluids	EngSc	3203	3S	U
081104	Statics	EngSc	2003	3S	L
081104	Dynamics	EngSc	3003	3S	U
081199	Mechanics of materials	EngSc	3103	3S	U
090599	Personal health & safety	HelEd	1103	3S	L
100313	Nutrition in health	HmEc	1213	3S	L
120201	Intro to literature	Engl	1113	3S	L
120201	Masterpieces Wstrn lit	Engl	1123	3S	L
120305	Grammar	Engl	2153	3S	L
120307	Engl lit from beg to 1700	Engl	2113	3S	L
120307	Engl lit from 1700 to pre	Engl	2123	3S	L
120307	American lit to Civil War	Engl	3313	3S	U
120307	Lit of the United States	Engl	3323	3S	U
120307	Intro to Shakespeare	Engl	3653	3S	U
120310	Composition	Engl	1013	3S	L
120310	Composition—continuation	Engl	1023	3S	L
120310	Essay writing	Engl	2013	3S	L
120310	Intermediate composition	Engl	3003	3S	U
120399	Vocabulary building	Engl	1153	3S	L
121005	Elementary French	Frnch	1003	3S	L
121005	Advanced grammar & comp	Frnch	4003	3S	U
121008	Elementary French	Frnch	1013	3S	L
121010	Intermediate French	Frnch	2003	3S	L
121010	Intermediate French	Frnch	2013	3S	L
121105	Intro to German	Ger	1003	3S	L
121105	Intro to German	Ger	1013	3S	L
121108	Modern German prose	Ger	2003	3S	L
122505	Elementary Spanish	Span	1003	3S	L
122505	Elementary Spanish	Span	1013	3S	L
122505	Advanced grammar & comp	Span	4003	3S	U
122508	Spanish readings	Span	3133	3S	U
122510	Intermediate Spanish	Span	2003	3S	L
122510	Intermediate Spanish	Span	2013	3S	L
1299	Life and lit in Bible	Engl	1033	3S	L
1299	Lit of the New Testament	Engl	1233	3S	L
1302	Business law I	Acctg	2222	2S	L
1302	Business law II	Acctg	2322	2S	L
150307	Genetics	Bot	3203	3S	U
150316	Survey of botany	Bot	1913	3S	L
150317	Bacteria in human affairs	Bact	2003	3S	L
150399	Nature study	Bot	1022	2S	L
1509	Man and his environment	Bot	2533	3S	L
1599	Conservation of nat resou	Zoolo	3133	3S	U
160199	Patterns in math	Math	1103	3S	L
160302	College algebra	Math	1203	3S	L
160401	Calculus I	Math	2555	5S	L
160401	Calculus II	Math	2565	5S	L
160401	Calculus III	Math	2573	3S	L
160408	Finite math	Math	2053	3S	L
160602	Plane trigonometry	Math	1213	3S	L
161101	Math of finance	Math	1503	3S	L
180403	Intro to philosophy	Philo	2003	3S	L
180599	Logic	Philo	2203	3S	L
190106	Organ & admin of phy ed	PhyEd	4213	3S	U
190110	Tests & measure in phy ed	PhyEd	3313	3S	U
200501	Abnormal psychology	Psych	3023	3S	U
200503	Applied psychology	Psych	2023	3S	L
200503	Mental hygiene	Psych	3083	3S	U
200504	Infancy and early childhd	Psych	3033	3S	U
200504	Childhood and adolescence	Psych	3093	3S	U
200599	Exceptional children	Psych	4013	3S	U
200603	Psychological tests	Psych	4053	3S	U
200799	Social psychology	Psych	3013	3S	U
200804	Educational psychology	Psych	4033	3S	U
200902	Personnel psychology	Psych	3043	3S	U
2099	General psychology	PolSc	2003	3S	L
210403	Problems of child welfare	SoWel	3633	3S	U
220102	Intro to anthropology	Anthr	2023	3S	L
220104	Indians of North America	Anthr	3213	3S	U
220201	Principles of economics I	Econ	2013	3S	L
220201	Prin of economics II	Econ	2023	3S	L
220202	Economic dev of the US	Econ	1123	3S	L

NCES No.	Course Title	Dept.	Course No.	Credits	Level
220302	Economic geography	Geog	2023	3S	L
220305	Physical geography	Geog	1003	3S	L
220306	World regional geography	Geog	2003	3S	L
220399	Human geography	Geog	1123	3S	U
220399	United States & Canada	Geog	3253	3S	U
220402	Dip hist of US 1775-1890	Hist	4263	3S	U
220402	Dip hist of US 1890-pres	Hist	4273	3S	U
220406	Cultural hist of Germany	Ger	2013	3S	L
220406	Inst ideas of Wstrn man	WCiv	1003	3S	L
220406	Study of civ 1650-present	WCiv	1013	3S	L
220421	Col & Rev Amer 1607-1783	Hist	4403	3S	U
220427	Latin American civilizatn	Span	4223	3S	U
220432	The Amer Repub 1492-1877	Hist	2003	3S	L
220432	US as wld power 1877-1965	Hist	2013	3S	L
220470	American Negro history	Hist	3403	3S	U
220471	Hist of the Amer Indian	Hist	3103	3S	U
220501	American national govt	PolSc	2003	3S	L
220511	State and local govt	PolSc	2203	3S	L
220599	Intro to political science	PolSc	1503	3S	L
220602	Criminology	Socio	3023	3S	U
220603	Population problems	Socio	3013	3S	U
220605	Marriage and the family	Socio	2043	3S	L
220606	General sociology	Socio	2013	3S	L
220613	Social problems	Socio	2033	3S	L
220614	Black ghetto	Socio	4123	3S	U

Noncredit courses

NCES No.	Course Title	Dept.	Course No.	Credits	Level
040203	Business records control	AdSci	1		NC
040203	Business records control	AdSci	2		NC
041303	Principles of real estate		NC-1		NC

(37) UNIVERSITY OF CALIFORNIA

Independent Study, Department NN
2223 Fulton Street
Berkeley, California 94720
Phone: (415) 642-4124

Enrollment on a noncredit basis accepted in some credit courses. Gifted high school students are permitted to enroll in undergraduate courses for credit. Overseas enrollment accepted. For more information about courses listed here, please contact the Independent Study Office for the appropriate catalog of courses.

NCES No.	Course Title	Dept.	Course No.	Credits	Level
	High school courses				
010599	Horticulture	Agri	AG901		H
030302	Hist & appreciation music	Music	MU900		H
030501	Begin drawing & painting	VisAr	A901		H
040101	Accounting 1st semester	Bus	B905		H
040101	Accounting 2nd semester	Bus	B906		H
049900	General business	Bus	B907		H
0810	Beginning drafting	EngAS	800A		H
0810	Beginning drafting	EngAS	800B		H
100699	Marriage & family living	HmEc	H903		H
110413	Auto mechanics	PrArt	P904		H
110504	Photography	VisAr	P900		H
120202	The short story	Engl	E908		H
120202	The novel	Engl	E911		H
120305	Ninth-grade English	Engl	E900		H
120305	Ninth-grade English	Engl	E901		H
120305	Tenth-grade English	Engl	E902		H
120305	Tenth-grade English	Engl	E903		H
120305	Eleventh-grade English	Engl	E904		H
120305	Eleventh-grade English	Engl	E905		H
120305	Twelfth-grade English	Engl	E906		H
120305	Twelfth-grade English	Engl	E907		H
120305	Business English	Engl	E912		H
120305	Basic English	Engl	E915		H
120308	Improving reading skills	Engl	E913		H
120310	Composition	Engl	E909		H
120399	Effective study methods	StSkl	ST900		H
121009	First-year French	Frnch	F900		H
121009	First-year French	Frnch	F901		H
121009	Second-year French	Frnch	F902		H
121009	Second-year French	Frnch	F903		H
121109	First-year German	Ger	G900		H

NCES No.	Course Title	Dept.	Course No.	Credits	Level
121109	First-year German	Ger	G901		H
121109	Second-year German	Ger	G902		H
121109	Second-year German	Ger	G903		H
121699	First-year Latin	Latin	L900		H
121699	First-year Latin	Latin	L901		H
121699	Second-year Latin	Latin	L902		H
121699	Second-year Latin	Latin	L903		H
122509	First-year Spanish	Span	S900		H
122509	First-year Spanish	Span	S901		H
122509	Second-year Spanish	Span	S902		H
122509	Second-year Spanish	Span	S903		H
130799	Business law	Bus	B909		H
150399	Biology	Bio	SC903		H
150399	Biology	Bio	SC904		H
150399	Biology with laboratory	Bio	SC901		H
150399	Biology with laboratory	Bio	SC902		H
150799	Physics with laboratory	Phys	SC905		H
150799	Physics with laboratory	Phys	SC906		H
150799	Descriptive physics	Phys	SC907		H
150799	Descriptive physics	Phys	SC908		H
1509	Earth science	Sci	SC909		H
160103	General mathematics	Math	M914		H
160103	General mathematics	Math	M915		H
160301	Business & consumer math	Math	M917		H
160301	Business & consumer math	Math	M918		H
160301	Remedial arithmetic	Math	M912		H
160302	Elementary algebra	Math	M900		H
160302	Elementary algebra	Math	M901		H
160302	Advanced algebra	Math	M908		H
160302	Advanced algebra	Math	M909		H
160601	Plane geometry	Math	M904		H
160601	Plane geometry	Math	M905		H
160602	Trigonometry	Math	M910		H
190509	Health science	HSci	SC900		H
190603	Driver education	DrEd	D900		H
200104	Psychology	Psych	SS911		H
220201	Economics	Econ	SS909		H
220399	World geography	Geog	SS901		H
220399	World geography	Geog	SS902		H
220432	American history	Hist	SS905		H
220432	American history	Hist	SS906		H
220433	World history	Hist	SS903		H
220433	World history	Hist	SS904		H
220502	Civics	PolSc	SS900		H
220599	Modern problems	Socio	SS908		H
220606	Sociology	Socio	SS910		H

College courses

NCES No.	Course Title	Dept.	Course No.	Credits	Level
020103	Basic interior design	Des	407	3Q	U
030301	Elementary counterpoint	Music	6	4Q	L
030302	Introduction to music	Music	27	4Q	L
030302	Introduction to harmony	Music	5	4Q	L
030399	History of jazz	Music	7	4Q	L
030501	Two-dimensional design	VisAr	416	3Q	U
030501	Italic lettering	VisAr	424	3Q	U
030501	Beginning drawing	VisAr	5	3Q	L
030502	Fundamental discoveries	VisAr	415	3Q	U
030502	Collage	VisAr	419	3Q	U
030502	Acrylic painting	VisAr	417	3Q	U
030603	Intro to modern painting	ArHis	11	1Q	L
030603	Intro to contemporary art	ArHis	13	1Q	L
030603	Ancient art: Egypt	ArHis	152A	4Q	U
030603	Ancient art: Greece I	ArHis	152E	4Q	U
030603	Ancient art: Greece II	ArHis	152F	4Q	U
040101	Intro to accounting I	Bus	1	5Q	L
040101	Accounting: intermediate	Bus	118	4Q	U
040101	Accounting: advanced	Bus	119	4Q	U
040101	Administrative accounting	Bus	125	4Q	U
040101	Intro to accounting II	Bus	2	5Q	L
040103	Auditing	Bus	126	5Q	U
040106	Cost accounting	Bus	124	5Q	U
040114	Federal tax: individuals	Bus	167	5Q	U
040114	Fed tax: partners & corps	Bus	168	5Q	U
040306	Return on investment	Bus	430.2	3Q	U
040306	Investment management	Bus	430	3Q	U
040601	Business communications	Bus	109	4Q	U
040903	Leadership & org devel	Bus	176	4Q	U
040904	Mgmt theory & policy	Bus	190	4Q	U
040904	Finance planning & mgmt	Bus	135	5Q	U
040905	Intro to bus org & mgmt	Bus	492.8	4Q	U
040999	Mgmt of new enterprises	Bus	112	5Q	U
041011	Marketing	Bus	160	5Q	U

NCES No.	Course Title	Dept.	Course No.	Credits	Level
041103	Mgr's guide to behavior	Bus	490.5	3Q	U
041104	Industrial relations	Bus	150	4Q	U
041104	Labor relations	Bus	451.9	4Q	U
041106	Office mgmt & control	Bus	492.9	4Q	U
041203	Production management	Bus	145	4Q	U
041301	Residential appraisal	Bus	408	4Q	U
041303	Real estate principles	Bus	406.8	4Q	U
041305	Real estate economics	Bus	406.9	4Q	U
041306	Real estate tax planning	Bus	449.1	4Q	U
041306	Real estate finance	Bus	407	4Q	U
041308	Land titles	Bus	405.8	4Q	U
041308	Real estate law	Bus	405.9	4Q	U
041309	Real estate practice	Bus	406	4Q	U
0499	Principles of purchasing	Bus	453	5Q	U
050101	Ads: strategy & design	Bus	440.3	3Q	U
050608	Reporting & newswriting	Jrnl	22	4Q	L
050699	Tech writing & editing	EngAS	412	4Q	U
050699	Publications production	EngAS	413	4Q	U
060705	Introductory FORTRAN	CmpSc	114	4Q	U
060705	Introductory COBOL	CmpSc	6	4Q	L
061103	Survey of computers	CmpSc	20	4Q	L
061104	Business data processing	Bus	482.5	4Q	U
070199	History of education	Educ	101	4Q	U
070302	Elementary education	Educ	125	4Q	U
070303	Secondary curriculum	Educ	144	4Q	U
070404	Adult ed matls & methods	Educ	355.1	3Q	U
070499	Adult ed principles	Educ	355.4	3Q	U
070499	Indiv study & research	Educ	399.1	VC	U
070512	The reading program	Educ	147	4Q	U
070512	Literature in elem school	Educ	148	4Q	U
070512	Language in elem school	Educ	155	4Q	U
070512	Secondary lit & comp	Engl	300	5Q	U
070512	Basic reading and writing	Educ	315.4	3Q	U
070515	Science in elem school	Educ	143	3Q	U
070516	Elem curriculum arith	Educ	140	3Q	U
070516	Math for elem teachers	Educ	157	5Q	U
070522	Elem curriculum:soc sci	Educ	141	3Q	U
070701	Counseling & guidance	Educ	362.3	4Q	U
070803	Mentally gifted students	Educ	352.3	3Q	U
071103	Measurement & evaluation	Educ	364.8	3Q	U
080901	Semiconductor devices	EngAS	142	4Q	U
080903	Intro to electronics	EngAS	17	4Q	L
081102	Elem fluid mechanics	EngAS	103A	4Q	U
081103	Mech of deformable solids	EngAS	108	4Q	U
081199	Engineering mechanics	EngAS	36	3Q	L
082602	Surveying	EngAS	4	3Q	L
0899	Intro to control systems	EngAS	171A	4Q	U
090799	Alcohol, indiv & society	PubHl	413.8	3Q	U
090799	Solving alcohol problems	PubHl	413.9	3Q	U
090799	Childbirth education	PubHl	420	4Q	U
100302	Clinical nutrition	NutSc	105A	3Q	U
100311	Survey of nutritional sci	NutSc	10	5Q	L
100313	Nutrition (survey)	NutSc	140	5Q	U
100603	Death and dying	Nrsng	403	3Q	U
120202	Folklore in America	Anthr	193	5Q	U
120202	Shakespeare	Engl	117S	5Q	U
120202	Amer lit 1914 to 1940	Engl	146	4Q	U
120202	The hero and the city	Engl	179	5Q	U
120202	Mystery fiction	Engl	103.9	5Q	U
120202	English novel	Engl	125A	5Q	U
120202	English novel	Engl	125B	5Q	U
120202	Amer fiction to 1900	Engl	135A	5Q	U
120202	Amer fiction 1900 to pres	Engl	135B	5Q	U
120202	Western novel 19th cent	Engl	152.1	5Q	U
120202	Western novel 20th cent	Engl	152.2	5Q	U
120302	English language history	Engl	436	5Q	U
120305	First-yr reading & comp	Engl	1A	5Q	L
120305	First-yr reading & comp	Engl	1B	5Q	L
120305	Freshman comp & lit	Engl	2A	5Q	L
120305	Freshman comp & lit	Engl	2B	5Q	L
120310	Advanced Engl composition	Engl	119.1	5Q	U
120310	The writer within	Engl	413	3Q	U
120310	Writing to grow	Engl	425	3Q	U
120399	Grammar & composition	Engl	22	4Q	L
120709	Elementary Chinese	Chi	1A	5Q	L
120709	Elementary Chinese	Chi	1B	5Q	L
121009	Elementary French	Frnch	1	5Q	L
121009	Elementary French	Frnch	2	5Q	L
121009	Intermediate French	Frnch	3	5Q	L
121009	Intermediate French	Frnch	4	5Q	L
121108	Readings: German culture	Ger	135	4Q	U
121109	Elementary German	Ger	1	5Q	L
121109	Elementary German	Ger	2	5Q	L
121109	Elementary German	Ger	3	5Q	L
121109	Intermediate German	Ger	4	5Q	L
121207	Myths of Greece & Rome	Clas	25	4Q	L
121409	Elementary Italian I	Ital	15	4Q	L
121409	Elementary Italian II	Ital	16	4Q	L
121509	Elem modern Japanese	Jap	9A	4Q	L
122509	Elementary Spanish	Span	1	5Q	L
122509	Elementary Spanish	Span	2	5Q	L
122509	Elementary Spanish	Span	3	5Q	L
122509	Intermediate Spanish	Span	4	5Q	L
122509	Span in bus & professions	Span	401	3Q	U
1299	Icelandic lit 1800–WW I	Scand	156	3Q	U
1299	Icelandic lit WW I–1950	Scand	157	3Q	U
1299	Elementary mod Icelandic	Scand	180	5Q	U
1299	Elementary mod Icelandic	Scand	181	5Q	U
130799	Intro to business law	Bus	18	5Q	L
150199	Intro to gen astronomy	Astro	10	4Q	L
150307	General genetics	Gen	100	5Q	U
150307	Genetics in man	Zoo	101	5Q	U
150316	Plants in California	Bot	113	5Q	U
150316	Plants and man	Bot	115	4Q	U
150323	Modern biology	Zoo	4	5Q	L
150327	Pest control course br 1	EntSc	401	4Q	U
150327	Pest control course br 2	EntSc	402	4Q	U
150327	Pest control course br 3	EntSc	403	4Q	U
150399	Human physiology	Zoo	3	5Q	L
150401	Introductory chemistry	Chem	25	4Q	U
150403	Introductory biochemistry	Bioch	105	4Q	U
150408	Organic chemistry	Chem	18A	3Q	L
150408	Organic chemistry	Chem	18B	3Q	L
150409	Physical chemistry	Chem	100	4Q	U
150410	Surface chemistry	Chem	120	4Q	U
150501	Marine geology	Geol	105	4Q	U
150501	Geology of California	Geol	109	4Q	U
150501	Intro physical geology	Geol	3	4Q	U
150708	Quant theory atom struc	Phys	113	4Q	U
150799	General physics	Phys	7A	4Q	L
150799	General physics	Phys	7B	4Q	L
160302	Intermediate algebra	Math	D	3Q	L
160499	First-yr anal geom & calc	Math	1.1	5Q	L
160499	First-yr anal geom & calc	Math	1.2	5Q	L
160499	First-yr anal geom & calc	Math	1.3	5Q	L
160602	Plane trigonometry	Math	C	3Q	L
160802	Intro statistical methods	Econ	40	4Q	L
160803	Intro to statistics	Stat	2	5Q	L
161105	Numerical methods	Math	143	4Q	U
161105	Num methods computer lab	Math	143L	VC	U
161199	Advanced engineering math	Math	114A	5Q	U
161199	Advanced engineering math	Math	114B	5Q	U
161199	Advanced engineering math	Math	114C	5Q	U
161201	Mathematics of finance	Bus	432	4Q	U
180402	History of philosophy	Philo	20A	5Q	L
180403	History of philosophy	Philo	20B	5Q	L
180405	History of Buddhist phil	Philo	169	4Q	U
180701	Individual & society	Philo	13	4Q	L
180701	Ethical & political phil	Philo	2	4Q	L
180701	Theory of knowledge	Philo	4	4Q	L
180799	Women's perspectives	Philo	185A	3Q	U
190311	Competitive sport—youth	PhyEd	125	3Q	U
200504	Adolescence	Psych	139	4Q	U
200504	Child development	Psych	140.1	5Q	U
200504	Devel of minority youth	Psych	486	3Q	U
200799	Psych of communication	Psych	156.1	4Q	U
200799	Social psychology	Psych	160	5Q	U
200804	Learning & the learner	Educ	110	3Q	U
200804	Child growth & developmnt	Educ	142	4Q	U
2099	General psychology	Psych	1	5Q	L
220102	Gen anthro: cultural	Anthr	9	5Q	L
220106	Intro to physical anthro	Anthr	1	5Q	L
220109	Indians of California	Anthr	176	5Q	U
220201	Microeconomics	Econ	1	4Q	L
220201	Econ principles, problems	Econ	100	4Q	U
220201	Macroeconomics	Econ	3	5Q	L
220208	Taxation: myth & reality	Econ	168	3Q	U

NCES No.	Course Title	Dept.	Course No.	Credits	Level
220211	Labor econ & relations	Econ	148	5Q	U
220214	International economics	Econ	190	4Q	U
220432	Amer intellectual history	Hist	102.1	5Q	U
220432	US through Civil War	Hist	17A	4Q	L
220432	US since Civil War	Hist	17B	4Q	L
220432	The American West	Hist	189.1	5Q	U
220432	Western civilization	Hist	8A	4Q	L
220432	Western civilization	Hist	8B	4Q	L
220432	Western civilization	Hist	8C	4Q	L
220453	Mod hist of the Americas	Hist	09	5Q	L
220470	Mexican-American history	Hist	107.2	5Q	U
220501	American institutions	PolSc	100	5Q	U
220510	Intro political theory	PolSc	7	5Q	L
220601	Introduction to sociology	Socio	10	4Q	L
220602	Crime, justice in America	Socio	100.1	3Q	U
220602	Crime & delinquency	Socio	172	4Q	U
220602	Punishments & corrections	Socio	175	4Q	U
2299	America & future of man	Hum	101	3Q	U
2299	Making of Amer society	Hum	106	3Q	U
2299	The American dream	Hum	429	3Q	U
2299	Molding of Amer values	Hum	439.1	3Q	U
2299	Moral choices in society	Hum	442	3Q	U
	Noncredit courses				
030302	Elements of music	Music	800	NC	
040101	CPA review: accounting	Bus	804	NC	
040199	CPA review: theory	Bus	805	NC	
040601	English for business	Bus	800	NC	
041307	Real estate investments	Bus	808	NC	
0499	Govt contracts for bus	Bus	807	NC	
060203	Bus bkkping by computer	CmpSc	802	NC	
0810	Beginning engr drafting	EngAS	800A	NC	
0810	Beginning engr drafting	EngAS	800B	NC	
0899	Engineering fundamentals	EngAS	843	NC	
090307	Radiologic technology	HSci	800A	NC	
090307	Radiologic technology	HSci	800B	NC	
120305	Grammar for ESL students	Engl	803	NC	
120310	Elementary composition	Engl	804	NC	
120310	Magazine article writing	Engl	801	NC	
120310	Advanced article writing	Engl	808	NC	
120310	Short story theory	Engl	816	NC	
120310	Short story writing	Engl	817	NC	
120310	Writing: Jung and Perls	Engl	802	NC	
120310	Poetry writing	Engl	815	NC	
160302	Elementary algebra	Math	852A	NC	
160302	Elementary algebra	Math	852B	NC	

(38) UNIVERSITY OF COLORADO

Ms. Eloise Pearson
Program Administrator
Division of Continuing Education
University of Colorado
Campus Box 178
Boulder, Colorado 80390
Phone: (303) 492-6409

Enrollment on a noncredit basis accepted in all credit courses. Gifted high school students are permitted to enroll in undergraduate courses for credit. Overseas enrollment accepted. Students work directly with instructors. Overseas students are allowed two years to complete work; others, one year. Six-month extensions are available (fee). Noncredit (CEUs) paralegal education courses are now available.

NCES No.	Course Title	Dept.	Course No.	Credits	Level
	High school courses				
030502	Beginning drawing & paint	Art	001A	HF	H
040101	Beginning accounting	Bus	024A	HF	H
040101	Beginning accounting	BusEd	023A	HF	H
040299	Office procedures & pract	Bus	013A	HF	H
040299	Office procedures & pract	BusEd	014A	HF	H
040302	Consumer education	BusEd	019A	HF	H
040601	Business English	Bus	011A	HF	H
0499	General business	BusEd	021A	HF	H
070899	Study skills	Study	001A	HF	D
080199	Aerospace age	Aero	001A	HF	H
080999	Basic elec & electronics	Sci	009A	HF	H
090119	Health science	Sci	001A	HF	H
090119	Health science	Sci	002A	HF	H

NCES No.	Course Title	Dept.	Course No.	Credits	Level
100699	Persl adju, marriage, fam	HmEc	011A	HF	H
120305	Ninth-grade English	Engl	031A	HF	H
120305	Ninth-grade English	Engl	032A	HF	H
120305	Tenth-grade English	Engl	033A	HF	H
120305	Tenth-grade English	Engl	034A	HF	H
120305	Eleventh-grade English	Engl	035A	HF	H
120305	Eleventh-grade English	Engl	036A	HF	H
120305	Twelfth-grade English	Engl	037A	HF	H
120305	Twelfth-grade English	Engl	038A	HF	H
120305	Basic English	Engl	001N	HF	H
120307	The short story	EngLL	009A	HF	H
120307	The novel	EngLL	015A	HF	H
120307	Poetry	EngLL	021A	HF	H
120307	American short story	Engl	011N	HF	H
120308	Improvmt of reading skill	Engl	003A	HF	H
120308	Improvmt of reading skill	Engl	004A	HF	H
120310	Composition	Engl	023N	HF	H
150301	Basic biology	Sci	015A	HF	H
150301	Basic biology	Sci	016A	HF	H
150301	Advanced biology	Sci	019A	HF	H
150799	Physics	Sci	035A	HF	H
150799	Physics	Sci	036A	HF	H
160199	General mathematics	Math	005A	HF	H
160199	General mathematics	Math	006A	HF	H
160301	Remedial arithmetic	Math	001A	HF	D
160302	Beginning algebra	Math	031A	HF	H
160302	Beginning algebra	Math	032A	HF	H
160302	Advanced algebra	Math	035A	HF	H
160302	Advanced algebra	Math	036A	HF	H
160601	Geometry	Math	033N	HF	H
160601	Geometry	Math	034N	HF	H
160602	Trigonometry	Math	037N	HF	H
161101	Bus & consumer math	Math	009X	HF	H
161101	Bus & consumer math	Math	010X	HF	H
200199	Psychology	SocSt	007N	HF	H
220399	World geography	SocSc	021A	HF	H
220421	American history	SocSt	033N	HF	H
220421	American history	SocSt	034N	HF	H
220433	World history	SocSc	031A	HF	H
220433	World history	SocSc	032A	HF	H
220501	American government	SocSt	035N	HF	H
220502	Civics	SocSc	001N	HF	H
220599	Modern problems	SocSc	037A	HF	H
220606	Sociology	SocSt	003N	HF	H
	College courses				
020103	Interior decoration	InDec	15	2C	V
020299	Mechanical perspective	InDec	15	2C	V
030302	Rudiments of music	Mus	108	3S	L
030503	Art for elementary teachr	FA	363	2S	U
040106	Cost accounting	Bus	332	3S	U
040111	Intro to managerial acctg	Bus	202	3S	L
040113	Intro to financial acctg	Bus	200	3S	L
040904	Prin of office managemt	Bus	140	3S	U
040905	Child adm organ & mgt	ChEd	45	2C	V
040999	Child adm parents & pers	ChEd	43	2C	V
041301	Real estate appraisal I	RE	2.	1C	V
041303	Real estate basics	RE	1	1C	V
041306	Real estate finance	RE	22	1C	V
041308	Real estate law	RE	12	1C	V
070499	Child curriculum planning	ChEd	21	3C	V
070512	Lit for adolescents	TEd	444	3S	U
070512	Children's literature	TEd	456	3S	U
070613	Safety education	PE	345	2S	U
070701	Child guidance techniques	ChEd	20	3C	V
081502	Occupational safety mgt	Eng	400	3S	U
090199	Environmental health	PE	295	3S	L
090199	School health education	PE	340	2S	U
100301	Child adm nutrition	ChEd	41	2C	V
100601	Child development 1	ChEd	10	3C	V
100601	Child development 2	ChEd	11	3C	V
100601	Child development 1	ChEd	10A	3C	V
100601	Child development 2	ChEd	11A	3C	V
120103	Hist & grammar of Eng lan	Engl	484	3S	U
120201	Existentialist literature	ComLi	484	3S	U
120202	Lit for adolescents	EngLL	481	3S	U
120304	Studies in lang fiction	Engl	382	3S	U
120308	Intro to fiction	EngLL	120	3S	L
120308	Intro to drama	EngLL	130	3S	L
120308	Great Books	Engl	260	3S	L
120308	Great Books	Engl	261	3S	L
120308	Modern short story	EngLL	220	3S	L

NCES No.	Course Title	Dept.	Course No.	Credits	Level
120308	Contemporary literature	Engl	253	3S	L
120308	Survey of American lit I	EngLL	365	3S	U
120308	Survey of American lit II	EngLL	366	3S	U
120308	Bible as literature	Engl	360	3S	U
120308	Chaucer	EngLL	395	3S	U
120308	Shakespeare	EngLL	397	3S	U
120308	Shakespeare	EngLL	398	3S	U
120310	General expository writng	A&S	100	3S	L
120310	Advanced expository wrtng	A&S	110	3S	L
120310	Intro to creative writing	Engl	119	3S	L
120310	Intermediate fiction wksp	Engl	305	3S	U
120310	Report writing	Engl	315	3S	U
120399	Images of women	EngLL	226	3S	L
1299	Intro to poetry	Engl	140	3S	L
130103	Evidence & investigation	Pl Ed	10	3C	V
130199	Litigation, civ proc, dis	Pl Ed	11	3C	V
131599	Legal research	Pl Ed	12	3C	V
160302	College algebra	Math	101	3S	L
160499	Analyt geom & calculus I	Math	130	5S	L
160499	Analyt geom & calculus II	Math	230	5S	L
160602	College trigonometry	Math	102	2S	L
160699	College algebra & trig	Math	110	5S	L
181199	Philosophy & religion	Phil	105	3S	L
200199	Intro to psychology	Psych	100	3S	L
2002	Intro to biopsychology	Psych	205	3S	L
200505	Psychology of adjustment	Psych	230	3S	L
200508	Child & adolescent psych	Psych	264	3S	L
200799	Social psychology	Psych	440	3S	U
220102	Principles of anthro I	Anthr	103	3S	L
220102	Principles of anthro II	Anthr	104	3S	L
220106	Intro to physical anthr I	Anthr	201	3S	L
220106	Intro to phys anthr II	Anthr	202	3S	L
220201	Prin of economics I	Econ	201	3S	L
220201	Prin of economics II	Econ	202	3S	L
220399	Environ sys climate & veg	Geog	100	3S	L
220399	Env sys landforms & soil	Geog	101	3S	L
220402	Dipl his of Europe 20th c	Hist	438	3S	U
220428	Hist of Colorado	Hist	258	3S	L
220431	Hist of Russia thr 17th c	Hist	493	3S	U
220431	Imperial Russia	Hist	494	3S	U
220431	Russ Revolution & Sov reg	Hist	495	3S	U
220432	Hist of US to 1865	Hist	151	3S	L
220432	Hist of US since 1865	Hist	152	3S	L
220432	Early American frontier	Hist	457	3S	U
220432	Later American frontier	Hist	458	3S	U
220453	Hist of modern Far East	Hist	271	3S	L
220499	Hist of Western civiliztn	Hist	101	3S	L
220499	Hist of Western civiliztn	Hist	102	3S	L
220501	American government I	PolSc	101	3S	L
220503	Intro to comp politics	PolSc	201	3S	L
220511	American government II	PolSc	102	3S	L
220599	Intro to political sci	PolSc	100	3S	L
220606	Intro to sociology	Soc	211	3S	L

Noncredit course

NCES No.	Course Title	Dept.	Course No.	Credits	Level
120399	Vocabulary building	Engl	108	NC	L

39 UNIVERSITY OF FLORIDA

Mr. Harold Markowitz Jr.
Director, Department of Independent Study by Correspondence
Division of Continuing Education
University of Florida
1938 West University Avenue, Room 1
Gainesville, Florida 32603
Phone: (904) 392-1711

Enrollment on a noncredit basis accepted in all credit courses. Gifted high school students are permitted to enroll in undergraduate courses for credit. Overseas enrollment accepted. Credit courses meet on-campus course/degree requirements. No external degree offered. The Department of Independent Study by Correspondence represents all public universities in Florida. The tuition rate for Florida residents is the same as on campus; slight increase for out-of-state students.

The university is planning extensive curriculum revisions; many courses not listed below may now be available. Current brochures on university, high school, or noncredit courses will be sent on request.

High school courses

NCES No.	Course Title	Dept.	Course No.	Credits	Level
120303	Tenth-grd English 1st sem	EH	10A	HF	H
120303	Tenth-grd English 2nd sem	EH	10B	HF	H
120304	Eleventh-grd Eng 1st sem	EH	11A	HF	H
120304	Eleventh-grd Eng 2nd sem	EH	11B	HF	H
120305	Ninth-grd English 1st sem	Engl	9A	HF	H
120305	Ninth-grd English 2nd sem	Engl	9B	HF	H
120307	Twelfth-grd Engl 1st sem	EH	12A	HF	H
120307	Twelfth-grd Engl 2nd sem	EH	12B	HF	H
130799	Business law 1st sem	BusLw	11A	HF	H
130799	Business law 2nd sem	BusLw	11B	HF	H
160302	Second-yr algebra 1st sem	Ms	10A	HF	H
160302	Second-yr algebra 2nd sem	Ms	10B	HF	H
160302	First-yr algebra 1st sem	Ms	9A	HF	H
160302	First-yr algebra 2nd sem	Ms	9B	HF	H
160601	Plane geometry 1st sem	Ms	3A	HF	H
160601	Plane geometry 2nd sem	Ms	3B	HF	H
160602	Trigonometry	Ms	12A	HF	H
1611	General math 1st sem	Ms	11A	HF	H
1611	General math 2nd sem	Ms	11B	HF	H
161201	Business math 1st sem	BusMs	10A	HF	H
161201	Business math 2nd sem	BusMs	10B	HF	H
200505	Project self-discovery	SS	14	HF	H
220399	World geography 1st sem	SS	9A	HF	H
220399	World geography 2nd sem	SS	9B	HF	H
220432	American history 1st sem	SS	11A	HF	H
220432	American history 2nd sem	SS	11B	HF	H
220433	World history 1st sem	SS	10A	HF	H
220433	World history 2nd sem	SS	10B	HF	H
220451	Probs of Am democ 1st sem	SS	12A	HF	H
220451	Probs of Am democ 2nd sem	SS	12B	HF	H
220501	American government	SS	13	HF	H
220503	Comparative political sys	SocHS	11CPS	HF	H

College courses

NCES No.	Course Title	Dept.	Course No.	Credits	Level
010199	Prin of food & res econom	AEB	3103	4S	U
010406	Beef cattle sci & rge mgt	AnSc	4242C	4S	U
010699	Field crop science	Agri	3210	3S	U
010699	Weed science	PIS	4601	3S	U
010702	General soils	Agri	3022C	4S	U
0199	The cult of citrus fruits	Agri	3210	3S	U
040101	Elementary accouting I	Acctg	2001	3S	L
040710	Risk mgmt and insurance	Ins	3015	3S	U
040903	Organizational behavior	Man	3109	3S	U
041001	Basic marketing concepts	Mar	3023	3S	U
041104	Mgmt of labor & ind rela	Man	4407	3S	U
0499	Productivity work ana/dsg	FSS	3423	3S	U
0499	Analysis of hospital comp	HFT	3000	3S	U
050101	Elements of advertising	Adv	3000	3S	U
050102	Radio-TV advertising	Adv	4103	3S	U
050104	Copywriting & visualizatn	Adv	4101	3S	U
050201	Survey of mass communictn	JMC	1000	2S	L
050605	Magazine & feature writng	Jou	4300	3S	U
0508	Writing for mass commun	JMC	2100	3S	L
0509	Intro to public relations	PuR	3000	3S	U
051201	Braille	EVI	3211	2S	U
070199	Social foundations of ed	EdF	3604	3S	U
070303	Expl cons ed for sec schl	Educ	4930	2S	U
070520	Educational psychology	EdPsy	4210	3S	U
070522	Pop dynamics & family pln	Educ	4930	2S	U
070812	Readings in visual disab	EVI	4313	3S	U
071103	Measurement & eval in ed	EdF	4430	3S	U
082601	Land surveying principles	Sur	3403	3S	U
082601	Land surveying computatn	Sur	3640	2S	U
0899	Engineering economy	Eg	4354	2S	U
100304	Man's food	FoS	2001	3S	L
100312	The science of nutrition	Hun	1201	3S	L
100312	Fund of human nutrition	Hun	2201		L
120202	Amer fiction: 20th cen	Engl	3124	3S	U
120299	Writing about literature	Lit	1102	3S	L
120299	British authors to 1700	Lit	2011	3S	L
120305	English grammar	Engl	2340	2S	U
120307	English novel: 18th cen	Engl	3112	3S	U
120307	English novel: 19th cen	Engl	3122	3S	U
120307	English novel: 20th cen	Engl	3132	3S	U
120310	Imaginative writing: fict	CrW	3110	3S	U
120310	Expos & argument writing	Engl	1101	3S	L
120310	Techn writ & bus comm	BTWr	3213	3S	U

NCES No.	Course Title	Dept.	Course No.	Credits	Level
120310	Advanced exposition	Engl	3310	3S	U
120310	Advanced profes writing	Engl	4260	3S	U
121199	Beginning German 1	Ger	1120	4S	L
121199	Beginning German 2	Ger	1121	3S	L
121199	Beginning German 3	Ger	1122	3S	L
1299	Non-Western lang: Aymara	Lang	3371	4S	U
130799	Business law	BuL	4100	3S	U
130799	Business law	BuL	4112	3S	U
130799	Business law	BuL	4305	4S	U
150102	Surv of solar sys astron	Ast	2003	3S	L
150103	Surv of stellar astronomy	Ast	2004	3S	L
150202	Intro to the atmosphere	Met	1010	3S	L
150401	Chemistry for lib studies	Chem	1020	3S	L
150599	Expl the geological sci	Gly	1000	3S	L
150599	Physical geology	Gly	2015	3S	L
150599	Historical geology	Gly	2100	3S	L
160305	Algebra and trigonometry	Mat	1132	4S	L
160399	Basic mathematics	Mat	1033	3S	L
160603	Analyt geometry & calc 1	Mat	3311	4S	U
160603	Analyt geometry & calc 2	Mat	3312	4S	U
180599	Intro to philosophy	Phi	2010	3S	L
180902	The Christian tradition	Rel	3505	3S	U
181103	Religion in America	Rel	2120	3S	L
181104	Introduction to religion	Rel	2000	3S	L
181104	Religion & cont culture	Rel	2130	2S	L
181201	Intro to Old Testament	Rel	2210	3S	L
181202	Intro to New Testament	Rel	2243	3S	L
190506	Personal & family health	HEd	2000	3S	L
190517	Various topics health ed	HEd	4905	3S	U
190599	Health ed & med terminol	HEd	3144	2S	U
200102	History of psychology	Psy	5605	3S	U
200199	Applied psychology	Psy	3101	3S	U
200199	General psychology	Psy	2013	3S	L
200501	Abnormal psychology	CIP	4144	3S	U
200504	Developmental psychology	DeP	3003	3S	U
200509	Psychology of personality	PPe	3004	3S	U
200799	Intr to social psychology	SoP	3004	3S	U
210401	Intro to soc work/soc wel	SoW	3203	3S	U
210403	Interv/recordg in soc wk	SoW	3350	2S	U
210404	Soc srvc for fam & chldrn	SoW	4242	3S	U
220201	Basic economics I	Econ	2013	3S	L
220201	Basic economics II	Econ	2023	3S	L
220299	Economic concepts & inst	Econ	2000	3S	L
220299	Child grwth & dev foun yr	ChD	3220	3S	U
220302	Conservation of resources	Geog	3370	3S	U
220399	Geography of Florida	Geog	3270	3S	U
220399	Geog for a changing world	Geog	1010	3S	L
220402	US diplomacy to 1920		4510	3S	U
220402	US diplomacy since 1920		4511	3S	U
220427	History of Mexico	Hist	4430	3S	U
220428	Florida 1821 to 1900	AmH	3422	2S	U
220428	Florida since 1945	AmH	3423	3S	U
220432	United States to 1877	AmH	2010	3S	L
220432	United States since 1877	AmH	2020	3S	L
220432	Labor history of the US	AmH	3501	3S	U
220452	Early Middle Ages	EuH	3121	3S	U
220452	The High Middle Ages	EuH	3122	3S	U
220453	Modern world to 1815	Hist	1022	3S	L
220453	Modern world since 1815	Hist	1030	3S	L
220501	American govt: national	PolS	1041	3S	L
220501	American federal govt	PolS	2041	3S	L
220511	Am state & local govt	PolS	2112	3S	L
220602	Criminology	Crim	3011	3S	U
220602	Law enforcement	Crim	3101	3S	U
220602	Corrections	Crim	3301	3S	U
220604	Juvenile delinquency	Soc	4130	3S	U
220605	Marriage & the family	MAF	2200	3S	L
220606	Principles of sociology	Soc	2000	3S	L
220613	Social problems	Soc	2020	3S	L
2299	Am cultural & soc institn	SocS	2110	3S	L
2299	Emerg of Amer ec/pol inst	SocS	2120	3S	L
2299	Intercultural interaction	IDS	4900	VC	U
2299	Law and society	IDS	4900	VC	U
2299	Community interaction	IDS	4910	VC	U
2299	US role in the world	ComS	3955	VC	U
2299	Contemporary health prob	ComS	4910	VC	U
2299	Volunteers and society	ComS	4900	VC	U
	Noncredit courses				
040702	Casualty ins: suretyship	CIS		NC	
C40709	Prop ins: fire & marine	PIFM		NC	
040799	Bail & bail bonds ins	BB		NC	

NCES No.	Course Title	Dept.	Course No.	Credits	Level
040799	Industrial fire	Fire		NC	
040799	Motor veh phys damage ins	Auto		NC	
070599	Prin of curriculum design	PCD		NC	
081304	Bas chem watr/wastewtr op	BCWWO		NC	
100602	Family plang & popu dynam	FP&PD		NC	
100702	Dietetic assistant	DAC		NC	
131203	Dut & resp of Fla tax coll	DRFTC		NC	
131203	Mgt for Fla tax collectrs	MFFTC		NC	
131203	Coll & dist of ad val tax	CDAVT		NC	
131203	Tax collector's role	TCRCL		NC	
190508	Basic nutr and diet modif	BNDM		NC	
220502	Our const and government	C&G		NC	
220502	English & government	E&G		NC	
220604	The prev of juv delinquen	TPOJD		NC	

④⓪ UNIVERSITY OF GEORGIA

Athens, Georgia 30602
Phone: (404) 542-3243

Enrollment on a noncredit basis accepted in all credit courses. Gifted high school students are permitted to enroll in undergraduate courses for credit. Overseas enrollment accepted for college and noncredit courses.

NCES No.	Course Title	Dept.	Course No.	Credits	Level
	College courses				
010599	Horticultural science	Hort	300	5Q	L
010603	Agricultural entomology	Agri	374	5Q	U
010999	Forest resources hist/pol	For	480	5Q	U
040101	Principles of acctg I	Acctg	110	5Q	L
040101	Principles of acctg II	Acctg	111	5Q	L
040114	Tax I	Acctg	540	5Q	U
040201	Business office procedure	Bus	310	5Q	U
040201	Principles of office mgmt	Bus	507	5Q	U
040208	Business communication	Bus	401	5Q	U
040301	Business finance	Bus	330	5Q	U
040306	Investments	Bus	431	5Q	U
040308	Money and banking	Bus	326	5Q	U
040399	American financial system	Bus	452	5Q	U
040902	Small-business management	Mgmt	554	5Q	U
040903	Organizational behavior	Mgmt	351	5Q	U
040999	Decision science	Mgmt	355	5Q	U
041001	Principles of marketing	Mktg	360	5Q	U
041001	Principles of retailing	Mktg	560	5Q	U
041005	Principles of advertising	Mktg	351	5Q	U
041203	Operations analysis	Mgmt	320	5Q	U
050699	Jrnlsm in secondry school	Jrnl	566	5Q	U
051108	Psych of speech commu	Commu	466	5Q	U
070199	Educ in modern America	Educ	304	5Q	U
070404	Early childhood education	Educ	333	5Q	U
070404	Prblms early child educ	Educ	400	5Q	U
070404	Elementary math methods	Educ	337	5Q	U
070404	Elem social studies mthds	Educ	340	5Q	U
070520	Psychology for teachers	Educ	305	5Q	U
090702	Community hygiene	HSci	310C	4Q	U
090799	Vectorborne-disease cont	HSci	313C	3Q	U
090799	Waterborne-disease cont	HSci	314C	3Q	U
090799	Foodborne-disease control	HSci	316C	3Q	U
100313	Nutrition	HmEc	351	5Q	U
100503	Interior design	HmEc	381	5Q	U
100699	Human growth and develop	Educ	295	5Q	L
120303	Derivatives frm Grk & Ltn	EngLL	310	5Q	U
120305	Composition part I	Engl	101	5Q	L
120305	Composition part II	Engl	102	5Q	L
120307	Western World literature	Engl	250	5Q	L
120307	Western World literature	Engl	251	5Q	L
120307	Survey of English lit I	Engl	131	5Q	L
120307	Survey of English lit II	Engl	132	5Q	L
120307	American literature	Engl	308	5Q	U
120307	Southern literature	Engl	320	5Q	U
120307	Poetry of Victorian era	Engl	405	5Q	U
120307	Contemporary novel	Engl	409	5Q	U
120307	Early American writing	Engl	420	5Q	U
120307	Children's literature	Engl	455	5Q	U

NCES No.	Course Title	Dept.	Course No.	Credits	Level
121005	Elementary French I	Frnch	151	5Q	L
121005	Elementary French II	Frnch	152	5Q	L
121005	Intermediate French I	Frnch	251	5Q	L
121005	Intermediate French II	Frnch	252	5Q	L
121105	Elementary German I	Ger	151	5Q	L
121105	Elementary German II	Ger	152	5Q	L
121105	Intermediate German I	Ger	251	5Q	L
121105	Intermediate German II	Ger	252	5Q	L
121605	Elementary Latin part I	CILL	201	5Q	L
121605	Elementary Latin part II	CILL	202	5Q	L
121605	Intermediate Latin	CILL	203	5Q	L
121608	Readings in Latin	CILL	304	5Q	U
122505	Elementary Spanish I	Span	151	5Q	L
122505	Elementary Spanish II	Span	152	5Q	L
122505	Intermediate Spanish I	Span	251	5Q	L
122505	Intermediate Spanish II	Span	252	5Q	L
130799	Business law part I	Bus	370	5Q	U
130799	Business law part II	Bus	576	5Q	U
150304	Ecology	Bio	350	5Q	U
160199	Introduction to math	Math	100	5Q	L
160203	Finite mathematics	Math	156	5Q	L
160302	Fundamentals of algebra	Math	103	5Q	L
160602	Trigonometry	Math	112	5Q	L
160603	Analyt geom & calculus	Math	166	5Q	L
160899	Statistics for social sci	Math	219	5Q	L
160899	Stat analysis for bus	Stat	312	5Q	U
180302	Introduction to ethics	Philo	305	5Q	U
180501	Intro to deductive logic	Philo	110	5Q	L
190501	Effcts of alcohol & drugs	Educ	521	5Q	U
190514	Health educ in pub school	Educ	300	5Q	U
200199	Elementary psychology	Psych	101	5Q	L
200501	Psychology of abnormal	Psych	423	5Q	U
200505	Psychology of adjustment	Psych	370	5Q	U
200508	Psychology of adolescence	Educ	332	5Q	U
200599	Psych of sex & sex deviat	Psy	326	5Q	U
210199	Principles of pub admin	PubAd	341	5Q	U
220102	Cultural anthropology	Anthr	452	5Q	U
220102	Introduction to anthropol	Anthr	102	5Q	L
220201	Prin of macroeconomics	Econ	105	5Q	L
220201	Prin of microeconomics	Econ	106	5Q	L
220207	Econ development of US	Econ	133	5Q	L
220211	Labor economics	Econ	386	5Q	U
220299	Government and business	Econ	478	5Q	U
220305	Earth science survey	Geog	104	5Q	L
220306	Geography developed world	Geog	101	5Q	L
220306	Underdeveloped world	Geog	102	5Q	L
220406	Classical culture: Greece	ClCiv	120	5Q	L
220406	Classical culture: Rome	ClCiv	121	5Q	L
220426	Western civiliz to 1500	Hist	111	5Q	L
220426	Western civiliz snce 1500	Hist	112	5Q	L
220428	History of Georgia	Hist	470	5Q	U
220432	American history to 1865	Hist	251	5Q	L
220432	American hist since 1865	Hist	252	5Q	L
220499	The ancient world	ArHis	210	3Q	L
220499	Mid Ages thru Renaissance	ArHis	211	3Q	L
220499	Baroque to modern world	ArHis	212	3Q	L
220501	American government	PolSc	101	5Q	L
220503	Comparative politics	PolSc	310	5Q	U
220505	International relations	PolSc	210	5Q	L
220511	State and local governmnt	PolSc	350	5Q	U
220599	Energy crisis & politics	PolSc	39R	5Q	U
220599	National security policy	PolSc	375	5Q	U
220599	Minority politics	PolSc	376	5Q	U
220601	Community organization	Socio	403	5Q	U
220602	Criminology	Socio	481	5Q	U
220604	Juvenile delinquency	Socio	407	5Q	U
220605	Sociology of marriage	Socio	103	5Q	L
220605	Sociology of the family	Socio	410	5Q	U
220606	Introductory sociology	Socio	105	5Q	L
220607	Social psychology	Socio	371	5Q	U
220607	Personality & soc struct	Socio	427	5Q	U
220607	Theories of social psych	Socio	470	5Q	U
220613	Contemporary soc problems	Socio	260	5Q	L
220615	American black society	Socio	402	5Q	U
220699	Social gerontology	Socio	365	5Q	U
220699	Sociology of aging	Socio	465	5Q	U
220699	Sociology of occupations	Socio	485	5Q	U

NCES No.	Course Title	Dept.	Course No.	Credits	Level
Noncredit courses					
090401	Biopharmaceutics	Pharm	002	NC	L
090403	Clinicl aspects drug abus	Pharm	003	NC	L
090499	Drug interactions	Pharm	001	NC	L
160302	Precollege algebra	Math	099	NC	L
220502	Citizenship	PolSc		NC	L

41 UNIVERSITY OF IDAHO

Ms. Patty Osborn
Coordinator
Correspondence Study Office
University of Idaho
Moscow, Idaho 83843
Phone: (208) 885-6641

Enrollment on a noncredit basis accepted in some credit courses. Gifted high school students are permitted to enroll in undergraduate courses for credit. Overseas enrollment accepted.

NCES No.	Course Title	Dept.	Course No.	Credits	Level
High school courses					
040104	Bookkeeping	FdAcg	I	HF	H
040104	Bookkeeping	FdAcg	II	HF	H
120305	Grammar and composition	FrEng	I	HF	H
120305	Grammar and composition	SoEng	I	HF	H
120305	English review grammar	SrEng	III	HF	H
120307	English lit and comp	FrEng	II	HF	H
120307	English lit and comp	SoEng	II	HF	H
120307	American lit and comp	JrEng	I	HF	H
120307	Modern lit and comp	JrEng	II	HF	H
120307	English lit and comp	SrEng	I	HF	H
120307	English novels and comp	SrEng	II	HF	H
121009	Elementary French	Frnch	I	HF	H
122009	Elementary Russian	Rus	I	HF	H
160301	General mathematics	GnMth	I	HF	H
160301	General mathematics	GnMth	II	HF	H
160302	Algebra	Alg	I	HF	H
160302	Algebra	Alg	II	HF	H
160604	Geometry	Geom	I	HF	H
160604	Geometry	Geom	II	HF	H
220432	American history	AmHis	I	HF	H
220432	American history	AmHis	II	HF	H
220501	Problems in Amer democ	PIAD	I	HF	H
220501	American government	AmGvt	II	HF	H
220699	Sociology	Socio	I	HF	H
College courses					
010107	Princ of farm/ranch mgmt	AgEc	C278	4S	L
010199	Ag in its soc/econ envir	AgEc	C101	3S	L
040101	Principles of accounting	Acctg	C201	3S	L
040101	Intermediate accounting	Acctg	C301	4S	U
040101	Intermediate accounting	Acctg	C302	4S	U
040111	Managerial accounting	Acctg	C202	3S	L
040203	Local govt records mgmt	BusEd	C312	2S	U
041001	Marketing	Bus	C321	3S	U
041001	Inter-marketing mgmt	Mktg	C320	3S	U
041303	Fundamntls of real estate	RIEs	C201	3S	L
041306	Real estate finance	Bus	C465	3S	U
041308	Real estate law	Bus	C464	3S	U
050199	Promotional strategy	Bus	C420	3S	U
060799	Digital computer prog	Engr	C131	2S	L
070306	Princ of vocational ed	VocEd	C351	2S	U
070309	Devel/org of extension ed	AgEd	C248	2S	L
070309	Intro to adult education	VocEd	C473	3S	U
070309	Psych of adult learners	VocEd	C474	3S	U
070515	Elem school science meths	Educ	C344	3S	U
070522	Social studies methods	Educ	C421	3S	U
0810	Engineering graphics	Engr	C101	2S	L
0810	Engineering graphics	Engr	C102	2S	L
081102	Fluid mechanics	EnSci	C320	3S	U
081104	Statics	EnSci	C210	3S	L
081104	Dynamics	EnSci	C220	3S	L
0812	Mechanics of materials	EnSci	C340	3S	U
082699	Elementary surveying	Engr	C201	3S	L
0899	Engineering economy	Engr	C363	2S	U
090799	El microbio/pub health	Bact	C154	3S	L
100202	Consumer education	ConEd	C471	3S	U
100313	Problems in nutrition	HmEc	C470	3S	U
120299	West in American lit	Engl	C326	3S	U
120305	Composition	Engl	C101	3S	L

NCES No.	Course Title	Dept.	Course No.	Credits	Level
120305	Composition	Engl	C102	3S	L
121009	Elementary French	Frnch	C0102	4S	L
1307	Legal envir of business	Bus	C265	3S	L
1307	Business law	Bus	C466	3S	U
1307	Business law	Bus	C467	3S	U
1402	Introduction to museology	Museo	C301	3S	U
150799	General physics	Phys	C113	3S	L
160301	Math for elem teachers	Math	C135	3S	L
160301	Math for elem teachers	Math	C136	3S	L
160302	College algebra	Math	C140	3S	L
160303	Prep for college math	Math	C110	4S	L
160602	Analytic trigonometry	Math	C179	2S	L
160603	Analytic geom and calc I	Math	C180	4S	L
160801	Intro to statistics	Math	C252	3S	L
1803	Ethics	Philo	C151	3S	L
180401	History of ancient philo	Philo	C309	3S	U
180403	History of modern philo	Philo	C310	3S	U
190107	Elem school physical ed	PhyEd	C252	2S	L
190107	Organization and admin	PhyEd	C496	3S	U
200104	Intro to psychology	Psych	C100	3S	L
200501	Abnormal psychology	Psych	C311	3S	U
200504	Developmental psychology	Psych	C205	3S	L
200504	Per/social devel in child	Psych	C309	3S	U
200509	Psychology of personality	Psych	C310	3S	U
200599	Human sexuality	Psych	C210	2S	L
200603	Meas and eval in psych	Psych	C402	3S	U
200799	Social psychology	Psych	C320	3S	U
210102	Public administration	PolSc	C451	3S	U
210111	Man and the environment	Bio	C200	3S	L
210111	Politics and pollution	PolSc	C152	1S	L
2201	Study of man	Anthr	C301	3S	U
220201	Principles of economics	Econ	C151	3S	L
220201	Principles of economics	Econ	C152	3S	L
220308	Comp urban plan devel	Geog	C439	3S	U
220423	History of the Far East	Hist	C470	3S	U
220424	History of England	Hist	C271	3S	L
220424	History of England	Hist	C272	3S	L
220428	Idaho and the Pacific NW	Hist		3S	U
220432	Intro to US history	Hist	C111	3S	L
220432	Intro to US history	Hist	C112	3S	L
220450	History of civilization	Hist	C101	3S	L
220450	History of civilization	Hist	C102	3S	L
220501	US govt: structure & funct	PolSc	C101	3S	L
220501	US govt: policies & issues	PolSc	C102	3S	L
220511	American state government	PolSc	C275	3S	L
220511	American local government	PolSc	C276	3S	L
220511	Local govt/intergovt rel	PolSc	C461	3S	U
220511	County government	PolSc	C476	3S	U
220602	Intro to criminal just ad	Cr	C201	3S	L
220604	Juvenile delinquency	Socio	C330	3S	U
220608	Rural sociology	Socio	C310	3S	U
220613	Social problems	Socio	C230	3S	L
220699	Introduction to sociology	Socio	C110	3S	L

Noncredit course

NCES No.	Course Title	Dept.	Course No.	Credits	Level
0809	Elem electrical theory	EE	C010	0S	L

㊷ **UNIVERSITY OF ILLINOIS**

Mr. Robert W. Batchellor
Head, Guided Individual Study
Guided Individual Study Division
University of Illinois
104a Illini Hall
725 South Wright Street
Champaign, Illinois 61820
Phone: (217) 333-1321/3758

Enrollment on a noncredit basis accepted in all credit courses. Gifted high school students are permitted to enroll in undergraduate courses for credit. Overseas enrollment is not encouraged; each case is judged on an individual basis. Overseas students need excellent English skills and dependable mail service. Credit courses meet on-campus degree requirements. External degrees are not offered. Enrollment by correspondence does not constitute admission to a degree program.

NCES No.	Course Title	Dept.	Course No.	Credits	Level
	College courses				
040101	Principles of acctg I	Acctg	X101	3S	L
040101	Principles of acctg II	Acctg	X105	3S	L
040101	Intermediate accounting	Acctg	X208	3S	U
040106	Cost accounting	Acctg	X266	3S	U
040109	Public-sector accounting	Acctg	X341	3S	U
040304	Financl markets & instit	Fin	X258	3S	U
040308	Money, credit, banking	Fin	X150	3S	L
040601	Bus & admin communication	BTWr	X251	3S	U
040604	Report writing	BTWr	X272	3S	U
0408	Intro to internationl bus	BusAd	X199B	3S	L
0408	Internat compar mangement	BusAd	X294A	3S	U
0408	Japanese managemt systems	BusAd	X294B	3S	U
0409	Intro to management	BusAd	X247	3S	U
040901	Business policy	BusAd	X389	3S	U
040999	Purchasing management	BusAd	X199A	3S	L
041001	Principles of marketing	BusAd	X202	3S	U
0501	Introduction to advertisg	Adv	X281	3S	U
0501	Advert in contemp society	Adv	X393	3S	U
050104	Advert creative strategy	Adv	X382	3S	U
070516	Metrics educ for teachers	VoTec	X399B	2S	U
070516	Math for elem teachers	Math	X202	5S	U
070516	Math for elem teachers	Math	X203	3S	U
0706	Tchg occ career prac arts	VoTec	X388	2S	U
070602	Career ed in elem school	VoTec	X399	2S	U
0707	Indiv counslg & group wrk	EdPsy	X199	3S	L
070799	Mental hyg & the school	EdPsy	X312	2S	U
071102	Const & use of tests	EdPsy	X391	4S	U
0810	Engineering graphics	GEngr	X103	3S	L
081104	Analyt mechan–statics	TAM	X150	2S	L
081104	Engr mechanics I–statics	TAM	X152	3S	L
081104	Analyt mechan–dynamics	TAM	X212	3S	U
081199	Elem mech of deform body	TAM	X221	3S	U
090504	First aid	Hl Ed	X181	2S	L
0907	Public health	Hl Ed	X110	3S	L
100601	Child dev for elem teachr	EdPsy	X236	3S	U
120307	Introduction to drama	EngLL	X102	3S	L
120307	Masterpieces of Amer lit	EngLL	X116	3S	L
120307	Intro to Shakespeare	EngLL	X118	3S	L
120307	Modern short story	EngLL	X246	3S	U
120307	American fiction	EngLL	X249	3S	U
120310	Principles of composition	Rhet	X105	4S	L
120310	Advan narrative writing	Rhet	X205	3S	U
1210	Elementary French	Frnch	X101	4S	L
1210	Elementary French	Frnch	X102	4S	L
1210	Modern French	Frnch	X103	4S	L
1210	Modern French	Frnch	X104	4S	L
121007	Intro Fr lit–17th-18th c	Frnch	X201	3S	U
121007	Intro Fr lit–19th-20th c	Frnch	X202	3S	U
1211	Elementary German	Ger	X101	4S	L
1211	Elementary German	Ger	X102	4S	L
1211	Intermediate German	Ger	X103	4S	L
1211	Intermediate German	Ger	X104	4S	L
1212	Elementary Greek	Greek	X101	4S	L
121610	Latin composition	Latin	X113	2S	L
121610	Latin composition	Latin	X114	2S	L
121641	Elementary Latin	Latin	X101	4S	L
121641	Elementary Latin	Latin	X102	4S	L
1220	First-year Russian	Rus	X101	4S	L
1220	First-year Russian	Rus	X102	4S	L
1220	Second-year Russian	Rus	X103	4S	L
1220	Second-year Russian	Rus	X104	4S	L
122007	19th-cent Rus lit in tran	Rus	X315	3S	U
1225	Elementary Spanish	Span	X101	4S	L
1225	Elementary Spanish	Span	X102	4S	L
1225	Reading & writing Spanish	Span	X123	4S	L
1225	Reading & writing Spanish	Span	X124	4S	L
122507	Span lit: Mid Ages–18th c	Span	X240	3S	U
122507	Span lit: 19th cen to pres	Span	X241	3S	U
122507	Spanish-Amer literature	Span	X242	3S	U
131102	Law and planning implemtn	Ur Pl	X308	3S	U
150311	Immunochem–humoral resp	Micro	X329A	2S	U
150311	Immunochem–cellular imm	Micro	X329B	1S	U
150311	Immunochem–autoimm dise	Micro	X329C	1S	U

NCES No.	Course Title	Dept.	Course No.	Credits	Level
1507	Gen phys: mech heat matter	Phys	X123	4S	L
1507	Gen phys: elec mag atm nuc	Phys	X124	4S	L
160302	College algebra	Math	X111	5S	L
160302	College algebra	Math	X112	3S	L
160306	Elem linear alg with appl	Math	X125	3S	L
160401	Calc & analyt geom I	Math	X120	5S	L
160401	Calc & analyt geom IIA	Math	X130	5S	L
160401	Calc & analyt geom IIIA	Math	X240	3S	L
160401	Calculus I	Math	X135	5S	L
160401	Calculus II	Math	X245	5S	L
160401	Calc & analyt geom IIB	Math	X132	5S	L
160401	Calc & analyt geom IIIB	Math	X242	5S	L
160406	Differ eq & orthog funct	Math	X345	3S	U
160602	Plane trigonometry	Math	X114	2S	L
160603	Analytic geometry	Math	X122	4S	L
1608	Descriptive statistics	Psych	X233	3S	U
1608	Inferential statistics	Psych	X234	2S	U
1611	Finite math: bus & soc sci	Math	X124	3S	L
1611	Calculus for social sci	Math	X134	4S	L
161101	Economic statistics I	Econ	X172	3S	L
161108	Statistical meth in psych	Psych	X235	5S	U
1905	Health and modern life	Hl Ed	X150	3S	L
190501	Drug-abuse education	Hl Ed	X393	2S	U
190503	Consumer health education	Hl Ed	X396	2S	U
190504	Concepts of disease prev	Hl Ed	X283	2S	U
190511	Safety education	S Ed	X280	3S	U
190512	Human sexuality	Hl Ed	X206	2S	U
190515	Sex educ for teachers	Hl Ed	X285	4S	U
190515	Hlth & safety ed elem sch	Hl Ed	X392	3S	U
2001	Intro to psychology	Psych	X100	3S	L
200401	Behavior modification	Psych	X337	3S	U
200406	Introduction to learning	Psych	X248	3S	U
200501	Abnormal psychology	Psych	X238	3S	U
200509	Psychology of personality	Psych	X250	3S	U
2007	Intro to social psychol	Psych	X201	3S	U
200804	Educational psychology	EdPsy	X211	3S	U
200901	Industrial psychology	Psych	X245	3S	U
220201	Introduction to economics	Econ	X101	4S	L
220209	Comparative econ systems	Econ	X255	3S	U
220305	Physical geography I	Geog	X102	4S	L
220305	Physical geography II	Geog	X103	4S	L
220401	Const dev of US to 1865	Hist	X369	3S	U
220401	Const dev of US snce 1865	Hist	X370	3S	U
220426	Hist of West civ to 1660	Hist	X111	4S	L
220426	Hist of West civ fr 1660	Hist	X112	4S	L
220432	US history to 1877	Hist	X151	4S	L
220432	US history 1877 to pres	Hist	X152	4S	L
220432	US in 20th century	Hist	X262	3S	U
220470	Afro-Amer hist to 1865	Hist	X253	3S	U
220470	Afro-Amer hist since 1865	Hist	X254	3S	U
2205	Intro to political sci	PolSc	X100	3S	L
220501	American government	PolSc	X150	3S	L
220503	Intro to compar politics	PolSc	X240	3S	U
220505	International relations	PolSc	X280	3S	U
220510	Contemp political theory	PolSc	X396	3S	U
220511	Municipal government	PolSc	X305	3S	U
2206	Introduction to sociology	Socio	X100	3S	L
220612	Stratification & soc clas	Socio	X223	3S	U
220699	Collective behavior	Socio	X240	3S	U

Noncredit courses

NCES No.	Course Title	Dept.	Course No.	Credits	Level
040601	Business communication	BTWr	X602	NC	
041004	Retail marketing managemt	BusAd	X612	NC	
090407	Chem basis of drug actn I	Pharm	X900	NC	
090407	Chem bas of drug actn II	Pharm	X901	NC	
090411	Contracep: new dir in prac	Pharm	X902	NC	
090411	Hypertens: new dir in prac	Pharm	X903	NC	
090411	Teratolog: new dir in prac	Pharm	X904	NC	
210302	Fire svc instructor I	FrSci	X901	NC	

43 UNIVERSITY OF IOWA

Ms. Phyllis Hopp
Office Coordinator
Guided Correspondence Study
University of Iowa
W400 Seashore Hall
Iowa City, Iowa 52242
Phone: (319) 353-4963

Enrollment on a noncredit basis accepted in all credit courses. Gifted high school students are permitted to enroll in undergraduate courses for credit. Educational advising service and study skills assistance are available. Continuing Education Units (CEUs) are awarded upon completion of all noncredit courses. The university accepts overseas enrollment for college-level and noncredit courses only. Courses with instruction level of B may be either upper-division collegiate or graduate.

College courses

NCES No.	Course Title	Dept.	Course No.	Credits	Level
030499	Basic playwriting	EngLL	8W155	3S	B
030499	Playwriting II	EngLL	8W156	3S	B
040301	Intro financial mgmt	Bus	6F100	3S	B
040306	Investments	Bus	6F111	3S	B
040502	Entrepreneurship new bus	Bus	6F127	3S	B
040502	Managing new or small bus	bus	6F128	3S	B
040708	General insurance	Bus	6F102	3S	B
040903	Organizational behavior	Bus	6K160	3S	B
040999	Production management	Bus	6K84	3S	L
041104	Collective bargaining	Bus	6L153	3S	B
050499	Pop culture & mass comm	Jrnl	19144	3S	B
050605	Free-lance writing	Jrnl	19148	3S	B
050699	Spec proj in mass comm	Jrnl	19180	VC	B
070401	Intro to education	Educ	7S101	3S	B
070404	Methods early child ed	Educ	7E157	3S	B
070404	Classroom management	Educ	7E170	VC	B
070505	Methods sec sch journalsm	Jrnl	19140	3S	B
070512	Lit for adolescents	Educ	7S193	3S	B
070512	Cor & eval hi sch writing	EngLL	8W110	2S	B
070512	Methods high sch reading	Educ	7S194	3S	B
070703	Fac career dev in schools	Educ	7X103	3S	B
070799	Sex role stereo & soc ed	Educ	7C140	3S	B
070799	Psych aspects roles	Educ	7C150	3S	B
0708	Exceptional persons	Educ	7U130	3S	B
070803	Education of the gifted	Educ	7U137	3S	B
070806	Mental retardation	Educ	7U135	3S	B
071102	Intro to educ measurement	Educ	7P150	3S	B
071299	Ind study nonmajors	Educ	7W193	3S	B
0810	Lettering	EngAS	105	1S	B
0810	Mechanical drawing	EngAS	107	2S	B
090118	Nrsng proc & pharmacology	Nrsng	96111	3S	B
100313	Nutrition	HmEc	17142	3S	B
100313	Advanced nutrition	HmEc	17145	3S	B
100602	Parent-child rltnshps	HmEc	17114	3S	B
100602	Parent-child-teacher rel	HmEc	17116	3S	B
120202	Maj 19th-cent Brit works	EngLL	863	3S	L
120202	Amer works before 1900	EngLL	864	3S	L
120202	Literature of Iowa	EngLL	8115	3S	B
120202	Chaucer	EngLL	8120	3S	B
120202	Shakespeare	EngLL	8122	3S	B
120202	Pop lits detective fictn	EngLL	8142	3S	B
120202	Science fiction I	EngLL	8181	3S	B
120202	Science fiction II	EngLL	8182	3S	B
120202	Women in literature	EngLL	8161	3S	B
120202	Chan concept women in lit	EngLL	8169	3S	B
120299	Studies in modern drama	EngLL	8168	3S	B
120307	Lit & cult 20th-cent Amer	EngLL	8106	3S	B
120307	Eng novel Scott to Butler	EngLL	8133	3S	B
120307	American novel 1900-1945	EngLL	8135	3S	B
120310	Expository writing	EngLL	8W10	3S	L
120310	Tech & scientific writing	EngLL	8W15	2S	L
120310	Creative writing	EngLL	8W23	3S	L
120310	Fiction writing	EngLL	8W151	3S	B
120310	Advanced fiction writing	EngLL	8W161	3S	B
120310	Writing for bus & indus	EngLL	8W113	3S	B
120310	Adv fiction writing II	EngLL	8W162	3S	B
121099	Elementary French	Frnch	91	4S	L
121099	Elementary French	Frnch	92	4S	L
121199	First-semester German	Ger	1311	3S	L
121199	Second-semester German	Ger	1312	3S	L
121641	Elementary Latin	Clas	201	4S	L

NCES No.	Course Title	Dept.	Course No.	Credits	Level
121641	Elementary Latin	Clas	202	4S	L
122508	Reading Spanish	Span	3551	3S	L
122599	Elementary Spanish I	Span	351	4S	L
122599	Elementary Spanish II	Span	352	4S	L
122599	Intermediate Spanish I	Span	3511	3S	L
122599	Intermediate Spanish II	Span	3512	3S	L
150399	Human biology	Zool	1121	3S	L
150401	Principles of chemistry	Chem	413	3S	L
150599	Introduction to geology	Geol	125	4S	L
160308	Elements of group theory	Math	22M50	3S	L
160399	Basic math techniques	Math	22M1	3S	L
160399	Mathematical techniques I	Math	22M2	3S	L
160399	Math techniques II	Math	22M3	3S	L
160399	Fundamentals college math	Math	22M10	4S	L
160399	Fundamentals college math	Math	22M11	4S	L
160401	Calculus I	Math	22M25	4S	L
160401	Calculus II	Math	22M26	4S	L
160401	Engineering calculus	Math	22M35	4S	L
160401	Quantitative methods	Math	22M7	4S	L
160603	Elementary functions	Math	22M20	3S	L
160802	Intro to stat methods	Educ	7P143	3S	B
181004	Sociology of religion	Socio	34167	3S	B
181104	Judeo-Christian tradition	Relig	3261	3S	L
181104	Religion and society	Relig	3262	3S	L
181199	Religion & women	Relig	32111	3S	B
181301	World of Old Testament	Relig	32105	3S	B
181302	World of New Testament	Relig	32122	3S	B
181399	Ind studies in relig (UG)	Relig	32195	3S	U
190106	Admin phy ed & athletics	PhyEd	27103	3S	B
190299	Human anatomy	PhyEd	2753	2S	L
190508	Nutrition work wth childn	HmEc	17124	3S	B
190702	Aging & leisure	RecEd	162	3S	B
190799	Contemp issues rec & leis	RecEd	146	3S	B
200199	Elementary psychology	Psych	311	VC	B
200501	Abnormal psychology	Psych	31163	3S	B
200799	Social psychology	Psych	31101	3S	B
200804	Ed psych & measurement	Educ	7P75	3S	L
200804	Learner characteristics	Educ	7P102	3S	B
200804	Educational psychology	Educ	7P131	3S	B
200805	Socialization sch child	Educ	7P109	3S	B
200901	Psych in bus & industry	Psych	3119	3S	L
210199	Intro to public admin	PolSc	30120	3S	B
220101	Intro Midwest prehistory	Anthr	11320	3S	L
220101	Hist of Iowa archaeology	Anthr	180	3S	B
220101	Iowa prehistory	Anthr	182	3S	B
220102	Intro study cult & soc	Anthr	1133	4S	L
220107	Women's roles cross-cult	Anthr	156	3S	B
220201	Principles of economics	Econ	6E1	4S	L
220201	Principles of economics	Econ	6E2	4S	L
220216	Problems in urban econ	Econ	6E137	3S	B
220301	Intro human geography	Geog	441	4S	L
220305	Intro physical geography	Geog	442	4S	L
220308	Urban geography	Geog	44135	3S	B
220426	Western civilization	Hist	1131	3S	L
220426	Western civilization	Hist	1132	3S	L
220426	20th-cent Europe Nazi era	Hist	16135	3S	B
220426	19th-cent Eur: imper era	Hist	16134	3S	B
220432	Amer history 1492-1877	Hist	1661	3S	L
220432	Amer history 1877-present	Hist	1662	3S	L
220432	Contemp US 1940-present	Hist	16168	3S	B
220432	Great Plains experience	Hist	16122	3S	B
220432	New Deal/new era 1920-40	Hist	16167	3S	B
220452	Medieval civilization	Hist	16110	3S	B
220501	Am const law & politics	PolSc	30116	3S	B
220503	Intro to world politics	PolSc	3060	3S	L
220511	Munic govt & politics	PolSc	30111	3S	B
220511	American state politics	PolSc	30113	3S	B
220511	Urban administration	PolSc	30121	3S	B
220511	Iowa govmt & politics	PolSc	30112	3S	B
220599	Intro American politics	PolSc	301	3S	L
220599	American political system	PolSc	30110	4S	B
220599	Ind study in pol science	PolSc	30190	VC	B
220602	Sociology of corrections	Socio	34145	3S	B
220602	Socio of law & crim just	Socio	34182	3S	B
220603	World population problems	Socio	34174	3S	B
220604	Juvenile delinquency	Socio	34141	3S	B
220605	American family	Socio	34161	3S	B
220606	Intro to socio principles	Socio	341	3S	L
220606	Intro to socio problems	Socio	342	3S	L

NCES No.	Course Title	Dept.	Course No.	Credits	Level
220606	Theories of sociology	Socio	34191	3S	B
220699	Women and society	Socio	34108	3S	B
Graduate courses					
070402	Spvsn & cur dev prekinder	Educ	7E268	3S	G
071103	Educ measurement & eval	Educ	7P257	3S	G
071299	Ind st inst des for major	Educ	7W293	VC	G
180999	Rdgs in Asian religions	Relig	32265	2S	G
181299	Rdg Jewish/Chrstn scripts	Relig	32260	2S	G
181399	Rdgs theol & rel thought	Relig	32263	2S	G
181399	Ind studies in relig grad	Relig	32290	3S	G
181599	Rdgs in religious ethics	Relig	32264	2S	G
190107	Phys ed program planning	PhyEd	28260	3S	G
Noncredit courses					
040206	Secretarial skills bldg	BusEd	BE99	NC	L
040299	Supervising sec services	BusEd	BE199	NC	B
040999	Personal time management	PubAf	PA10	NC	L
050102	Advertising basics: intro	BusAd	BI10	NC	L
090104	Interp card arrhythmias I	Nrsng	90676	NC	V
090104	Interp card arrhythm II	Nrsng	90677	NC	V
090104	Intro cong heart failure	Nrsng	90807	NC	V
090199	Medical terminology	HSci	HS100	NC	B
090799	Ag health probs in ind	Nrsng	90808	NC	V
160301	Practical math review	Math	SI30	NC	D
181001	Biblical archaeology	Relig	RS10	NC	B
220499	Finding your roots	Genea	GS99	NC	L

44 UNIVERSITY OF KANSAS

Ms. Nancy Colyer
Director, Independent Study
Division of Continuing Education
University of Kansas
Lawrence, Kansas 66045
Phone: (913) 864-4792

Enrollment on a noncredit basis accepted in all credit courses. Gifted high school students are permitted to enroll in undergraduate courses for credit. Overseas enrollment accepted.

NCES No.	Course Title	Dept.	Course No.	Credits	Level
College courses					
020906	Des rec facilities sp pop	Arch	757	3S	U
040101	Financial accounting	Bus	240	4S	L
040111	Managerial accounting	Bus	241	3S	L
040601	Business communication	Bus	355	3S	U
041006	Office mgt & supervision	Bus	500	3S	U
041103	Human relations in bus	Bus	747	3S	U
041105	Personnel management	Bus	544	3S	U
050199	Elements of advertising	Jour	240	3S	U
050608	Reporting I	Jrnl	350	3S	U
050699	Mass media & pop art Amer	Jour	605	3S	U
051103	Loving relationships	ComS	455	3S	U
051103	Life shaping	ComS	459	2S	U
051103	Dir hi schl forensic prog	ComS	559	3S	U
051103	Dev child aware via commu	ComS	741	3S	U
070199	Educational sociology	CI	324	2S	U
070199	Survey of American educ	EPA	312	2S	U
070201	Teacher & school admin	EPA	308	3S	U
070404	Teaching reading in sec sc	C&I	429	3S	U
070899	Intro to psyc & ed child	SpEd	725	3S	U
071103	Intro educ measurements	EPR	302	2S	U
080101	Space dynamics	AE	655	3S	U
100599	Housing	FEcon	420	3S	U
100601	Intro child behav & devel	HDFL	160	3S	L
100601	Intro child behav & devel	HDFL	432	3S	U
100601	Children and television	HDFL	325	3S	U
100699	Prin nutr & health in dev	HDFL	220	3S	L
100699	Prin of env design & fam	HDFL	102	3S	L
100699	Theories of human develop	HDFL	480	3S	U
120305	Composition & literature	Engl	101	3S	L
120305	Composition & literature	Engl	102	3S	L
120307	Introduction to poetry	Engl	210	3S	L
120307	Shakespeare	Engl	332	3S	U
120307	Literature for children	Engl	466	3S	U
120307	Directed readings: Austen	Engl	496	1S	U
120307	Directed readings: Conrad	Engl	496	1S	U
120307	Directed rdngs: Lawrence	Engl	496	1S	U
120307	Post–World War II Am novl	Engl	571	3S	U

NCES No.	Course Title	Dept.	Course No.	Credits	Level
120307	American literature I	Engl	320	3S	U
120307	American literature II	Engl	322	3S	U
120310	Technical writing	Engl	362	3S	U
120310	Creative writing: fiction	Engl	305	3S	U
120399	Grk & Lat elem in Eng lge	Clsx	232	3S	L
120399	Grk & Lat elem in Eng lge	Clsx	332	3S	U
121005	Elementary French I	Frnch	110	5S	L
121005	Elementary French II	Frnch	120	5S	L
121008	French for reading knowlg	Frnch	100	3S	L
121105	Elementary German I	Ger	104	5S	L
121105	Elementary German II	Ger	108	5S	L
121108	German reading course	Ger	100	4S	L
121605	Elementary Latin	Latin	104	5S	L
121605	Latin reading & grammar	Latin	108	5S	L
121607	Virgil's *Aeneid*	Latin	124	3S	L
122505	Elementary Spanish I	Span	104	5S	L
122508	Spanish reading course	Span	100	3S	L
122508	Intermediate Spanish I	Span	112	3S	L
150199	Introductory astronomy	Astro	191	3S	L
150202	Meteorology	Metr	320	3S	U
150301	Human reprod bio & behav	Bio	303	3S	U
150399	Human physiology	Bio	305	4S	U
150399	Can man survive?	Bio	521	3S	U
160299	Modern elementary math I	Math	109	3S	L
160299	Modern elementary math II	Math	110	3S	L
160302	Algebra	Math	101	3S	L
160401	Calculus	Math	115	3S	L
160401	Calculus	Math	116	3S	L
160603	Calculus & analyt geom I	Math	121	5S	L
160603	Calc & analyt geom III	Math	123	5S	L
180404	Intro to philosophy	Philo	140	4S	L
180599	Intro to logic	Philo	148	3S	L
181104	Relig & culture pub schl	Relig	591	3S	U
181199	Loving relationships	Rel	475	3S	U
181399	New Test to hist understd	Relig	315	3S	U
190104	Hist & foundtn phys ed	HPER	244	3S	L
190311	Coaching of basketball	HPER	252	2S	L
190311	Coaching of track & field	HPER	292	2S	L
190311	Coaching of football	HPER	240	3S	U
190505	Environmental health	HPER	449	2S	U
190599	Personal & commun health	HPER	260	3S	U
190703	Recreation program	HPER	489	3S	U
200199	General psychology	Psych	104	3S	L
200199	General psychology	Psych	304	3S	U
200399	Environmental psychology	Psych	467	3S	U
200599	Intro psych excep child	Educ	725	3S	U
200599	Psych of adolescence	Psych	626	3S	U
200599	Children and television	Psyc	325	3S	U
200799	Social psychology	Psych	260	3S	L
200804	Educational psychology	EPR	300	2S	U
220106	Intro physical anthropol	Anthr	104	4S	L
220106	Intro physical anthropol	Anthr	304	4S	U
220201	Introductory economics	Econ	104	4S	L
220207	American economic dvlpmnt	Econ	530	3S	U
220305	Intro physical geography	Geog	106	5S	L
220402	Am diplomat hist aft 1901	Hist	630	3S	U
220407	Inside Hitler's Germany	Hist	441	3S	U
220432	Hist US through Civil War	Hist	128	3S	L
220433	Hist US since Civil War	Hist	129	3S	L
220470	Intro African studies	AfAmS	104	3S	L
220471	Hist of American Indian	Hist	619	3S	U
220499	History of art	ArHis	200	3S	L
220499	Hist of Second World War	Hist	440	3S	U
220499	History of Kansas	Hist	620	3S	U
220501	Intro to US politics	PolSc	110	3S	L
220503	Intro to compar politics	PolSc	150	3S	L
220504	Contemp issues US politcs	PolSc	210	3S	L
220507	Library res public policy	PolSc	190	1S	U
220602	Causation of crime & delin	Soc	661	3S	U
220602	Corrections	Soc	662	3S	U
220606	Elements of sociology	Socio	104	3S	L
220612	Sociology of health & med	Soc	624	3S	U
220613	Sociology of aging	Soc	523	3S	U
220699	Socio prob & Amer values	Socio	160	3S	L

Noncredit courses

NCES No.	Course Title	Dept.	Course No.	Credits	Level
020102	Residential landscape des			NC	
020102	Res landscape design			NC	
020203	Self-suff home: site sel			NC	
040306	Stocks, bonds & beg invst			NC	
082699	Elementary surveying			NC	

NCES No.	Course Title	Dept.	Course No.	Credits	Level
090255	Renal anatomy	Nurs		NC	
090255	Intro to renal trans proc	Nurs		NC	
090255	Physiological role of kidn	Nurs		NC	
090255	Therapeu agent affec kidn	Nurs		NC	
090255	Diagnos of renal disease	Nurs		NC	
090255	Aspects of urinary nursng	Nurs		NC	
090255	Urinary tract infections	Nurs		NC	
090255	Nurs knowl of renal dis	Nurs		NC	
090255	Chronic renal failure	Nurs		NC	
090305	Spinal traction	PTher		NC	
090305	Class of musculoskel spin	PTher		NC	
090305	The shoulder joint	PTher		NC	
090305	Sex dysfunction of handic	PTher		NC	
090305	Cardiac rehabilitation	PTher		NC	
100604	Project self-discovery			NC	
120308	Fiction's world of horror			NC	
120308	Short story reluct readrs			NC	
200408	Straight thinking			NC	
200502	Career planning			NC	
200505	Life shaping			NC	

(45) UNIVERSITY OF KENTUCKY

Dr. E. Earl Pfanstiel
Director
Independent Study Program
University of Kentucky
Room 1, Frazee Hall
Lexington, Kentucky 40506
Phone: (606) 257-3466

Enrollment on a noncredit basis accepted in all credit courses. Gifted high school students are permitted to enroll in undergraduate courses for credit. Overseas enrollment is not encouraged; each case is judged on an individual basis.

High school courses

NCES No.	Course Title	Dept.	Course No.	Credits	Level
040101	Accounting I first half	BusHS	01	HF	H
040101	Accounting I second half	BusHS	02	HF	H
040205	Shorthand I first half	BusHS	09	HF	H
040205	Shorthand I second half	BusHS	10	HF	H
040207	Beginning typing first hf	BusHS	11	HF	H
040207	Typing I second half	BusHS	12	HF	H
049900	Business math first half	BusHS	03	HF	H
049900	Business math second half	BusHS	04	HF	H
049900	Business law	BusHS	06	HF	H
049900	Gen business first half	BusHS	07	HF	H
049900	Gen business second half	BusHS	08	HF	H
059900	Mass media/print/radio/TV	EngHS	21	HF	H
120305	Grammar grade 9	Engl	13	HF	H
120305	Grammar grade 10	Engl	15	HF	H
120305	Grammar grade 11	Engl	17	HF	H
120305	Grammar grade 12	Engl	19	HF	H
120307	Literature grade 9	Engl	14	HF	H
120307	Literature grade 10	Engl	16	HF	H
120307	Literature grade 11	Engl	18	HF	H
120307	Literature grade 12	Engl	20	HF	H
1210	French I, II, III, IV	LanHS	26	IU	H
1211	German I, II, III, IV	LanHS	24	IU	H
1211	Greek I	LanHS	22	IU	H
1216	Latin I, II	LanHS	23	IU	H
1225	Spanish I, II, III, IV	LanHS	25	IU	H
160301	General math first half	MatHS	29	HF	H
160301	General math second half	MatHS	30	HF	H
160302	Algebra I first half	MatHS	31	HF	H
160302	Algebra I second half	MatHS	32	HF	H
160302	Algebra II first half	MatHS	33	HF	H
160302	Algebra II second half	MatHS	34	HF	H
160601	Plane geometry first half	MatHS	35	HF	H
160601	Plane geometry second hf	MatHS	36	HF	H
190509	Personal-community health	Hlth	27	HF	H
190509	Pers-comm hlth second hf	Hlth	28	HF	H
200502	Psychology	Psych	43	HF	H
220399	World geog first half	Geog	39	HF	H
220399	World geog second half	Geog	40	HF	H
220432	US history first half	Hist	41	HF	H
220432	US history second half	Hist	42	HF	H

NCES No.	Course Title	Dept.	Course No.	Credits	Level
220601	Sociology first half	SocHS	44	HF	H
220601	Sociology second half	SocHS	45	HF	H
	College courses				
010199	Agricultural economics	Agri	B102	2S	L
010402	Agri animal science	Agri	106	4S	L
010407	Agri feeds and feeding	Agri	380	3S	U
010604	Agri plant science	Agri	104	4S	L
010607	Field crop production	Agri	386	3S	U
010703	Soil science management	Agri	366	3S	U
010901	Elements of forestry	Fores	100	3S	L
030303	Introduction to music	Music	200	3S	L
040101	Principles of accounting	Acctg	201	3S	L
040101	Prin of accounting II	Acctg	202	3S	L
040101	Intermediate accounting 1	Acctg	301	3S	U
040101	Intermediate accounting 2	Acctg	302	3S	U
040106	Cost accounting	Acctg	408	3S	U
040201	Office admin and services	BOE	445	3S	U
040205	Theory of shorthand I	BOE	112	3S	L
040205	Intermediate shorthand II	BOE	113	3S	L
040207	Beginning typewriting	BOE	117	3S	L
040207	Advanced typewriting	BOE	118	3S	L
040301	Corporate finance	BusAd	345	3S	U
040902	Business management	BusAd	335	3S	U
040903	Organizational behavior	BusAd	435	3S	U
041003	Marketing management	BusAd	330	3S	U
041104	Personnel and industrial	BusAd	336	3S	U
049900	Legal environment of bus	BusAd	340	3S	U
049900	Business law I	BusAd	341	3S	U
049900	Business law II	BusAd	441	3S	U
050608	Princ of news writing	Jrnl	203	3S	L
070516	Math for elem teachers I	Math	201	3S	L
070516	Math for elem teachers II	Math	202	3S	L
0899	Engineering tech writing	Engl	104	3S	L
100103	Clothing awareness select	HmEc	337	3S	U
100199	Introduction to textiles	HmEc	120	3S	L
100399	Food nutrition for man	HmEc	101	3S	L
100499	Personal/family finance	HmEc	251	3S	L
100602	Individual marriage & fam	HmEc	252	3S	L
110503	Basic engineering graphcs	Graph	105	2S	L
120201	Western lit Greeks–1660	Engl	261	3S	L
120201	Western lit 1660–present	Engl	262	3S	L
120201	Lit Old Testament	Engl	270	3S	L
120201	Lit New Testament	Engl	271	3S	L
120201	Women in literature	Engl	375	3S	U
120201	Shakespeare survey	Engl	425	3S	U
120201	American lit 1800-1860	Engl	451	3S	U
120201	American lit 1860-1900	Engl	452	3S	U
120303	English lit survey I	Engl	221	3S	L
120303	English lit survey II	Engl	222	3S	L
120310	Freshman composition	Engl	101	3S	L
120310	Advanced freshman comp	Engl	102	3S	L
120310	Writing for industry	Engl	103	3S	L
120399	Etymology	Engl	201	3S	L
120399	Medical terminology	Engl	131	3S	L
1210	Elementary French I	Frnch	101	3S	L
1210	Elementary French II	Frnch	102	3S	L
1210	Intermediate French I	Frnch	201	3S	L
1210	Intermediate French II	Frnch	202	3S	L
1211	Elementary German I	Ger	111	3S	L
1211	Elementary German II	Ger	112	3S	L
1212	Beginning Greek	Greek	151	3S	L
1212	Intermediate German I	Ger	201	3S	L
1212	Intermediate German II	Ger	202	3S	L
1216	Elementary Latin I	Latin	101	3S	L
1216	Elementary Latin II	Latin	102	3S	L
1225	Elementary Spanish I	Span	141	3S	L
1225	Elementary Spanish II	Span	142	3S	L
1225	Intermediate Spanish I	Span	241	3S	L
1225	Intermediate Spanish II	Span	242	3S	L
150199	Descriptive astronomy I	Astro	191	3S	L
150199	Descriptive astronomy II	Astro	192	3S	L
150301	Human biology	Bio	110	3S	L
150306	Evolution	Bio	508	3S	U
150307	Principles of genetics	Bio	404	3S	U
150311	Principles of microbiol	Bio	108	3S	L
150316	Plant biology	Bio	106	3S	L
150323	Animal biology	Bio	104	3S	L
150399	Animal-plant microbiology	Bio	103	3S	L
150399	Economic botany	Bio	465	3S	U
160302	Remedial algebra	Math	108R	3S	L
160302	College algebra	Math	109	3S	L

NCES No.	Course Title	Dept.	Course No.	Credits	Level
160401	Calculus I: integral	Math	113	4S	L
160401	Calculus II: differential	Math	114	4S	L
160401	Elementary calculus	Math	123	3S	L
160602	Trigonometry	Math	112	2S	L
160801	Descriptive statistics	Stat	292	1S	L
160899	Probability	Stat	293	1S	L
160899	Sampling and inference	Stat	294	1S	L
161101	Mathematics of finance	Math	121	3S	L
180399	Introductory ethics	Philo	130	3S	L
180501	Elementary logic	Philo	120	3S	L
180609	Great religions	Philo	440	3S	U
180799	Intro to philosophy	Philo	100	3S	L
200199	Intro to psychology	Psych	100	4S	L
200501	Abnormal psychology	Psych	533	3S	U
200504	Developmental psychology	Psych	223	3S	L
200901	Industrial psychology	Psych	502	3S	U
200902	Personnel psychology	Psych	503	3S	U
210401	Social welfare	SocW	222	3S	L
210402	Social work profession	SocW	322	4S	U
220201	Principles of economics I	Econ	260	3S	L
220201	Prin of economics II	Econ	261	3S	L
220204	Monetary economics	Econ	485	3S	U
220305	Physical geography	Geog	151	3S	L
220306	Regional geography	Geog	152	3S	L
220309	Weather and climate	Geog	251	3S	L
220399	Environmental geography	Geog	210	3S	L
220399	Human geography	Geog	252	3S	L
220424	British people I	Hist	202	3S	L
220424	British people II	Hist	203	3S	L
220425	History of Canada	Hist	558	3S	U
220426	History of Europe to 1713	Hist	104	3S	L
220426	Europe 1713 to present	Hist	105	3S	L
220432	US history through 1865	Hist	108	3S	L
220432	US history since 1865	Hist	109	3S	L
220432	US history since 1939	Hist	566	3S	U
220432	Civil War 1860-1877	Hist	567	3S	U
220432	History of the Old South	Hist	578	3S	U
220432	History of the New South	Hist	579	3S	U
220499	History of Kentucky	Hist	240	3S	L
220499	Afro-Amer history to 1865	Hist	260	3S	L
220499	Afro-Amer hist from 1865	Hist	261	3S	L
220501	American government	PolSc	101	3S	L
220507	Political parties	PolSc	470	3S	U
220511	State government	PolSc	255	3S	L
220511	Municipal government	PolSc	452	3S	U
220601	The community	Socio	220	3S	L
220602	Criminology	Socio	437	3S	U
220604	Juvenile delinquency	Socio	538	3S	U
220605	The family	socio	409	3S	U
220606	Introductory sociology	Socio	101	3S	L
220609	Relations in administratn	Socio	542	3S	U
220609	Dimensions of aging	Socio	528	3S	U
220610	Deviant behavior	Socio	436	3S	U
220613	Modern social problems	Socio	152	3S	L
	Noncredit course				
120310	Writing for college class	Engl	003	NC	D

46 UNIVERSITY OF MICHIGAN

Mr. Alfred W. Storey
Director, Extension Service
Department of Independent Study
University of Michigan
412 Maynard Street
Ann Arbor, Michigan 48109
Phone: (313) 764-5306

Enrollment on a noncredit basis accepted in all credit courses. Gifted high school students are permitted to enroll in undergraduate courses for credit. Overseas enrollment accepted.

NCES No.	Course Title	Dept.	Course No.	Credits	Level
	College courses				
0199	The environ & the citizen	NatrS	485	2S	B
0199	The environ & the citizen	NatrS	486	2S	B
030399	Topics in Amer cult: jazz	AmCul	301	3S	L
040101	Principles of accounting	Acctg	271	3S	L
050299	Tech & prof writing	Hums	498	3S	U
050399	Intro to film	Spch	220	3S	L

NCES No.	Course Title	Dept.	Course No.	Credits	Level
070499	Psych of tchg rdg & writg	Educ	C510	3S	B
120304	Lit & cult of Ireland	Engl	317	3S	L
120304	Contemporary Am novel	Engl	434	3S	U
120307	Great Books	GrBks	201	4S	L
120399	Teach Eng as a forgn lang	Educ	D448	3S	B
120399	Major American authors	Engl	475	3S	U
120399	Contemporary poetry	Engl	441	3S	U
1210	First special rdg course	Fr	111	4S	B
1210	Second special rdg course	Fr	112	4S	B
1211	First special rdg course	Ger	111	4S	B
1211	Second special rdg course	Ger	112	4S	B
1299	Asia through fiction	As St	441	3S	L
160306	Elementary linear algebra	Math	117	2S	L
160399	Algebra & analyt trig	Math	105	4S	L
160602	Analyt geom & calculus I	Math	115	4S	L
160602	Analyt geom & calculus II	Math	116	3S	L
2099	Intro to psychology	Psych	172	4S	L
2099	Psychology of aging	Psych	459	3S	U
2099	Intro to behavior modific	Psych	474	3S	U
220201	Principles of economics	Econ	201	4S	L
220306	Geog of North America	Geog	402	4S	L
220499	Pales & Arab-Israeli conf	Hist	592	3S	B
2299	Intro to women's studies	WmSt	240	4S	L
2299	Cross-disci studies	WmSt	342	3S	L
2299	Women and the arts	WmSt	344	3S	L
	Graduate courses				
0199	The environ & the citizen	NatrS	485	2S	B
0199	The environ & the citizen	NatrS	486	2S	B
070499	Psych of tchg rdg & writg	Educ	C510	3S	B
070512	Tchng Engl as a for lang	Educ	D4481	2S	B
1210	First special rdg course	Fren	111	4S	B
1210	Second special rdg course	Fren	112	4S	B
1211	First special rdg course	Ger	111	4S	B
1211	Second special rdg course	Ger	112	4S	B
2099	Intro to behavior modific	Psych	474	3S	B
220499	Pales & Arab-Israeli conf	Hist	592	3S	B
	Noncredit courses				
0199	The environ & the citizen	NatrS	485	NC	
0199	The environ & the citizen	NatrS	486	NC	
040601	Pract wrtg for business	BuC	I	NC	
050605	Writing nonfiction	Journ	1	NC	
050605	Wrtg fiction for mags	Journ	2	NC	
070512	Tchng Engl as a for lang	Educ	04481	NC	
1199	Fire service inst traing	Fire	I	NC	
120307	Great Books	GrBks	201	NC	

47 UNIVERSITY OF MINNESOTA

Ms. Deborah Nelson
Associate Director
Department of Independent Study
University of Minnesota
45 Wesbrook Hall
77 Pleasant Street, S.E.
Minneapolis, Minnesota 55455
Phone: (612) 373-3256

Enrollment on a noncredit basis accepted in all credit courses. Gifted high school students are permitted to enroll in undergraduate courses for credit. Overseas enrollment accepted.

NCES No.	Course Title	Dept.	Course No.	Credits	Level
	High school courses				
040101	Fundmntls of accountg A	Bus	9813	HF	H
040101	Fundmntls of accountg B	Bus	9814	HF	H
040205	Shorthand	Bus	9901	HF	H
0499	General business A	Bus	9821	HF	H
0499	General business B	Bus	9822	HF	H
1299	Ninth-grade English A	Engl	9831	HF	H
1299	Ninth-grade English B	Engl	9832	HF	H
1299	Tenth-grade English A	Engl	9833	HF	H
1299	Tenth-grade English B	Engl	9834	HF	H
1299	Eleventh-grade English A	Engl	9835	HF	H
1299	Eleventh-grade English B	Engl	9836	HF	H
1299	Twelfth-grade English A	Engl	9847	HF	H
1299	Twelfth-grade English B	Engl	9848	HF	H
1299	Straight thinking	Engl	9839	QT	H
1299	Youth in conflict	Engl	9840	QT	H
1299	Meaning/self-discov–lit	Engl	9841	QT	H

NCES No.	Course Title	Dept.	Course No.	Credits	Level
1299	Practical writing	Engl	9842	QT	H
1299	Advanced composition	Engl	9845	HF	H
1299	Comparative mythology	Engl	9844	QT	H
1299	Contemp lit and problems	Engl	9843	HF	H
1299	Black American experience	Engl	9919	QT	H
1299	American dream and drama	Engl	9846	HF	H
1299	Creative writing	Engl	9849	HF	H
150399	Biology A	Bio	9801	HF	H
150399	Biology B	Bio	9802	HF	H
150899	Physical science	Phys	9891	HF	H
160199	Math for consumer: basics	Math	9881	QT	H
160199	Math for consumer: banking	Math	9882	QT	H
160199	Math for consumer: spendng	Math	9883	QT	H
160199	Math for consumer: problms	Math	9884	QT	H
160302	Elementary algebra A	Math	9871	HF	H
160302	Elementary algebra B	Math	9871	HF	H
160302	Higher algebra A	Math	9885	HF	H
160302	Higher algebra B	Math	9886	HF	H
160601	Geometry A	Math	9887	HF	H
160601	Geometry B	Math	9888	HF	H
160602	Trigonometry	Math	9876	HF	H
200399	Environmental survival	Psych	9894	HF	H
2099	General psychology A	Psych	9941	HF	H
2099	General psychology B	Psych	9942	HF	H
220432	American history A	Hist	9922	HF	H
220432	American history B	Hist	9923	HF	H
220433	World history A	Hist	9920	HF	H
220433	World history B	Hist	9921	HF	H
220501	Probs of Amer democracy A	PolSc	9911	HF	H
220501	Probs of Amer democracy B	PolSc	9912	HF	H
	College courses				
010103	Agriculture mkts & prices	Agri	1400	4Q	L
010499	Principles of beekeeping	AnSci	0004C	3V	L
010499	Horse production	AnSc	1600	4Q	L
010504	Home landscape design	Hort	1010	3Q	L
010504	Residential landscp desig	Hort	3026	4Q	U
0114	Conserv of nat resources	For	1201	3Q	L
030302	Ear trng & sight singing	Music	1501	4Q	L
030302	Music appreciation	Music	5950	4Q	U
030402	Hist of American theater	ThArt	5186	4Q	U
030499	Playwriting	ThArt	5115	4Q	U
030599	Basic craft skills	ArHis	1048	4Q	L
0399	Art in Western civilizati	ArHis	1015	4Q	L
040101	Principles of acctg I	Acctg	1024	3Q	L
040101	Principles of acctg II	Acctg	1025	3Q	L
040101	Principles of acctg III	Acctg	1026	3Q	L
040114	Income tax accounting	Acctg	5135	4Q	U
040302	Consumer problems	Bus	1731	5Q	L
040302	Personal finance	Bus	1731	4Q	L
040501	Small business operations	Bus	1513	4Q	U
040710	Risk mgmt and insurance	Ins	3100	4Q	U
041001	Principles of marketing	Mktg	3000	3Q	U
041199	Development administratn	PA	5401	4Q	U
0499	Intro to modern business	Bus	1511	5Q	L
0499	Salesmanship	Bus	1537	3Q	L
050199	Principles of advertising	Jrnl	1201	4Q	L
050199	Psychology of advertising	Jrnl	5251	4Q	U
0506	Intro to mass communicatn	Jrnl	1001	2Q	L
050606	History of journalism	Jrnl	5601	4Q	U
050699	Communic & public opinion	Jrnl	5501	4Q	U
050699	Mass media in dynamic soc	Jrnl	5721	4Q	U
050699	Magazine writing	Jour	3173	4Q	U
051299	Parliamentary procedure	Commu	1226	1Q	L
060199	Intro to data processing	GC	1535	3Q	L
060799	Block diagram & programmg	CmpSc	1572	5Q	L
070102	Crit issues–contemp educa	Educ	5141	3Q	U
070199	Intro to philos of educ		EDUC		L
070199	School and society	Educ	3090	3Q	U
070299	Personal time management	Educ	5128	2Q	U
071199	Intro to statistics	Educ	3102	3Q	U
0799	How to study	Educ	1001	2Q	L
0799	Efficient reading	Educ	1147	3Q	L

NCES No.	Course Title	Dept.	Course No.	Credits	Level
0799	Vocabulary building	GC	1401	3Q	L
080199	Deformable body mechanics	ArAEg	3016	4Q	U
080399	Amer architecture to 1860	AmSt	3970	4Q	U
081502	Indust rel: manpwr mgmt	IR	3012	4Q	U
081503	Work measurment standards	IEOR	0103	5V	L
081599	Supervision I	IR	0001C	3V	L
081599	Indust rel: labor mktg	IR	3002	4Q	U
081999	Soils engineering	EngAS	0001C	4V	L
081999	Concrete materials	EngAS	0302C	3V	L
100301	Man's food	FScN	1010	4Q	L
100301	Tech of food processing	FScN	1102	4Q	L
100602	Family in world perspectv	FSoS	5210	5Q	U
100602	Parent-child relationship	GC	1722	4Q	L
100604	Dating/courtship/marriage	FSoS	1001	3Q	L
100604	Parenting: altern for 80s	FSoS	5240	4Q	U
100604	American families in tran	FSoS	5230	4Q	U
100699	Human sexual behavior	FSoS	5001	4Q	U
110599	Design I	Graph	1525	3Q	L
1199	Hazardous mat & processes	FPro	0002C	3V	L
1199	Hazardous mat & processes	FPro	0003C	3V	L
1199	Hazardous mat & processes	FPro	0004C	3V	L
1199	Fire prevention & control	FPro	0005C	3V	L
1199	Life safety systems	FPro	0006C	3V	L
1199	Private fire prot systems	FPro	0007C	3V	L
1199	Private fire prot systems	FPro	0008C	3V	L
1199	Fire dept administration	FPro	0009C	3V	L
1199	Anal approach to fire pro	GC	3061	4Q	U
1199	Fire administration	GC	3062	4Q	U
1199	Fire preven org and mgmt	GC	3063	4Q	U
1199	Personnel mgmt fire serv	GC	3064	4Q	U
1199	Fire-related human behav	GC	3066	4Q	U
1199	Disaster & fire defense	GC	3072	4Q	U
1199	Pol & legal found fire pr	GC	3065	4Q	U
1199	Fire pro struc & sys dsgn	GC	3075	4Q	U
120201	European folk tales	Engl	5414	4Q	U
120299	Individualism in Am life	AmSt	1101	4Q	L
120299	Religion in American life	AmSt	1102	4Q	L
120299	Ellery Queen detect stor	AmSt	1920	4Q	L
120299	American popular culture	AmSt	3920	4Q	U
120299	Tech terms–science med	Clas	1048	3Q	L
120299	Magic/witchcraft/occult	Clas	1019	4Q	L
120299	Religion: Greek & Hellenis	Clas	3071	4Q	U
120299	Madness/dev behav Greece	Clas	5005	4Q	U
120299	Am lit: major fig & themes	Engl	1016	4Q	L
120299	Intro to mod lit: poetry	Engl	1017	4Q	L
120299	Intro to mod lit: drama	Engl	1019	4Q	L
120299	Intro to literature I	Engl	1821	4Q	L
120299	Shakespeare I	Engl	3241	4Q	U
120299	Shakespeare II	Engl	3242	4Q	U
120299	American literature I	Engl	3411	4Q	U
120299	American literature II	Engl	3412	4Q	U
120299	American literature III	Engl	3413	4Q	U
120299	20th-century Engl novel	Engl	5153	4Q	U
120299	Chaucer	Engl	5221	4Q	U
120299	Literature for children	Engl	1363	4Q	L
120299	Afro-American literature	Engl	1816	3Q	L
120299	Reading short stories	Engl	1371	4Q	L
120299	Philosophy through lit	Engl	3352	4Q	U
120299	Humanities in mod world I	Hum	1101	3Q	L
120299	Hum in modern world II	Hum	1002	5Q	L
120299	Hum in modern world III	Hum	1103	3Q	L
120299	Hum in modern world IV	Hum	1104	3Q	L
120299	European heritage: Greece	Hum	1011	5Q	L
120299	European heritage: Rome	Hum	1012	5Q	L
120299	Mod sci fiction & fantasy	Engl	1005	4Q	L
120299	Survey English lit I	Engl	3111	4Q	U
120299	Survey English lit II	Engl	3112	4Q	U
120299	Survey English lit III	Engl	3113	4Q	U
120299	American short story	Engl	3455	4Q	U
120310	Introductory composition	Commu	1001	4Q	L
120310	Introductory composition	Commu	1002	4Q	L
120310	Intermed composition	Commu	1027	4Q	L
120310	Fiction writing	Commu	3030	4Q	U
120310	Business writing	Commu	1531	4Q	L
120310	Business writing	Commu	3531	4Q	U
120310	Journal & memoir writing	Engl	3030	4Q	U
1207	Beginning Chinese I	Chi	1011	5Q	L
1207	Beginning Chinese II	Chi	1012	5Q	L
1207	Beginning Chinese III	Chi	1013	5Q	L
1207	Religions in East Asia	Chi	1032	4Q	L
1207	Asian civ: China	Chi	3501	4Q	U
1209	Beginning Finnish I	Fin	1101	5Q	L
1210	Beginning French I	Frnch	1101	5Q	L
1210	Beginning French II	Frnch	1102	5Q	L
1210	Beginning French III	Frnch	1103	5Q	L
1210	French literary texts	Frnch	3104	5Q	U
1211	Beginning German I	Ger	1101	5Q	L
1211	Beginning German II	Ger	1102	5Q	L
1211	Beginning German III	Ger	1103	5Q	L
1211	Intermediate German	Ger	1301	5Q	L
121241	Beginning classical Greek	Greek	1101	5Q	L
1214	Beginning Italian I	Ital	1101	5Q	L
1215	Beginning Japanese I	Jap	1011	5Q	L
1215	Beginning Japanese II	Jap	1012	5Q	L
1215	Beginning Japanese III	Jap	1013	5Q	L
1215	Religions of East Asia	Jap	1032	4Q	L
121641	Beginning Latin I	CILL	1101	5Q	L
121641	Beginning Latin II	CILL	1102	5Q	L
121641	Beginning Latin III	CILL	1103	5Q	L
121641	Cicero	CILL	3105	3Q	U
121641	Vergil: *Aeneid*	CILL	3106	5Q	U
121641	Latin readings	CILL	1104	5Q	L
1218	Beginning Norwegian I	Nor	1101	5Q	L
1218	Beginning Norwegian II	Nor	1102	5Q	L
1220	Beginning Russian I	Rus	1101	5Q	L
1220	Beginning Russian II	Rus	1102	5Q	L
1220	Beginning Russian III	Rus	1103	5Q	L
1220	Scientific Russian I	Rus	1221	5Q	L
1220	Scientific Russian II	Rus	1222	2Q	L
1220	Scientific Russian III	Rus	1223	2Q	L
1225	Beginning Spanish I	Span	1101	5Q	L
1225	Beginning Spanish II	Span	1102	5Q	L
1225	Beginning Spanish III	Span	1103	5Q	L
1225	Intermediate Spanish	Span	1104	4Q	L
1225	Reading and composition	Span	1105	5Q	L
1225	Civ: pre-Columb to 1825	Span	1502	4Q	L
1226	Beginning Swedish I	Swed	1101	5Q	L
1299	Beginning Polish I	Plsh	1101	5Q	L
1299	Modern Judaism	JwSt	3126	4Q	U
1299	The Holocaust	JwSt	3521	4Q	U
1299	Tales of H C Andersen	Scan	3602	4Q	U
130202	Law of contracts & agency	Law	3058	4Q	U
130703	Partner corp & real prope	Law	3078	4Q	U
130907	Personal prop wills & est	Law	3088	4Q	U
1399	Law in society	Law	1235	5Q	L
1399	Practical law	Law	1534	5Q	L
140199	Descriptive cataloging	LibSc	1401	3Q	L
150102	Solar astronomy	Astro	1161	5Q	L
150103	Stellar astronomy	Astro	1162	5Q	L
1503	General biology	Bio	1011	5Q	L
150304	Intro to ecology	EnvD	3001	4Q	U
150599	Physical geology	Geol	1001	5Q	L
150599	Historical geology	Geol	1006	3Q	L
150799	Introduction to physics	Phys	1031	5Q	L
150799	Introduction to physics	Phys	1032	5Q	L
150799	General physics	Phys	1271	5Q	L
150799	General physics	Phys	1281	4Q	L
150799	General physics	Phys	1291	4Q	L
160199	Precalculus	Math	1201	5Q	L
160302	Intermediate algebra	GC	1445	5Q	L
160304	College alg/analyt geom	Math	1111	5Q	L
160306	Linear alg & lin diff equ	Math	3221	5Q	U
160401	Intro to calculus	Math	1142	5Q	L
160402	Analysis IV	Math	3211	5Q	U
160406	Differential equations	Math	3066	4Q	U
160412	Analysis I	Math	1211	5Q	L
160412	Analysis II	Math	1221	5Q	L
160412	Analysis III	Math	1231	5Q	L
160602	Trigonometry	Math	1008	3Q	L
180301	Moral choices–contemp soc	GC	3355	4Q	U
180399	Ethics	GC	1355	4Q	L
180401	Greek philosophy-history	Philo	3001	5Q	U
180402	Descartes through Hume	Philo	3003	5Q	U
180403	Kant through Nietzsche	Philo	3004	5Q	U
180501	Logic	Philo	1001	3Q	L

NCES No.	Course Title	Dept.	Course No.	Credits	Level
180999	Religions of East Asia	Relig	1032	4Q	L
181099	Psychical phenom in relig	Relig	3521	4Q	U
181101	Science and religion	Philo	1011	4Q	L
190199	Therapeutic recreation	Rec	5210	3Q	U
190799	Camp administration	Rec	5170	3Q	U
200501	Abnormal psychology	Psych	3604	4Q	U
200504	Psych of human developmnt	Psych	1283	5Q	L
200509	Intro to personality	Psych	3101	4Q	U
200599	Child psychology	Psych	1301	4Q	L
200599	Adolescent psychology	Psych	5303	4Q	U
200905	Psychology of advertising	Psych	5751	4Q	U
2099	General psychology	Psych	1001	5Q	L
220102	Intro to soc & cult anthr	Anthr	1102	5Q	L
220102	Culture and personality	Anthr	5141	5Q	U
220199	Indians of North America	Anthr	3211	5Q	U
220199	Human origins	Anth	1101	5Q	L
220201	Principles of macroeconom	Econ	1001	4Q	L
220201	Principles of microeconom	Econ	1002	4Q	L
220204	Money and banking	Econ	3701	4Q	U
220211	Labor mkt behav & regulat	Econ	5537	4Q	U
220299	Macroeconomic theory	Econ	3102	4Q	U
220299	Economic security	Econ	5534	4Q	U
220306	Geog of US and Canada	Geog	3101	4Q	U
220306	Geog of Minnesota	Geog	3111	4Q	U
220306	Geog of South America	Geog	3121	4Q	U
220306	Geog of USSR	Geog	3181	4Q	U
220306	Geog of Twin Cities	Geog	3972	4Q	U
220306	Minnesota resources	Geog	3841	4Q	U
220423	Asian civilizations	Hist	3451	4Q	U
220423	Asian civilizations	Hist	3452	4Q	U
220423	Asian civilizations	Hist	3453	4Q	U
220426	English history	Hist	3151	4Q	U
220426	English history	Hist	3152	4Q	U
220426	Dipl hist Eur: 19th-20th c	Hist	5284	4Q	U
220426	Dipl hist Eur: 19th-20th c	Hist	5285	4Q	U
220426	Dipl hist Eur: 19th-20th c	Hist	5286	4Q	U
220426	Europe during World W II	Hist	3224	4Q	U
220428	Minnesota history	GC	1221	5Q	L
220432	American history	Hist	1301	4Q	L
220432	American history	Hist	1302	4Q	L
220450	Ancient civilization I	Hist	1051	3Q	L
220450	Ancient civilization II	Hist	1052	3Q	L
220450	Ancient civilization III	Hist	1053	3Q	L
220450	Readings in ancient civ	Hist	1061	2Q	L
220450	Readings in ancient civ	Hist	1062	2Q	L
220450	Readings in ancient civ	Hist	1063	2Q	L
220450	Ancient Near East I	Hist	5051	3Q	U
220450	Ancient Near East II	Hist	5052	3Q	U
220450	Ancient Near East III	Hist	5053	3Q	U
220452	Medieval & Renaissance	Hist	3101	4Q	U
220452	Medieval & Renaissance	Hist	3101	4Q	U
220452	Medieval & Renaissance	Hist	3101	4Q	U
220453	Intro mod European hist	Hist	1001	4Q	L
220453	Intro mod European hist	Hist	1002	4Q	L
220453	Intro mod European hist	Hist	1003	4Q	L
220499	Jewish-Christian relation	Hist	3611	4Q	U
220499	Jewish-Christian relation	Hist	3612	4Q	U
220501	American govt & politics	PolSc	1001	5Q	L
220504	World politics	PolSc	1025	3Q	L
220507	Political parties	PolSc	5737	4Q	U
220599	American foreign policy	PolSc	1026	4Q	L
220599	Govt & pol of Sov Union	PolSc	5443	4Q	U
220599	Govt & pol–African countr	PolSc	5448	4Q	U
220599	Chinese govt and politics	PolSc	5454	4Q	U
220599	Power & the individual	GC	3238	4Q	U
220601	American community	Socio	1002	4Q	L
220602	Elements of criminology	Socio	3103	4Q	U
220603	World population problems	Soc	3551	4Q	U
220607	Intro to soc psychology	Socio	5201	4Q	U
220610	Crime & justice in Amer	GC	1236	4Q	L
220699	Introduction to sociology	Socio	1001	4Q	L
220699	Death in America	Socio	5960	4Q	U
220699	Soc of law & soc control	Soc	3102	4Q	U
220699	Analytical social theory	Soc	5701	4Q	U

Noncredit courses

NCES No.	Course Title	Dept.	Course No.	Credits	Level
030499	Independent playwriting	ThArt	0001	NC	
120310	Preparatory composition	Commu	0001	NC	
120310	Grammar review	Commu	0002	NC	
120310	Writing of poetry	Commu	0011	NC	
120310	Advanced writg of poetry	Commu	0012	NC	

NCES No.	Course Title	Dept.	Course No.	Credits	Level
120310	Independent writing	Commu	0017	NC	
120310	Short manuscript criticsm	Commu	0018	NC	
1210	French for grad students	Frnch	0001	NC	
1211	German for grad students	Ger	0221	NC	
1211	German for grad students	Ger	0222	NC	
1225	Spanish for grad students	Span	0221	NC	
160399	Basic mathematics	Math	0001	NC	
160399	Basic mathematics	Math	0002	NC	
160399	Basic mathematics	Math	0003	NC	
160399	Basic mathematics	Math	0004	NC	

48 UNIVERSITY OF MISSISSIPPI

Mrs. Christine S. White
Coordinator of Independent Study
Department of Independent Study
University of Mississippi
Yerby Center for Continuing Education
University, Mississippi 38677
Phone: (601) 232-7313

Gifted high school students are permitted to enroll in undergraduate courses for credit. Overseas enrollment accepted for college courses.

NCES No.	Course Title	Dept.	Course No.	Credits	Level
	College courses				
030302	History of music	Music	202	3S	L
030302	Music literature I	Music	101	3S	L
030399	Opera	Music	203	1S	L
030502	Art appreciation	Art	281	3S	L
030602	Mat and tech of painter	Art	105	1S	L
040101	Intro to accounting prin	Acctg	201	3S	L
040101	Intro to accounting prin	Acctg	202	3S	L
040199	Administrative accounting	Acctg	301	3S	U
040199	Children's lit, K-8	LibSc	301	3S	U
040201	Admin practices & proced	OfAdm	561	3S	U
040206	Secretarial proced/admin	OfAdm	351	3S	U
040301	Business finance I	Fin	331	3S	U
040308	Money and banking	Econ	303	3S	U
040308	Money and banking	Fin	303	3S	U
040601	Business communication	OfAdm	271	3S	L
040604	Business reports	OfAdm	372	3S	U
040799	Risk and insurance	Fin	341	3S	U
040902	Found of voc bus educ	BusEd	201	3S	L
041001	Marketing principles	Mktg	351	3S	U
041099	Buyer-seller comm	Mktg	354	3S	U
041099	Intro to retailing	Mktg	361	3S	U
041301	Real estate valuatn & app	Fin	353	3S	U
041306	Real estate fin mort bank	Fin	355	3S	U
041309	Real estate	Fin	351	3S	U
050199	Intro to advertising	Mktg	353	3S	U
050699	School publications	SecEd	528	3S	U
050699	Intro to advertising	Jrnl	385	3S	U
050699	School publications	Jrnl	399	3S	U
051199	Ana and phy speech hear	ComDi	205	3S	L
061103	Computers and society	CmpSc	231	3S	L
070499	Pub sch curriculum	SecEd	401	3S	U
070520	Psychology of adolescence	Educ	309	3S	U
070522	Science in the elem sch	ElEd	303	3S	U
070522	Soc studies in the el sch	ElEd	401	3S	U
070599	Arith in the elem school	ElEd	403	3S	U
070602	Career education	Culns	300	3S	U
070610	Found of elem reading	Read	300	3S	U
070610	Tchng rdng in elem school	Read	415	3S	U
070610	Diagnostic tchng of readg	Read	417	3S	U
070610	Readg in the sec school	Read	429	3S	U
070701	Principles of guidance	Educ	539	3S	U
070799	Psyc of human grwth & dev	Educ	333	3S	U
071199	Elem statistics in educ	EdRes	501	3S	U
100313	Nutrition	HmEc	311	3S	U
100601	Child development	ElEd	305	3S	U
100601	Child care and developmnt	HmEc	321	3S	U
100602	Marriage and family rel	HmEc	325	3S	U
120299	Shakespeare	Engl	301	3S	U
120299	Shakespeare	Engl	302	3S	U
120299	Backgro of Am lit culture	Engl	403	3S	U
120299	Am novel before 1914	Engl	573	3S	U
120299	Am novel after 1914	Engl	574	3S	U

NCES No.	Course Title	Dept.	Course No.	Credits	Level
120299	Survey of English lit	Engl	308	3S	U
120299	Survey of English lit	Engl	309	3S	U
120299	Sur of Am lit to Civ War	Engl	303	3S	U
120299	Sur Am lit since Civ War	Engl	304	3S	U
120299	Faulkner's fiction	Engl	466	3S	U
120302	Hist of the English lang	Engl	406	3S	U
120305	Advanced English grammar	Engl	401	3S	U
120310	English composition	Engl	101	3S	L
120310	English composition	Engl	102	3S	L
120310	Advanced composition	Engl	321	3S	U
121105	Elementary German	Ger	101	3S	L
121105	Elementary German	Ger	102	3S	L
121105	Second-year German	Ger	201	3S	L
121105	Second-year German	Ger	202	3S	L
121641	Intro to Latin	Latin	101	3S	L
121641	Intro to Latin	Latin	102	3S	L
121641	Intermediate Latin	Latin	202	3S	L
121641	Latin review and reading	Latin	203	3S	L
121641	Latin review and reading	Latin	204	3S	L
122505	Elementary Spanish	Span	101	3S	L
122505	Elementary Spanish	Span	102	3S	L
122505	Second-year Spanish	Span	201	3S	L
122505	Second-year Spanish	Span	202	3S	L
140199	Children's literature I	LibSc	305	3S	U
140199	Children's literature II	LibSc	306	3S	U
150102	Descriptive astronomy	Astro	101	3S	L
150102	Descriptive astronomy	Astro	102	3S	L
150399	Survey of biology	Bio	102	3S	L
150399	Wildlife conservation	Bio	231	3S	L
150399	Survey of botany	Bio	211	3S	L
150499	Environmental chemistry	Chem	201	3S	L
150499	Environmental chemistry	Chem	202	3S	L
150799	Phys of sound and music	Phys	111	1S	L
150799	Phys of light color art	Phys	112	1S	L
150799	Descriptive oceanography	Phys	151	3S	L
150899	Physical science	Phys	105	3S	L
150899	Physical science	Phys	106	3S	L
160299	Math for elem teachers I	Math	245	3S	L
160299	Math for elem teachers II	Math	246	3S	L
160302	College algebra	Math	121	3S	L
160401	Unif calc & analyt geom	Math	261	3S	L
160401	Unif calc & analyt geom	Math	262	3S	L
160401	Unif calc & analyt geom	Math	263	3S	L
160401	Unif calc & analyt geom	Math	264	3S	L
160406	Elem differential equatns	Math	353	3S	U
160499	Elem math analysis I	Math	267	3S	L
160499	Elem math analysis II	Math	268	3S	L
160602	Trigonometry	Math	123	3S	L
180299	Recent ethical issues	Philo	515	3S	U
180499	History of philosophy	Philo	301	3S	U
180499	History of philosophy	Philo	302	3S	U
180599	Logic	Philo	203	3S	L
180609	Phil of religion	Philo	307	3S	U
180799	Phil of contemporary soc	Philo	102	3S	L
180999	World religions	Relig	205	3S	L
181299	New Testament thought	Relig	306	3S	U
190509	Personal and comm health	PhyEd	191	3S	L
190511	Safety education	PhyEd	507	3S	U
190599	First aid	PhyEd	203	3S	L
190599	Health and safety pub sch	PhyEd	505	3S	U
200804	Educational psychology	Educ	307	3S	U
220201	Principles of economics	Econ	201	3S	L
220201	Principles of economics	Econ	202	3S	L
220299	Economic fluctuations	Econ	509	3S	U
220402	Am diplomacy to 1898	Hist	315	3S	U
220402	Am diplomacy since 1898	Hist	316	3S	U
220409	Reform movement in the US	Hist	331	3S	U
220424	England to 1688	Hist	281	3S	L
220424	England since 1688	Hist	282	3S	L
220426	Modern Europe to 1660	Hist	151	3S	L
220426	Modern Europe since 1660	Hist	152	3S	L
220428	Miss. 1540 to the present	Hist	311	3S	U
220432	The US to 1877	Hist	201	3S	L
220432	The US since 1877	Hist	202	3S	L
220472	Women's movemnt in the US	Hist	332	3S	U
220599	Criminal investigation	PolSc	333	3S	U
220602	Criminology	Socio	431	3S	U

NCES No.	Course Title	Dept.	Course No.	Credits	Level
220604	Juvenile delinquency	Socio	333	3S	U
220615	The prison community	Socio	421	3S	U
Noncredit course					
121199	PhD German	Ger	95	NC	L

49 UNIVERSITY OF MISSOURI

Dr. Roger G. Young
Director
Center for Independent Study
University of Missouri
400 Hitt Street
Columbia, Missouri 65211
Phone: (314) 882-2491

Enrollment on a noncredit basis accepted in all credit courses. Gifted high school students are permitted to enroll in undergraduate courses for credit. Overseas enrollment is not encouraged; each case is judged on an individual basis. One feature of the Missouri program is unique among university correspondence programs—computer-assisted lesson service. More than half of the University of Missouri's independent study curriculum consists of courses that provide computer responses to lessons that students submit.

NCES No.	Course Title	Dept.	Course No.	Credits	Level
High school courses					
010499	Functional horsemanship	Agri	HU	H
0199	Agriculture	Agri	IU	H
030599	Art	Art	HF	H
040104	Bookkeeping	Acctg	IU	H
040299	Clerical practice	Bus	HF	H
041004	Retail merchandising	Bus	HU	H
041099	Retailing	Bus	HU	H
0499	General business	Bus	IU	H
0499	Salesmanship	Bus	IU	H
0499	You & the world of work	Bus	HF	H
0506	Intro to journalism	Engl	HF	H
070703	Career planning	HmEc	HU	H
0810	General drafting	IndAr	1U	H
0810	Technical drafting	IndAr	HU	H
100202	Consumer econ: econ envir	Bus	HF	H
100202	Econ: making decisions	Bus	HF	H
100601	Chld dev concep to adoles	HmEc	HF	H
100602	Marriage & parenting	HmEc	HF	H
100604	Personal adj & dating	HmEc	HF	H
100604	Project self-discovery	HmEc	HF	H
120305	Ninth-grade English	Engl	IU	H
120305	Tenth-grade English	Engl	IU	H
120305	Eleventh-grade English	Engl	IU	H
120305	Twelfth-grade English	Engl	IU	H
120307	Afro-Amer lit: early years	Engl	HF	H
120307	Amer envir through lit	Engl	HF	H
120307	American lit to 1890	Engl	HF	H
120307	Contemp Afro-Amer prose	Engl	HF	H
120307	Eng lit thru Shakespeare	Engl	HF	H
120307	Man and myth	Engl	HF	H
120307	Readings in short story	Engl	HF	H
120307	Science fiction	Engl	HF	H
120307	Search for iden thru lit	Engl	HF	H
120307	Shrt stry reluc readers	Engl	HF	H
120307	Readings in Amer novel	Engl	HU	H
120307	Sci fiction reluct reader	Engl	HU	H
120308	Reading & study skills	Engl	HU	H
120399	Thnkng clear: mkng sense	Engl	HF	H
121005	French I	Lang	1U	H
122505	Spanish I	Lang	1U	H
1302	Consumer & business law	Law	HU	H
1399	You and the law	Law	HF	H
1503	Survey of living world	Bio	HF	H
1503	Spec topics life science	Bio	HF	H
150401	Chemistry	Chem	IU	H
150599	Environmental geology	Geol	HF	H
150599	Physical geology	Geol	HU	H
150599	Underground world caves	Sci	HU	H
1507	Physics	Phys	IU	H
150704	AC electronics	Phys	HF	H
150704	DC electronics	Phys	HF	H
1599	Conserv of nat resources	EnvSc	HF	H

NCES No.	Course Title	Dept.	Course No.	Credits	Level
160301	General mathematics	Math		1U	H
160302	Elementary algebra I	Math		IU	H
160399	Modern algebra II & trig	Math		IU	H
160601	Modern math: plane geom	Math		1U	H
161201	Business mathematics	Math		HU	H
181002	World religions	Relig		HF	H
190599	Health and hygiene	HSci		HF	H
1906	Driver education	DriEd		HF	H
2001	Psych: found human behavr	Psych		HU	H
2001	Personal & social psych	Psych		HU	H
200508	Youth in conflict	Psych		HU	H
2201	Anthropology	Anthr		HF	H
220109	Indians of Missouri	Anthr		HF	H
2203	Geography	Geog		HF	H
220428	Missouri history	Hist		HF	H
220432	Amer history to 1865	Hist		HF	H
220432	Amer history since 1865	Hist		HF	H
220433	World history to 1814	Hist		HF	H
220433	World history since 1814	Hist		HF	H
220450	Ancient history	Hist		HF	H
220452	Medieval history	Hist		HF	H
220453	Modern history	Hist		IU	H
220470	Black Amer experience	Hist		HF	H
220499	Immigrants' experience	Hist		HF	H
220501	American government	PolSc		HF	H
220505	International relations	PolSc		HF	H
220509	Civics: natl/state/local	PolSc		HU	H
220509	Civics: polit proc/prob	PolSc		HU	H
2206	Sociology	Socio		HF	H
2299	Contemporary world	SoSci		HF	H

College courses

NCES No.	Course Title	Dept.	Course No.	Credits	Level
010103	Gen agricultural mktng	AgEcn	220	3S	U
010301	Planning farm buildings	AgEng	103	3S	L
0105	Basic home horticulture	Hort	20	3S	L
030302	Theory (written)	Music	21	2S	L
040101	Accounting I	Acctg	36	3S	L
040111	Accounting II	Acctg	37	3S	L
040306	Investments	Finan	333	3S	B
040311	Principles of finance	Finan	123	3S	L
040904	Fundamentals of mgmt	Mgmt	202	3S	U
041001	Principles of marketing	Mktg	204	3S	U
0411	Personnel management	Mgmt	310	3S	B
050606	Hist & prin of journalism	Jrnl	100	3S	L
050699	High school journalism	Jrnl	380	2S	B
070199	Hist found Amer education	Educ	B351	3S	B
070516	Algebra for elem teachers	Math	7	3S	L
070516	Geometry for el teachers	Math	8	3S	L
070516	Teaching math elem school	Educ	T267	2S	U
070519	Org & adm of PE programs	Educ	H199	2S	L
070610	Teaching of reading	Educ	T315	3S	B
0708	Survey of special educ	Educ	L101	2S	L
0708	Psych ed exceptionl indiv	Educ	313	3S	B
070806	Intro mental retardation	Educ	311	3S	B
071101	Intro ed measure & eval	Educ	A240	2S	U
071102	Educational statistics I	Educ	R370	3S	B
0810	Engr draw & descrip geom	EngrT	10	3S	L
081103	Mech of materials	EngrM	110	3S	L
081104	Engr mech: dynamics	EngrM	150	2S	L
081104	Engr mech: dynamics	EngrM	160	3S	L
090601	Problems: hospital mgmt	HSMgt	300	3S	B
090602	Am health-care system	HSMgt	210HM	3S	U
090699	Health-planning principls	HSMgt	250HM	3S	U
090699	Prin health-care finance	HSMgt	270HM	3S	U
090699	Long-term-care admin	HSMgt	325	3S	B
090699	Econ of health care	HSMgt	340HM	3S	B
105327	Insects in environment	Entom	101	3S	L
120299	Classical mythology	Class	60	3S	L
120299	Intro to folklore	Engl	285	3S	U
120307	Literary types	Engl	12	3S	L
120307	Afro-American literature	Engl	104	3S	L
120307	Intro to Shakespeare	Engl	135	3S	L
120307	American literature	Engl	175	3S	L
120307	Gothic fiction	Engl	101	3S	L
120307	Women's exp modern fictn	Engl	101	3S	L
120307	Eng lit: beging to 1784	Engl	201	3S	U
120310	Composition	Engl	1	3S	L
120310	Creative wrtng: short stry	Engl	50	3S	L
120310	Technical writing	Engl	161	3S	L
120310	Exposition	Engl	60	3S	L

NCES No.	Course Title	Dept.	Course No.	Credits	Level
120310	Creative writing: poetry	Engl	70	3S	L
121005	Elementary French I	Frnch	1	5S	L
121005	Elementary French II	Frnch	2	5S	L
121008	French reading	Frnch	103	3S	L
122505	Elementary Spanish I	Span	1	5S	L
122505	Elementary Spanish II	Span	2	5S	L
122508	Spanish reading	Span	103	3S	L
150202	Introductory meteorology	AtmSc	50	3S	L
150599	Physical geology	Geol	2	4S	L
150599	Man and his earth	Geol	101	3S	L
160199	Basic concepts mod math	Math	12	3S	L
160302	Basic algebra	Math	3	2S	L
160302	College algebra	Math	10	3S	L
160401	Elements of calculus	Math	61	3S	L
160401	Analytic geom & calculus	Math	80	5S	L
160401	Calculus II	Math	175	5S	L
160401	Calculus III	Math	201	4S	U
160401	Calc for soc & nat sci I	Math	207	3S	U
160406	Differential equations	Math	304	3S	B
160408	Finite mathematics	Math	60	3S	L
160602	Trigonometry	Math	9	2S	L
160802	Elementary statistics	Stat	31	3S	L
161101	Business mathematics	Math	4	3S	L
180501	Logic	Philo	15	3S	L
1808	General intro to philo	Philo	1	3S	L
180902	Life & teachings of Jesus	Relig	122	3S	L
181002	Major world religions	Relig	130	3S	L
181202	Intro to the Old Testmnt	Relig	110	3S	L
181202	Intro to the New Testmnt	Relig	121	3S	L
181202	Life & letters of Paul	Relig	124	3S	L
190502	Community health	FCMed	25	2S	L
1907	Intro to leisure studies	RecPk	10	3S	L
190701	Intro leisure serv mgmt	RecPk	151	3S	L
200199	General psychology	Psych	1	3S	L
200501	Abnormal psychology	Psych	180	3S	L/U
200504	Psych & ed devel of child	Educ	A207	3S	U
200599	Child psychology	Psych	170	3S	L
200599	Adolescent psychology	Psych	271	3S	U
200799	Social psychology	Psych	260	3S	U
200804	Educational psychology	Educ	A102	2S	L
2101	Intro to public admin	PolSc	310	3S	B
2201	General anthropology	Anthr	1	3S	L
220201	Fundamentals of econ I	Econ	1	3S	L
220302	Economic geography	Geog	100	3S	L
220305	Physical geography 1	Geog	111	3S	L
220306	Reg & nations of world I	Geog	1	3S	L
220306	Reg & nations of world II	Geog	2	3S	L
220402	Am foreign pol snce WW II	Hist	173	3S	L
220431	History of the USSR	Hist	355C	3S	B
220432	Foundations Western civ	Hist	1	4S	L
220432	American history to 1865	Hist	3	3S	L
220432	American hist since 1865	Hist	4	3S	L
220450	Roman culture	Class	116	3S	L
220499	History of the Old South	Hist	327	3S	B
220499	Period of Amer Revolution	Hist	364	3S	B
220499	Contemporary Europe	Hist	231	3S	U
220501	American government	PolSc	1	3S	L
220599	Intro to political sci	PolSc	11	3S	L
220601	Collective behavior	Socio	215	3S	B
220605	The family	Socio	214	3S	U
220606	Intro to sociology	Socio	1	3S	L
220608	Rural sociology	RuSoc	1	3S	L
220610	Social deviance	Socio	50	3S	L
220615	Ethn & racial minorities	Socio	127	3S	L
220615	Aging in American society	Socio	322	3S	B

Graduate courses

NCES No.	Course Title	Dept.	Course No.	Credits	Level
070309	Prog devlpmt & evaluation	ExtEd	403	3S	G
0704	Secondary school curric	Educ	T445	3S	G
070404	Fund of ext tchng of adul	ExtEd	406	3S	G
070610	Issues & trends reading	Educ	T420	3S	G
200508	Psych of elem sch child	Educ	A407	3S	G
220432	Special topics Amer hist	Hist	400	3S	G

Noncredit courses

NCES No.	Course Title	Dept.	Course No.	Credits	Level
080799	City and county planning	CivEg		NC	
100310	Science in food	HmEc		NC	
100399	Your family's food	HmEc		NC	
100402	Today's homemaker	HmEc		NC	
100601	Those impor preschool yrs	HmEc		NC	
210303	Hazardous materials	Sfty		NC	L
210503	So you're a park bd memb	PubAd		NC	
220502	Citizenship	PolSc		NC	

㊿ UNIVERSITY OF NEBRASKA–LINCOLN

Mr. Monty E. McMahon
Director, Independent Study
Division of Continuing Studies
University of Nebraska–Lincoln
269 Nebraska Center for Continuing Education
33rd and Holdrege
Lincoln, Nebraska 68583-0900
Phone: (402) 472-1926

Enrollment on a noncredit basis accepted in all credit courses. Gifted high school students are permitted to enroll in undergraduate courses for credit. Overseas enrollment accepted. The independent study high school program is accredited by the State Department of Education and the North Central Association of Colleges and Schools and is authorized to grant a fully accredited high school diploma. A special diploma program for adults (18 years or older) is also available.

NCES No.	Course Title	Dept.	Course No.	Credits	Level
	High school courses				
010599	Horticulture	Agri	009A	HF	H
010599	Horticulture	Agri	011A	HF	H
0199	General agriculture	Agri	001A	HF	H
0199	General agriculture	Agri	002A	HF	H
030302	Beginning piano	Music	001A	HF	H
030302	Intermediate piano	Music	003A	HF	H
030302	Harmony	Music	007A	HF	H
030302	Music theory	Music	005N	HF	H
030399	History & apprec of music	Music	011A	HF	H
040101	Beginning accounting	BusEd	023A	HF	H
040101	Beginning accounting	BusEd	024A	HF	H
040205	Beginning shorthand	BusEd	016A	HF	H
040205	Beginning shorthand	BusEd	015N	HF	H
040205	Beginning shorthand	BusEd	016N	HF	H
040206	Secretarial practice	BusEd	017A	HF	H
040207	Typing with one hand	BusEd	001A	HF	H
040207	Beginning typing	BusEd	003A	HF	H
040207	Beginning typing	BusEd	004A	HF	H
040207	Advanced typing	BusEd	005A	HF	H
040207	Advanced typing	BusEd	006A	HF	H
040299	Office proced & practice	BusEd	013A	HF	H
040299	Office proced & practice	BusEd	014A	HF	H
040699	Business English	BusEd	011A	HF	H
0499	General business	BusEd	021A	HF	H
0499	General business	BusEd	022A	HF	H
050608	Journalism	Engl	025A	HF	H
0799	Effective methds of study	StSki	001A	HF	H
080199	The aerospace age	Aero	001A	HF	H
090199	Health science	Sci	001A	HF	H
090199	Health science	Sci	002A	HF	H
100104	Clothing construction	HmEc	007N	HF	H
100699	Persl adju, marriage, fam	HmEc	011A	HF	H
1099	Etiquette	HmEc	001A	HF	H
1099	General homemaking	HmEc	003A	HF	H
1099	General homemaking	HmEc	004A	HF	H
110412	Small-engine care/operatn	IndEd	005A	HF	H
110412	Small-engine maint/repair	IndEd	006A	HF	H
110413	Automotive mechanics	IndEd	007A	HF	H
110413	Automotive mechanics	IndEd	008X	HF	H
110413	Automotive mechanics	IndEd	007A	HF	H
110503	Beg drawing and painting	Art	001A	HF	H
110503	Advanced drawing	Art	007A	HF	H
110503	Advanced watercolor	Art	009A	HF	H
110504	Photography	Photo	001N	HF	H
1199	General shop	IndEd	001A	HF	H
1199	General shop	IndEd	002A	HF	H
120305	Basic English 1	Engl	001N	HF	H
120305	Basic English 2	Engl	002N	HF	H
120307	The short story	Engl	009A	HF	H
120307	American short story	Engl	011A	HF	H
120307	The novel	Engl	015A	HF	H
120307	Poetry	Engl	021A	HF	H
120307	Fiction and drama	Engl	052A	HF	H
120308	Improvg reading skills	Engl	003A	HF	H
120308	Improvg reading skills	Engl	004A	HF	H
120308	Guided reading	Engl	005A	QT	H
120308	Guided reading	Engl	006A	QT	H
120308	Guided reading	Engl	007A	HF	H
120310	Composition	Engl	023A	HF	H
120399	Tenth-grade English	Engl	033A	HF	H
120399	Tenth-grade English	Engl	034A	HF	H
120399	Eleventh-grade English	Engl	035A	HF	H
120399	Eleventh-grade English	Engl	036A	HF	H
120399	Twelfth-grade English	Engl	037A	HF	H
120399	Twelfth-grade English	Engl	038A	HF	H
120399	Poetry analysis, comp	Engl	051A	HF	H
120399	Ninth-grade English	Engl	031N	HF	H
120399	Ninth-grade English	Engl	032N	HF	H
120399	Tenth-grade English	Engl	033N	HF	H
120399	Tenth-grade English	Engl	034N	HF	H
1210	First-year French	Lang	F001A	HF	H
1210	First-year French	Lang	F002A	HF	H
1210	Second-year French	Lang	F003A	HF	H
1210	Second-year French	Lang	F004A	HF	H
1210	First-year French	Lang	001N	HF	H
1211	First-year German	Lang	G001A	HF	H
1211	First-year German	Lang	G002A	HF	H
1211	Second-year German	Lang	G003A	HF	H
1211	Second-year German	Lang	G004A	HF	H
1216	First-year Latin	Lang	L001A	HF	H
1216	First-year Latin	Lang	L002A	HF	H
1216	Second-year Latin	Lang	L003A	HF	H
1216	Second-year Latin	Lang	L004A	HF	H
1216	Third-year Latin	Lang	L005A	HF	H
1216	Third-year Latin	Lang	L006A	HF	H
1225	Second-year Spanish	Lang	S003A	HF	H
1225	Second-year Spanish	Lang	S003X	HF	H
1225	Second-year Spanish	Lang	S004X	HF	H
1225	First-year Spanish	Lang	001N	HF	H
1225	First-year Spanish	Lang	002N	HF	H
130799	Business law	BusEd	025A	HF	H
150399	Basic biology	Sci	015A	HF	H
150399	Basic biology	Sci	016A	HF	H
150399	Advanced biology	Sci	019A	HF	H
150399	Advanced biology	Sci	020A	HF	H
150401	Chemistry	Sci	031A	HF	H
150401	Chemistry	Sci	032A	HF	H
150401	Chemistry	Sci	032A	HF	H
150799	Physics	Sci	035A	HF	H
150799	Physics	Sci	036A	HF	H
1508	General science	Sci	011A	HF	H
1508	General science	Sci	012A	HF	H
160301	Remedial arithmetic	Math	001A	HF	H
160302	Beginning algebra	Math	031A	HF	H
160302	Beginning algebra	Math	032A	HF	H
160302	Advanced algebra	Math	035A	HF	H
160302	Advanced algebra	Math	036A	HF	H
160399	General mathematics	Math	005A	HF	H
160399	General mathematics	Math	006A	HF	H
160399	Precalculus	Math	041A	HF	H
160399	Precalculus	Math	042A	HF	H
160601	Geometry	Math	034A	HF	H
160601	Solid geometry	Math	039A	HF	H
160601	Geometry	Math	033R	HF	H
160601	Geometry	Math	033N	HF	H
160602	Trigonometry	Math	037N	HF	H
160603	Analytic geom & calculus	Math	051A	HF	H
160603	Analytic geom & calculus	Math	052A	HF	H
161299	Business & consumer math	Math	009X	HF	H
161299	Business & consumer math	Math	010X	HF	H
1699	The slide rule	Math	013A	TN	H
190699	Driver education	Dr	001A	HF	H
200199	Psychology	SocSt	007N	HF	H
220201	Economics	BusEd	027N	HF	H
220208	Consumer education	BusEd	019A	HF	H
220399	World geography	SocSt	021A	HF	H
220399	World geography	SocSt	022A	HF	H
220432	American history	SocSt	033N	HF	H
220432	American history	SocSt	034N	HF	H
220433	World history	SocSt	031A	HF	H
220433	World history	SocSt	032A	HF	H
220501	American government	SocSt	035N	HF	H
220501	American government	SocSt	036N	HF	H
220502	Civics	SocSt	001N	HF	H
220606	Sociology	SocSt	003N	HF	H
2299	Modern problems	SocSt	037A	HF	H
	College courses				
030599	Intro art history & crit	Art	167X	3S	L
040101	Intermediate accounting	Acctg	313X	3S	U
040101	Introductory accounting	Acctg	201X	3S	L
040101	Introductory accounting	Acctg	202X	3S	L
040111	Managerial accounting	Acctg	308X	3S	U
040207	Elementary typewriting	BusEd	115X	1S	L

NCES No.	Course Title	Dept.	Course No.	Credits	Level
040207	Intermediate typewriting	BusEd	116X	3S	L
040311	Finance	Fin	361X	3S	U
040708	Principles of insurance	Econ	307X	3S	U
040999	Administrative policy	Mgmt	435X	3S	B
041103	Human resources mgmt	Mgmt	360X	3S	U
041199	Personnel administration	Mgmt	361X	3S	U
041202	Elem quantitative methods	Econ	245X	3S	L
041299	Ele quantitative methods	Mgmt	245X	3S	L
041301	Real estate appraisal	RlEs	441X	3S	U
041303	Real estate prin & prac	Fin	382X	3S	U
041303	Real est princ & practice	RlEs	382X	3S	U
041304	Real estate management	RlEs	345X	3S	U
041306	Real estate finance	Fin	482X	3S	U
041306	Real estate finance	RlEs	482X	3S	U
041307	Real estate investments	RlEs	439X	3S	U
050401	Adv broadcast writing	Jrnl	407X	3S	U
050608	Newswriting, reporting	Jrnl	282X	3S	L
070199	Intro philosophy educ	EdPSF	331X	3S	U
070404	Teaching social studies	CrIns	307X	3S	U
070613	Driver education 1	CrIns	345X	3S	U
0799	Ed psych & measurements	EdPsy	362X	3S	U
081104	Engineering statics	EnMec	223X	3S	L
081104	Mechanics elastic bodies	EnMec	325X	3S	U
081503	Intro industrial dcs mdls	IndEg	206X	3S	U
090504	Emergency health care	HPE&R	170X	3S	L
090999	Elements health promotion	HPE&R	101X	3S	L
100313	Introduction to nutrition	HNFSM	151X	3S	L
120299	Composition & short story	Engl	103X	3S	L
120307	Genre survey	Engl	100X	3S	L
120307	Genre survey: novel, story	Engl	200AX	3S	L
120307	Genre surv: poetry, drama	Engl	200BX	3S	L
120307	Novel 1900 to present	Engl	205BX	3S	L
120307	Shakespeare	Engl	230AX	3S	L
120310	Expository writing	Engl	254X	3S	L
120310	Business writing	Engl	255X	3S	L
120310	Special topics in writing	Engl	258X	2S	L
1220	Beginning Russian	Rus	101X	5S	L
1220	Beginning Russian	Rus	102X	5S	L
1225	Second-year Spanish	Span	201X	3S	L
1225	Second-year Spanish	Span	202X	3S	L
1299	Scientific Greek & Latin	Clas	116X	2S	L
150304	Introductory ecology	LfSci	220X	3S	L
150327	Beekeeping	Entom	109X	2S	L
150799	Gen phys for life sci	Phys	141X	4S	L
150799	Gen phys for life sci	Phys	142X	4S	L
150799	General physics	Phys	211X	4S	L
150799	General physics	Phys	212X	4S	L
160302	Algebra	Math	100X	2S	L
160302	Algebra	Math	101X	2S	L
160602	Trigonometry	Math	102X	2S	L
160603	Analytic geometry	Math	17X	3S	L
160603	Analyt geom & calculus I	Math	106X	5S	L
160603	Analyt geom & calculus II	Math	107X	5S	L
160603	Analyt geom & calculus III	Math	208X	5S	L
180599	Elementary logic	Philo	110X	3S	L
181202	Philo of Old Testament	Philo	251X	3S	L
181202	Philo of New Testament	Philo	252X	3S	L
190105	Intro to phys education	HPE&R	175X	3S	L
190311	Coaching of basketball	HPE&R	311X	2S	U
1906	Education for safety	HPE&R	340X	3S	U
190699	Driver education I	HPE&R	345X	3S	U
200299	Biopsychology	Psych	273X	3S	L
200504	Human dev and the family	HuDev	160X	3S	L
200504	Child dev and guidance	HuDev	270X	3S	L
200508	Psychology of women	Psych	421X	3S	U
200509	Psychology of personality	Psych	287X	3S	L
200599	Elementary psychology I	Psych	170X	3S	L
200599	Elementary psychology II	Psych	171X	3S	L
200599	Aspects of alcoholism	Psych	222X	3S	L
220199	General anthropology	Anthr	111X	3S	L
220201	Principles of economics	Econ	211X	3S	L
220201	Principles of economics	Econ	212X	3S	L
220299	Statistics	Econ	215X	3S	L
220301	Intro human geography	Geog	140X	3S	U
220302	Intro economic geography	Geog	120X	3S	L
220306	Geography of US	Geog	271X	3S	L
220306	Geography of Africa	Geog	379X	3S	U
220426	History early mod Europe	Hist	212X	3S	L
220426	History of modern Europe	Hist	101X	3S	L

NCES No.	Course Title	Dept.	Course No.	Credits	Level
220428	History of Nebraska	Hist	359X	3S	U
220432	American history to 1877	Hist	201X	3S	L
220432	Amer history aft 1877	Hist	202X	3S	L
220450	History of ancient world	Hist	210X	3S	L
220452	History of Middle Ages	Hist	211X	3S	L
220501	Amer natl and state govt	PolSc	100X	3S	L
220507	Political parties	PolSc	230X	3S	L
220599	Contemporary foreign govt	PolSc	104X	3S	L
220599	Contemporary foreign govt	PolSc	104X	3S	L
220602	Delinquency and crime	Socio	209X	3S	L
220605	Marriage and the family	Socio	225X	3S	L
220606	Intro to sociology	Socio	153X	3S	L
220608	Rural sociology	AgEco	276X	3S	L
220608	Rural sociology	Socio	241X	3S	L
220699	Nationality, race relatns	Socio	217X	3S	L
Noncredit courses					
010399	Irrigation theory-prac	Irr	1X	NC	L
110412	Small-engine care/operatn	IndEd	005A	NC	L
110412	Small-engine maint/repair	IndEd	006A	NC	L
110413	Automotive mechanics	IndEd	007A	NC	L
110504	Photography	Photo	001N	NC	L
120299	Nebraska folklore	Folk	1X	NC	L
120305	Basic English 1	Engl	001N	NC	L
120305	Basic English 2	Engl	002N	NC	L
160302	Algebra	Math	90X	NC	L
210302	Fire and arson invest	ArsIn	1X	NC	L
210304	Orient law enforcement	PoSci	1X	NC	L
210304	Intro to law enforcement	PoSci	2X	NC	L
210305	Fundamentals of electrcty	ElIns	1X	NC	L
210305	Fundamentals of electrcty	ElIns	2X	NC	L
210305	Inspection procedures	ElIns	3X	NC	L
210305	Administrative policy	ElIns	6X	NC	L
210399	Field inspec & plan rview	BlgIn	1X	NC	L

(51) UNIVERSITY OF NEVADA RENO

Ms. Catherine D. Sanders
Correspondence Studies Assistant
Independent Study Department, Continuing Education
University of Nevada Reno
Room 333, College Inn
Reno, Nevada 89557
Phone: (702) 784-4652

Gifted high school students are permitted to enroll in undergraduate courses for credit. Overseas enrollment accepted. Gifted high school students may take courses if accepted into the UNR Superior Student Program.

NCES No.	Course Title	Dept.	Course No.	Credits	Level
College courses					
040101	Introductory accounting I	Acctg	C201	3S	L
040101	Introduct accounting II	Acctg	C202	3S	L
040301	Corporation finance	ManSc	C365	3S	U
040903	Organzatn & interpers beh	ManSc	C323	3S	U
040999	Operations management	ManSc	C352	3S	U
041001	Marketing principles	ManSc	C310	3S	U
041199	Personnel administration	ManSc	C367	3S	U
0499	Orientation to hotel ind	HoA	C101	3S	L
050199	Principles of advertising	Jrnl	C356	2S	U
050605	The feature article	Jrnl	C468	2S	U
0509	Pub reltns, prin, pract	Jrnl	C301	2S	U
070199	Legal foundations of educ	EdFM	C210	2S	U
070404	Science tchg & reasng dev	C&I	C481	3S	U
070404	Five teaching skills	C&I	C481	1S	U
070599	Curriculum dev in env ed	C&I	C449	3S	U
070899	Ed of the exceptnl child	C&I	C310	3S	U
100313	Human nutrition	HmEc	C121	3S	L
100601	Child dev: prenatal to 6	HmEc	C131	3S	U
100699	Chld & fmls: multi-eth soc	HmEc	C438	3S	U
120307	Introduction to the novel	Eng	C247	3S	L
120399	Vocabulary and meaning	Eng	C181	2S	L
120399	Introduction to drama	Eng	C253	2S	L
120399	Introduction to poetry	Eng	C261	2S	L
121099	Elementary French I	Frnch	C101	4S	L
121199	Second-year German I	Ger	C203	3S	L
121199	Second-year German II	Ger	C204	3S	L
1214	Elementary Italian I	Ital	C101	4S	L
1214	Elementary Italian II	Ital	C102	4S	L

NCES No.	Course Title	Dept.	Course No.	Credits	Level
122507	Survey of Spanish lit	Span	C357	3S	U
122599	Elementary Spanish I	Span	C101	4S	L
122599	Elementary Spanish II	Span	C102	4S	L
150323	General zoology	Bio	C160	3S	L
150399	General biology	Bio	C103	3S	L
160302	Intermediate algebra	Math	C101	2S	L
160399	College algebra	Math	C110	3S	L
160602	Plane trigonometry	Math	C102	2S	L
160603	Analytic geometry	Math	C140	3S	L
161101	Mathematics of finance	Math	C210	3S	L
1699	Elementary school math I	Math	C173	3S	L
1699	Elementary school math II	Math	C174	3S	L
1699	Elements of calculus	Math	C265	3S	L
200501	Abnormal psychology	Psych	C441	3S	U
200509	Personality	Psych	C435	3S	U
200599	Psychology of adolescence	Psych	C231	3S	L
200599	Child psychology	Psych	C233	3S	L
200804	Educational psychology	Psych	C321	3S	U
2099	General psychology	Psych	C101	3S	L
220101	Introdctn to archaeology	Anthr	C202	3S	L
220199	Introdctn to anthropology	Anthr	C101	3S	L
220199	Intr to hum evol & prehis	Anthr	C102	3S	L
220199	Ethn groups in cont socts	Anthr	C205	3S	L
220299	Princpls of statistics I	Econ	C261	3S	L
220299	Princpls of statistics II	Econ	C262	3S	L
220299	Prin of microeconomics	Econ	C102	3S	L
220299	Prin of macroeconomics	Econ	C101	3S	L
220301	Intro to cultural geog	Geog	C106	3S	L
220424	England & the British Emp	Hist	C393	3S	U
220424	England & the Brit Emp II	Hist	C394	3S	U
220426	European civilization	Hist	C105	3S	L
220426	European civilization	Hist	C106	3S	L
220428	Nevada history	Hist	C217	3S	L
220501	Prin of Amer const govt	PolSc	C103	3S	L
220511	Constitution of Nevada	PolSc	C100	1S	L
	Noncredit courses				
161202	Fund of the metric system	Math	CC	NC	D
220502	Citizenship for new Amer	PolSc	CA	NC	D

(52) UNIVERSITY OF NEW MEXICO

Ms. Mary W. Bullock
Division Registrar
Continuing Education and Community Services
University of New Mexico
805 Yale Boulevard, N.E.
Albuquerque, New Mexico 87131
Phone: (505) 277-2105

Overseas enrollment accepted.

NCES No.	Course Title	Dept.	Course No.	Credits	Level
	College courses				
040101	Intro to accounting	ASM	202	3S	L
040601	Business communications	BusEd	265	3S	L
0701	Philosophies of educ	EdFdn	415	3S	U
0701	Sociology of education	EdFdn	421	3S	U
070199	Foundations of education	EdFdn	290	3S	L
070199	History of American educ	EdFdn	411	3S	U
070512	Tchng of reading elem sch	ElEd	331	3S	U
070516	Math for elem sch tchrs I	Math	111	3S	L
070516	Math for elem sch tchs II	Math	112	3S	L
0809	Circ anal I–int el eng I	Engr	203	3S	L
090255	Intro to concepts in nurs	Nurs	225	4S	L
090255	Nurs pathophysiology I	Nurs	239	3S	L
090255	Nurs pathophysiology II	Nurs	240	3S	L
090255	Body fluid & electrolytes	Nurs	408	3S	U
090799	Personal & comm health	HEd	171	3S	L
120302	History of Engl language	Engl	445	3S	U
120307	Children's literature	ElEd	441	3S	U
120307	Survey of early Engl lit	Engl	294	3S	L
120307	Survey of later Engl lit	Engl	295	3S	L
120307	American literature	Engl	296	3S	L
120310	Writing standard English	Engl	100	3S	L
120310	Expository writing	Engl	220	3S	L
120310	Creative writing: fiction	Engl	221	3S	L
120399	Writing, reading in expos	Engl	101	3S	L
120399	Writing, reading lit	Engl	102	3S	L
1225	Elementary Spanish	Span	101	4S	L
1225	Elementary Spanish	Span	102	4S	L
1225	Intermediate Spanish	Span	201	3S	L
1225	Intermediate Spanish	Span	202	3S	L
122505	Advanced grammar & comp	Span	301	3S	U
122599	Advan comp & conversation	Span	302	3S	U
140199	Fundamentals of lib sci	LibSc	424	3S	U
140804	Classification & catalog	LibSc	427	3S	U
1501	Intro to astronomy	Astro	101	3S	L
150499	Inter organic & biochem	Chem	212	4S	L
150599	Physical geology	Geol	101	3S	L
160301	Arith for college studnts	Math	010	0S	L
160301	Basic algebra	Math	020	0S	L
160302	Intermediate algebra	Math	120	3S	L
160302	College algebra	Math	121	3S	L
160302	Algebra & trigonometry	Math	150	4S	L
160401	Calculus I	Math	162	4S	L
160401	Calculus II	Math	163	4S	L
160401	Calculus III	Math	264	4S	L
160499	Vector analysis	Math	311	3S	U
1607	Intro to prob & statistic	Math	102	3S	L
170102	Military hist of the US	Hist	375	3S	U
180405	Chinese philosophy	Phil	336	3S	U
180599	Introduction to logic	Phil	156	3S	L
1899	Intro to philoso problems	Phil	110	3S	L
200799	Social psychology	Psych	371	3S	U
2099	Introductory psychology	Psych	107	3S	L
220201	Principles & problems	Econ	200	3S	L
220201	Principles of economics	Econ	201	3S	L
220204	Money and banking	Econ	315	3S	U
2204	Survey of music history I	Music	161	3S	L
2204	Sur of music history II	Music	162	3S	L
2204	Spanish civilization	Span	345	3S	U
220428	History of New Mexico	Hist	360	3S	U
220428	Hist of SW, Span period	Hist	380	3S	U
220432	Hist of US to 1877	Hist	161	3S	L
220432	Hist of US since 1877	Hist	162	3S	L
220433	Western civilization	Hist	101	3S	L
220433	Western civilization	Hist	102	3S	L
220599	The political world	PolSc	110	3S	L
220599	American politics	PolSc	200	3S	L
220606	Introduction to sociology	Soc	101	3S	L
220613	Social problems: sel topcs	Soc	211	3S	L
220614	The urban community	Soc	351	3S	U

(53) UNIVERSITY OF NORTH CAROLINA

Mr. Norman H. Loewenthal
Assistant Director of Extension and Continuing Education for Independent Study
Independent Study by Extension
University of North Carolina
Abernethy Hall 002A
Chapel Hill, North Carolina 27514
Phone: (919) 962-1106

Enrollment on a noncredit basis accepted in all credit courses. Only in exceptional cases are gifted high school students permitted to enroll in undergraduate courses for credit. Overseas enrollment accepted. Statewide program; institutional code precedes course number. C—University of North Carolina at Chapel Hill; A—Appalachian State University; S—North Carolina State University; G—University of North Carolina at Greensboro; E—East Carolina University; U—University of North Carolina at Asheville; W—Winston-Salem University; Z—Elizabeth City State University.

NCES No.	Course Title	Dept.	Course No.	Credits	Level
	College courses				
010406	Poultry production	AnSci	S200	3S	L
020699	Gen environmental science	EnvSc	Z101	3S	L
030302	Fundamentals of music	Music	C21	3S	L
030399	Music appreciation	Music	C41	3S	L
030402	Intro to the theater	ThArt	C15	3S	L
030499	Playwriting	ThArt	C155	3S	L
030599	History of Western art	VisAr	C31	3S	L
030599	American art history surv	VisAr	S203	3S	L
040101	Acctg I prin of fin acctg	Acctg	S260	3S	L
040101	Accounting principles I	Acctg	C71	3S	L
040101	Intro to managerial acctg	Acctg	C72	3S	L

NCES No.	Course Title	Dept.	Course No.	Credits	Level
040601	Business English	Commu	C32	3S	L
040601	Business English	Commu	C32A	2S	L
040601	Wrtg for business & indus	Commu	E3880	3S	U
041004	Principles of marketing	Mktg	A3050	3S	U
041303	Real estate	RIEs	A3850	3S	U
0499	Business law	Bus	S307	3S	L
0602	Intro to computers & uses	CmpSc	S200	3S	L
070199	Educ in American society	Educ	C41	3S	L
070303	The secondary school	Educ	C99	3S	L
070401	Curriculum construction	Educ	C100	3S	U
070516	Math in the elem school	Educ	C156	3S	U
070516	Teaching math	Educ	U342	3S	U
070899	Intro to study exc child	Educ	C130	3S	U
0799	Educational psychology	Educ	C71	3S	L
0799	Org & mgmt youth club act	Educ	S457	3S	U
080901	Electrical circuits I	EEg	S211	3S	L
081304	Water supplies & treatmnt	EnEg	E3300	3S	U
090242	Long-term care for aged	HsHCA	C176	3S	U
100599	History of American homes	HmEc	E5385	3S	U
1199	Technology and change	Int	W4604	3S	U
120301	Social dialects	Engl	C192	3S	U
120305	Modern English grammar	Engl	C36	3S	L
120307	English literature	Engl	C22	3S	L
120307	American literature I	Engl	S265	3S	L
120307	Contemporary literature	Engl	C24	3S	L
120307	The English novel	Engl	C43	3S	L
120307	Shakespeare	Engl	C58	3S	L
120307	Amer lit: beginning-1865	Engl	C81	3S	L
120307	Eng & Amer drama 20th cen	Engl	C95	3S	L
120307	Survey of English lit	Engl	C20	3S	L
120310	English comp & rhetoric	Engl	C1	3S	L
120310	Composition & rhetoric	Engl	S111	3S	L
120310	English comp & rhetoric	Engl	C2	3S	L
120310	Composition & rhetoric	Engl	S112	3S	L
120310	Creative writing short st	Engl	C34F	3S	L
120310	Advanced short story wrtg	Engl	C35	3S	L
120310	Creative writing poetry	Engl	C35P	3S	L
120310	Intro to fiction	Engl	C23	3S	L
121009	Elementary French	Frnch	C1	4S	L
121107	German literature	Ger	C21	3S	L
121109	Elementary German	Ger	C1	3S	L
121109	Elementary German	Ger	C2	3S	L
121109	Intermediate German	Ger	C3	3S	L
121109	Intermediate German	Ger	C4	3S	L
121409	Elementary Italian	Ital	C1	3S	L
121409	Elementary Italian	Ital	C2	3S	L
121409	Intermediate Italian	Ital	C3	3S	L
121409	Intermediate Italian	Ital	C4	3S	L
121607	Selections of Latin poetr	Latin	C21	3S	L
121607	Latin poetry	Latin	C22	3S	L
121609	Elementary Latin	Latin	C1	3S	L
121609	Elementary Latin	Latin	C2	3S	L
121609	Intermediate Latin	Latin	C3	3S	L
121609	Intermediate Latin	Latin	C4	3S	L
122009	Elementary Russian	Rus	C1	3S	L
122009	Elementary Russian	Rus	C2	3S	L
122009	Intermediate Russian	Rus	C3	3S	L
122009	Intermediate Russian	Rus	C4	3S	L
122507	Modern Spanish literature	Span	C22	3S	L
122509	Intermediate Spanish	Span	C3	3S	L
122509	Intermediate Spanish	Span	C4	3S	L
1299	Medical word form & etym	Clas	C25	3S	L
150316	Plants and life	Bot	C10	3S	L
150401	General chemistry	Chem	C11	3S	L
150401	General chemistry	Chem	C21	3S	L
150401	Intro to chemical concept	Chem	C10	2S	L
150599	Physical geology	Geol	C11	4S	L
150599	General physical geology	Geol	S101	3S	L
1506	Surv coastal marine envmt	Ocean	E2125	3S	L
1507	General physics	Phys	S204	3S	L
1507	General physics	Phys	S207	3S	L
160302	Algebra & trigonometry	Math	S111	4S	L
160401	Analytic geom & calc I	Math	S102	4S	L
160401	Analytic geom & calc II	Math	S201	4S	L
160401	Analytic geom & calc III	Math	S202	4S	L
160601	Elem functions & coo geom	Math	C30	3S	L
160899	Intro stat for engineers	Stat	S361	3S	U
161101	Mathematics of finance	Math	S122	3S	L
170102	American military history	Hist	C77	3S	L
180399	Introduction to ethics	Philo	C22	3S	L
180502	Introd symbolic logic	Philo	C21	3S	L
181199	Religion in American life	Relig	S321	3S	U
181201	Intro to Old Testament	Relig	C21	3S	L
181202	Intro to New Testament	Relig	C22	3S	L
1899	Intro to philosophy	Philo	C20	3S	L
1899	Problems & types of philo	Philo	S205	3S	L
190303	Hist of American sport	Hist	S333	3S	U
200199	General psychology	Psych	C10	3S	L
200501	Abnormal psychology	Psych	G341	3S	U
220102	Cultural anthropology	Anthr	S252	3S	L
220199	Intro to anthropology	Anthr	C41	3S	L
220201	Economics I	Econ	S201	3S	L
220301	Cultural geography	Geog	G201	3S	L
220305	Physical geography	Geog	C38	3S	L
220305	Environmental phys geog	Geog	S208	3S	L
220306	Geography of Anglo-Amer	Geog	C157	3S	U
220402	Diplom hist of US to 1914	Hist	C143	3S	U
220402	Diplom hist of US to pres	Hist	C144	3S	U
220421	Amer history 1607-1877	Hist	C21	3S	L
220424	English history	Hist	C44	3S	L
220424	English history	Hist	C45	3S	L
220426	Modern European history	Hist	C48	3S	L
220426	Modern European history	Hist	C49	3S	L
220427	Latin Amer hist colo-revo	Hist	C46	3S	L
220427	Latin Amer hist natl per	Hist	C47	3S	L
220427	Latin Amer since 1826	Hist	S216	3S	L
220428	North Carolina 1548-1835	Hist	C161	3S	U
220428	North Carolina 1835-197-	Hist	C162	3S	U
220431	Russia & Sov Un 1861-pres	Hist	C31	3S	L
220432	Amer history 1865-1972	Hist	C22	3S	L
220432	United States 1845-1914	Hist	S243	3S	L
220450	Ancient history	Hist	C41	3S	L
220450	Ancient world to 180 AD	Hist	S207	3S	L
220499	Wes civ earlst—mid 17th c	Hist	C11	3S	L
220499	Western civ to present	Hist	C12	3S	L
220499	Western civ since 1400	Hist	S205	3S	L
2205	Urban politics	PolSc	W3370	3S	U
220501	Intro to govt in US	PolSc	C41	3S	L
220501	American politics	PolSc	U100	3S	L
220501	American govtl system	PolSc	S201	3S	L
220505	American foreign policy	PolSc	U280	3S	L
220511	State govt in the US	PolSc	C42	3S	L
220602	Criminology	Socio	S306	3S	U
220604	Juvenile delinquency	Socio	S425	3S	U
220605	Contemporary family life	Socio	S204	3S	L
220605	Family & society	Socio	C30	3S	L
220606	Principles of sociology	Socio	S202	3S	L
220606	Intro to sociology	Socio	C10	3S	L
220614	Urban sociology	Socio	S402	3S	U
220699	Black-white relations	Socio	C22	3S	L
220699	Population problems	Socio	C21	3S	L
220699	Human behavior	Socio	S301	3S	U
220699	Corrections & penology	Socio	G413	3S	U
220699	The black family	AfAmS	C65	3S	U
2299	Death & dying	Int	U395	3S	U
2299	Energy & man	UnStu	S495	3S	U

Noncredit courses

NCES No.	Course Title	Dept.	Course No.	Credits	Level
090101	Dental anatomy & physiol	DLT	C26	NC	V
090101	Prosthodontic techniques	DLT	C30A	NC	V
090101	Professionalism	DA	C1	NC	V
090101	Legal & ethical considtns	DA	C2	NC	V
090101	Office management	DA	C3	NC	V
090101	Anatomy & physiology	DA	C4	NC	V
090101	Dental anatomy	DA	C5	NC	V
090101	Pathology	DA	C6	NC	V
090101	Pharmacology	DA	C7	NC	V
090101	Microbiology & steriliztn	DA	C8	NC	V
090101	Med emerg in dentl office	DA	C9	NC	V
090101	Histology	DA	C10	NC	V
090101	Oral pathology	DA	C11	NC	V
090101	Communication	DA	C12	NC	V
090101	Psychology	DA	C13	NC	V
090101	Nutrition	DA	C14	NC	V
090101	Preventive dentistry	DA	C15	NC	V
090101	Dental radiology equipmt	DA	C16	NC	V
090101	Radiographic anat & biol	DA	C17	NC	V
090101	Dental radiograph techn	DA	C18	NC	V

NCES No.	Course Title	Dept.	Course No.	Credits	Level
090101	Restorative materials	DA	C19	NC	V
090101	Impressions & models	DA	C20	NC	V
090101	Dental casting	DA	C21	NC	V
090101	Denture prosthetics	DA	C22	NC	V
090101	Dental practice orientatn	DA	C23	NC	V
090101	Dental surgery	DA	C24	NC	V
090101	Restorative dentistry	DA	C25	NC	V
090101	Pedodontics/orthodontics	DA	C26	NC	V
090101	Fundamentals in practice	DA	C27	NC	V
090101	Dental surgery practice	DA	C28	NC	V
090101	Restorative dent practice	DA	C29	NC	V
090101	Pedodont & orthodont prac	DA	C30	NC	V
090242	Aging in America	Geron		NC	V
120310	English composition	Engl	CO	NC	D
160302	Contemporary algebra	Math	CR	NC	D
160601	Plane geometry	Math	CA	NC	D
220502	Citizenship	Citz	C1	NC	D

(54) UNIVERSITY OF NORTH DAKOTA

Ms. Rebecca C. Monley
Director
Department of Correspondence Study, Outreach Programs
University of North Dakota
Box 8277, University Station
Grand Forks, North Dakota 58202
Phone: (701) 777-3044

Enrollment on a noncredit basis accepted in all credit courses. Only in exceptional cases are gifted high school students permitted to enroll in undergraduate courses for credit. No overseas enrollment accepted. Students in high school who have completed 14 units may enroll in undergraduate courses for credit with the approval of their principal.

NCES No.	Course Title	Dept.	Course No.	Credits	Level
	College courses				
030599	Art history survey	VisAr	210	3S	L
030599	American art & architect	VisAr	315	3S	U
040101	Elements of accounting	Acctg	102	3S	L
040101	Elements of accounting	Acctg	201	3S	L
040106	Cost accounting	Acctg	208	2S	L
040203	Records management	BVEd	210	3S	L
040301	Corporation finance	Mgmt	303	3S	U
040904	Principles of management	Mgmt	300	3S	U
040999	Production management	Mgmt	301	3S	U
041001	Principles of marketing	Mktg	301	3S	U
041005	Retailing	Mktg	303	3S	U
041099	Cooperative marketing	Mktg	390	2S	U
041099	Salesmanship	Mktg	204	2S	L
041099	Marketing information	Mktg	400	3S	U
041099	Consumer & market behav	Mktg	401	3S	U
0411	Personnel management	Mgmt	302	3S	U
041301	Real estate appraisal	Mktg	329	3S	U
041303	Principles of real estate	Mktg	324	3S	U
041306	Real estate finance	Mktg	326	3S	U
0501	Advertising and sales pro	Mktg	302	3S	U
050608	Reporting	Jrnl	201	3S	L
061103	Introduction to computers	CmpSc	101	2S	L
070803	Career/voc ed of excep ch	Educ	421	3S	U
070899	Prescriptive teaching	Educ	318	3S	U
0810	Engineering graphics	Graph	101	2S	L
0810	Descriptive geometry	Graph	102	2S	L
120305	Modern grammar	Engl	309	3S	U
120307	Survey of English lit	EngLL	301	2S	U
120307	Survey of English lit	EngLL	302	3S	U
120307	Survey of American lit	EngLL	303	3S	U
120307	Survey of American lit	EngLL	304	3S	U
120307	Shakespeare	EngLL	315	3S	U
120307	Shakespeare	EngLL	316	3S	U
120308	Introduction to fiction	EngLL	211	2S	L
120308	Introduction to poetry	EngLL	213	2S	L
120308	Introduction to drama	EngLL	217	2S	L
120310	Composition I	Engl	101	3S	L
120310	Composition II	Engl	102	3S	L
120310	Advanced composition	Engl	203	2S	L
120310	Technical & business writ	Engl	209	2S	L
120310	Creative writing	Engl	305	2S	U
1210	Beginning French	CILL	101	4S	L

NCES No.	Course Title	Dept.	Course No.	Credits	Level
1210	Beginning French	CILL	102	4S	L
1210	Second-year French	CILL	201	4S	L
1210	Second-year French	CILL	202	4S	L
1210	Third-year French	CILL	301	3S	U
1210	Third-year French	CILL	302	3S	U
1211	Beginning German	CILL	101	4S	L
1211	Beginning German	CILL	102	4S	L
121641	First-year college Latin	CILL	101	4S	L
121641	First-year college Latin	CILL	102	4S	L
121641	Second-year college Latin	CILL	201	4S	L
121641	Second-year college Latin	CILL	202	4S	L
121707	American Indian lit	EngLL	367	3S	U
1218	Beginning Norwegian	CILL	101	4S	L
1218	Beginning Norwegian	CILL	102	4S	L
1218	Second-year Norwegian	CILL	201	4S	L
1218	Second-year Norwegian	CILL	202	4S	L
1225	Beginning Spanish	CILL	101	4S	L
1225	Beginning Spanish	CILL	102	4S	L
1225	Second-year Spanish	CILL	201	4S	L
1225	Second-year Spanish	CILL	202	4S	L
122507	Survey of Span-Amer lit	CILL	403	2S	U
1305	Business law I	Acctg	315	3S	U
1305	Business law II	Acctg	316	3S	U
160199	Mathematics	Math	110	3S	L
160302	College algebra A	Math	103	3S	L
160302	College algebra B	Math	103	3S	L
160302	Intermediate algebra	Math	102	3S	L
160305	Algebraic struc of no sys	Math	277	4S	L
160602	Trigonometry	Math	105	2S	L
160603	Analyt geom & calculus I	Math	211	4S	L
160603	Analyt geom & calculus II	Math	212	4S	L
160603	Analytic geom & calc III	Math	213	4S	L
1610	Applied mathematics	Math	351	3S	U
180702	Philosophy of voc ed	BVEd	444	3S	U
181002	World religions	Relig	203	3S	L
181099	Introduction to religion	Relig	101	3S	L
181502	Contemporary moral issues	Relig	205	2S	L
181599	Relig values in marriage	Relig	235	2S	L
181599	Death and dying	Relig	345	2S	U
181599	Intro to humanities	Hum	101	4S	L
190599	School health education	HSci	403	2S	U
210502	Playgrounds & comm rec	Rec	222	3S	L
220201	Principles of econ I	Econ	201	3S	L
220201	Principles of econ II	Econ	202	3S	L
220301	Cultural geography	Geog	151	3S	L
220426	Western civ to 1500	Hist	101	3S	L
220426	Western civ since 1500	Hist	102	3S	L
220501	American government I	PolSc	101	3S	L
220501	American government II	PolSc	102	3S	L
220602	Criminology	Socio	252	3S	L
220605	The family	Socio	335	4S	U
220606	Introduction to sociology	Socio	101	3S	L
220607	Social psychology	Socio	361	4S	U
220608	Rural sociology	Socio	331	3S	U
220699	Aging	Socio	352	3S	U
	Noncredit courses				
041304	Real estate management			NC	
090118	Pharmacology for nurses			NC	
090699	Long-term-care admin			NC	
100309	Dietetic assist's course			NC	
100309	B & c nutrit for diet per			NC	
100309	School food service			NC	
1299	ESO reading course			NC	
220599	Naturalization course			NC	

(55) UNIVERSITY OF NORTHERN COLORADO

Greeley, Colorado 80639
Phone: (303) 356-2442

Enrollment on a noncredit basis accepted in all credit courses. Gifted high school students are permitted to enroll in undergraduate courses for credit. Overseas enrollment accepted for college courses.

NCES No.	Course Title	Dept.	Course No.	Credits	Level
	College courses				
040101	Principles of acctg I	Acctg	220	4Q	L
040101	Principles of acctg II	Acctg	221	4Q	L

NCES No.	Course Title	Dept.	Course No.	Credits	Level
040904	Principles of management	Bus	150	4Q	L
0506	Intro to journalism	Jrnl	100	2Q	L
0506	Profiles 20th-cen jourlst	Jrnl	496	3Q	U
0506	Using news media	Jrnl	413	3Q	U
0701	Foundations of education	EdF	366	4Q	U
0701	Philosophy of education	EdF	367	3Q	U
070899	Hndcpd stu in reg clsrm	EdSE	405	3Q	U
100504	Cnsmr aspct of hshld equi	HmEc	374	4Q	U
120299	Intro to Greek & Roman pr	Hum	111	4Q	L
120299	Middle Ages & Renaissance	Hum	112	4Q	L
120299	Studies in sci fiction	Engl	325	4Q	U
120299	Comm on a theme	Engl	105	4Q	L
1503	Biological science	Sci	104	3Q	L
150401	Introduction to chemistry	Chem	100	3Q	L
160102	Intro to history of math	Math	464	3Q	U
160302	Intermediate algebra	Math	123	5Q	L
160602	Plane trigonometry	Math	125	5Q	L
2007	Psych of fam relations	Psy	499	3Q	U
220306	World geography	Geog	100	5Q	L
220306	Geography of Colorado	Geog	350	3Q	U
220432	US history I	Hist	170	4Q	L
220432	US history II	Hist	171	4Q	L
220432	US history III	Hist	172	4Q	L
220433	World history I	Hist	130	4Q	L
220433	World history II	Hist	131	4Q	L
220433	World history III	Hist	132	4Q	L
2205	Politics & environment	EnSt	240	3Q	L
220501	National govt of the US	PSci	100	5Q	L
220501	President and bureaucracy	PSci	302	3Q	U
220511	State & local government	PSci	201	5Q	L
220699	Human ecology	Soc	479	3Q	U

(56) UNIVERSITY OF NORTHERN IOWA

Dr. Virginia Hash
Acting Associate Dean
Extension and Continuing Education
University of Northern Iowa
144 Gilchrist Hall
Cedar Falls, Iowa 50614
Phone: (319) 273-2121

Only in exceptional cases are gifted high school students permitted to enroll in undergraduate courses for credit. Overseas enrollment is not encouraged; each case is judged on an individual basis.

NCES No.	Course Title	Dept.	Course No.	Credits	Level
	College courses				
070199	History of education	Educ	26134	3S	B
070404	Methods in elem science	Educ	21142	2S	B
070404	Social studies elem sch	Educ	21143	2S	B
070404	Group eval techniques	Educ	25181	3S	B
070505	Writing exposition	Educ	62003	3S	L
070512	Modern drama	Educ	62115	3S	B
070512	20th-cent British novel	Educ	62120	3S	B
070512	Shakespeare	Educ	62148	3S	B
070512	British novel thru Hardy	Educ	62156	3S	B
070512	Lit for adolescents	Educ	62165	3S	B
070512	Intro to literature	Educ	62031	3S	L
100313	Basic nutrition	HmEc	31030	2S	L
100604	Personal relationships	HmEc	31051	2S	L
150202	Elements of weather	ErSci	87021	3S	L
150599	Fundamentals of geology	Geol	87128	4S	B
160103	Survey of math ideas	Math	80020	3S	L
160103	Metric system measurement	Math	80136	2S	B
160803	Statistical methods	Stat	80172	3S	U
181104	Religions of the world	Relig	64124	3S	B
181104	Individual readings relig	Relig	64189	VC	B
200804	Child psychology	Psych	20100	2S	B
200804	Development of young chld	Psych	20109	3S	B
200804	Psych of adolescence	Psych	20116	2S	B
200804	Social psychology educ	Psych	20140	3S	B
220299	Econ for general educ	Econ	92024	3S	U
220305	Communicatng through maps	Geog	97050	2S	L
220306	Regional geog Middle East	Geog	97150	3S	B
220308	Urban geography	Geog	97132	3S	U
220399	World geography	Geog	97025	3S	U

NCES No.	Course Title	Dept.	Course No.	Credits	Level
220399	History of Iowa	Hist	96130	3S	B
220423	Foreign area stdy: India	Hist	68125	3S	U
220426	Modern Europe to 1815	Hist	96154	3S	U
220426	Modern Europe snc 1815	Hist	96155	3S	U
220432	US history to 1877	Hist	96014	3S	U
220432	US history since 1877	Hist	96015	3S	U
220432	Recent US history	Hist	96116	3S	B
220432	The black in US history	Hist	96122	3S	B
220432	US foreign relations	Hist	96138	3S	B
220472	Women's studies: intro	Hist	68040	3S	L
220499	Humanities I	Hist	68021	4S	U
220499	Humanities II	Hist	68022	4S	U
220501	Intro to Amer politics	PolSc	94014	3S	U
220601	Principles of sociology	Socio	98058	3S	U
220602	Corrections & punishment	Socio	98126	3S	B
220605	The family	Socio	98105	2S	U
220613	Social problems	Socio	98060	3S	U
220615	Minority group relations	Socio	98130	3S	B

(57) UNIVERSITY OF OKLAHOMA

Mr. Hugh Harris
Director, Independent Study Department
University of Oklahoma
1700 Asp Avenue, Room B-1
Norman, Oklahoma 73037
Phone: (405) 325-1921

Enrollment on a noncredit basis accepted in all credit courses. Overseas enrollment accepted. Oklahoma residents may call toll free to 1-800-942-5702.

NCES No.	Course Title	Dept.	Course No.	Credits	Level
	High school courses				
0114	Conservatn nat resources	SocSt		HF	H
030502	Art understanding	Art	D	HF	H
040104	Bookkeeping	Acctg	A	HF	H
040104	Bookkeeping	Acctg	B	HF	H
040205	Elementary shorthand	Shthd	A	HF	H
040205	Elementary shorthand	Shthd	B	HF	H
040207	Begin type for one hand	Typew	AH	HF	H
040207	Typewrit first yr fir sem	Typew	A	HF	H
040207	Typewrit first yr sec sem	Typew	B	HF	H
040207	Typewrit second yr fir se	Typew	C	HF	H
040207	Typewrit second yr sec se	Typew	D	HF	H
040601	Business Engl first sem	Engl	K	HF	H
040604	Business Engl second sem	Engl	L	HF	H
0499	General business	Bus	A	HF	H
0499	General business	Bus	B	HF	H
0506	Creative prose writing	Jrnl		HF	H
0506	The school newspaper	Jrnl		HF	H
100109	Clothes	HmEc	B	HF	H
1004	Food and furnishing	HmEc	D	HF	H
100401	General homemaking	HmEc	C	HF	H
100601	Relationships child grow	HmEc	A	HF	H
110503	Beginning lettering	Art	B	HF	H
110503	Beginning drawing	Art	C	HF	H
110503	Drawing II	Art	E	HF	H
1203	Engl ninth gr first sem	Engl	A	HF	H
1203	Engl ninth gr second sem	Engl	B	HF	H
1203	Engl tenth gr first sem	Engl	C	HF	H
1203	Engl tenth gr second sem	Engl	D	HF	H
1203	Engl eleventh gr fir sem	Engl	E	HF	H
1203	Engl eleventh gr sec sem	Engl	F	HF	H
1203	Engl twelth gr fir sem	Engl	G	HF	H
1203	Engl twelth gr sec sem	Engl	H	HF	H
121005	French first yr first sem	Frnch	A	HF	H
121005	French first yr second se	Frnch	B	HF	H
121005	French second yr first se	Frnch	C	HF	H
121005	French second yr sec sem	Frnch	D	HF	H
121641	Latin first yr first sem	Clas	A	HF	H
121641	Latin first yr second sem	Clas	B	HF	H
121641	Latin second yr first sem	Clas	C	HF	H
121641	Latin second yr second se	Clas	D	HF	H
122505	Spanish first yr fir sem	Span	A	HF	H
122505	Spanish first yr sec sem	Span	B	HF	H
122505	Spanish second yr fir sem	Span	C	HF	H
122505	Spanish second yr sec sem	Span	D	HF	H
1302	Applied business law	Law	A	HF	H
1503	Biology first sem	Bio	A	HF	H

NCES No.	Course Title	Dept.	Course No.	Credits	Level
1503	Biology second sem	Bio	B	HF	H
160301	General math first sem	Math	K	HF	H
160301	General math second sem	Math	M	HF	H
160302	Algebra first sem	Math	A	HF	H
160302	Algebra second sem	Math	B	HF	H
160302	Algebra third sem	Math	E	HF	H
160302	Algebra fourth sem	Math	F	HF	H
160601	Modern geometry first sem	Math	C	HF	H
160601	Modern geometry sec sem	Math	D	HF	H
160602	Trigonometry	Math	G	HF	H
161201	Business mathematics	Math	L	HF	H
1905	Modern health	Scien	C	HF	H
2001	Psychology	Psych		HF	H
220201	Basic economics	Econ		HF	H
220208	Consumer econ first sem	Econ	A	HF	H
220208	Consumer econ second sem	Econ	B	HF	H
220208	Democracy	Dem		HF	H
2203	World geography first sem	Geog	A	HF	H
2203	World geography sec sem	Geog	B	HF	H
220428	Oklahoma history	Hist	O	HF	H
220432	American hist first sem	Hist	E	HF	H
220432	American hist second sem	Hist	F	HF	H
220433	World history first sem	Hist	J	HF	H
220433	World history second sem	Hist	K	HF	H
220501	American govt first sem	Govt	A	HF	H
220501	American govt second sem	Govt	B	HF	H
220502	Problems Amer democracy	Dem	A	HF	H
220502	Problems Amer democracy	Dem	B	HF	H
2206	Sociology	Socio		HF	H
2299	Etiquette everyday mannrs	HmEc		HF	H

College courses

NCES No.	Course Title	Dept.	Course No.	Credits	Level
030302	Understanding of music	Music	1113	3S	L
030402	History of the theater I	Drama	2713	3S	L
030402	History of the theater II	Drama	2723	3S	L
040101	Elementary accounting I	Acctg	2113	3S	L
040101	Elementary accounting II	Acctg	2123	3S	L
040106	Cost accounting	Acctg	3313	3S	U
040108	Intermed accounting I	Acctg	3113	3S	U
040108	Intermed accounting II	Acctg	3123	3S	U
040301	Business finance	Fin	3303	3S	U
040302	Personal finance	Fin	1203	3S	L
040308	Money and banking	Fin	3403	3S	U
040601	Adv business communicatn	BuCom	3223	3S	U
040604	Business report writing	BuCom	3113	3S	U
040904	Prin orgn and management	Mgmt	3013	3S	U
041001	Intro to marketing	Mktg	3013	3S	U
0411	Personnel management	Mgmt	3513	3S	U
041303	Real estate principles	Fin	3503	3S	U
0501	Intro to advertising	Jrnl	2303	3S	L
0506	Prof writing: fundamentals	Jrnl	3504	4S	U
0506	Prof writ: appr to fiction	Jrnl	3514	4S	U
0506	Prof writ: magazine writ	Jrnl	3534	3S	U
0509	Prin of public relations	Jrnl	3413	3S	U
0704	Curric develop elem schs	Educ	5533	3S	U
070402	Supvsn sec sch publicat	Jrnl	4703	3S	U
070503	Public school art	Art	3142	2S	U
070504	Business mathematics	Educ	1303	3S	L
070512	Lang arts elementary schs	Educ	4252	2S	U
070512	Teaching of English	Engl	4913	3S	U
070516	Arithmetic elementary sch	Educ	4152	2S	U
070516	Arithmetic for elem teach	Math	2213	3S	L
070522	Social studies elem schs	Educ	4322	2S	U
0708	Educ exceptional children	Educ	3412	2S	U
080703	Hydrology	EngAS	5843	3S	U
080901	Electrical science	EngAS	2613	3S	L
080903	Electronics	EngAS	3413	3S	U
0810	Graphics and design	EngAS	1213	3S	L
081102	Fluid mechanics	EngAS	3223	3S	U
081102	Hydromechanic processes	EngAS	3552	2S	U
081104	Rigid-body mechanics	EngAS	2113	3S	L
0812	Thermodynamics	EngAS	3213	3S	U
0815	Intro to industrial engrg	EngAS	2012	2S	L
081503	Fund of engrg economy	EngAS	4223	3S	U
0819	Strength of materials	EngAS	2153	3S	L
0819	Struct and prop materials	EngAS	3313	3S	U
1001	Textiles	HmEc	2443	3S	L
100109	Sociodynamics of fashion	HmEc	3452	2S	U
100313	Elementary nutrition	HmEc	1823	3S	L
120201	Ancient mythology	Clas	2373	3S	L
120201	People and nature in lit	Engl	2053	3S	L

NCES No.	Course Title	Dept.	Course No.	Credits	Level
120201	Read world lit to 1700	Engl	2713	3S	L
120201	Lit stu Bible Old Testam	Engl	2813	3S	L
120201	Lit stu Bible New Testam	Engl	2823	3S	L
120201	Modern continental drama	Engl	4373	3S	U
120201	Read world lit to 1700	Engl	2433	3S	L
120201	The Bible as literature	Engl	2813	3S	L
120204	Lit criticism Plato–Pope	Engl	4153	3S	U
120302	History of Engl language	Engl	4413	3S	U
120305	Prin English comp I	Engl	1113	3S	L
120305	Prin English comp II	Engl	1213	3S	L
120307	Engl lit 1375 to 1700	Engl	2543	3S	L
120307	Engl lit 1700 to present	Engl	2653	3S	L
120307	American literature	Engl	2773	3S	L
120307	American literature II	Engl	2883	3S	L
120307	Milton maj prose min poet	Engl	4613	3S	U
120307	Milton maj poems Chr doct	Engl	4623	3S	U
120307	American drama	Engl	4793	3S	U
120307	Shakespeare hist & comedy	Engl	4843	3S	U
120307	Shakespeare trag & poems	Engl	4853	3S	U
120307	Milton	Engl	4623	3S	U
121003	French civilization	Frnch	4313	3S	L
121005	Beginning French I	Frnch	1115	5S	L
121005	Beginning French II	Frnch	1225	5S	L
121007	Sur Frnch lit to 1800	Frnch	4153	3S	U
121007	Sur Frnch lit 19th-20th c	Frnch	4163	3S	U
121008	French reading I	Frnch	2113	3S	L
121008	French reading II	Frnch	2223	3S	L
121010	French composition I	Frnch	2322	2S	L
121010	French composition II	Frnch	2422	2S	L
121010	Advanced Frnch compositn	Frnch	3423	3S	U
121105	Beginning German I	Ger	1115	5S	L
121105	Beginning German II	Ger	1225	5S	L
121107	Hist German lit to 1750	Ger	4153	3S	U
121108	Begin German for read I	Ger	1013	3S	L
121108	Begin German for read II	Ger	1023	3S	L
121108	Mod Ger prose & poetry I	Ger	2113	3S	L
121108	Mod Ger prose & poetry II	Ger	2223	3S	L
121108	Scientific German I	Ger	3013	3S	U
121108	Scientific German II	Ger	3123	3S	U
121110	German composition I	Ger	2322	2S	L
121110	German composition II	Ger	2422	2S	L
121241	Beginning Greek I	Greek	1113	3S	L
121241	Beginning Greek II	Greek	1213	3S	L
121299	Medical vocabulary	Clas	1162	2S	L
121341	Beginning Hebrew I	Heb	1113	3S	L
121341	Beginning Hebrew II	Heb	1213	3S	L
121341	Intermediate Hebrew	Heb	2113	3S	L
121405	Beginning Italian I	Ital	1115	5S	L
121405	Beginning Italian II	Ital	1225	5S	L
121505	Beginning Japanese I	Jap	1115	5S	L
121505	Beginning Japanese II	Jap	1225	5S	L
121641	Beginning Latin I	Latin	1115	5S	L
121641	Beginning Latin II	Latin	1215	5S	L
121641	Latin reading	Latin	2013	3S	L
121641	Vergil: sel from *Aeneid*	Latin	2153	3S	L
121641	Intermed prose: Cicero	Latin	2513	3S	L
121641	Intermed prose: Livy	Latin	2513	3S	L
121641	Lyric poetry: Catullus	Latin	2603	3S	L
121699	Latin derivatives	Clas	1112	2S	L
121707	American Indian lit	Engl	4050	VC	U
1220	Beginning Russian I	Russ	1115	5S	L
1220	Beginning Russian II	Russ	1225	5S	L
122503	Spanish civilization	Span	4313	3S	U
122505	Beginning Spanish I	Span	1115	5S	L
122505	Beginning Spanish II	Span	1225	5S	L
122507	Sur Sp-Am lit 1888-pres	Span	4103	3S	U
122507	Sur Spanish lit to 1700	Span	4153	3S	U
122507	Sur Spanish lit from 1700	Span	4163	3S	U
122508	Spanish reading I	Span	2113	3S	L
122508	Spanish reading II	Span	2223	3S	L
122510	Spanish composition I	Span	2322	2S	L
122510	Spanish composition II	Span	2422	2S	L
122510	Advan Spanish comp	Span	3423	3S	U
1299	Soviet lit in English	MLang	3533	3S	U
1299	Russian lit in translatn	Russ	2003	3S	L
1304	Elementary criminal law	PolSc	4813	3S	U
130402	Criminal legal procedure	PolSc	4803	3S	U
1307	Legal environ of business	BuLaw	3323	3S	U
1309	Real property	BuLaw	4613	3S	U
1501	General astronomy	Astro	1504	4S	L

NCES No.	Course Title	Dept.	Course No.	Credits	Level
1504	Chemis for nonsci majors	Chem	1614	4S	L
150408	Organic chemistry	Chem	3053	3S	U
150408	Organic chemistry I	Chem	3053	3S	U
150408	Organic chemistry II	Chem	3153	3S	U
160302	Begin algebra for col stu	Math	0133	5U	D
160302	Intermediate algebra	Math	1213	3S	L
160302	College algebra	Math	1513	3S	L
160306	Linear algebra	Math	3333	3S	U
160401	Calculus I	Math	1823	3S	L
160401	Calculus II	Math	2423	3S	L
160401	Calculus III	Math	2434	3S	L
160602	Trigonometry	Math	1612	2S	L
160603	Analytic geometry	Math	1812	2S	L
160802	Elements of statistics	Econ	2843	3S	L
160802	Elementary statistics	Math	3703	3S	U
1611	Math for bus/life/soc sci	Math	1443	3S	L
1611	Calculus I: bus/life/so sc	Math	1743	3S	L
1611	Engineering mathematics I	Math	3114	4S	U
1611	Math for bus/life/soc sci	Math	1443	3S	L
1611	Calculus for bus/life/soc	Math	2123	3S	L
1801	Aesthetics: beauty and art	Philo	3053	3S	U
1803	History of ethics	Philo	3253	3S	U
180401	Hist Greek and Roman phil	Philo	3313	3S	U
180402	Hist medieval philosophy	Philo	3323	3S	U
180403	Hist modern philosophy	Philo	3333	3S	U
1805	Introduction to logic	Philo	1113	3S	L
190106	Org & admin health phy ed	PhyEd	4943	3S	U
190107	Adaptive phy ed program	PhyEd	3882	2S	U
190110	Tests and meas in phy ed	PhyEd	4923	3S	U
190203	Physiology of exercise	Zool	3132	2S	U
190205	Kinesiology	PhyEd	3713	3S	U
190311	Theory of baseball	PhyEd	3052	2S	U
190311	Theory of basketball	PhyEd	3072	2S	U
190311	Theory of track and field	PhyEd	3082	2S	U
190311	Theory of wrestling	PhyEd	3092	2S	U
1905	Health education	Educ	2913	3S	L
1905	Health education	PhyEd	2913	3S	L
190704	Leadership in recreation	PhyEd	2932	2S	L
2001	Elements of psychology	Psych	1113	3S	L
200504	Intro developmental psych	Psych	1403	3S	L
200509	Intro to personality	Psych	1193	3S	L
200901	Industrial psychology	Psych	3363	3S	U
2101	Intro public administratn	PolSc	2173	3S	L
210111	Conservation	Geog	3253	3S	U
210304	Intro law enforcement	PolSc	2803	3S	L
210304	Police administration I	PolSc	3803	3S	U
210304	Prin criminal investigatn	PolSc	3853	3S	U
210403	Community leadership	SocWk	3113	3S	U
210403	Social work with groups	SocWk	3223	3S	U
210403	Spec prob: alcohol, drugs	SocWk	5010	3S	U
210405	Soc welfare chang world	SocWk	5310	3S	U
2201	General anthropology	Anthr	1113	3S	L
220101	Intro to archaeology	Anthr	2113	3S	L
220104	High civiliz ancient Amer	Anthr	3893	3S	U
220104	Nat people/western N Amer	Anthr	3823	3S	U
220107	Intro to social anthropol	Anthr	2203	3S	L
220201	Principles of economics I	Econ	2113	3S	L
220201	Prin of economics II	Econ	2123	3S	L
220214	Internat econ problems	Econ	3613	3S	U
2203	Human geography	Geog	1103	3S	L
220302	Prin economic geography	Geog	1213	3S	L
220306	World geography by region	Geog	3603	3S	U
220306	Regl geog of US & Canada	Geog	4913	3S	U
220402	US diplomat hist to 1900	Hist	3563	3S	U
220402	US diplomat hist to 1900	PolSc	3563	3S	U
220403	Econ development of US	Econ	1013	3S	L
220423	East Asian civizn to 1800	Hist	1723	3S	L
220423	Mod East Asia since 1800	Hist	1733	3S	L
220424	England to 1603	Hist	2313	3S	L
220424	England since 1603	Hist	2323	3S	L
220424	England to 1688	Hist	2313	3S	L
220424	England since 1688	Hist	2323	3S	L
220426	Sur ancient medieval Euro	Hist	1013	3S	L
220426	Europe 1500 to 1815	Hist	1223	3S	L
220426	Europe since 1815	Hist	1233	3S	L
220427	Hispanic Amer 1492-1810	Hist	2613	3S	L
220427	Hispanic Amer 1810-pres	Hist	2623	3S	L
220428	History of Oklahoma	Hist	2503	3S	L
220429	Hebrew civ in ancie times	Clas	3413	3S	U
220429	Hebrew civ in ancie times	Hist	3413	3S	U
220432	United States 1492-1865	Hist	1483	3S	L
220432	United States 1865-pres	Hist	1493	3S	L
220450	Ancient history	Hist	1033	3S	L
2205	Intro to political sci	PolSc	1603	3S	L
220501	Govt of the United States	PolSc	1113	3S	L
220505	Intro to internatl relat	PolSc	2503	3S	L
220505	Great powers in world pol	PolSc	3503	3S	U
220507	American polit parties	PolSc	2403	3S	L
220509	Government of Oklahoma	PolSc	3303	3S	U
220511	State government	PolSc	2303	3S	L
220511	Urban govt and politics	PolSc	3313	3S	U
220602	Sociology: crime and delin	Socio	3523	3S	U
220605	The family	Socio	3723	3S	U
220606	Intro to sociology	Socio	1113	3S	L
	Noncredit courses				
0506	Creative prose writing	Jrnl		NC	H
0506	Creative prose writing	Jrnl		NC	D
0506	Prof writ I fundamentals	Jrnl		NC	D
0506	Prof writ II appr fiction	Jrnl		NC	D
0506	Prof writ III fiction	Jrnl		NC	D
0506	Prof writ IV nonfiction	Jrnl		NC	D
110503	Lettering	Art		NC	D
110503	Drawing fundamentals	Art		NC	D
110503	Drawing methods	Art		NC	D
120305	English review	Engl		NC	D
121243	New Testament Greek	Greek		NC	L
220502	Citizenship for aliens	PolSc		NC	D

58 UNIVERSITY OF SOUTH CAROLINA

Ms. Sylvia A. Brazell
Director, Correspondence Study
Continuing Education
University of South Carolina
915 Gregg Street
Columbia, South Carolina 29208
Phone: (803) 777-2188

Only in exceptional cases are gifted high school students permitted to enroll in undergraduate courses for credit. Overseas enrollment accepted for high school and college courses.

NCES No.	Course Title	Dept.	Course No.	Credits	Level
	High school courses				
040101	High school acctg I	BAdm	BE023	HF	H
040101	High school acctg II	BAdm	BE024	HF	H
040901	General business I	BAdm	BE021	HF	H
040901	General business II	BAdm	BE022	HF	H
100604	Etiquette	HmEc	HE001	HF	H
120399	Ninth-grade English I	Engl	EN031	HF	H
120399	Ninth-grade English II	Engl	EN032	HF	H
120399	Tenth-grade English I	Engl	EN033	HF	H
120399	Tenth-grade English II	Engl	EN034	HF	H
120399	Eleventh-grade English I	Engl	EN035	HF	H
120399	Eleventh-grade English II	Engl	EN036	HF	H
120399	Twelfth-grade English I	Engl	EN037	HF	H
120399	Twelfth-grade English II	Engl	EN038	HF	H
120399	Business English	Engl	BE011	HF	H
120399	Remedial English	Engl	EN001	HF	H
130299	Business law	BAdm	BE025	HF	H
150301	Basic biology I	Sci	S1015	HF	H
150301	Basic biology II	Sci	S1016	HF	H
1599	General science I	Sci	S1011	HF	H
1599	General science II	Sci	S1012	HF	H
160302	Beginning algebra I	Math	MA031	HF	H
160302	Beginning algebra II	Math	MA032	HF	H
160302	Advanced algebra I	Math	MA035	HF	H
160302	Advanced algebra II	Math	MA036	HF	H
160601	Geometry I	Math	MA033	HF	H
160601	Geometry II	Math	MA034	HF	H
160601	Solid geometry	Math	MA039	HF	H
160602	Trigonometry	Math	MA037	HF	H
161201	Business & consumer math	Math	MA009	HF	H
161201	Business & consumer math	Math	MA010	HF	H
161299	Remedial arithmetic	Math	MA001	HF	H
190599	Health science I	Sci	S1001	HF	H
190599	Health science II	Sci	S1002	HF	H
200104	Psychology	SoStu	SS007	HF	H

NCES No.	Course Title	Dept.	Course No.	Credits	Level
220201	Economics	SoStu	BE027	HF	H
220305	World geography I	SoStu	SS021	HF	H
220305	World geography II	SoStu	SS022	HF	H
220432	American history I	SoStu	SS033	HF	H
220432	American history II	SoStu	SS034	HF	H
220433	World history I	SoStu	SS031	HF	H
220433	World history II	SoStu	SS032	HF	H
220501	American government	SoStu	SS035	HF	H
220502	Civics	SoStu	SS001	HF	H
220606	Sociology	SoStu	SS003	HF	H
	College courses				
040101	Fundamentals of acctg	BAdm	C-225	3S	L
040101	Fundamentals of acctg	BAdm	C-226	3S	L
040101	Functional accounting I	GStd	C-161	3S	L
040101	Functional accounting II	GStd	C-162	3S	L
040103	Auditing theory	BAdm	C-535	3S	U
040106	Advanced cost accounting	BAdm	C-334	3S	U
040107	Acctg con sys & data proc	BAdm	C-539	3S	U
040108	Intermediate accounting	BAdm	C-331	3S	U
040108	Intermediate accounting	BAdm	C-332	3S	U
040108	Advanced accounting	BAdm	C-537	3S	U
040109	Governmental accounting	BAdm	C-534	3S	U
040114	Federal tax procedure	BAdm	C-531	3S	U
040201	Office procedures	GStd	C-239	3S	L
040205	Shorthand I	GStd	C-145	3S	L
040301	Commer bank prac & policy	BAdm	C-465	3S	U
040399	Commer & central banking	BAdm	C-301	3S	U
040710	Prin of risk & insurance	BAdm	C-341	3S	U
040903	Personnel organ & superv	GStd	C-244	3S	L
040904	Prin of management	BAdm	C-371	3S	U
040999	Retailing management	BAdm	C-551	3S	U
041001	Marketing	BAdm	C-350	3S	U
041004	Marketing management	BAdm	C-558	3S	U
041005	Marketing communications	BAdm	C-352	3S	U
041005	Promot policies & strat	BAdm	C-454	3S	U
041005	Prin of retailing	GStd	C-165	3S	L
041099	Channels and institutions	BAdm	C-353	3S	U
041099	Consumer behavior	BAdm	C-455	3S	U
041099	Marketing research	BAdm	C-457	3S	U
041099	Marketing environment	BAdm	C-550	3S	U
041099	Industrial marketing	BAdm	C-557	3S	U
041303	Intro real est & urb dev	BAdm	C-366	3S	U
070301	Child development	GStd	C-189	3S	L
070301	Early childhood education	GStd	C-191	3S	L
070401	Elem sch curr & organ	Educ	C-441	3S	U
070401	Organ & curr middle sch	Educ	C-451	3S	U
070509	Health educ elem schools	HEdu	C-331	3S	U
070515	Science in elem school	Educ	C-515	3S	U
070516	Basic concepts elem math	Math	C-501	3S	U
070516	Basic concepts elem math	Math	C-502	3S	U
070516	Tch soc stu lang elem sch	Educ	C-444	3S	U
070520	Intro to educ psychology	Educ	C-335	3S	U
070522	Teach soc stu & lan arts	Educ	C-443	3S	U
070803	Psych of exceptnl child	Psych	C-528	3S	U
070805	Spec learn disab sch chil	Psych	C-529	3S	U
090710	Personal & commun health	HEdu	C-221	3S	L
100206	Personal finance	BAdm	C-369	3S	U
110699	Transportation	BAdm	C-549	3S	U
120103	Vocabulary & semantics	Engl	C-452	3S	U
120201	The short story	Engl	C-435	3S	U
120201	Adv rhe & comp for teach	Engl	C-459	3S	U
120203	Major writers Americ lit	Engl	C-287	3S	L
120203	Maj writers British lit	Engl	C-288	3S	L
120203	Chaucer	Engl	C-401	3S	U
120203	Shakespeare's tragedies	Engl	C-405	3S	U
120203	Shakespeare's comedies	Engl	C-406	3S	U
120204	Contemporary drama	Engl	C-284	3S	L
120204	Contemporary poetry	Engl	C-286	3S	L
120204	Early English drama	Engl	C-470	3S	U
120204	Theo of literary criticsm	Engl	C-483	3S	U
120205	Effective English	Engl	C-245	3S	L
120205	Children's literature	Engl	C-484	3S	U
120205	Adolescent literature	Engl	C-485	3S	U
120299	Contemporary fiction	Engl	C-282	3S	L
120299	Modern English literature	Engl	C-423	3S	U
120305	Composition	Engl	C-101	3S	L
120307	Composition & literature	Engl	C-102	3S	L
121004	Intro French	ForLa	C-101	4S	L
121004	Intro French	ForLa	C-102	3S	L
121004	Intermediate French	ForLa	C-201	3S	L
121004	Intermediate French	ForLa	C-202	3S	L
121104	Intermediate German	ForLa	C-201	3S	L
121104	Intermediate German	ForLa	C-202	3S	L
121641	Intro Latin	ForLa	C-101	4S	L
121641	Intro Latin	ForLa	C-102	3S	L
122504	Intro Spanish	ForLa	C-101	4S	L
122504	Intro Spanish	ForLa	C-102	3S	L
122504	Intermediate Spanish	ForLa	C-201	3S	L
122504	Intermediate Spanish	ForLa	C-202	3S	L
130101	Police admin & operations	GStd	C-172	3S	L
130202	Survey of commercial law	BAdm	C-324	3S	U
130202	Commercial law I	BAdm	C-347	3S	U
130202	Commercial law II	BAdm	C-348	3S	U
130402	Intro to criminal justice	GStd	C-171	3S	L
130402	Criminal investigation	GStd	C-271	3S	L
130404	Crim law & court proced	GStd	C-272	3S	L
130499	Crime & delinquency	GStd	C-177	3S	L
150102	Descriptive astronomy I	Astro	C-111	3S	L
150310	Oceans and man	MSci	C-210	3S	L
150799	General physics I	Phys	C-201	4S	L
160199	Math analysis I	Math	C-121	3S	L
160199	Math analysis II	Math	C-122	3S	L
160199	Precalculus mathematics	Math	C-125	3S	L
160701	Finite mathematics	Math	C-203	3S	L
160803	Elementary statistics	Math	C-201	3S	L
161101	Business mathematics	GStd	C-144	3S	L
180499	Hist of modern philosophy	Philo	C-202	3S	L
180501	Intro to logic I	Philo	C-110	3S	L
180501	Intro to logic II	Philo	C-111	3S	L
180599	Intro to philosophy	Philo	C-102	3S	L
190105	Intro to physical educ	PEdu	C-132	3S	L
190106	Organ & admin of phy educ	PEdu	C-553	3S	U
190107	Elem school phy educ prog	PEdu	C-505	3S	U
190110	Measuremnt & eval phy edu	PEdu	C-545	3S	U
190311	Foundations of coaching	PEdu	C-302	3S	U
190311	Scientific bases for coachg	PEdu	C-330	3S	U
200104	Intro to psychology	Psych	C-101	3S	L
200499	Psychological statistics	Psych	C-225	3S	L
200501	Abnormal psychology	Psych	C-410	3S	U
200504	Abnorm behavior in childn	Psych	C-510	3S	U
200504	Psych of child developmnt	Psych	C-520	3S	U
200505	Psychology of adjustment	Psych	C-103	3S	L
200599	Psychology of marriage	Psych	C-301	3S	U
200599	Human sexual behavior	Psych	C-300	3S	U
200599	Sensation and perception	Psych	C-450	3S	U
200599	Psych of adolescence	Psych	C-521	3S	U
210101	Intro to public admin	GInt	C-370	3S	U
210103	Public financial mgmt	GInt	C-571	3S	U
210199	Public personnel admin	GInt	C-572	3S	U
220201	Principles of economics	BAdm	C-221	3S	L
220201	Principles of economics	BAdm	C-222	3S	L
220201	Principles of economics	BAdm	C-223	3S	L
220201	Economic foundations	BAdm	C-224	3S	L
220201	Basic economics	GStd	C-149	3S	L
220202	History of econ thought	BAdm	C-408	3S	U
220211	Labor economics	BAdm	C-406	3S	U
220299	Gov policy toward bus	BAdm	C-379	3S	U
220303	Man's impact on environmt	Geog	C-343	3S	U
220305	Intro to weather & clim	Geog	C-202	4S	L
220306	Geog of North America	Geog	C-424	3S	U
220424	History of Great Britain	Hist	C-311	3S	U
220424	History of Great Britain	Hist	C-312	3S	U
220426	Intro European civilizat	Hist	C-101	3S	L
220426	Intro European civilizat	Hist	C-102	3S	L
220426	Contemporary Europe	Hist	C-321	3S	U
220426	Contemporary Europe	Hist	C-322	3S	U
220427	Latin America found soc	Hist	C-361	3S	U
220428	South Carolina	GStd	C-109	3S	L
220428	Hist of SC 1670-1865	Hist	C-341	3S	U
220428	Hist of SC since 1865	Hist	C-342	3S	U
220432	The United States	GStd	C-108	3S	L
220432	Hist of US discov to pres	Hist	C-201	3S	L
220432	Hist of US discov to pres	Hist	C-202	3S	L
220432	Civ War & reconstruction	Hist	C-334	3S	U
220432	Rise of indust America	Hist	C-335	3S	U
220432	US history since 1945	Hist	C-337	3S	U
220501	American national govt	GInt	C-201	3S	L
220501	Contem US foreign policy	GInt	C-341	3S	U
220501	The legislative process	GInt	C-462	3S	U

NCES No.	Course Title	Dept.	Course No.	Credits	Level
220504	Comparative politics	GInt	C-316	3S	U
220504	Ideology & world politics	GInt	C-430	3S	U
220504	US & world prob: perspctv	GInt	C-101	3S	L
220504	US & world prob: perspctv	GInt	C-102	3S	L
220505	International relations	GInt	C-315	3S	U
220505	International integration	GInt	C-516	3S	U
220599	Pol & govt of Indian subc	GInt	C-585	3S	U
220606	Introductory sociology	Socio	C-101	3S	L
	Noncredit courses				
040707	Cons perspec life insur	BAdm		NC	
041303	Fundmntls of real estate	BAdm		NC	
220502	Citizenship	SoStu		NC	

(59) UNIVERSITY OF SOUTH DAKOTA

Ms. Sharon Brown
Director, Independent Studies
Statewide Educational Services
University of South Dakota
Center for Continuing Education
Vermillion, South Dakota 57069
Phone: (605) 677-5281

Enrollment on a noncredit basis accepted in all credit courses. Gifted high school students are permitted to enroll in undergraduate courses for credit. Overseas enrollment accepted.

NCES No.	Course Title	Dept.	Course No.	Credits	Level
	High school courses				
030502	Drawing & painting	Art	VX	HF	H
040101	High school accounting 1	BusEd	IXX	HF	H
040101	High school accounting 2	BusEd	XX	HF	H
040205	Elementary shorthand	BusEd	VX	HF	H
040207	Elem & personal typing 1	BusEd	IX	HF	H
040207	Elem & personal typing 2	BusEd	IIX	HF	H
040207	Advanced typewriting	BusEd	IIIX	HF	H
0499	General business 1	BusEd	XIIIX	HF	H
0499	General business 2	BusEd	XIVX	HF	H
0499	Business English	BusEd	XXIX	HF	H
0506	Journalism	Engl	IXX	HF	H
070899	Effective methods of stdy	StuSk	IIIX	HF	H
090119	Modern health	Sci	IX	HF	H
100104	Clothing & construction	HmEc	VX	HF	H
100312	Nutrition education	HmEc	IIIX	HF	H
100504	Household equipment	HmEc	VIIX	HF	H
100604	Personal & social relatns	HmEc	XXIX	HF	H
100701	Modern etiquette	Etiq	IX	HF	H
100701	General homemaking 1	HmEc	HE003	HF	H
100701	General homemaking 2	HmEc	HE004	HF	H
110199	General shop	IndEd	VIIX	HF	H
120305	Ninth-grade English 1	Engl	IX	HF	H
120305	Ninth-grade English 2	Engl	IIX	HF	H
120307	Tenth-grade English 1	Engl	IIIX	HF	H
120307	Tenth-grade English 2	Engl	IVX	HF	H
120307	Eleventh-grade English 1	Engl	VX	HF	H
120307	Eleventh-grade English 2	Engl	VIX	HF	H
120307	Twelfth-grade English 1	Engl	VIIX	HF	H
120307	Twelfth-grade English 2	Engl	VIIIX	HF	H
120307	The short story	Engl	XIIIX	HF	H
120307	The novel	Engl	XIXX	HF	H
120308	Guided reading	Engl	XIX	HF	H
120308	Improvemnt of rdg skill 1	Engl	XXVX	HF	H
120308	Improvemnt of rdg skill 2	Engl	XXVIX	HF	H
120310	Composition	Engl	XVX	HF	H
120432	American history 2	Hist	SS034	HF	H
120432	American history 3	Hist	VIXA	HF	H
121005	Beginning French 1	ForLa	XXXIX	HF	H
121105	Beginning German 1	ForLa	XXIX	HF	H
121105	Beginning German 2	ForLa	XXIIX	HF	H
121605	Beginning Latin 1	ForLa	IX	HF	H
121605	Beginning Latin 2	ForLa	IIX	HF	H
122505	Beginning Spanish 1	ForLa	XLIX	HF	H
122505	Beginning Spanish 2	ForLa	XLIIX	HF	H
1503	Biology 1	Sci	VX	HF	H
1503	Biology 2	Sci	VIX	HF	H
150899	General science 1	Sci	IIIX	HF	H
150899	General science 2	Sci	IVX	HF	H
1509	Earth science	Sci	XVX	HF	H
160301	General mathematics 1	Math	XIX	HF	H

NCES No.	Course Title	Dept.	Course No.	Credits	Level
160301	General mathematics 2	Math	XIIX	HF	H
160301	Remedial arithmetic	Math	XXX	HF	H
160302	Elementary algebra 1	Math	IX	HF	H
160302	Elementary algebra 2	Math	IIX	HF	H
160302	Advanced algebra 1	Math	VX	HF	H
160302	Advanced algebra 2	Math	VIX	HF	H
160601	Geometry 1	Math	IIIX	HF	H
160601	Geometry 2	Math	IVX	HF	H
160603	Analytic geometry & calc	Math	XVX	HF	H
161201	Business & consumer math	Math	XX	HF	H
161201	Bus and consumer math 1	Math	IXX	HF	H
161201	Bus and consumer math 2	Math	XX	HF	H
161202	Bus and consumer math 1	Math	IXX	HF	H
161202	Bus and consumer math 2	Math	XX	HF	H
200101	Psychology	SocSt	XVIX	HF	H
220201	Economics	SocSt	XIIX	HF	H
2203	World geography 1	SocSt	IX	HF	H
2203	World geography 2	SocSt	IIX	HF	H
220432	American history 1	Hist	SS033	HF	H
220433	World history 1	SocSt	IIIXA	HF	H
220433	World history 2	SocSt	IVX	HF	H
220433	World history 3	SocSt	VIIX	HF	H
220501	American government	Socio	XIIIX	HF	H
220612	Sociology	SocSt	XVX	HF	H
220613	Modern problems	SocSt	VIIIX	HF	H
220699	Pers and soc relations	Socio	XXIX	HF	H
	College courses				
040101	Principles of accounting1	Bus	210	3S	L
040102	Principles of acctg 2	Bus	211	3S	L
070302	Geography for elem tchrs	Educ	162	2S	L
070302	Teaching art in elem sch	Educ	206	4S	L
070303	Reading dev in content	Educ	452	3S	U
070607	Elem & personal typing	Educ	111	2S	L
070607	Intermediate typing	Educ	112	3S	L
070701	Guidance in elem schools	Educ	415	2S	U
120305	English grammar	Engl	203	3S	L
120307	Intro to literary genres	Engl	163	3S	L
120307	World literature	Engl	213	3S	L
120307	Intro to British lit	Engl	221	3S	L
120307	Intro to British lit 2	Engl	222	3S	L
120307	Intro to American lit	Engl	241	3S	L
120307	American lit 2	Engl	242	3S	L
120310	English composition	Engl	101	3S	L
120310	Advanced composition	Engl	200	3S	L
120310	Communications: technical	Engl	101	3S	L
120310	Technical writing	Engl	103	3S	L
121005	First-year French 1	Frnch	101	4S	L
121005	First-year French 2	Frnch	102	4S	L
121006	Second-year French 1	Frnch	203	3S	L
121006	Second-year French 2	Frnch	204	3S	L
121007	French lit 1	Frnch	353	3S	U
121007	French lit 2	Frnch	354	3S	U
121105	German 1	Ger	101	4S	L
121105	German 2	Ger	102	4S	L
121106	Second-year German 1	Ger	203	3S	L
121106	Second-year German 2	Ger	204	3S	L
121201	Greek literature in trans	Clas	362	3S	U
121205	Greek etymology	Clas	103	2S	L
121207	Homer's *Iliad*	Clas	211	3S	L
121207	Plato	Clas	311	3S	U
121299	Greek art & archaeology	Clas	331	2S	U
121601	Latin literature in trans	Clas	363	3S	U
121605	Latin etymology	Clas	102	2S	L
121605	Latin refresher & rdg 1	Clas	201	3S	L
121605	Latin readings 2	Clas	202	3S	L
121608	Vergil: *The Aeneid*	Clas	213	3S	L
121608	Vergil: *The Aeneid*	Clas	214	3S	L
121610	Writing of Latin 1	Clas	301	1S	U
121610	Writing of Latin 2	Clas	302	1S	U
121641	Classical mythology	Clas	361	2S	U
121699	Roman social institutions	Clas	341	2S	U
121699	Latin individual work 1	Clas	371	2S	U
121699	Latin individual work 2	Clas	372	2S	U
122508	Reading in Spanish 1	Span	291	2S	L
122508	Reading in Spanish 2	Span	292	2S	L
122509	Conv & comp: Spanish 1	Span	311	3S	U
122509	Conv & comp: Spanish 2	Span	312	3S	U
150199	Astronomy	Astro	203	3S	L
151109	Communication disorders	Commu	131	3S	L
160103	Foundations of math	Math	351	3S	U
160199	Modern concepts for el ed	Math	341	3S	U

NCES No.	Course Title	Dept.	Course No.	Credits	Level
160199	Basic math concepts	Math	140	3S	L
160203	Finite mathematics	Math	141	3S	L
160203	Finite mathematics	Math	340	3S	U
160302	Elem mathematics 1	Math	111	4S	L
160302	Elem mathematics 2	Math	112	4S	L
160306	Linear algebra	Math	315	3S	U
160401	Elem calculus 1	Math	123	4S	L
160401	Elem calculus 2	Math	224	4S	L
160401	Elem calculus 3	Math	225	4S	L
160406	Differential equations	Math	321	3S	U
160602	Trigonometry	Math	120	2S	L
160802	Intro to statistics	Math	381	3S	U
190104	Hist & prin of phys educ	PhyEd	340	3S	U
200103	General psychology	Psych	101	3S	L
200509	Personal adjustment	Psych	165	3S	L
210304	Intro to criminal justice	CJus	201	3S	L
210304	Police community relation	CJus	202	3S	L
220201	Principles of economics 1	Bus	201	3S	L
220201	Principles of economics 2	Bus	202	3S	L
220207	American bus development	Bus	103	3S	L
220306	World geography	Geog	111	3S	L
220428	South Dakota and politics	Socio	315	3S	U
220432	American history 1	Hist	251	3S	L
220432	American history 2	Hist	252	3S	L
220432	American frontier	Hist	361	3S	U
220432	American South	Hist	370	3S	U
220433	Western civilization 1	Hist	121	3S	L
220433	Western civilization 2	Hist	122	3S	L
220501	American government	PolSc	100	3S	L
220602	Intro to crime and delin	Socio	250	3S	L
220602	Criminology	Socio	351	3S	U
220602	Penology	Socio	352	3S	U
220604	Juvenile delinquency	Socio	451	3S	U
220605	Courtship & marriage adj	Socio	280	3S	L
220606	Intro to sociology	Socio	100	3S	L
220609	Methods of social res	Socio	310	3S	U
220613	Social problems	Socio	150	3S	L
220699	Field of social work	Socio	200	3S	L

Noncredit courses

NCES No.	Course Title	Dept.	Course No.	Credits	Level
041303	Real estate 1			NC	V
041303	Real estate 2			NC	V
041309	Real estate 3			NC	V

(60) UNIVERSITY OF SOUTHERN MISSISSIPPI

Mr. William Lewis
Director of Independent Study
University of Southern Mississippi
Southern Station Box 5056
Hattiesburg, Mississippi 39406-5056
Phone: (601) 266-4206

Enrollment on a noncredit basis accepted in all credit courses. Gifted high school students are permitted to enroll in undergraduate courses for credit. Overseas enrollment accepted.

NCES No.	Course Title	Dept.	Course No.	Credits	Level
	High school courses				
040104	Bookkeeping 1st half	Bus		HF	H
040104	Bookkeeping 2nd half	Bus		HF	H
040205	Shorthand elem 1st half	Bus		HF	H
040205	Shorthand elem 2nd half	Bus		HF	H
040207	Typewriting elem 1st half	Bus		HF	H
040207	Typewriting elem 2nd half	Bus		HF	H
040207	Typewriting adv 1st half	Bus		HF	H
040207	Typewriting adv 2nd half	Bus		HF	H
040601	Business English	Bus		HF	H
0499	General business 1st half	Bus		HF	H
0499	General business 2nd half	Bus		HF	H
050699	Journalism	Jrnl		HF	H
100199	Homemaking II 1st half	HmEc		HF	H
100313	Homemaking I 2nd half	HmEc		HF	H
100499	Homemaking II 2nd half	HmEc		HF	H
100601	Child development	HmEc		HF	H
100602	Family living	HmEc		HF	H
100699	Homemaking I 1st half	HmEc		HF	H
120299	English IV 2nd half	Engl		HF	H
120305	English I 1st half	Engl		HF	H
120307	English I 2nd half	Engl		HF	H

NCES No.	Course Title	Dept.	Course No.	Credits	Level
120307	English II 1st half	Engl		HF	H
120307	English II 2nd half	Engl		HF	H
120307	English III 1st half	Engl		HF	H
120307	English III 2nd half	Engl		HF	H
120310	English IV 1st half	Engl		HF	H
1210	French I 1st half	Frnch		HF	H
1210	French I 2nd half	Frnch		HF	H
1210	French II 1st half	Frnch		HF	H
1210	French II 2nd half	Frnch		HF	H
1225	Spanish I 1st half	Span		HF	H
1225	Spanish I 2nd half	Span		HF	H
1225	Spanish II 1st half	Span		HF	H
1225	Spanish II 2nd half	Span		HF	H
130799	Business law	Bus		HF	H
150399	Biology 1st half	Bio		HF	H
150399	Biology 2nd half	Bio		HF	H
150401	Chemistry 1st half	Chem		HF	H
150401	Chemistry 2nd half	Chem		HF	H
1599	General science 1st half	Sci		HF	H
1599	General science 2nd half	Sci		HF	H
160299	Fundamental math I 1st hf	Math		HF	H
160299	Fundamental math I 2nd hf	Math		HF	H
160299	Fundamental math II 1st hf	Math		HF	H
160299	Fundamental math II 2nd hf	Math		HF	H
160302	Algebra elem 1st half	Math		HF	H
160302	Algebra elem 2nd half	Math		HF	H
160302	Algebra adv 1st half	Math		HF	H
160302	Algebra adv 2nd half	Math		HF	H
160601	Geometry 1st half	Math		HF	H
160601	Geometry 2nd half	Math		HF	H
161201	Business arithmetic	Bus		HF	H
1699	Senior math adv 1st half	Math		HF	H
1699	Senior math adv 2nd half	Math		HF	H
220201	Economics	Econ		HF	H
220399	World geography	Geog		HF	H
220432	American history 1st half	Hist		HF	H
220432	American history 2nd half	Hist		HF	H
220433	World history 1st half	Hist		HF	H
220433	World history 2nd half	Hist		HF	H
220501	American government	PolSc		HF	H
220502	Civics	PolSc		HF	H
220511	Mississippi history	Hist		HF	H
220599	Problems in American dem	PolSc		HF	H
220699	Sociology	Socio		HF	H

NCES No.	Course Title	Dept.	Course No.	Credits	Level
	College courses				
040101	Prin of accounting I	Acc	201	3S	L
040101	Prin of accounting II	Acc	202	3S	L
040199	Personal finance	Fin	320	3S	U
040301	Business finance	Fin	389	3S	U
040604	Business writing	BEd	300	3S	U
040708	General insurance	REI	325	3S	U
040999	Managerial communications	GBA	375	3S	U
041001	Principles of marketing	Mkt	300	3S	U
041199	Principles of management	Mgt	360	3S	U
041303	Real estate principles	REI	330	3S	U
041308	Real estate law	RIEs	340	3S	U
050605	Feature writing	Jou	301	3S	L
061099	Statistical methods I	CSs	211	3S	L
061099	Statistical methods II	CSs	212	3S	L
070401	Cir of secondary school	CIS	470	3S	U
070516	Math for elem teachers II	Mat	310	3S	U
070516	Math teach jr hi sch math	Mat	410	3S	U
070701	Principles of guidance	REF	336	3S	U
071199	Tests & measurements	REF	469	3S	U
0810	Engineering drawing I	IVE	323	3S	U
0810	Engineering drawing II	IVE	324	3S	U
090305	Neurology	Thy	454	3S	U
090305	Pathology	Thy	455	3S	U
120201	Shakespeare comedy & trag	Eng	454	3S	U
120202	Drama	Eng	200	3S	L
120299	Literature of the South	Eng	485	3S	U
120305	Language	Eng	101	3S	L
120307	Literature	Eng	102	3S	L
120310	Intro poetry writing	Eng	322	3S	U
120310	Intro short fiction writg	Eng	321	3S	U
120310	Short story writing	Eng	421	3S	U
120310	Poetry writing	Eng	422	3S	U

NCES No.	Course Title	Dept.	Course No.	Credits	Level
120399	Fiction	Eng	201	3S	L
120399	Poetry	Eng	202	3S	L
121105	Beginning German I	FL	121	3S	L
121105	Beginning German II	FL	122	3S	L
121105	Intermediate German	FL	221	3S	L
130799	Legal environment bus	GBA	295	3S	L
150199	General astronomy I	Ast	111	3S	L
150199	General astronomy II	Ast	112	3S	L
150301	Biological science I	PS	106	3S	L
150301	Biological science II	PS	107	3S	L
150399	History of biology	Bio	401	3S	U
150399	Biogeography	Bio	460	3S	U
150399	Introductory chemistry	Che	100	3S	L
150599	Physical geology	Gly	101	3S	L
150599	Historical geology	Gly	103	3S	L
150899	Physical science I	PS	104	3S	L
1509	Physical science II	PS	105	3S	L
160103	Appl algebra prob solv	Mat	112	3S	L
160199	Math for arts & hum	Mat	120	3S	L
160199	Math for elem teachers I	Mat	210	3S	L
160302	College algebra	Mat	101	3S	L
160401	Calculus I & analyt geom	Mat	276	3S	L
160401	Calculus I & analyt geom	Mat	277	3S	L
160602	Plane trigonometry	Mat	103	3S	L
180599	Introduction to logic	Phi	253	3S	L
1808	Intro to philosophy	Phi	151	3S	L
181101	Introduction to religion	Rel	131	3S	L
181202	The Christian tradition	Rel	335	3S	U
190104	Survey hist & phil of PE	PEd	222	3S	L
190106	Organ & admin of PE	PEd	426	3S	U
190311	Org & adm of athletics	AAC	303	3S	U
190311	Basic tech of coach footb	AAC	320	3S	U
190311	Bas tech of coach basktbl	AAC	321	3S	U
190311	Adv tech of coach footbll	AAC	421	3S	U
190311	Adv tech of coach basktbl	AAC	422	3S	U
190311	Coaching baseball	AAC	423	3S	U
190311	Coaching track & field	AAC	424	3S	U
190502	Community health	Hth	321	3S	U
190509	Personal health	Hth	101	3S	L
190704	Recreation leadership	Rec	323	3S	U
200199	General psychology	Psy	110	3S	L
200408	Mental hygiene	Psy	231	3S	L
200599	Human growth & dev I: chil	EPy	370	3S	U
200599	Hum growth & dev II: adol	EPy	372	3S	U
200805	Educational psychology	EPy	374	3S	U
210304	Traffic law	CJ	332	3S	U
220102	Language & culture	Ant	311	3S	U
220104	Mythology & folklore	Ant	412	3S	U
220106	Physical anthropology	Ant	301	3S	U
220199	Gen or intro anthropology	Ant	101	3S	L
220199	Anthropological theory	Ant	413	3S	U
220201	Principles of economics I	Eco	255	3S	L
220201	Principles of economics II	Eco	255	3S	L
220299	Introduction to economics	Eco	200	3S	L
220306	World regional geography	Ghy	103	3S	L
220306	Geography of US & Canada	Ghy	402	3S	L
220432	United States to 1877	His	140	3S	L
220432	United States since 1877	His	141	3S	L
220433	World civ to AD 1648	Hth	101	3S	L
220433	World civ since AD 1648	His	102	3S	L
220501	American government	PS	101	3S	L
220505	US foreign policy	PS	330	3S	U
220505	Intro internatnl politics	PS	331	3S	U
220509	State & local politics	PS	301	3S	U
220510	Introduction to pol sci	PS	220	3S	L
220602	Intro to criminal justice	CJ	200	3S	L
220602	Criminology	Soc	341	3S	U
220605	Marriage & human sex	Hth	430	3S	U
220605	The family	Soc	314	3S	U
220606	Intro to sociology	Soc	101	3S	L
220699	Intro to social work	Soc	230	3S	L

⑥① UNIVERSITY OF TENNESSEE

Dr. Kenneth L. Burton
Director
Center for Extended Learning
University of Tennessee
420 Communications Building
Knoxville, Tennessee 37996
Phone: (615) 974-5134

Enrollment on a noncredit basis accepted in all credit courses. Gifted high school students are permitted to enroll in undergraduate courses for credit. Overseas enrollment accepted. Courses in criminal justice are part of an external degree program.

NCES No.	Course Title	Dept.	Course No.	Credits	Level
	High school courses				
030501	Art: cartooning I	Art	1HS	HF	H
030501	Art: cartooning II	Art	2HS	HF	H
04	General business	Bus	1HS	HF	H
04	General business	Bus	2HS	HF	H
040104	Bookkeeping	Bus	1HS	HF	H
040104	Bookkeeping	Bus	2HS	HF	H
0402	Clerical practice	Bus	1HS	HF	H
040601	Business English	Bus	1HS	HF	H
040601	Business English	Bus	2HS	HF	H
041001	Salesmanship	Bus	1HS	HF	H
041001	Salesmanship	Bus	2HS	HF	H
0506	Journalism	Engl	13HS	HF	H
100604	Project self-discovery	SocSt	1HS	HF	H
120305	Ninth-grade lang skills	Engl	F-1H	HF	H
120305	Tenth-grade lang skills	Engl	S-1H	HF	H
120305	Eleventh-grade lang skills	Engl	J-1H	HF	H
120305	Twelfth-grade lang skills	Engl	SR-1H	HF	H
120305	Ninth-grade English	Engl	1HS	HF	H
120307	Ninth-grade English	Engl	2HS	HF	H
120307	Tenth-grade English: lit	Engl	4HS	HF	H
120307	Eleventh-gr Eng: Amer lit	Engl	6HS	HF	H
120307	Twelfth-gr Eng: Brit lit	Engl	8HS	HF	H
120307	British novel I	Engl	12HS	HF	H
120307	British novel II	Engl	2-12H	HF	H
120307	Science fiction	Engl	14HS	HF	H
120308	Ninth-grade rdg skills	Engl	F-2H	HF	H
120308	Tenth-grade rdg skills	Engl	S-2H	HF	H
120308	Eleventh-grade rdg skills	Engl	J-2H	HF	H
120308	Twelfth-grade rdg skills	Engl	SR-2H	HF	H
120310	Tenth-grade English	Engl	3HS	HF	H
120310	Eleventh-grade English	Engl	5HS	HF	H
120310	Twelfth-grade English	Engl	7HS	HF	H
120310	Creative writ: articles	Engl	9HS	HF	H
120310	Creative writ: stories	Engl	10HS	HF	H
120310	Creative writ: poetry	Engl	11HS	HF	H
1210	French I 1st sem	Frnch	1HS	HF	H
1210	French I 2nd sem	Frnch	2HS	HF	H
1210	French II 1st sem	Frnch	3HS	HF	H
1210	French II 2nd sem	Frnch	4HS	HF	H
1216	Latin	Lat	1HS	HF	H
1225	Spanish I 1st sem	Span	1HS	HF	H
1225	Spanish I 2nd sem	Span	2HS	HF	H
1225	Spanish II 1st sem	Span	3HS	HF	H
1225	Spanish II 2nd sem	Span	4HS	HF	H
1307	Business law	Bus	1HS	HF	H
1307	Business law	Bus	2HS	HF	H
15	General science	Sci	1HS	HF	H
15	General science	Sci	2HS	HF	H
1503	Biology	Bio	1HS	HF	H
1503	Biology	Bio	2HS	HF	H
160301	Business arithmetic	Bus	1HS	HF	H
160301	Business arithmetic	Bus	2HS	HF	H
160302	Algebra I 1st sem	Math	1HS	HF	H
160302	Algebra I 2nd sem	Math	2HS	HF	H
160302	Algebra II 1st sem	Math	3HS	HF	H
160302	Algebra II 2nd sem	Math	4HS	HF	H
160601	Geometry: plane 1st sem	Math	5HS	HF	H
160601	Geometry: plane 2nd sem	Math	6HS	HF	H
160602	Trigonometry	Math	7HS	HF	H
181202	Bible: New Testament	Relig	1HS	HF	H
181202	Bible: Old Testament	Relig	2HS	HF	H
1901	Physical education	PhyEd	1HS	HF	H
190510	Physical fitness	Hlth	7HS	HF	H
190510	Physical fitness	Hlth	8HS	HF	H
190603	Driver ed: gen safety	HSci	1HS	HF	H
2001	Psychology	Psych	1HS	HF	H
2001	Psychology	Psych	2HS	HF	H

NCES No.	Course Title	Dept.	Course No.	Credits	Level
2202	Economics	SocSt	1HS	HF	H
2202	Economics	SocSt	2HS	HF	H
2203	World geography	SocSt	1HS	HF	H
2203	World geography	SocSt	2HS	HF	H
2204	Ancient & medieval hist	Hist	1HS	HF	H
2204	Ancient & medieval hist	Hist	2HS	HF	H
220432	American history	Hist	7HS	HF	H
220432	American history	Hist	8HS	HF	H
220433	World history	Hist	5HS	HF	H
220433	World history	Hist	6HS	HF	H
220453	Modern history	Hist	3HS	HF	H
220453	Modern history	Hist	4HS	HF	H
220501	American government	SocSt	1HS	HF	H
220501	American government	SocSt	2HS	HF	H
220502	Civics	SocSt	1HS	HF	H
220502	Civics	SocSt	2HS	HF	H
2206	Sociology	Socio	1HS	HF	H
220605	Adjust & marriage prep	Socio	2HS	HF	H
	College courses				
0101	Land economics	AgEco	4330K	3Q	U
010999	Introduction to forestry	For	1620K	3Q	L
040103	Theory & pract: auditing	Acctg	4110M	3Q	U
040106	Survey: man cost acctg	Acctg	2130K	3Q	L
040106	Managerial cost acctg	Acctg	3210K	3Q	U
040106	Managerial cost acctg	Acctg	3220K	3Q	U
040108	Fundamentals of acctg	Acctg	2110K	3Q	L
040108	Fundamentals of acctg	Acctg	2120K	3Q	L
040108	Intermediate accounting	Acctg	3110K	3Q	U
040108	Intermediate accounting	Acctg	3120K	3Q	U
040108	Intermediate accounting	Acctg	3130K	3Q	U
040114	Federal income tax	Acctg	3430K	3Q	U
040201	Mgt: concepts/theo & prac	Bus	315C	3S	U
040201	Personnel management	Bus	332C	3S	U
040201	Principles of management	Bus	350C	3S	U
040201	Office management	OffAd	400C	3S	U
040203	Records management	OffAd	309C	3S	U
040301	Corporation finance	Bus	3120M	3Q	U
040301	Corporation finance	Bus	3130M	3Q	U
040308	Money and banking	Econ	301C	3S	U
040601	Business communication	OffAd	219C	3S	U
050603	Radio-TV news	Brdcs	3610K	3Q	U
050605	Writing feature articles	Jrnl	3120K	3Q	U
050608	Writing for mass media	Jrnl	2210K	3Q	L
0701	Education in the US	Educ	201C	3S	L
070201	Principles of bus educatn	Educ	4010M	3Q	U
070302	Teaching reading: elem sch	Educ	420C	3S	U
070303	Teaching read: secon sch	Educ	421C	3S	U
070604	Org/opr: distributive ed	Educ	4310K	3Q	U
070604	Coord technqs, distrib ed	Educ	4330K	3Q	U
0708	Ed of exceptional childrn	Educ	250C	3S	L
070804	Psy & ed of hearng impair	Educ	4250K	3Q	U
070804	Curr: el/sec sch, hearg im	Educ	4280K	3Q	U
071103	Educational measurement	Educ	412C	2S	U
080901	Elec eng: circuits I	EEg	2010K	3Q	L
080901	Elec eng: circuits II	EEg	2020K	3Q	L
081599	Engineering economy	IndEg	4520K	3Q	U
100313	Elementary nutrition	Nutrn	1230M	3Q	U
100601	Lrng experiences w parent	ChFam	4420K	3Q	U
100601	Child-care staff comptncs	ChFam	4710K	3Q	U
110699	Intro to transportation	Trans	3110K	3Q	U
110699	Traffic management	Trans	3120K	3Q	U
110699	Carrier liability & claim	Trans	4910K	3Q	U
110699	Trans law & procedures	Trans	4920K	3Q	U
120302	History of the Eng lang	Engl	4420M	3Q	U
120305	Modern English grammar	Engl	4430M	3Q	U
120307	Lit of the Western world	Engl	2112M	3Q	L
120307	Lit of the Western world	Engl	2132M	3Q	L
120307	English masterpieces	Engl	2510K	4Q	L
120307	English masterpieces	Engl	2520K	4Q	L
120307	American masterpieces	Engl	2530K	4Q	L
120307	Intro to drama	Engl	2660K	4Q	L
120307	Prose in the 18th century	Engl	3630M	3Q	U
120307	Western European culture	Engl	3640M	3Q	U
120307	Western European culture	Engl	3650M	3Q	U
120307	Women in literature	Engl	3750M	3Q	U
120307	Women in literature	Engl	3760M	3Q	U
120307	Shakespeare	Engl	4010K	3Q	U
120307	Shakespeare	Engl	4020K	3Q	U
120307	The British novel	Engl	4310K	3Q	U
120307	The British novel	Engl	4320K	3Q	U
120307	The British novel	Engl	4340K	3Q	U
120307	Intro study English lang	Engl	4410M	3Q	U
120307	Southern literature	Engl	4650M	3Q	U
120307	Poetry of John Milton	Engl	4850M	3Q	U
120307	Chaucer: *Canterbury Tales*	Engl	4920M	3Q	U
120307	Nineteenth-cen Amer novel	Engl	4050M	3Q	U
120310	English composition	Engl	1010K	3Q	L
120310	English composition	Engl	1020K	3Q	L
120310	English composition	Engl	1031K	3Q	L
120310	Technical writing	Engl	2010M	3Q	L
120399	Medical & scientif vocab	Engl	3150M	4Q	U
1210	Elementary French	Frnch	1110K	3Q	L
1210	Elementary French	Frnch	1120K	3Q	L
1210	Elementary French	Frnch	1130K	3Q	L
1210	Elementary French	Frnch	1520K	4Q	L
1210	French lit 17th century	Frnch	4110K	3Q	U
1210	French lit 17th century	Frnch	4120K	3Q	U
1210	French lit 17th century	Frnch	4130K	3Q	U
1210	French lit 18th century	Frnch	4310K	3Q	U
1210	French lit 18th century	Frnch	4320K	3Q	U
1210	French lit 18th century	Frnch	4330K	3Q	U
1210	Intermediate French	Frnch	2110K	3Q	L
1210	Intermediate French	Frnch	2120K	3Q	L
1210	Intermediate French	Frnch	2130K	3Q	L
1211	Elementary German	Ger	1110K	3Q	L
1211	Elementary German	Ger	1120K	3Q	L
1211	Elementary German	Ger	1130K	3Q	L
1211	Intermediate German	Ger	2110K	3Q	L
1211	Intermediate German	Ger	2120K	3Q	L
1211	Intermediate German	Ger	2130K	3Q	L
1214	Elementary Italian	Ital	1110K	3Q	L
1214	Elementary Italian	Ital	1120K	3Q	L
1214	Elementary Italian	Ital	1130K	3Q	L
1225	Spanish	Span	1510K	4Q	L
1225	Spanish	Span	1520K	4Q	L
1225	Intermediate Spanish	Span	2510K	4Q	L
1225	Intermediate Spanish	Span	2520K	4Q	L
1225	Aspects of Spanish lit	Span	3510K	4Q	U
1225	Aspects of Spanish lit	Span	3520K	4Q	U
1225	Spanish civilization	Span	4410K	3Q	U
1225	Latin American civilizatn	Span	4430K	3Q	U
1304	Criminal law	Soc	4000M	3Q	U
130799	Environmental busines law	Bus	4110K	3Q	U
130799	Law-bus organ & regulatn	Bus	4120K	3Q	U
130799	Adm regulatn of business	Bus	4130K	3Q	U
130799	Business law	Bus	4330K	3Q	U
140199	Books & rel mater childrn	LibSc	4510M	3Q	U
140199	Books & rel mat young peo	LibSc	4520M	3Q	U
150401	Chemistry, man & society	Chem	11C	3S	L
150599	Elements of geology	Geol	1110M	4Q	L
150599	Elements of geology	Geol	1120M	4Q	L
150599	Elements of geology	Geol	1130M	4Q	L
160299	Logic and sets	Math	3100K	3Q	L
160301	Basic con of element math	Math	2012K	4Q	L
160302	College algebra	Math	1540K	4Q	L
160303	Structure-number system	Math	2110K	3Q	L
160303	Structure-number system	Math	2120K	3Q	L
160303	Structure-number system	Math	2130K	3Q	L
160306	Linear algebra gen math	Math	1560K	4Q	L
160401	Introductory calculus	Math	1550K	4Q	L
160401	Single-variable calculus	Math	1840K	4Q	L
160401	Single-variable calculus	Math	1850K	4Q	L
160401	Single-variable calculus	Math	1860K	4Q	L
160401	Multi cal & matrix algebr	Math	2840K	4Q	L
160401	Multi cal & matrix algebr	Math	2850K	4Q	L
160803	Statistics for engnrng	Stat	3450K	3Q	U
18	Off-campus study	Philo	4102K	4Q	U
180399	Bioethics	Zool	3410K	3Q	U
180902	Images of Jesus	Relig	3311K	4Q	U
181104	Intro to religions world	Relig	2610K	4Q	L
181104	Issues in relig studies	Relig	2612K	4Q	L
181104	Hist of West rel tho & in	Relig	3060K	3Q	U
181104	Hist West rel thoug & ins	Relig	3070K	3Q	U
190502	Com hlth: death education	HEd	4140K	3Q	U
190509	Princ of personal health	HEd	1110K	3Q	L
190509	Personal hygiene	HEd	100C	3S	L
190511	Princ of general safety	HEd	3520K	3Q	U
200202	Bio foundations of behav	Psych	2520K	4Q	L
200501	Psych of the individual	Psych	2540K	4Q	L
200501	Abnormal psychology	Psych	3650K	4Q	U
200508	Child psychology	Psych	3550K	4Q	U
200599	Psych as a social science	Psych	2530K	4Q	L

NCES No.	Course Title	Dept.	Course No.	Credits	Level
200799	Social psychology	Psych	3120K	4Q	U
200804	Ed psych: child study	Educ	203C	2S	L
200804	Ed psych: adolescence	Educ	204C	2S	L
200804	Ed psych	Educ	207C	3S	L
2099	General psychology	Psych	2500K	4Q	L
2099	Psych statistics	Psych	3150K	4Q	U
210304	Intro to criminal justice	Soc	2000M	3Q	L
210304	Criminal investigation	Soc	3100M	3Q	U
210304	Criminal procedure I	Soc	3210M	3Q	U
210304	Criminal procedure II	Soc	3220M	3Q	U
210304	Criminal procedure III	Soc	3230M	3Q	U
210304	Police & community reltns	Soc	3300M	3Q	U
210304	Police mngmt systems	Soc	3500M	3Q	U
210304	Intro to security	Soc	3900M	3Q	U
210304	Criminalistics	Soc	4100M	3Q	U
210304	Crim just ethcs & sp prob	Soc	4600M	3Q	U
220102	Human culture	Anthr	2530K	4Q	L
220302	Economic geography	Geog	2110K	4Q	L
220302	Economic geography	Geog	2120K	4Q	L
220305	Weather & climate	Geog	206C	3S	L
220306	Geography Latin America	Geog	202C	3S	L
220306	Geography of Asia	Geog	205C	3S	L
220306	Geography of Soviet Union	Geog	3880K	4Q	U
220306	Regnl geog of US & Canada	Geog	3910K	4Q	U
220399	Introduction to geography	Geog	1610K	4Q	L
220399	Introduction to geography	Geog	1620K	4Q	L
220399	Geography of resources	Geog	3490K	4Q	L
2204	Dev of Western civilizatn	Hist	1510K	4Q	L
2204	Dev of Western civilizatn	Hist	1520K	4Q	L
220408	Wstn relig thought & inst	Relig	3060K	3Q	U
220427	History of Latin America	Hist	3870K	3Q	U
220427	History of Latin America	Hist	3880K	3Q	U
220427	History of Latin America	Hist	3890K	3Q	U
220428	History of Tennessee	Hist	3311	3Q	U
220428	History of Tennessee	Hist	3321	3Q	U
220432	History of United States	Hist	2510K	4Q	L
220432	History of United States	Hist	2520K	4Q	L
220501	US gov & polit: fndatns	PolSc	2510K	4Q	L
220501	US gov & polit: institutn	PolSc	2520K	4Q	L
220599	International relations	PolSc	3210M	3Q	U
220602	Corrections	Socio	4120M	3Q	U
220602	Criminology	Socio	4130M	3Q	U
220603	Collective behavior	Socio	3010K	4Q	U
220603	Sociology of aging	Socio	3690K	4Q	U
220605	Marriage & family relatns	Socio	2180M	3Q	L
220610	Socio of social problems	Socio	1520K	4Q	L
220610	Sociology of deviant beha	Socio	3510M	3Q	U
220612	Social stratification	Socio	3350K	4Q	U
220612	Race, class, and power	Socio	3410M	3Q	U
220612	Urban problems	Socio	3420K	4Q	U
220613	Social psychology	Socio	3130K	4Q	U
220614	Urban environment	Socio	3410K	4Q	L
220699	General sociology	Socio	1510K	4Q	L
220699	Intro to social research	Socio	3910K	4Q	U
220699	Elem statistical methods	Socio	3920K	4Q	U
220699	Formal organization	Socio	4560K	4Q	U
220699	Social movements	Socio	4930K	4Q	U

Noncredit courses

NCES No.	Course Title	Dept.	Course No.	Credits	Level
010406	Beekeeping			NC	H
030501	Basic cartooning		1	NC	H
030501	Advanced cartooning		2	NC	H
030501	Intr to pencil drawing			NC	L
040207	Typing	Bus	I	NC	L
041199	Personnel super & mgt			NC	L
041399	Real estate	RIEs	I	NC	L
041399	Real estate	RIEs	II	NC	L
081802	Basic oceanic navigation		1	NC	L
081802	Intermdt oceanic navigatn		2	NC	L
081802	Celestial navigation		3	NC	L
090404	Tennessee pharmacy laws	Pharm	333	NC	U
090404	Phamaceutcl jurisprudence	Pharm	334	NC	U
090408	Contemporary drug therapy	Pharm	316	NC	U
090408	Drug interactions	Pharm	322	NC	U
090408	Disease proc & app therap	Pharm	327	NC	U
090411	Cmnty pharm mgt/plng/dev	Pharm	232	NC	U
090411	Cmnty pharm mgt/op proc	Pharm	313	NC	U
090411	Nonprescription drugs I	Pharm	335	NC	U
090411	Nonprescription drugs II	Pharm	336	NC	U
090411	Intr to self-care consltg	Pharm	337	NC	U
090411	Weight-control counseling	Pharm	338	NC	U
090411	Patnt medcatn prof/phrmct	Pharm	342	NC	U
090411	Patnt medcatn recrd/nurse	Pharm	343	NC	U
100603	Gerontology			NC	L
100604	Project self-discovery			NC	H
120305	English: develpmntl skill	Engl	1	NC	H
120308	How to study			NC	L
120308	English: reading skills	Engl	2	NC	H
120310	How to write almost anyth			NC	L
120310	Creative writng: articles		1	NC	L
120310	Creative writng: stories		2	NC	L
120310	Creative writng: poetry		3	NC	L
1212	Greek		1N	NC	H
1212	Greek		2N	NC	H
1212	Greek		3N	NC	H
160199	Everyday math	Math		NC	L
160302	Refresher algebra	Math		NC	L
160602	Trigonometry	Math		NC	L
181202	Bible: What ds Bible say?	Relig	1M	NC	L
181202	Bible: mighty acts of God	Relig	2M	NC	L
181202	Bible: What's right?	Relig	3M	NC	L
181202	Bible: intr New Testament	Relig	4M	NC	L
181202	Bible: intr Old Testament	Relig	5M	NC	L
181202	Bible: Wht's relig livng?	Relig	6M	NC	L
181202	Bible: life/lit New Testa	Relig	7M	NC	L
181202	Bible: life/lit Old Testa	Relig	8M	NC	L
181202	Bible: Protestant denomns	Relig	10M	NC	L
2099	Mind over memory		1	NC	H

62 UNIVERSITY OF TEXAS AT AUSTIN

Ms. Olga Garza
Supervisor of Student Services
Extension and Correspondence Studies
University of Texas at Austin
Education Annex F-38
Austin, Texas 78712
Phone: (512) 471-5616

Enrollment on a noncredit basis accepted in all credit courses. Gifted high school students are permitted to enroll in undergraduate courses for credit. Overseas enrollment accepted. High school credit may be earned by examination, in keeping with state and school policies.

NCES No.	Course Title	Dept.	Course No.	Credits	Level
	High school courses				
040104	Accounting 1st sem	Acctg		HF	H
040104	Accounting 2nd sem	Acctg		HF	H
0404	Data processing 1st sem	DP		HF	H
040502	Free-enterprise system	FES		HF	H
0499	Gen business 1st sem	GB		HF	H
0499	Gen business 2nd sem	GB		HF	H
120302	American lit 1500-1900	Engl	17	HF	H
120305	Sr comp and lit soc crtsm	Engl	20	HF	H
120305	Review of grammar & comp	Engl	21	HF	H
120307	Freshman lit survey	Engl	13	HF	H
120307	Sophomore lit survey	Engl	15	HF	H
120307	Junior composition & lit	Engl	18	HF	H
120307	Eng lit srvy bng to 1900	Engl	19	HF	H
120307	Wish and nightmare	Engl	22	HF	H
120307	Fiction's world of horror	Engl	24	HF	H
120307	Science fiction	Engl	25	HF	H
120307	The Arthurian Legend	Engl	28	HF	H
120307	Biographies British Amer	Engl	29	HF	H
120307	Twentieth-century Eng lit	Engl	31	HF	H
120307	Twentieth-century Am lit	Engl	33	HF	H
120310	Freshman comp and lit	Engl	14	HF	H
120310	Sophomore comp and lit	Engl	16	HF	H
120310	Writing with style	Engl	30	HF	H
121605	First-year Latin 1st sem	Lat	I	HF	H
121605	First-year Latin 2nd sem	Lat	I	HF	H
121605	Second-year Latin 1st sem	Lat	II	HF	H
121605	Second-year Latin 2nd sem	Lat	II	HF	H
122505	Beginner's Span 1st sem	Span	I	HF	H
122505	Beginner's Span 2nd sem	Span	I	HF	H
122505	Intermed Spanish 1st sem	Span	II	HF	H

NCES No.	Course Title	Dept.	Course No.	Credits	Level
122505	Intermed Spanish 2nd sem	Span	II	HF	H
130799	Business law 1st sem	BL		HF	H
130799	Business law 2nd sem	BL		HF	H
1503	Biology I 1st sem	Bio	I	HF	H
1503	Biology I 2nd sem	Bio	I	HF	H
1508	Physical science 1st sem	PS		HF	H
1508	Physical science 2nd sem	PS		HF	H
160301	Fund of math 1st sem	FOM		HF	H
160301	Fund of math 2nd sem	FOM		HF	H
160302	Intro algebra 1st sem	IA		HF	H
160302	Intro algebra 2nd sem	IA		HF	H
160302	Algebra 1st sem	Alg		HF	H
160302	Algebra 2nd sem	Alg		HF	H
160302	Algebra 3rd sem	Alg		HF	H
160302	Algebra 4th sem	Alg		HF	H
160601	Geometry 1st sem	Geo		HF	H
160601	Geometry 2nd sem	Geo		HF	H
160602	Trigonometry one semester	Trg		HF	H
161202	Math of cons econ 1st sem	MCE		HF	H
161202	Math of cons econ 2nd sem	MCE		HF	H
180599	Philosophy one semester	Phl		HF	H
190312	Physical educ I 1st sem	PEd	I	HF	H
190312	Physical educ I 2nd sem	PEd	I	HF	H
190509	Health education I	HEd	I	HF	H
190509	Health education II	HEd	II	HF	H
220301	Wld geog studies 1st sem	WGS		HF	H
220301	Wld geog studies 2nd sem	WGS		HF	H
220432	Amer hist 1st sem	AH		HF	H
220432	Amer hist 2nd sem	AH		HF	H
220433	Wld hist studies 1st sem	WHS		HF	H
220433	Wld hist studies 2nd sem	WHS		HF	H
220499	Advanced Texas studies	ATS		HF	H
220501	American govt 1st sem	AG		HF	H
220501	American govt 2nd sem	AG		HF	H
220606	Sociology one semester	Socio		HF	H

College courses

NCES No.	Course Title	Dept.	Course No.	Credits	Level
040301	Business finance	Fin	357	3S	U
040308	Money bankng econ cndtns	Fin	354	3S	U
040604	Bus rpt wrtng behav comm	BC	324	3S	U
040903	Organizational behav admn	Mgmt	336	3S	U
040999	Operations management	Mgmt	335	3S	U
041001	Principles of marketing	Mktg	337	3S	U
041199	Personnel management	Mgmt	325	3S	U
041299	Elementary business stat	Sta	309	3S	L
041299	Intermed bus statistics	Sta	362	3S	U
041303	Intr real est urb lnd dev	RE	358	3S	U
070199	Psych found of elem educ	EdP	332E	3S	U
070199	Psych found of secnd educ	EdP	332S	3S	U
070309	Hum lrn dev: adult years	EdC	371.3	3S	U
070516	Modern topics elem math I	Math	316K	3S	L
070516	Modern topics el math II	Math	316L	3S	L
070516	Tching problems geometry	Math	333L	3S	U
071102	Intro to statistics	EdP	371	3S	U
090499	Pharm and med terminology	Pharm	313K	3S	L
100313	Introductory nutrition	HmEc	311	3S	L
120307	Mstrwks Eng lt th 18th c	Engl	312L	3S	L
120307	Intro to literature I	Engl	314K	3S	L
120307	Shakespeare: selected plys	Engl	321	3S	U
120307	American lit 1865 to pres	Engl	338	3S	U
120307	Intro to lit II black lit	Engl	314L	3S	L
120310	Rhetoric and composition	Engl	306	3S	L
120310	Literature & composition	Engl	307	3S	L
120310	Technical writing	Engl	317	3S	L
120310	Creative writing	Engl	325	3S	L
121005	First-year French I	Frnch	406	4S	L
121005	First-year French II	Frnch	407	4S	L
121005	Second-year French I	Frnch	312K	3S	L
121005	Second-year French II	Frnch	312L	3S	L
121105	First-year German I	Ger	406	4S	L
121105	First-year German II	Ger	407	4S	L
121108	Second-year German I	Ger	312K	3S	L
121108	Second-year German II	Ger	312L	3S	L
121241	First-year Greek I	Greek	506	5S	L
121241	First-year Greek II	Greek	507	5S	L
121241	Greek poetry and prose	Greek	312	3S	L
121243	New Testmnt Gk: The Gospel	Greek	319	3S	L
121243	Nw Tst Gk: Gsp/Acts/Pl/Ept	Greek	328	3S	U

NCES No.	Course Title	Dept.	Course No.	Credits	Level
121405	First-year Italian I	Ital	406	4S	L
121405	First-year Italian II	Ital	407	4S	L
121405	Second-year Italian I	Ital	312K	3S	L
121641	First-year Latin I	Latin	506	5S	L
121641	First-year Latin II	Latin	507	5S	L
121641	Latin prose reading	Latin	311	3S	L
122005	First-year Russian I	Rus	406	4S	L
122205	First-year Czech I	Czech	406	4S	L
122205	First-year Czech II	Czech	407	4S	L
122505	First-year Spanish I	Span	406	4S	L
122505	First-year Spanish II	Span	407	4S	L
122505	Second-year Spanish I	Span	312K	3S	L
122505	Second-year Spanish II	Span	312L	3S	L
122510	Advanced composition	Span	327	3S	U
130201	Commercial transactions	BL	366	3S	U
130299	Business law first course	BL	323	3S	U
140803	Museum education	AEd	376	3S	U
150103	Introductory astronomy	Astro	302	3S	L
150302	Cellular & molecular biol	Bio	302	3S	L
150303	Structure-fnctn organisms	Bio	303	3S	L
150803	Mechanics	Phys	301	3S	L
150899	Gen phys mech heat sound	Phys	302K	3S	L
150899	Gen phys elec mag lt nuc	Phys	302L	3S	L
150899	Elem phys nontech mech ht	Phys	609AI	3S	L
150899	Elem phys nontech elec mg	Phys	609B	3S	L
160302	College algebra	Math	301	3S	L
160303	First crs theory numbers	Math	328K	3S	U
160305	Intro algebraic structure	Math	343K	3S	U
160307	Lin alg and matrix theory	Math	311	3S	L
160401	Calculus I	Math	808A	4S	L
160401	Calculus II	Math	808B	4S	L
160401	Calculus III	Math	325	3S	U
160602	Trigonometry	Math	304E	3S	L
160603	Analytic geometry	Math	305E	3S	L
160699	Elem fnctns coord geom	Math	305G	3S	L
160702	Probability I	Math	362K	3S	U
160801	Elem statistical methods	Math	316	3S	L
161101	Math for bus and econ	Math	603A	3S	L
161101	Math for bus and econ	Math	603B	3S	L
161299	Mathematics of investment	Math	303F	3S	L
180501	Introduction to logic	Philo	312	3S	L
190515	Health educ in elem schls	HEd	333	3S	U
200104	Intro to psychology	Psych	301	3S	L
200403	Stat methds in psychology	Psych	317	3S	U
200501	Abnormal psychology	Psych	352	3S	U
200599	Child psychology	Psych	342	3S	U
220102	Cultural anthropology	Anthr	302	3S	L
220103	Amer Ind cultrs N of Mex	Anthr	336L	3S	U
220106	Physical anthropology	Anthr	301	3S	L
220106	Fossil man	Anthr	348	3S	U
220201	Intro to econ I: macroecon	Econ	302	3S	L
220201	Intro to econ II: microeco	Econ	303	3S	L
220301	Geography of the world	Geog	305	3S	L
220302	Economic geography	Res	325	3S	U
220302	Econ geog and locatn thry	Geog	335	3S	U
220305	Physical geography	Grg	301C	3S	L
220424	English civ before 1603	Hist	304K	3S	L
220424	English civ since 1603	Hist	304L	3S	L
220427	Latin America before 1810	Hist	346K	3S	L
220432	The US 1492-1865	Hist	315K	3S	L
220432	The US since 1865	Hist	315L	3S	L
220452	Westrn civ in med times	Hist	309K	3S	L
220453	Westrn civ in mdrn times	Hist	309L	3S	L
220501	American government	Gov	610A	3S	L
220501	American government	Gov	610B	3S	L
220504	Intl politics snce 2nd WW	Gov	323M	3S	U
220505	American foreign relatns	Gov	344	3S	U
220511	Texas government	Gov	105	1S	L
220603	Population and society	Socio	369K	3S	U
220606	Intro to stdy of sociolgy	Socio	302	3S	L
220615	Racial and ethnic rltns	Socio	344	3S	U
220699	Sex roles	Socio	333K	3S	U

Noncredit courses

NCES No.	Course Title	Dept.	Course No.	Credits	Level
090253	Dental office procedures	DOP		NC	V
090253	Dental charting	DC		NC	V
090253	Dental chairside techniqs	DCT		NC	V
120310	Writing with style	Engl	001N	NC	H

NCES No.	Course Title	Dept.	Course No.	Credits	Level
220502	Citizenship I	Cit	I	NC	D
220502	Citizenship II	Cit	II	NC	D

(63) **UNIVERSITY OF UTAH**

Dr. James P. Pappas
Director
Division of Continuing Education, Correspondence Study
University of Utah
1152 Annex
Salt Lake City, Utah 84112
Phone: (801) 581-6472

Enrollment on a noncredit basis accepted in all credit courses. Gifted high school students are permitted to enroll in undergraduate courses for credit. Overseas enrollment accepted for college and noncredit courses.

NCES No.	Course Title	Dept.	Course No.	Credits	Level
	College courses				
030302	Mideastern music	Music	327	3Q	U
030302	Poetry, prose & music	Music	511	3Q	U
030303	Music fund for elem tchrs	Music	159	2Q	L
030303	Music ed in elem school	Music	371	3Q	U
030502	Intro to the visual arts	Art	100	5Q	L
040101	Elementary accounting	Acctg	121	3Q	L
040101	Elementary accounting	Acctg	122	3Q	L
040111	Management accounting	Acctg	350	4Q	U
040114	Federal tax accounting	Acctg	509	4Q	U
040114	Federal tax accounting	Acctg	510	4Q	U
040205	Gregg shorthand	SecTr	161	4Q	L
040207	Fundmntls of typewriting	SecTr	140	2Q	L
040207	Intermediate typewriting	SecTr	141	2Q	L
040301	Business finance	Finan	303	4Q	U
040302	Personal finance	Finan	120	4Q	L
040306	Investment principles	Finan	336	4Q	U
040308	Money and banking	Econ	320	3Q	U
040601	Bus comm & research des	Mgmt	518	4Q	U
040708	Risk and insurance	Finan	324	4Q	U
041001	Principles of marketing	Mktg	301	4Q	U
050103	Intro to advertising	Mktg	350	4Q	U
050601	The editing process	JMC	301	4Q	U
050605	Magazine article writing	JMC	451	3Q	U
070204	Public school finance	EdAdm	530	3Q	U
070206	Educational law	EdAdm	634	3Q	U
070299	Conceptual prob in educ	EdAdm	652	3Q	U
070399	Introduction to education	Educ	151	2Q	L
070401	Kindergarten/early ch ed	Educ	520	3Q	U
070404	Storytelling in elem sch	Educ	102	3Q	L
070404	Fdtns el sch curriculum	Educ	503	6Q	U
070404	Tching science in el sch	Educ	449	3Q	U
070404	Social studies in el sch	Educ	450	3Q	U
070404	Art for elementary school	Educ	514	3Q	U
070404	Child literature in sch	Educ	440	3Q	U
070404	Mathematics in el school	Educ	408	3Q	U
070404	Language arts in el sch	Educ	430	3Q	U
070404	Reading as develop prcess	Educ	420	4Q	U
070404	Tching reading early chil	Educ	421	5Q	U
070404	Tching reading inter grds	Educ	422	5Q	U
070404	Tching reading content ar	Educ	558	4Q	U
070404	Child dev curriculum chge	Educ	602	3Q	U
070404	Modern pro in dev reading	Educ	659	3Q	U
070404	Tching reading secon schs	Educ	423	5Q	U
070404	Gen secondary tching meth	Educ	575	3Q	U
070404	Art for secondary schs	Art	491	3Q	U
070404	Real number system	Math	405	4Q	U
070404	Teach use of books librs	ESLR	553	3Q	U
070404	Methods/skills arts/craft	RecLe	320	3Q	U
070599	Behavior prob in school	Educ	611	3Q	U
070613	Intro to driver education	HSci	350	3Q	U
070613	Organ and admin driver ed	HSci	351	3Q	U
070613	Driver ed individual stdy	HSci	692	VC	U
070801	Intro to special educ	SpEd	502	3Q	U
071203	Intro to instruction med	ESLR	512	3Q	U
071203	Intro to instruction med	ESLR	512	5Q	U
071203	Prin of graphic communica	ESLR	513	4Q	U
071204	Organ school media prog	ESLR	551	3Q	U
071205	Instructional TV programg	ESLR	570	3Q	U
071299	Eval and sel of ed media	ESLR	503	3Q	U
071299	Cat and class spec mater	ESLR	541	3Q	U

NCES No.	Course Title	Dept.	Course No.	Credits	Level
0810	Engineering drawing	CivEg	101	2Q	L
081399	Energy and man	FueEg	141	4Q	L
082199	Elements of metallurgy	MetEg	361	3Q	U
090403	Alcohol and drugs	HSci	548	3Q	U
090901	Personal health problems	HSci	101	3Q	L
090901	School health program	HSci	312	3Q	U
100312	Fundmntls of nutrition	FdNut	144	3Q	U
120299	Amer lit 1900-1945	Engl	519	5Q	U
120299	Amer lit since 1945	Engl	520	4Q	U
120299	Shakespeare: early plays	Engl	540	5Q	U
120299	American folklore	Engl	573	5Q	U
120305	Modern English grammar	Engl	343	5Q	U
120310	Intro to expository writg	Engl	101	4Q	L
1299	First-year Persian	Persi	101	5Q	L
1299	First-year Persian	Persi	102	5Q	L
130799	Business law	Mgmt	341	4Q	U
140199	Intro to cat and classif	ESLR	540	4Q	U
140804	Reference work	ESLR	351	4Q	U
140899	Selection of lib material	ESLR	533	4Q	U
140902	Library work with child	ESLR	326	5Q	U
140904	Use of books and library	ESLR	102	2Q	L
150199	Cultural astronomy	Phys	106	4Q	L
150202	Intro to meteorology	Meteo	101	4Q	L
150202	Dynamics-thermodynamics	Meteo	561	3Q	U
150202	Dynamics-basic equations	Meteo	562	3Q	U
150202	Dynamics-basic hydrodyna	Meteo	563	3Q	U
150304	Human ecology	Bio	175	3Q	U
150306	Evolution	Bio	350	3Q	U
150307	Human genetics	Bio	335	3Q	U
150399	Introductory physiology	Bio	201	5Q	L
150799	Elementary physics	Phys	101	5Q	L
150799	General mechanics sound	Phys	111	4Q	L
150799	General heat elec magneti	Phys	112	4Q	L
150799	General light modern phy	Phys	113	4Q	L
150799	For sc eng: mechanics	Phys	171	4Q	L
150799	For sc eng: elec magneti	Phys	172	4Q	L
150799	For sc eng: heat/lght/sd	Phys	173	4Q	L
150799	Science and soc futurism	Phys	100	3Q	L
160302	Intermediate algebra	Math	101	5Q	L
160302	College algebra	Math	105	5Q	L
160401	Calculus I	Math	111	4Q	L
160401	Calculus I	Math	112	4Q	L
160401	Calculus I	Math	113	4Q	L
160602	Plane trigonometry	Math	106	5Q	L
160803	Elementary statistics	Math	107	4Q	L
190199	Intro to physical educ	PhyEd	250	2Q	L
190203	Physiology of exercise	PhyEd	282	2Q	L
190203	Medical aspects	PhyEd	283	2Q	L
190306	Sport psychology	PhyEd	278	2Q	L
190311	Nordic ski practicum	PhyEd	284	4Q	L
190511	Accident prevention	HSci	104	3Q	L
190512	Human sexuality	HSci	300	3Q	U
190704	The recreation program	RecLe	332	5Q	U
190709	Outdoor recreation	RecLe	530	3Q	U
190799	Recreat and leisure mod s	RecLe	192	5Q	U
200199	Psychology	Psych	101	5Q	L
200501	Psych of abnormal behav	Psych	340	4Q	U
200503	Survey of clinical stat	Psych	332	3Q	U
200603	Elementary statistics	Psych	150	4Q	L
200799	Social psychology	Psych	341	4Q	U
220101	Prehistory of No America	Anthr	541	3Q	U
220101	Archaeology of Southwest	Anthr	320-3	3Q	U
220102	Intro to cultural anthro	Anthr	101	5Q	L
220106	Intro to physical anthro	Anthr	102	5Q	L
220109	Civiliz of the Aztecs	Anthr	320-1	5Q	U
220109	Indians of North America	Anthr	304	5Q	U
220109	Civilization of the Maya	Anthr	320-2	5Q	U
220201	Economics as social sci	Econ	105	5Q	L
220202	Economic history of US	Econ	274	4Q	L
220211	Labor economics	Econ	310	4Q	U
220301	World cultural geography	Geog	160	5Q	L
220306	Geog of Mexico and Cen Am	Geog	355	4Q	U
220306	Geography of Utah	Geog	360	3Q	U
220408	The Reformation	Hist	510	5Q	U
220426	Europe since 1914	Hist	310	5Q	U
220427	The Mexican nation	Hist	561	5Q	U
220428	History of Utah	Hist	586	5Q	U
220432	American civilization	Hist	170	5Q	L
220450	Hist of civilizat: ancient	Hist	101	5Q	L
220453	Hist of civilizat: modern	Hist	103	5Q	L

NCES No.	Course Title	Dept.	Course No.	Credits	Level
220501	American national govt	PolSc	110	5Q	L
220505	Intro to intl politics	PolSc	210	5Q	L
220599	Intro to political sci	PolSc	101	5Q	L
220606	Intro to sociology	Socio	101	5Q	L
	Noncredit courses				
041107	Intro to business mgmt	Mgmt	10R	NC	V
041303	Real estate principles	Finan	24	NC	V
160302	Preparatory algebra	Math	50	NC	L
1906	Motor vehicle acc reconst			NC	L
220502	Naturalization			NC	V

(64) UNIVERSITY OF WASHINGTON

Dr. Kathleen A. J. Murphy
Program Director, Independent Study
University of Washington
222 Lewis Hall
Mail Stop DW-30
Seattle, Washington 98195
Phone: (206) 543-2350

Enrollment on a noncredit basis accepted in all credit courses. Gifted high school students are permitted to enroll in undergraduate courses for credit. Overseas enrollment accepted.

NCES No.	Course Title	Dept.	Course No.	Credits	Level
	College courses				
010901	Interp the environment	For M	C353	5Q	U
030302	Symphony music: 19th cen	Music	C123	2Q	L
030302	History of jazz	Music	C331	3Q	U
040311	Money, natl income, price	B Ecn	C301	4Q	U
0408	Interntnl enviro business	IntBu	C300	5Q	U
0408	Bus enviro: indust country	IntBu	C340	4Q	U
041001	Marketing concepts	Mktg	C301	4Q	U
041004	Retailing	Mktg	C470	4Q	U
041005	Advertising	Mktg	C340	4Q	U
050299	The mass media	Commu	C150	5Q	L
060701	Intro FORTRAN programming	Engr	C141	4Q	L
071103	Basic educ statistics	EdPsy	C490	3Q	U
081104	Engineering statics	Engr	C210	4Q	L
090255	Interaction: parent-child	Nurs	C436	3Q	U
090305	Phys ther in public schls	Rehab	C413	3Q	U
090905	Chronic dis: epilepsy	Nurs	C353	3Q	U
100601	Normal devel & atypic inf	Psych	C498	3Q	U
120199	Intro Romance linguistics	Rom	C402	5Q	U
120299	Mod Europ lit in translat	Engl	C371	5Q	U
120299	Mod Jewish lit in trans	Engl	C372	5Q	U
120307	Science fiction & fantasy	Engl	C489B	3Q	U
120307	Popular literature	Engl	C221	5Q	L
120307	Chldrn's lit reconsidered	Engl	C223	5Q	L
120307	Chaucer	Engl	C311	5Q	U
120307	Late Renaissance	Engl	C321	5Q	U
120307	Milton	Engl	C322	5Q	U
120307	Amer lit: early nation	Engl	C352	5Q	U
120307	Amer lit: later 19th cent	Engl	C353	5Q	U
120307	Amer lit: early modern	Engl	C354	5Q	U
120307	Amer lit: contemp America	Engl	C355	5Q	U
120307	Utopias and social ideals	Engl	C417	5Q	U
120307	Shakespeare: survey	Engl	C231	5Q	L
120307	Shakespeare to 1603	Engl	C314	5Q	U
120307	Shakespeare after 1603	Engl	C315	5Q	U
120307	Reading literature	Engl	C200	5Q	L
120307	The contemporary novel	Engl	C359	5Q	U
120307	The modern novel	Engl	C340	5Q	U
120307	Fantasy	Engl	C370	5Q	U
120307	The Bible as literature	Engl	C309	5Q	U
120307	Studies in autobiog lit	Engl	C489	5Q	U
120310	College writing	Engl	C171	3Q	L
120310	Begin verse writing	Engl	C274	5Q	L
120310	Intermediate verse writng	Engl	C386	5Q	L
120310	Intermediate verse writng	Engl	C387	5Q	L
120310	Advanced verse writing	Engl	C422	5Q	U
120310	Advanced verse writing	Engl	C423	5Q	U
120310	Advanced verse writing	Engl	C424	5Q	U
120310	Intermed expos writing	Engl	C271	5Q	L
120310	Advanced expos writing	Engl	C379	5Q	U
120310	Begin short story writing	Engl	C277	5Q	L
120310	Advan short story writing	Engl	C388	5Q	U

NCES No.	Course Title	Dept.	Course No.	Credits	Level
120399	Technical writing	Engr	C331	3Q	U
120805	Elem Danish	Dan	C101	5Q	L
120808	Elem Danish	Dan	C102	5Q	L
120809	Elem Danish	Dan	C103	5Q	L
120905	Elem Finnish	Finn	C101	5Q	L
120908	Elem Finnish	Finn	C102	5Q	L
121005	Elem French	Fren	C111	5Q	L
121005	Elem French	Fren	C112	5Q	L
121005	Elem French	Fren	C113	5Q	L
121008	Elem French reading	Fren	C105	5Q	L
121105	First-year German	Germ	C111	5Q	L
121105	First-year German	Germ	C112	5Q	L
121105	First-year German	Germ	C113	5Q	L
121107	Advan 2nd-year German	Germ	C203	3Q	L
121108	Basic 2nd-year German	Germ	C201	5Q	L
121108	Inter 2nd-year German	Germ	C202	5Q	L
121341	Elementary Hebrew	Hebr	C101	5Q	L
121405	Elem Italian	Ital	C111	5Q	L
121405	Elem Italian	Ital	C112	5Q	L
121405	Elem Italian	Ital	C113	5Q	L
121410	Inter Italian	Ital	C213	5Q	L
121805	Elem Norwegian	Norw	C101	5Q	L
121807	Norwegian contemp novel	Norw	C300	3Q	U
121808	Elem Norwegian	Norw	C102	5Q	L
121809	Elem Norwegian	Norw	C103	5Q	L
122205	First-year Russian	Russ	C101	5Q	L
122205	First-year Russian	Russ	C102	5Q	L
122504	Cultural bkground lit	Span	C461	5Q	U
122505	Elem Spanish	Span	C111	5Q	L
122505	Basic grammar review	Span	C122	5Q	L
122508	Elem Spanish	Span	C112	5Q	L
122509	Elem Spanish	Span	C113	5Q	L
122510	Inter Spanish	Span	C211	5Q	L
122510	Inter Spanish	Span	C212	5Q	L
122510	Inter Spanish	Span	C213	5Q	L
122510	Advan syntax and comp	Span	C301	5Q	U
122510	Advan syntax and comp	Span	C302	5Q	U
122605	Elem Swedish	Swed	C101	5Q	L
122608	Elem Swedish	Swed	C102	5Q	L
122609	Elem Swedish	Swed	C103	5Q	L
130899	Women and the law	Wom S	C310	5Q	L
150101	Astronomy	Astr	C101	5Q	L
150201	Survey of the atmosphere	AtmSc	C101	5Q	L
150401	Chemical science	Chem	C100	5Q	L
150401	General chemistry	Chem	C140	4Q	L
150401	General chemistry	Chem	C150	4Q	L
1506	Survey of oceanography	Ocean	C101	5Q	L
160399	Appl of algebra to busin	Math	C156	5Q	L
160403	Calculus with analyt geom	Math	C124	5Q	L
160405	Appl of calculus to busin	Math	C157	5Q	L
160406	Calculus with analyt geom	Math	C125	5Q	L
160407	Calculus with analyt geom	Math	C126	5Q	L
160408	Elem diff equations	Math	C238	3Q	L
160507	Elementary functions	Math	C105	5Q	L
160802	Basic statistics	Stat	C220	5Q	L
160802	Basic statistics wth appl	Stat	C301	5Q	U
160802	Elements of stat methods	Stat	C311	5Q	U
161299	Math for elem schl tchrs	Math	C170	3Q	L
180502	Introduction to logic	Phil	C120	5Q	L
181002	Intro to Eastern religion	Relig	C202	5Q	L
200501	Deviant personality	Psych	C305	5Q	U
200504	Normal devel & atypic inf	Psych	C498	3Q	U
200504	Developmental psychology	Psych	C306	5Q	U
200509	Intro to pers and ind dif	Psych	C205	4Q	U
200604	Basic educ statistics	EdPsy	C490	3Q	U
200702	Social psychology	Psych	C345	5Q	U
200799	Psych as a social science	Psych	C101	5Q	L
220101	Meth & princ archaeology	Archy	C499	5Q	U
220102	Intro to study of man	Anthr	C100	5Q	L
220102	Anthro studies of women	Anthr	C353	5Q	U
220103	Pacific NW Indians	Anthr	C311	5Q	U
220107	Principles social anthro	Anthr	C202	5Q	L
220201	Intro to economics	Econ	C200	5Q	L
220202	Econ hist of Westrn world	Econ	C260	5Q	L
220213	Intro microeconomics	Econ	C201	5Q	L
220302	Economic geography	Geog	C207	5Q	L
220308	Geography of cities	Geog	C277	5Q	L
220428	Hist Washington and NW	Hist	C432	5Q	U
220472	Anthrop study of women	Wom S	C353	5Q	U
220504	Pub bureauc in pol order	PolSc	C470	5Q	U
220505	Intro to intntl relations	PolSc	C203	5Q	L

NCES No.	Course Title	Dept.	Course No.	Credits	Level
220505	American foreign policy	PolSc	C321	5Q	U
220506	Intro to Amer politics	PolSc	C202	5Q	L
220507	Politics & mass communic	PolSc	C305	5Q	U
220509	The American democracy	PolSc	C351	5Q	U
220510	Intro to politics	PolSc	C101	5Q	L
220605	The family	Socio	C352	5Q	U
220606	Survey of sociology	Socio	C110	5Q	L
220610	Sociology of deviance	Socio	C271	5Q	L
220613	Race relations	Socio	C362	5Q	U
	Noncredit courses				
160302	Intermediate algebra	Math	C101	NC	H
160399	Elementary algebra: survey	Math	CA	NC	H
160399	Elementary algebra: survey	Math	CB	NC	H
160602	Plane trigonometry	Math	C104	NC	H
160603	Analytic geometry: survey	Math	CC	NC	H
160603	Analytic geometry: survey	Math	CD	NC	H

(65) UNIVERSITY OF WISCONSIN–EXTENSION

Dr. Donald F. Kaiser
Director, Independent Study
University of Wisconsin–Extension
432 North Lake Street
Madison, Wisconsin 53706
Phone: (608) 263-2055

Enrollment on a noncredit basis accepted in some credit courses. Gifted high school students are permitted to enroll in undergraduate courses for credit. Overseas enrollment accepted. In addition to college credit, high school, and continuing education (noncredit) courses, the university offers correspondence courses in vocational-technical subjects.

NCES No.	Course Title	Dept.	Course No.	Credits	Level
	High school courses				
020402	Architectural drawing	Arch	A88	HF	H
030302	Beginning music theory I	Music	H30	1U	H
030302	Beginning music theory II	Music	H31	1U	H
030599	Elements of art	VisAr	H41	HF	H
030599	Basic drawing	VisAr	A20	HF	H
030699	Study of Western art	ArHis	A15	1U	H
040104	Basic bookkeeping I	Bus	A30	HF	H
040104	Basic bookkeeping II	Bus	A31	HF	H
040104	Advanced bookkeeping I	Bus	H40	HF	H
040104	Advanced bookkeeping II	Bus	H41	HF	H
040205	Gregg shorthand I	Bus	A42	HF	H
041005	Retail selling	Bus	A82	QT	H
0499	General business I	Bus	H25	HF	H
0499	Stocks, bonds & investing	Bus	A69	QT	H
050608	High school journalism	Jrnl	H30	HF	H
080102	General aeronautics	AraEg	V68	HF	H
0804	Automotive engines	EngAS	A60	HF	H
0804	Automotive chassis	EngAS	A61	HF	H
0804	Diesel engines	EngAS	A64	HF	H
080999	Electricity fundamentals	EngAS	W72	HF	H
090799	Family & community health	HSci	H30	HF	H
110407	Intro to refrigeration	EngAS	W97	HF	H
120305	First-yr high sch Engl I	Engl	H10	HF	H
120305	First-yr high sch Eng II	Engl	H11	HF	H
120307	American literature	Lit	H30	HF	H
120307	American literature	Lit	H31	HF	H
120307	English literature	Lit	H41	HF	H
120310	Grammar & composition	Engl	H12	HF	H
120310	Second-yr high sch Eng I	Engl	H20	HF	H
120310	Second-yr high sch Eng II	Engl	H21	HF	H
120310	Writing & grammar review	Engl	H42	HF	H
120310	Creative writing	Engl	H45	HF	H
121005	First-sem high sch French	Frnch	H10	HF	H
121005	Second-sem h s Frnch	Frnch	H11	HF	H
121008	Third-sem high sch Frnch	Frnch	H20	HF	H
121008	Fourth-sem high sch Frnch	Frnch	H21	HF	H
121008	Fifth-sem high sch French	Frnch	H30	HF	H
121008	Sixth-sem high sch French	Frnch	H31	HF	H
121008	Seventh-sem h s Frnch	Frnch	H40	HF	H
121008	Eighth-sem high sch Frnch	Frnch	H41	HF	H
121105	First-sem high sch German	Ger	H10	HF	H
121105	Second-sem high sch Ger	Ger	H11	HF	H
121108	Third-sem h s German	Ger	H20	HF	H
121108	Fourth-sem high sch Ger	Ger	H21	HF	H

NCES No.	Course Title	Dept.	Course No.	Credits	Level
121108	Fifth-sem high sch German	Ger	H30	HF	H
121108	Sixth-sem high sch German	Ger	H31	HF	H
121108	Seventh-sem h s German	Ger	H40	HF	H
121108	Eighth-sem high sch Ger	Ger	H41	HF	H
121605	First-sem high sch Latin	CILL	H10	HF	H
121605	Second-sem high sch Latin	CILL	H11	HF	H
121605	Third-sem high sch Latin	CILL	H20	HF	H
121608	Fourth-sem high sch Latin	CILL	H21	HF	H
122005	First-sem high sch Russn	Rus	H10	HF	H
122005	Second-sem h s Russian	Rus	H11	HF	H
122005	Third-sem h s Russian	Rus	H20	HF	H
122005	Fourth-sem h s Russian	Rus	H21	HF	H
122009	Russian conversation/comp	Rus	A70	1U	H
122010	Fifth-sem h s Russian	Rus	H30	HF	H
122010	Sixth-sem h s Russian	Rus	H31	HF	H
122010	Seventh-sem h s Russian	Rus	H40	HF	H
122010	Eighth-sem h s Russian	Rus	H41	HF	H
122505	First-sem h s Spanish	Span	H10	HF	H
122505	Second-sem h s Spanish	Span	H11	HF	H
122505	Third-sem h s Spanish	Span	H20	HF	H
122505	Fourth-sem h s Spanish	Span	H21	HF	H
122505	Seventh-sem h s Spanish	Span	H40	HF	H
122505	Eighth-sem h s Spanish	Span	H41	HF	H
122510	Fifth-sem h s Spanish	Span	H30	HF	H
122510	Sixth-sem h s Spanish	Span	H31	HF	H
140903	Using h s libry media ctr	LibSc	H30	HF	H
150302	General biology I	Bio	H20	HF	H
150303	General biology II	Bio	H21	HF	H
150899	Gen physical science I	Meas	H20	HF	H
150899	Gen physical science II	Meas	H21	HF	H
160301	Shop arithmetic I	Meas	A50	HF	H
160301	Practical arithmetic	Meas	A52	HF	H
160302	First-semester algebra	Math	H10	HF	H
160302	Second-semester algebra	Math	H11	HF	H
160302	Advanced algebra I	Math	H30	HF	H
160302	Advanced algebra II	Math	H31	HF	H
160302	College algebra	Math	H39	HF	H
160306	Introductory linear math	Math	H43	HF	H
160601	Geometry I	Math	H20	HF	H
160601	Geometry II	Math	H21	HF	H
160602	Plane trigonometry	Math	H40	HF	H
161299	Math for electricity I	Meas	A56	HF	H
161299	Math for electricity II	Meas	A57	HF	H
220299	Contemporary economics	Econ	H40	HF	H
220305	Physical geography	Geog	H22	HF	H
220432	US history to 1877	Hist	H30	HF	H
220432	US history since 1877	Hist	H31	HF	H
220501	American govt today	PolSc	H30	HF	H
	College courses				
010104	Cooperation	Agri	422	3S	U
010902	Introduction to forestry	Bio	100	2S	L
030302	Apprec & history of music	Music	101	2S	L
030302	Apprec & history of music	Music	102	2S	L
030599	Creative design	Art	131	3S	L
030699	History of Western art	ArHis	105	4S	L
040101	Elementary accounting I	Bus	201	3S	L
040101	Elementary accounting II	Bus	202	3S	L
040101	Intermediate accounting I	Bus	301	3S	L
040101	Intermediate acctg II	Bus	302	3S	L
040106	Cost accounting I	Bus	323	3S	U
040106	Advanced cost accounting	Bus	413	3S	U
040111	Managerial accounting	Bus	300	3S	L
040306	Investments	Bus	322	3S	L
040306	Principles of finance	Bus	320	3S	U
040307	Financial management	Bus	427	3S	L
040710	Prin of risk management	Bus	560	3S	U
040903	Organization behavior	Bus	346	3S	L
040905	Organization & mgt	Bus	233	3S	L
040999	Intro Amer bus enterprise	Bus	120	3S	L
040999	Production management	Bus	341	3S	L
040999	Purchasing—matrls mgmt	Bus	436	3S	U
041001	Principles of marketing	Bus	311	3S	L
041199	Personnel administration	Bus	303	3S	U
0499	Business law I	Bus	305	3S	U
050103	Advertising copy & layout	Jrnl	450	4S	L
050605	Writing feature articles	Jrnl	305	3S	L
050608	Newswriting	Jrnl	203	3S	L
0507	Publications design	Jrnl	207	2S	L
0509	Public relations	Jrnl	525	3S	U
060799	FORTRAN programming	EngAS	211	2S	U

NCES No.	Course Title	Dept.	Course No.	Credits	Level
061103	Intro to computers	CmpSc	113	3S	L
070309	Voc tech adult education	Educ	502	2S	L
070499	School curriculum design	Educ	300	3S	L
070499	Early childhood education	Educ	482	1S	L
070509	Health info for teachers	Educ	340	3S	L
070512	Children's literature	Educ	649	3S	L
070602	Career education	Educ	498	3S	L
070899	The exceptnl individual	Educ	300	3S	L
070899	Children with handicaps	Educ	496	2S	L
070902	Human relation–education	Educ	465	3S	L
070999	Family day care	Educ	481	1S	L
080799	Critical path network	EngAS	590	2S	L
081104	Dynamics	EngAS	222	3S	U
081104	Statics	EngAS	221	3S	U
081199	Mechanics of materials	EngAS	303	3S	U
081599	Industrial engineering	EngAS	114	3S	L
081799	Economic analysis—engr	EngAS	312	3S	U
082099	Intro numerical control	EngAS	428	2S	L
082199	Intro to materials sci	EngAS	360	3S	U
090799	Nursing in the school	HSci	470	2S	U
100206	Consumer education	Bus	344	3S	L
100601	The child: his nature	Educ	120	3S	L
100601	Development in adolescenc	Educ	321	3S	L
100604	Human ability & learning	Educ	301	3S	U
110119	Art & science of welding	EngAS	137	3S	L
120103	Intro to linguistics	Engl	320	3S	L
120201	Fantasy & science fiction	Lit	357	3S	L
120302	Hist of English language	Engl	323	3S	L
120305	Structure of English lang	Engl	329	3S	L
120307	Intro to literature	Engl	200	3S	L
120307	Contemporary literature	Engl	209	3S	L
120307	American literature	Engl	211	3S	L
120307	American literature	Engl	212	3S	L
120307	Shakespearian drama	Engl	217	3S	L
120307	Shakespearian drama	Engl	218	3S	L
120307	Saul Bellow	Engl	311	1S	L
120307	Willa Cather	Engl	312	1S	L
120307	Doris Lessing	Engl	313	1S	L
120307	Eudora Welty	Engl	314	1S	L
120307	Virginia Woolf	Engl	315	1S	L
120307	Sherwood Anderson	Engl	365	1S	L
120307	Ernest Hemingway	Engl	431	1S	L
120307	William Faulkner	Engl	433	1S	L
120307	Graham Greene	Engl	434	1S	L
120307	The English novel	Engl	460	3S	L
120307	Camus in translation	Engl	230	1S	L
120307	De Beauvoir in translation	Engl	231	1S	L
120307	Colette in translation	Engl	232	1S	L
120307	Malraux in translation	Engl	260	1S	L
120307	Thomas Mann	Engl	190	1S	L
120307	Günter Grass	Engl	191	1S	L
120307	Scandinavian experience	Engl	295	1S	L
120307	Unamuno	Engl	256	1S	L
120307	Wisconsin authors	Engl	216	3S	L
120310	Technical writing	EngAS	279	3S	L
120310	Technical writing I	EngAS	273	1S	L
120310	Technical writing II	EngAS	274	1S	L
120310	Technical writing III	EngAS	275	1S	L
120310	Intermediate composition	Engl	201	2S	L
120310	Intro to creative writing	Engl	203	2S	L
120399	Freshman English	Engl	102	3S	L
120542	First-semester Arabic	Heb	101	4S	L
120542	Second-semester Arabic	Heb	102	4S	L
121005	First-semester French	Frnch	103	4S	L
121005	Second-semester French	Frnch	104	4S	L
121005	Third-semester French	Frnch	203	3S	U
121005	Fourth-semester French	Frnch	204	3S	U
121007	French lit: 17th & 18th c	Frnch	221	3S	U
121007	French lit: 19th century	Frnch	222	3S	U
121007	French lit: 20th century	Frnch	223	3S	U
121007	Modern French dramatists	Frnch	644	3S	U
121007	André Malraux	Frnch	360	1S	U
121007	Camus	Frnch	441	1S	U
121007	Simone de Beauvoir	Frnch	442	1S	U
121007	Colette	Frnch	443	1S	U
121010	Intermediate composition	Frnch	227	2S	U
121010	Advanced composition	Frnch	324	2S	U
121099	Business French	Frnch	219	2S	U
121099	Applied German philology	Ger	662	3S	U
121105	First-semester German	Ger	103	4S	L
121105	Second-semester German	Ger	104	4S	L
121105	Third-semester German	Ger	203	3S	U
121105	Fourth-semester German	Ger	204	3S	U
121107	Intro German literature	Ger	221	3S	U
121107	Intro German literature	Ger	222	3S	U
121107	The classical period	Ger	302	3S	U
121107	Contemporary German lit	Ger	305	3S	U
121107	Goethe's *Faust*	Ger	633	3S	U
121107	Thomas Mann	Ger	699A	1S	U
121107	Günter Grass	Ger	699B	1S	U
121110	Intermediate composition	Ger	223	3S	U
121110	Intermediate composition	Ger	224	3S	U
121241	Elementary Greek	Greek	103	4S	L
121241	Elementary Greek	Greek	104	4S	L
121241	Plato	Greek	104P	2S	L
121241	Homer: *The Iliad*	Greek	210	3S	L
121243	Xenophon & New Testament	Greek	204	3S	L
121341	First-sem Hebrew—biblical	Heb	101B	4S	L
121341	Scnd-sem Hebrew—bibl	Heb	104	2S	L
121341	Biblical texts: Esther	Heb	201	2S	L
121341	Exodus & Leviticus	Heb	321	2S	L
121341	Biblical texts: Joshua	Heb	322	2S	L
121341	Aramaic: Daniel & Ezra	Heb	501	2S	U
121342	First-sem Hebrew—modern	Heb	101M	4S	L
121342	Scnd-sem Hebrew—mod	Heb	103	2S	L
121342	Mod Hebrew conversation	Heb	225	3S	L
121399	Sefarad-Spanish Jewry	Heb	365	3S	U
121399	Jewish cultural hist I	Heb	471	3S	L
121399	Jewish cultural hist II	Heb	472	3S	L
121405	First-semester Italian	Ital	103	4S	L
121405	Second-semester Italian	Ital	104	4S	L
121405	Third-semester Italian	Ital	203	3S	L
121405	Fourth-semester Italian	Ital	204	3S	L
121641	Elementary Latin	Clas	103	4S	L
121641	Elementary Latin	Clas	104	4S	L
121641	Cicero's *Orations*	Clas	203	4S	L
121641	Vergil	Clas	204	4S	L
121641	General survey (Latin)	Clas	301	3S	U
121641	General survey (Latin)	Clas	302	3S	U
121641	Intermediate Latin comp	Clas	505	2S	U
121641	Advanced Latin comp	Clas	506	2S	U
121641	Horace: *Satires & Epistles*	Clas	512	3S	U
121642	Medieval Latin	Clas	563	2S	U
121805	Beginning Norwegian I	Ger	101	4S	L
121805	Beginning Norwegian II	Ger	102	4S	L
121905	First-sem Portuguese	Span	101	4S	L
121905	Second-sem Portuguese	Span	102	4S	L
122005	First-semester Russian	Rus	101	4S	L
122005	Second-semester Russian	Rus	102	4S	L
122005	Third-semester Russian	Rus	201	3S	U
122005	Fourth-semester Russian	Rus	202	3S	U
122505	First-semester Spanish	Span	101	4S	L
122505	Second-semester Spanish	Span	102	4S	L
122505	Third-semester Spanish	Span	203	3S	U
122505	Fourth-semester Spanish	Span	204	3S	U
122507	Spanish literature	Span	221	3S	U
122507	Spanish literature	Span	222	3S	U
122507	Modern Spanish readings	Span	228	3S	U
122507	Modern Spanish readings	Span	229	3S	U
122507	Spanish-American readings	Span	230	3S	U
122507	Miguel de Unamuno	Span	407	1S	U
122510	Intermediate composition	Span	224	2S	U
122599	Latin-Amer civilization	Span	246	2S	U
122705	First-semester Yiddish	Heb	101	4S	L
122705	Second-semester Yiddish	Heb	102	4S	L
1299	Greek & Latin medical trm	Clas	205	3S	L
1299	Greek drama in English	Clas	313	2S	L
1299	Classical mythology	Clas	370	3S	L
150202	Weather & climate	EngAS	100	2S	L
150316	Survey of botany	Bio	100	3S	L
150401	General chemistry I	EngAS	103	3S	L
150401	General chemistry II	EngAS	104	3S	L
150599	General geology	Geol	100	3S	L
150799	General physics I	EngAS	103	3S	L
150799	General physics II	EngAS	104	3S	L
160302	Intermediate algebra	Math	101	4S	L
160302	College algebra	Math	112	3S	L
160302	College algebra	Math	112A	3S	L
160306	Matrix & linear algebra	Math	340	3S	U
160399	Algebra & trigonometry	Math	114	5S	L
160399	Algebra & trigonometry	Math	114A	5S	L

NCES No.	Course Title	Dept.	Course No.	Credits	Level
160401	Calculus & related topics	Math	211	5S	U
160406	Differential equations	Math	417	3S	U
160406	Differential equations	Math	305	2S	U
160499	Calculus & analyt geom I	Math	221	5S	U
160499	Calculus & analyt geom II	Math	222	5S	U
160499	Calculus & analyt geom III	Math	223	5S	U
160602	Plane trigonometry	Math	113	2S	U
160899	Intro statistical methods	Math	301	3S	U
180199	Intro to philosophy	Philo	101	4S	L
180301	Introduction to ethics	Philo	241	4S	L
180502	Beginning logic	Philo	211	4S	L
190599	Women & their bodies		103	3S	L
200504	Child psychology	Psych	560	3S	L
200505	Psych of human adjustment	Psych	205	3S	L
200509	Psychology of personality	Psych	507	3S	L
200599	Intro to psychology	Psych	202	3S	L
200701	Intro to socl psychology	Psych	530	3S	L
210401	Social welfare programs	SocWk	205	3S	L
210499	Child welfare services	SocWk	462	3S	U
220102	Intro to anthropology	Psych	100	3S	L
220201	Introductory economics	Bus	101	4S	L
220201	Principles of economics	Bus	103	3S	L
220201	Principles of economics	Bus	104	3S	L
220302	Economic geography	Geog	102	3S	L
220305	Physical environment	Geog	120	3S	L
220399	Environmntl conservation	Geog	339	3S	L
220424	England to 1688	Hist	123	3S	L
220424	British his: 1688-present	Hist	124	3S	L
220428	History of Wisconsin	Hist	390	3S	L
220431	History of Soviet Russia	Hist	419	3S	U
220432	American hist 1492-1865	Hist	101	3S	L
220432	American hist 1865-pres	Hist	102	3S	L
220450	Ancient hist: Near East	Hist	111	3S	L
220450	Ancient hist: Roman Empire	Hist	112	3S	L
220470	Black-white experience I	Hist	203	3S	L
220470	Black-white experience II	Hist	204	3S	L
220471	Red Man in white America	Hist	274	3S	L
220472	Woman in Western culture	Hist	205	3S	L
220472	Women in America	Hist	206	3S	L
220499	History of World War II	Hist	357	2S	U
220501	American national govermt	PolSc	101	3S	L
220599	Public personnel administ	PolSc	470	3S	U
220605	Marriage and family	Socio	212	3S	L
220606	Introductory sociology	Socio	100	3S	L
220613	Social problems	Socio	220	3S	L
220615	Race-cultural minorities	Socio	224	3S	L
220699	Social stratification	Socio	633	3S	U
2299	Soc institutions—women	Socio	102	3S	L

Noncredit courses

NCES No.	Course Title	Dept.	Course No.	Credits	Level
010104	Cooperatives	Agri	A40	NC	L
010499	Elementary horse science	VetSc	A50	NC	L
010502	Flower gardening I	Hort	A50	NC	L
010502	Flower gardening II	Hort	A51	NC	L
010503	Garden center operation	Hort	A60	NC	L
010599	Flower arranging	Hort	A52	NC	L
010999	Eco-sploring	Bio	A10	NC	L
020402	Architectural drawing	EngAS	A88	NC	L
020502	Concrete structures	EngAS	A347	NC	U
030599	Basic drawing	Art	A20	NC	L
030599	Study of Western art	ArHis	A15	NC	L
040101	Intro to accounting I	Bus	A32	NC	L
040101	Intro to accounting II	Bus	A33	NC	L
040101	Intermediate accounting I	Bus	A35	NC	L
040101	Intermed accounting II	Bus	A36	NC	L
040104	Basic bookkeeping—Bus I	Bus	A30	NC	L
040104	Basic bookkeeping—Bus II	Bus	A31	NC	L
040106	Cost accounting	Bus	A37	NC	U
040106	Advanced cost accounting	Bus	A38	NC	U
040109	Governmental accounting	Bus	A39	NC	U
040111	Managerial accounting	Bus	A34	NC	L
040205	Gregg shorthand I	Bus	A42	NC	L
040302	Consumer education	Bus	A48	NC	L
040601	Business correspondence	Bus	A20	NC	L
040999	Management supervision	Bus	M50	NC	L
040999	Assertiveness in business	Bus	A46	NC	L
041004	Sales management	Bus	A86	NC	U
041005	Retail selling	Bus	A82	NC	L
041005	Selling	Bus	A85	NC	L
041006	Service selling	Bus	A88	NC	L

NCES No.	Course Title	Dept.	Course No.	Credits	Level
041099	Route operations	Bus	A89	NC	L
041301	Appraising real estate	Bus	A75	NC	L
0499	Stocks, bonds & investing	Bus	A69	NC	L
0499	Finding the job you want	Bus	A21	NC	L
0499	Customer relations—auto	Bus	A83	NC	L
050103	Advertising copy & layout	Jrnl	A450	NC	L
050199	Business promotion	Bus	A87	NC	L
050499	Publicity techniques	Jrnl	A55	NC	L
050601	Manuscript editing	Engl	A52	NC	L
050699	Writing for fun & profit	Jrnl	A60	NC	L
050699	Publications design	Jrnl	A207	NC	L
050699	Article writing success	Jrnl	A70	NC	L
070602	Career education	Educ	A498	NC	L
070899	Rehab: perspectives	Educ	A500	NC	U
070899	Rehab: commun resources	Educ	A501	NC	U
070899	Rehab: client assessment	Educ	A502	NC	U
070899	Rehab: counseling approach	Educ	A503	NC	U
070899	Rehab: placement methods	Educ	A504	NC	U
070902	Human relations—educ	Educ	A465	NC	L
070999	Child care—day care	Educ	A40	NC	L
070999	Family day care	Educ	A41	NC	L
080102	General aeronautics	EngAS	V68	NC	L
080199	Photogrammetry	EngAS	A359	NC	L
0804	Automotive engines	EngAS	A60	NC	L
0804	Automotive chassis	EngAS	A61	NC	L
0804	Diesel engines	EngAS	A64	NC	L
080701	Function analysis	EngAS	A362	NC	U
080999	Electricity fundamentals	EngAS	W72	NC	L
081301	Air pollution	EngAS	A412	NC	L
081303	Solid-waste landfills	EngAS	A180	NC	L
081304	Water & wastewater	EngAS	A411	NC	L
081399	Environmntl engr: policy	EngAS	A410	NC	L
081399	Occupational health	EngAS	A413	NC	L
081399	Environmntl engr: topics	EngAS	A420	NC	L
081399	Sanitary sewer design	EngAS	A450	NC	U
081599	Safety supervision	EngAS	A80	NC	L
081599	Safety engineering	EngAS	A81	NC	L
081599	Safety management	EngAS	A84	NC	U
082601	Elementary surveying I	EngAS	A251	NC	L
082601	Elementary surveying II	EngAS	A252	NC	L
082699	Advanced surveying	EngAS	A253	NC	U
0899	Engineering refresher	EngAS	A50	NC	U
0899	Intro to quality control	EngAS	A142	NC	U
0899	Intro to value analysis	EngAS	A361	NC	L
090255	Relf of pain—nurse's role	HSci	N50	NC	U
090255	Nursing—person & cancer	HSci	N55	NC	U
090255	Family maternity care	HSci	N65	NC	U
090255	Management for nurses	HSci	N75	NC	U
090255	Curriculum in nursing	HSci	N30	NC	U
090255	Teaching in nursing	HSci	N35	NC	U
090255	Patient education	HSci	N40	NC	U
090255	Geriatric nursing	HSci	N45	NC	U
090255	Adult patient assessment	HSci	N60	NC	U
090255	Counseling procedures	HSci	N80	NC	U
100309	The food server	HmEc	A10	NC	L
110119	Welding processes	EngAS	A139	NC	L
110119	Weld inspection I	EngAS	A232	NC	U
110119	Weld inspection II	EngAS	A233	NC	U
110119	Weld inspection III	EngAS	A234	NC	U
110399	Steam-plant operation	EngAS	A92	NC	L
110407	Intro to refrigeration	EngAS	W97	NC	L
110407	Air conditioning I	EngAS	V117	NC	L
110407	Air conditioning II	EngAS	V118	NC	L
110407	Air conditioning III	EngAS	V119	NC	U
120308	Power reading	Jrnl	A65	NC	L
120310	Expository writing	Engl	A53	NC	L
120310	Intermediate composition	Engl	A63	NC	L
120310	Writing nonfiction books	Engl	A64	NC	L
120399	Vocabulary building	Engl	A51	NC	L
121008	French-reading knowledge	Frnch	A60	NC	L
121108	Reading German	Ger	A60	NC	L
121199	Business German	Ger	A70	NC	L
121408	Reading Italian	Ital	A60	NC	L
122008	Russian for reading	Rus	A60	NC	L
122009	Russian conversation	Rus	A70	NC	L
122208	Reading Polish	Slav	A60	NC	L
122208	Reading Polish	Slav	A61	NC	L
122508	Spanish for reading	Span	A60	NC	L
160301	Shop arithmetic I	EngAS	A50	NC	L
160301	Practical arithmetic	EngAS	A52	NC	L
160302	Review of college algebra	Math	A39	NC	L

NCES No.	Course Title	Dept.	Course No.	Credits	Level
160401	Review of basic calculus	Math	A42	NC	U
160401	Review of inter calculus	Math	A43	NC	U
160401	Review of vector calculus	Math	A45	NC	U
160601	Geometry I	Math	A20	NC	L
160601	Geometry II	Math	A21	NC	L
160602	Review of trigonometry	Math	A40	NC	L
161299	Math for electricity I	EngAS	A56	NC	L
161299	Math for electricity II	EngAS	A57	NC	L
220499	Genealogical research	Hist	A10	NC	L

⑥⑥ UNIVERSITY OF WYOMING

Dr. Heikki I. Leskinen
Coordinator, Correspondence Study
University of Wyoming
Box 3294, University Station
Laramie, Wyoming 82071
Phone: (307) 766-6323

Enrollment on a noncredit basis accepted in all credit courses. Gifted high school students are permitted to enroll in undergraduate courses for credit. Overseas enrollment accepted. The required books can be rented or purchased. High school courses may be taken by combined oral-correspondence study method. The enrollment fee comprises tuition, handling, course syllabus, and audiovisual materials. A refundable deposit is required for audiovisual material, however. Students may, in some courses, contract for a grade of A, B, or C.

NCES No.	Course Title	Dept.	Course No.	Credits	Level
	High school courses				
010902	Intro to forestry sem 1	Sci	E1	HF	H
010902	Intro to forestry sem 2	Sci	E2	HF	H
030302	Music theory	Music	A1	HF	H
030502	Introduction to art	Art	A1	HF	H
040104	Bookkeeping I sem 1	Acctg	A1	HF	H
040104	Bookkeeping I sem 2	Acctg	A2	HF	H
0499	General business	Bus	A1	HF	H
0499	Business law	Bus	C1	HF	H
100202	Consumer economics	HmEc	AA	QT	H
100205	Consumer rights	HmEc	AC	QT	H
100206	Personal finance	HmEc	AB	QT	H
100312	Everyday foods sem 1	HmEc	B1	HF	H
100314	Everyday foods sem 2	HmEc	B2	HF	H
100604	Adult living sem 1	HmEc	C1	HF	H
100604	Adult living sem 2	HmEc	C2	HF	H
1099	Etiquette	HmEc	D1	HF	H
120305	Grammar	Engl	A1	HF	H
120307	Comp & lit: 9th gr sem 1	EngLL	C1	HF	H
120307	Comp & lit: 9th gr sem 2	EngLL	C2	HF	H
120307	Comp & lit: 10th gr sem 1	EngLL	D1	HF	H
120307	Comp & lit: 10th gr sem 2	EngLL	D2	HF	H
120307	Comp & lit: 11th gr sem 1	EngLL	E1	HF	H
120307	Comp & lit: 11th gr sem 2	EngLL	E2	HF	H
120307	Comp & lit: 12th gr sem 1	EngLL	F1	HF	H
120307	Comp & lit: 12th gr sem 2	EngLL	F2	HF	H
121005	First-year French sem 1	Frnch	A1	HF	H
122505	First-yr Spanish sem 1	Span	A1	HF	H
150304	Environmental science	Sci	C1	HF	H
160301	General mathematics	Math	A1	HF	H
160302	Algebra I sem 1	Math	C1	HF	H
160302	Algebra II sem 1	Math	E1	HF	H
160302	Algebra I sem 2	Math	C2	HF	H
160601	Geometry I sem 1	Math	D1	HF	H
161201	Business mathematics	Bus	B1	HF	H
200199	Intr to psychology	SocSt	K1	HF	H
220215	Economics	SocSt	B1	HF	H
220401	United States Constituton	SocSt	F1	HF	H
220432	History of the US sem 1	SocSt	E1	HF	H
220432	History of the US sem 2	SocSt	E2	HF	H
220433	World history	SocSt	D1	HF	H
220501	United States government	SocSt	G1	HF	H
220606	Principles of sociology	SocSt	H1	HF	H
220613	Social problems	SocSt	T1	HF	H
	College courses				
010106	Econ of world food & agri	Agri	686D	3S	U
010199	Econ with applic to agric	Agri	571F	3S	L
010406	Livestock prod & mgt beef	AnSci	522D	3S	L
010407	Prin of animal nutrition	AnSci	611D	3S	U

NCES No.	Course Title	Dept.	Course No.	Credits	Level
010407	Feeds and feeding	AnSc	310D	4S	L
010601	Weed science & technology	Agri	607D	3S	U
010603	Agricultural entomology	Agri	555D	3S	L
030302	Introduction to music	Music	300D	3S	L
030302	Theory I—written	Music	301F	3S	L
030302	Theory I—written	Music	301G	3S	L
030399	America's ethnic music	Music	312D	2S	L
030402	Intro to theater	ThArt	352M	3S	L
030502	Intro to hist & crit art	ArHis	380D	3S	L
040101	Elementary accounting	Acctg	301F	3S	L
040101	Elementary accounting	Acctg	301G	3S	L
040106	Cost accounting	Acctg	611D	3S	U
040203	Indexing and filing	EdBus	331D	2S	L
040203	Records management	EdBus	631D	3S	U
040207	Intermediate typing	EdBus	301D	3S	L
040301	Managerial finance	Fin	625D	3S	U
040306	Intro investment mgt	Fin	601D	3S	U
040708	Principles of insurance	Fin	671D	3S	U
040904	Management & organization	Mgmt	621D	3S	U
041001	Elements of marketing	Mktg	621D	3S	U
041099	Advertising	Mktg	623D	3S	U
041199	Personnel management	Mgmt	641D	3S	U
041303	Principles of real estate	Fin	661D	3S	U
0499	Introduction to business	Bus	300D	3S	L
050605	Journalistic writing	Jrnl	511D	3S	L
051001	Broadcast fundamentals	Radio	501D	3S	L
051107	Public communication	Commu	301D	2S	L
051108	Intro to human communcatn	Commu	304D	3S	L
0599	Intr to mass media	Bdcst	500D	3S	L
061103	Intro to computer science	CmpSc	301F	3S	L
070103	Educational sociology	Educ	704D	2S	U
070199	Issues in contempry educ	Educ	696D	2S	U
070299	Tchr & elemen sch adminis	Educ	625M	2S	U
070299	Tchr & second sch adminis	Educ	642M	2S	U
070302	Educ trends in elem educ	Educ	707M	2S	U
070304	The middle school	Educ	644M	3S	U
071102	Educ tests & measurements	Educ	706M	2S	U
071203	Intro to educ comun & tec	Educ	676D	3S	U
080703	Hydrology	CivEg	680D	3S	U
0810	Graphics	Graph	300D	3S	L
081104	Statics	EngAS	401D	3S	L
081104	Dynamics	EngAS	402D	3S	L
090101	Intro comparative biochem	Bioch	597D	4S	L
100206	Personal finance	HmEc	511D	3S	L
100305	Intr to food science	FSc	553D	3S	L
100313	Nutrition	HmEc	3600	2S	L
100503	Applied design	HmEc	301D	3S	L
100601	Child development	HmEc	554D	4S	L
100601	Later childhood & adolesc	HmEc	654D	2S	U
100602	Foundations of marriage	HmEc	542D	3S	L
120201	World lit: Renaiss—20th c	EngLL	501G	3S	L
120305	Freshman English sem 1	Engl	301F	3S	L
120305	Freshman English sem 2	Engl	301G	3S	L
120307	Amer lit: colonial-Melvile	EngLL	522F	3S	L
120307	Amer lit: Whitman-Faulkner	EngLL	522G	3S	L
120307	Shakespeare: comedies	EngLL	620M	3S	U
120307	Shakespeare: trag/Rom his	EngLL	621M	3S	U
120310	Composition	Engl	564D	3S	L
120310	Scientific & tech writing	Engl	611D	3S	L
121005	First-year French sem 1	Frnch	302F	4S	L
121008	Second-year French	Frnch	420D	3S	L
121108	Second-year German	Ger	420D	4S	L
122505	First-year Spanish sem 1	Span	302F	4S	L
122505	First-year Spanish sem 2	Span	302G	4S	L
122508	Second-year Spanish	Span	420D	4S	L
130202	Business law I	Bus	531D	3S	L
140303	Libraries & librarianship	LibSc	338D	2S	L
140307	Admin of sch lib/med cntr	LibSc	638D	3S	U
140401	Cataloging & classficatn	LibSc	640D	3S	U
140408	Selectin of instruc matrls	LibSc	637D	3S	U
140902	Literature for children	LibSc	512D	3S	L
140903	Libry/media matrls teengr	LibSc	514D	3S	L
150316	Descriptive astronomy	Astro	402D	2S	L
150316	General botany	Bot	302D	4S	L
150403	Food biochemistry	FSc	672D	3S	U
150501	Introduction to geology	Geol	300D	2S	L
160301	Theory of arith sem 1	Math	507F	3S	L
160301	Theory of arith sem 2	Math	507G	3S	L

NCES No.	Course Title	Dept.	Course No.	Credits	Level
160302	Precalculus algebra	Math	302F	3S	L
160306	El linear alg & matrix ty	Math	501D	3S	L
160399	Precalculus mathematics	Math	303D	5S	L
160401	Calculus & analyt geom I	Math	311F	4S	L
160401	Calculus & analyt geom II	Math	311G	4S	L
160602	Precalculus trigonometry	Math	302G	3S	L
160603	Calculus & analyt geom I	Math	311F	4S	L
160802	Fundmntls of statistics	Stat	301D	4S	L
161201	Math analysis for busines	Math	313F	4S	L
190502	Personl & commun hlth	Educ	380D	3S	L
200199	General psychology	Psych	302D	4S	L
200504	The child	Psych	530D	3S	L
200504	Exceptional children	Psych	531D	2S	L
200504	Adjustment	Psych	533D	3S	L
200702	Social psychology	Psych	575D	3S	L
210103	Intro to public admin	PolSc	530D	3S	L
210404	Intro to aging services	SocWk	648D	3S	U
210404	Child welfare services	SocWk	652D	3S	U
210404	Permanency planning child	SocWk	653D	3S	U
210405	Hum behavior & soc envir	SocWk	553F	3S	L
210499	Interviewing tools	SocWk	330D	1S	L
210499	Intr to social work	SocWk	378D	3S	L
210499	Social work research	SocWk	656D	3S	U
220101	Intro to archaeology	Anthr	303D	3S	L
220102	Intr to antr II: cult & soc	Anthr	302D	3S	L
220106	Intr to anthr I: human org	Anthr	301D	3S	L
220201	Prin of econ sem 1	Econ	301F	3S	L
220201	Prin of econ sem 2	Econ	301G	3S	L
220213	Intermed thry microecon	Econ	630F	3S	U
220301	Intro to human geography	Geog	302D	3S	L
220426	Hist of Westn Eurpn civza	Hist	310F	3S	L
220426	Hist of Westn Eurpn civza	Hist	310G	3S	L
220428	History of Wyoming	Hist	360D	2S	L
220428	Hist of the American West	Hist	361D	2S	L
220432	Gen survey of US history	Hist	341F	3S	L
220432	Gen survey of US history	Hist	341G	3S	L
220471	Hist of Indians of the US	Hist	540D	3S	L
220501	Gov of the US & Wyo const	PolSc	305D	3S	L
220606	Sociological principles	Socio	301D	3S	L
220607	Human interaction	Socio	540D	3S	L
220613	Social problems	Socio	302D	3S	L
	Noncredit courses				
040502	Intr to small-bus retail	Bus	10	NC	
040502	Practicum: small-bus ret	Bus	11	NC	
040502	Design small-bus retail	Bus	12	NC	
0508	Handwriting analysis	GnKno	10	NC	
0799	The school board	Educ	10	NC	
160199	Metric system	Math	10	NC	
180901	Buddhism	Rel	10	NC	
180902	Christianity	Rel	11	NC	
180903	Hinduism	Rel	12	NC	
180904	Islam	Rel	13	NC	
180905	Judaism	Rel	14	NC	
220421	Amer issues before constu	Hist	10	NC	
220510	Capitalism	PolSc	10	NC	
220510	Communism	PolSc	11	NC	
220510	Socialism	PolSc	12	NC	

67 UPPER IOWA UNIVERSITY

Mrs. Linda L. Crossett
Director
Expanded Campus Programs
Upper Iowa University
Alexander-Dickman Hall
Fayette, Iowa 52142
Phone: (319) 425-3311

Only in exceptional cases are gifted high school students permitted to enroll in undergraduate courses for credit. Overseas enrollment accepted for college courses.

NCES No.	Course Title	Dept.	Course No.	Credits	Level
	College courses				
030302	Introduction to music	Music	100	3S	L
030402	Introduction to theater	ThArt	110	3S	L
030502	Introduction to art	Art	100	3S	L
040101	Accounting I	Bus	121	3S	L

NCES No.	Course Title	Dept.	Course No.	Credits	Level
040101	Accounting II	Bus	122	3S	L
040902	Small-business management	Bus	370	3S	U
040904	Principles of management	Bus	260	3S	U
040905	Organizational behavior	Bus	360	3S	U
041001	Marketing principles	Bus	350	3S	U
041005	Retailing	Bus	355	3S	U
041103	Personnel management	Bus	361	3S	U
041106	Supervision	Bus	362	3S	U
090302	Normal nutr and diet mod	Nurs	230	3S	L
090602	Intro to health-care syst	Nurs	331	3S	L
120305	Basic composition	Engl	101	3S	L
120307	Intro to literature	Engl	102	3S	L
130101	Administrative law	PolSc	445	3S	U
130302	Am constitutional law II	PolSc	412	3S	U
130304	Amer constitutional law I	PolSc	411	3S	U
130701	Business law I	Bus	302	3S	U
130703	Business law II	Bus	303	3S	U
150301	General biology	Bio	130	3S	L
150304	Introduction to ecology	Bio	242	3S	L
150401	Basic chemistry	Chem	130	3S	L
160306	Quantitative methods I	Math	109	3S	L
160801	Elementary statistics	Math	220	3S	L
200504	Developmental psychology	Psy	230	3S	L
200509	General psychology	Psy	190	3S	L
210102	Prin of public admin	PolSc	364	3S	U
210103	Cases in public admin	PolSc	430	3S	U
210199	Public budgeting process	PolSc	440	3S	U
220201	Principles of economics I	Bus	211	3S	L
220201	Prin of economics II	Bus	212	3S	L
220201	History of econ thought	Bus	410	3S	U
220202	American economic history	Bus	210	3S	L
220426	Mod Europe 1815-present	Hist	304	3S	L
220432	American civilization I	Hist	110	3S	L
220432	American civilization II	Hist	111	3S	L
220433	World civilization I	Hist	100	3S	L
220433	World civilization II	Hist	101	3S	L
220501	US government	PolSc	100	3S	L
220506	Congress and legislation	PolSc	370	3S	U
220507	Political parties	PolSc	361	3S	U
220511	State & local government	PolSc	230	3S	L
220606	Principles of sociology	Soc	110	3S	L
220613	Social problems	Soc	220	3S	L

68 UTAH STATE UNIVERSITY

Mrs. Shirley Andreasen
Program Administrator
Independent Study Division, UMC 50
Utah State University
Eccles Conference Center
Logan, Utah 84322
Phone: (801) 750-2131

Enrollment on a noncredit basis accepted in all credit courses. Gifted high school students are permitted to enroll in undergraduate courses for credit. Overseas enrollment accepted.

NCES No.	Course Title	Dept.	Course No.	Credits	Level
	College courses				
010102	Farm bsns decision making	AgEd	210	3Q	L
010103	Marketing farm products	AgEc	260	3Q	L
010107	Farm & ranch management	AgEc	410	3Q	U
010402	Horse production practice	AnSci	219	3Q	L
010402	Breeding farm animals	AnSci	456	4Q	U
010404	Prin of reproduction	AnSci	520	3Q	U
010406	Funds of livestock produc	AnSci	110	3Q	L
010406	Livestock industries	AnSci	111	2Q	L
010406	Lactation of farm animals	AnSci	535	3Q	U
010407	Feeding farm animals	AnSci	245	3Q	L
010407	Animal feeds & feeding	AnSci	245	5Q	U
010602	World crops	PlSci	250	3Q	U
010604	Intro to agric plant sci	PlSci	100	4Q	L
010604	Vegetable production	PlSci	440	3Q	U
010604	Fruit production	PlSci	450	4Q	U
010701	General soils	Soils	358	4Q	U
010701	General soils laboratory	Soils	359	1Q	U
010702	Soil identif & interpreta	Soils	514	5Q	U
010801	General fishery biology	WlfSc	350	5Q	U
010901	Principles of forestry	For	300	3Q	U

NCES No.	Course Title	Dept.	Course No.	Credits	Level
010901	Principles of conservatn	For	410	3Q	U
0110	Recreat use of wild land	OR	350	3Q	U
011299	Wildlife law enforcement	WlfSc	410	3Q	U
020102	Intro to landscape archit	LAEP	103	5Q	U
030502	Survey of Western art	Art	275	3Q	L
030502	Survey of Western art	Art	276	3Q	L
030502	Survey of Western art	Art	277	3Q	L
030602	Exploring art	Art	101	3Q	L
030602	Basic lettering	Art	330	3Q	U
040101	Introductory accounting	Acctg	201	3Q	L
040101	Introductory accounting	Acctg	202	3Q	L
040106	Industrial cost acctg	Acctg	331	4Q	U
040111	Managerial accounting	Acctg	203	3Q	L
040201	Intro to business	BusAd	135	3Q	
040301	Corporation finance	BusAd	340	4Q	U
040399	Managing personal finan	BusEd	314	3Q	U
040502	Entrepren/new venture mgt	BusAd	435	4Q	U
040601	Business communications	BusEd	255	3Q	L
040902	Management concepts	BusAd	311	4Q	U
040902	Administrative sys mgt	BusEd	541	3Q	U
040999	Retailing management	BusAd	454	4Q	U
041001	Fundmntls of marketing	BusAd	350	4Q	U
041103	Behav dimensions in mgt	BusAd	360	4Q	U
050102	Basic advertising design	Art	331	3Q	U
050301	Biology & the citizen	Bio	101	5Q	U
070516	Metric educ for teachers	ElEd	345	1Q	U
070516	Math for elem teachers	Math	201	3Q	L
070522	Teaching social studies	ElEd	420	3Q	U
070610	Teaching of reading	ElEd	415	3Q	U
070799	Child abuse & neglect	SpEd	300	3Q	U
070803	Educ of exceptnl children	SpEd	301	3Q	U
070803	Intro instr for excp chld	SpEd	305	3Q	U
070803	Ed of gifted & talented	ElEd	584	3Q	U
070804	Educational audiology	Com D	528	3Q	U
071103	Measurement & eval in edu	SecEd	604	5Q	U
080205	Soils, water & environmnt	Soils	200	2Q	L
080703	Water res eng hydraulics	CEE	352	4Q	U
080703	Engineering hydraulics	CEE	553	5Q	U
081102	Elem fluid mechanics	CEE	350	5Q	U
081104	Engr mechanics statistics	Engr	200	3Q	L
081104	Engr mechanics dynamics	Engr	202	3Q	L
090106	Fundmntls of epidemiology	Bio	430	3Q	U
090111	Personal health	Bio	115	2Q	L
090113	Communicable disease cont	Bio	412	3Q	U
090114	Elementary microbiology	Bio	111	4Q	L
090119	Human physiology	Bio	130	5Q	L
090301	Phonetics	Com D	275	3Q	L
090702	Environmental health	Bio	410	4Q	U
090702	Insect/rodent vector cont	Bio	413	3Q	U
090702	Waterborne-disease contrl	Bio	414	3Q	U
090702	Foodborne-disease control	Bio	416	3Q	U
090799	School health program	Bio	457	4Q	U
100312	Nutrition for men	NFS	122	3Q	L
100312	Nutrition update	NFS	585	3Q	U
120201	Comp lit 19th & 20th cent	Engl	533	3Q	U
120202	Greek literature	Engl	428	5Q	U
120299	Children's literature	Engl	416	3Q	U
120299	Lit for adolescents	Engl	417	3Q	U
120305	Elements of grammar	Engl	109	3Q	L
120305	Vocabulary	Engl	110	3Q	L
120305	Grammar	Engl	410	3Q	U
120307	World lit before 1650	Engl	216	5Q	L
120307	World lit 1650 to present	Engl	217	5Q	L
120308	Intro to short stories	Engl	118	3Q	L
120308	Intro to the novel	Engl	119	3Q	L
120308	Mythology	Engl	126	3Q	L
120310	Writing poetry	Engl	501	3Q	U
120310	Writing short stories	Engl	502	3Q	U
140499	Cataloging & classificatn	IM	521	3Q	U
140799	Eval & sel of instr mater	IM	511	3Q	U
150201	Weather and climate	Bmet	517	4Q	U
150302	General biology	Bio	120	5Q	L
150304	General ecology	RngSc	384	5Q	U
150327	Insects affecting man	Bio	190	4Q	L
150327	Biology of honeybees	Bio	191	2Q	L
150599	Introductory geology	Geol	101	5Q	L
160199	Math concepts for el tchr	Math	301	5Q	U
160301	Basic mathematics	Math	001	5Q	L

NCES No.	Course Title	Dept.	Course No.	Credits	Level
160302	Elementary algebra	Math	002	5Q	L
160302	Intro to college algebra	Math	101	5Q	L
160302	College algebra	Math	105	5Q	L
160401	Calculus I	Math	215	3Q	L
160401	Calculus II	Math	216	3Q	L
160602	Plane trigonometry	Math	106	3Q	L
160801	Business statistics	BusAd	296	5Q	L
190510	Fitns fr th plsntly plump	HPER	299	3Q	L
190510	Dynamic fitness	HPER	300	3Q	L
220201	Economics I	Econ	200	5Q	L
220201	Economics II	Econ	201	5Q	L
220208	Microeconomics	Econ	501	4Q	U
220431	Spec st: Musc/Imp Russia	Hist	489	3Q	U
220432	American civilization	Hist	170	5Q	L
220432	Civil War & Reconstructn	Hist	438	3Q	U
220452	Comp civil: anc & medievl	Hist	101	3Q	L
220453	Comp civilizs: modern	Hist	103	3Q	L
220453	Comp civs: early modern	Hist	102	3Q	L
220453	Recent America 1945-pres	Hist	446	3Q	U

⑥⑨ **WASHINGTON STATE UNIVERSITY**

Dr. Von V. Pittman Jr.
Acting Director
Office of Continuing University Studies
Washington State University
208 Van Doren Hall
Pullman, Washington 99164-5220
Phone: (509) 335-3557

Enrollment on a noncredit basis accepted in all credit courses. Gifted high school students are permitted to enroll in undergraduate courses for credit. Overseas enrollment accepted for college and noncredit courses. One of our courses, Spe 325x, Language and Human Behavior, is accepted toward meeting the certification requirements of the American Speech, Language, and Hearing Association for a speech therapist.

NCES No.	Course Title	Dept.	Course No.	Credits	Level
	College courses				
010407	Animal nutrition	AS	307X	3S	U
010505	Turfgrass culture	Agron	301X	2S	U
010509	Plants and gardens	Hort	101X	3S	L
010603	Agricultural entomology	Entom	340X	3S	U
010702	Soils	Soils	201X	3S	L
030399	Survey of music literat	Mus	160X	3S	L
040101	Prin of accounting I	Acctg	230X	3S	L
040101	Prin of accounting II	Acctg	231X	3S	L
040710	Risk and insurance	Ins	320X	3S	U
041303	Real estate	RE	305X	3S	U
041303	Law of real estate	B Law	414X	3S	U
041309	Real estate administratn	RE	406X	3S	U
051103	Language/human behavior	Spe	325X	3S	U
080799	Statics	CE	211X	3S	L
080901	Electrical circuits I	EE	261X	3S	U
100399	Nutrition for man	HNF	130X	3S	L
120103	Language/human behavior	Spe	325X	3S	U
120202	Reading literature	Engl	108X	3S	L
120299	Topics in Eng/detect fict	Engl	495X	3S	U
120299	Contemporary Amer fiction	Engl	250X	1S	U
120307	English lit to 1750	Engl	209X	3S	L
120307	English lit 1750 to 1900	Engl	210X	3S	L
120307	American lit to 1855	Engl	245X	3S	L
120307	American lit since 1855	Engl	246X	3S	L
120307	Shakespeare	Engl	305X	3S	U
120307	Shakespeare	Engl	306X	3S	U
120307	Engl novel: Defoe to Eliot	Engl	366X	3S	U
120307	Engl novel: Meredith-prsnt	Engl	367X	3S	U
120307	English Romantic lit	Engl	416X	3S	U
120307	Victorian literature	Engl	417X	3S	U
120310	English composition	Engl	101X	3S	L
120310	Expository writing	Engl	201X	3S	L
1225	First-semester Spanish	Span	101X	4S	L
1225	Second-semester Spanish	Span	102X	4S	L
130401	Criminal law	Crm J	320X	3S	U
130403	Intro to juvenile justice	Crm J	240X	3S	L
130799	Law and business I	B Law	210X	3S	L
180401	Hum in ancient world	Hum	101X	3S	L
180499	Intro to philosophy	Phil	101X	3S	L
190599	Sci concepts for nurs I	Nurs	305X	3S	U

NCES No.	Course Title	Dept.	Course No.	Credits	Level
190599	Sci concepts for nurs II	Nurs	315X	3S	U
200501	Abnormal psychology	Psych	333X	3S	U
200504	Developmental psychology	Psych	360X	3S	U
220201	Contemporary economics	Econ	201X	4S	L
220426	Classcl/Christian Europe	Hist	101X	3S	L
220426	Europe since Louis XIV	Hist	102X	3S	L
220427	Latin Amer: colonial per	Hist	230X	3S	L
220427	Latin Amer: national per	Hist	231X	3S	L
220450	Hum in ancient world	Hum	101X	3S	L
220499	History of the Pacific NW	Hist	422X	3S	U
220501	Amer national government	Pol S	101X	3S	L
220511	State-local government	Pol S	206X	3S	L
220605	Marital sexual lifestyles	Soc	150X	3S	L
220605	The family	Soc	351X	3S	U
220606	Intro to sociology	Soc	101X	3S	L
	Noncredit courses				
100207	Nutrition: What's for you?	HNF	078X	NC	V
100312	Nutrition: What's for you?	HNF	078X	NC	V

NCES No.	Course Title	Dept.	Course No.	Credits	Level
210599	Recreat for the elderly	Rec	490	3S	U
220199	Anthropology of religion	Anthr	324	3S	U
220211	Labor instit & pub policy	Econ	340	3S	U
220299	Managerial economics	Econ	332	3S	U
220399	Climatology	Geog	424	3S	U
220399	Population geography	Geog	443	3S	U
220432	American history to 1877	Hist	105	3S	L
220432	American hist since 1877	Hist	106	3S	U
220432	Business in Am history	Hist	302	3S	U
220432	US military history	Hist	304	3S	U
220432	The American West	Hist	308	3S	U
220432	Am Revol & the new nation	Hist	413	3S	U
220499	Germany under Hitler	Hist	438	3S	U
220501	Int to Am govt & politics	PolSc	122		L
220599	Supreme Court	PolSc	319	3S	U
220599	Pol campaigns & elections	PolSc	350	3S	U
220602	Criminology	Socio	355	3S	U
220604	Juvenile delinquency	Socio	425	3S	U
220605	The family	Socio	460	3S	U
220615	Minority peoples	Socio	411	3S	U

70 WESTERN ILLINOIS UNIVERSITY

Ms. Joyce E. Nielsen
Director, Independent Study Program
Non-Traditional Programs
Western Illinois University
309 Sherman Hall
Macomb, Illinois 61455
Phone: (309) 298-1929

Overseas enrollment is not encouraged; each case is judged on an individual basis. Registration for courses follows the on-campus semester timetable; please request course listings for future terms. Persons wishing information about the external degree program should contact Board of Governors Degree Program, Non-Traditional Programs, 309 Sherman Hall, Western Illinois University.

NCES No.	Course Title	Dept.	Course No.	Credits	Level
	College courses				
040111	Managerial accounting	Acctg	343	3S	U
040301	Business finance	Mktg	312	3S	U
040308	Money, banking and credit	Econ	325	3S	U
040399	Personal investing	Mktg	305	3S	U
040710	Risk mgmt & insurance	Mktg	351	3S	U
040904	Principles of management	Mgmt	349	3S	U
040904	Management and society	Mgmt	481	3S	U
040999	Intro to operations mgmt	Mgmt	352	3S	U
041001	Principles of marketing	Mktg	327	3S	U
041004	Retailing management	Mktg	343	3S	U
041005	Advtg & promotional conc	Mktg	331	3S	U
041103	Personnel management	Mgmt	353	3S	U
070602	Career educ & persnl devl	Educ	241	2S	L
070899	Current trends in spec ed	Educ	475	3S	U
100313	Intro to nutrition	HmEc	109	3S	L
120305	Modern English grammar	Engl	370	3S	U
120307	Introduction to poetry	Engl	200	3S	L
120307	Women and literature	Engl	301	3S	U
120307	Lit of crime & detection	Engl	302	3S	U
120307	Spec studies in English	Engl	309	3S	U
120307	Romantic literature	Engl	320	3S	U
120307	Afro-American fiction	Engl	346	3S	U
120307	World of F S Fitzgerald	Engl	475	3S	U
120399	Scientific & tech writing	Engl	381	3S	U
150301	Biology	Bio	303	4S	U
150303	Human biology	Bio	304	4S	U
150306	Intro to organ evolution	Bio	319	4S	U
150599	Environmental geology	Geol	375	3S	U
180301	Moral philosophy	Philo	330	3S	U
180501	Logic & reasoning	Philo	115	3S	L
200799	Fire-related human behavr	Psych	475	3S	U
210299	Fire protect struc design	InArt	475	3S	U
210302	Pol & legal fnd fire prot	LEA	475	3S	U
210302	Adv fire administration	LEA	481	3S	U
210302	Anlyt appr to fire protec	LEA	482	3S	U
210302	Psnl mgmt for fire serv	LEA	483	3S	U
210302	Fire-prvn organ & mgmt	LEA	484	3S	U
210302	Disaster & fire def plang	HSci	477	3S	U
210401	Soc serv & welfare policy	Socio	311	3S	U
210501	Outdoor recreat perspect	Rec	376	3S	U

71 WESTERN MICHIGAN UNIVERSITY

Mrs. Geraldine Schma
Director of Self-Instructional Programs
Office of Self-Instructional Programs
Western Michigan University
Ellsworth Hall, Room B-102
Kalamazoo, Michigan 49008
Phone: (616) 383-0788

Enrollment on a noncredit basis accepted in all credit courses. Gifted high school students are permitted to enroll in undergraduate courses for credit. Overseas enrollment is not encouraged; each case is judged on an individual basis. WMU is selective in the correspondence courses offered. Not all courses offered on campus are available for instruction by correspondence. Students have up to one year to complete a course. All courses are offered on either a noncredit or undergraduate credit basis. New courses are continually added. There is no external degree program, but courses meet on-campus course/degree requirements or may be transferred to other universities.

NCES No.	Course Title	Dept.	Course No.	Credits	Level
	College courses				
010699	Plants of SW Michigan	Bio	225	3S	L
010699	Trees & shrubs	Bio	224	2S	L
010699	Economic botany	Bio	599	3S	U
020699	Energy & the way we live	AmSt	333	2S	L
020699	Connections: tec & change	A&Sci	501	2S	U
050299	Mass media: messgs/manip	GHum	316	4S	U
050402	Technical communication	InEg	102	3S	L
050499	Popular culture	AmSt	333	4S	U
070303	Teaching of rdg sec sch	Educ	322	3S	U
070306	Prin of vocatnl education	InArt	512	3S	U
070306	Prin of vocational educat	IndEd	512	3S	U
070511	Teaching industrial educa	InArt	344	3S	U
070511	Teaching of indust educat	IndEd	344	3S	U
070599	Course planng & construct	IndEd	342	3S	L
070603	Coord techniq in co-op ed	DisEd	573	3S	U
070604	Organ/operatn of dist ed	DisEd	570	2S	U
070604	Tchng technqs in dist ed	DisEd	572	3S	U
070799	Prin & phil of guidance	CP	580	2S	U
100699	Amer families in transitn	AmSt	333	2S	L
100699	Working: changes/choices	AmSt	333	2S	L
100699	Death & dying: ch/change	A&Sci	501	2S	U
120299	The British novel	Eng	344	4S	U
120299	World of mystery fiction	AmSt	499	2S	L
120299	Children's literature	Eng	282	4S	U
120308	Personal readg efficiency	Educ	103	2S	L
120310	Thought & language: expos	Eng	105	4S	L
120399	Personal vocabulary devel	Educ	101	2S	L
120399	Effctv rdg for coll stu	Educ	104	2S	L
150499	History of chemistry	Chem	580	3S	U
160202	Logic	Phil	520	4S	U
180501	Logic	Phil	320	4S	U
190504	Healthful living	Bio	111	2S	L
190599	Healthful living	Bio	111	2S	L
200202	Intro to human behavior	Psy	150		L

NCES No.	Course Title	Dept.	Course No.	Credits	Level
200501	Abnormal psychology	Psych	250	3S	U
200508	Child psychology	Psych	160	3S	L
200599	Intro to human behavior	Psych	150	3S	L
200901	Psy in business & indust	Psy	344	3S	U
220201	Principles of econ: micro	Econ	201	3S	L
220201	Principles of econ: macro	Econ	202	3S	L
220204	Money & credit	Econ	420	4S	U
220211	Labor problems	Econ	410	3S	U
220472	Women: past, pres, future	GHum	409	4S	U
220499	Intro to non-Westrn world	GenS	304	4S	U
220505	International relations	PolSc	250	4S	U
220505	International relations	PSci	250	4S	U
220599	Poli topics: admin behavr	PSci	270	1S	U
220601	American society	Soc	100	3S	L
220602	Criminology	Socio	362	3S	U
220604	Juvenile delinquency	Socio	564	3S	U
220606	Principles of sociology	Socio	200	3S	L
220607	Intro to social psych	Soc	320	3S	L
220615	Intro to social gerontol	Soc	352	3S	U
220699	Intro to criminal justice	Soc	264	3S	L

NCES No.	Course Title	Dept.	Course No.	Credits	Level
220426	Modern Europe 1914-1945	Hist	428	5Q	U
220428	Hist/govern of Washington	Hist	391	3Q	U
220428	History of Hawaiian Islds	Hist	417C	3Q	U
220428	Survey of community hist	Hist	491	2Q	U
220432	American history to 1865	Hist	103	5Q	L
220432	American hist since 1865	Hist	104	5Q	L
220470	Intro to Asian-Amer study	EthSt	205	3Q	U
220470	Comparative minority st	EthSt	301	3Q	U
220499	Trans-Mississippi West	Hist	465	4Q	U
220602	Criminology	Socio	352	5Q	U
220605	Sociology of the family	Socio	360	5Q	U
220610	Sociology: deviant behav	Socio	351	5Q	U
220699	Introduction to sociology	Socio	202	5Q	L
220699	Sociology of sexual behav	Socio	338	5Q	U

(72) WESTERN WASHINGTON UNIVERSITY

Ms. Janet Howard
Independent Study Coordinator
Independent Study Office
Western Washington University
Old Main 400
Bellingham, Washington 98225
Phone: (206) 676-3320

Enrollment on a noncredit basis accepted in some credit courses. Gifted high school students are permitted to enroll in undergraduate courses for credit. Overseas enrollment accepted for college courses.

NCES No.	Course Title	Dept.	Course No.	Credits	Level
	College courses				
040101	Prin of financial acctg	Acctg	241	4Q	L
040101	Prin of financial acctg	Acctg	242	4Q	L
040104	Basic acctg procedures	Acctg	150	3Q	L
040109	Fund and governmental acc	Acctg	367	3Q	U
040111	Prin of managerial acctg	Acctg	243	4Q	L
070199	Foundation of education	Educ	411	4Q	U
070199	History of American educ	Educ	413	4Q	U
070899	Intro to exceptional chld	Educ	360	3Q	U
071102	Eval in secondary school	Psych	371	3Q	U
071102	Eval in elementary school	Psych	372	2Q	U
100313	Human nutrition	HmEc	250	3Q	L
1199	Hist and phil of voc ed	Tech	491	3Q	U
1199	Community/indus resources	Tech	496	1Q	U
120307	Medieval literature	Engl	306	4Q	U
120307	Renaissance literature	Engl	307	4Q	U
120307	Romantic literature	Engl	309	4Q	U
120307	American lit to 1870	Engl	317	4Q	U
120307	American lit 1870 to 1914	Engl	318	4Q	U
120307	American lit 1914 to 1945	Engl	319	4Q	U
120307	Bible as literature	Engl	336	5Q	U
12305	Language and exposition	Engl	101	4Q	L
150201	Climatology	Geog	331	5Q	U
160102	Intro to mathematics	Math	151	3Q	L
160301	Theory of arithmetic	Math	281	4Q	L
160302	Algebra	Math	103	5Q	L
160302	College algebra	Math	105	5Q	L
160401	Calc with app to bus/econ	Math	156	4Q	L
160401	Survey of calculus	Math	200	5Q	L
160602	Trigonometry	Math	104	3Q	L
160603	Calc/analytic geometry	Math	124	5Q	L
160801	Intro to statistics	Math	240	3Q	L
180599	Introductio to logic	Philo	102	3Q	L
200406	Psych: human lrng/instruct	Psych	351	3Q	U
200504	Developmental psychology	Psych	316	5Q	U
200504	Child development & educ	Psych	352	3Q	U
200508	Adolescent psychology	Psych	353	4Q	U
220102	Intro to cultural anthrop	Anthr	201	5Q	L
220423	Korea: people/cult/history	SEAs	311	5Q	U

Use this alphabetical listing to quickly locate the name of any subject-matter area in the Index; then turn to the section of the Index that corresponds to the number following the subject listing. For example, if you are interested in advertising, find Advertising below (Advertising 0501), and then (after carefully reading the key to the Index on its first page) turn to section 0501 of the Index to determine which colleges and universities offer courses in that area.

Abnormal Psychology	200501
Accident and Health Insurance	040705
Accounting	0401
Accounting Principles	040101
Accounting Systems	040102
Administrative and Office Services	0402
Administrative Law	130101
Administrative Management	210103
Administrative Procedures	040201
Administrative Theory	210101
Adult-Continuing Education Systems	070309
Advertising	0501
Advertising Evaluation	050101
Advertising Media	050102
Advertising Production	050103
Aerodynamics	080101
Aeronautics	080102
Aerospace and Aeronautical Engineering and Technology	0801
Aesthetics	1801
African History	220420
African Languages	1204
Agency Law	130701
Agricultural Appraisal	010101
Agricultural Credit and Finance	010102
Agricultural Design, Construction, and Maintenance	010301
Agricultural Economics	0101
Agricultural Electrification	010302
Agricultural Engineering and Technology	0802
Agricultural Marketing	010103
Agricultural Occupations	070601
Agricultural Organizations	010104
Agricultural Technology	0103
Agriculture and Renewable Natural Resources	01
Air-Pollution Control	081301
Algebra	160302
Algebraic Geometry	160304
Algebraic Structures	160305
Analytic Geometry	160603
Anatomy	090101
Ancient History	220450
Animal Anatomy	150324
Animal Diseases, Parasites, and Insects	010403
Animal Genetics	150326
Animal Genetics and Reproduction	010404
Animal Management and Production	010406
Animal Nutrition	010407
Animal or Animal Products Selection and Evaluation	010402
Animal Sciences	0104
Anthropology	2201
Anthropology of Religion	181001
Arabic	1205
Archaeology	220101
Architectural Design	020101
Architectural Drafting	020402

Architectural Engineering and Technology	0803
Architecture and Environmental Design	02
Archives	140701
Arithmetic	160301
Arithmetic and Algebra	1603
Arts, Visual and Performing	03
Arts, Visual and Performing, Teaching of	070503
Asian History	220423
Assemblers	060801
Astronomy	1501
Atmospheric Sciences	1502
Audiology and Speech Pathology	090301
Auditing	040103
Automotive Engineering and Technology	0804
Bacteriology	150317
Banking and Finance	0403
Behavior Analysis	200401
Bibliographies	140703
Bilingual Education Programs	070611
Biochemistry (Chemistry)	150403
Biochemistry (Health-Care Sciences)	090102
Biological Behavior	150301
Biology	1503
Biopharmaceutics	090401
Biopsychology	2002
Bookkeeping	040104
Botany, General	150316
Braille	051201
British History	220424
Buddhism	180901
Building Construction	080301
Business	04
Business and Corporate Finance	040301
Business and Industrial Economics	220213
Business Communication	040601
Business Data Systems	0404
Business Mathematics	161201
Business Policy	040901
Business Report Writing	040604
Business Research Methods	041201
Business, Teaching of	070504
Calculus	160401
Calculus of Variations	160412
Canadian History	220425
Career Development	200502
Career Education	070602
Career Information and Counseling	070703
Casualty Insurance	040702
Cataloging of Collections	140401
Cell Biology	150302
Chemical Engineering and Technology	0806
Chemistry	1504
Child Development	100601
Chinese	1207
Christianity	180902
Christology	181406
Citizenship	220502
Civil and Administrative Procedure	1301
Civil Engineering and Technology	0807
Civil Liberties	130302
Classical Analysis	1604
Classical Applied Mathematics (Physical Systems)	1610
Classification of Collections	140402
Climatology	150201

Engineering Science	0812	God	181401
English Language Structure and Grammar	120305	Governmental Regulation of Business	1305
English Language, Study and Uses of	1203	Government, American	220501
Entomology	150327	Graphic Arts	1105
Entrepreneurship	0405	Graphics and Drafting for Engineering and	
Environmental Design	0201	Technology	0810
Environmental Engineering and		Graph Theory	160204
Technology	0813	Greek	1212
Environmental Health Administration	090703	Greenhouse and Nursery	010503
Environmental-Health Education	190505	Group Games, Contests, and Self-Testing	
Environmental Psychology	2003	Activities	190103
Environmental Technology	0206	Group Processes	200702
Epidemiology	090106	Group Theory	160308
Ethical Principles of Psychology	200101		
Ethics	1803	Handicapped, Early Education of	070801
Ethnography	220103	Health Care and Health Sciences	09
Ethnology	220104	Health Care and Health Sciences, Teaching	
European History	220426	of	070509
Evidence	130103	Health-Care Assisting	090253
Evolution	150306	Health-Care Delivery Systems	090602
Exercise	190102	Health Education	1905
Existentialism	180603	Health-Education Administration	190513
		Health-Education Curriculum	190514
Family Development	100602	Health-Education Instruction	190515
Family-Health Education	190506	Health Planning	090901
Family Medicine	090272	Hearing Handicapped, Education of	070804
Farm and Ranch Management	010107	Heating and Cooling Maintenance and	
Film and Public Policy	050301	Repair	110407
Film as Communication	0503	Hebrew	1213
Financial Institutions	040304	Hinduism	180903
Finite Differences and Functional		History—Thematic, Area, Period, and	
Equations	160408	Person	2204
Finite Probability	160701	Home Economics	10
Finite Sets	160203	Home Furnishings	100501
Finnish	1209	Home Management	1004
Fire Protection	210302	Home Planning and Interior Design	100503
First Aid	090504	Horticulture, Ornamental	0105
Fisheries	0108	Hospital and Health-Care Administration	0906
Fisheries Biology	010801	Hospital Organization and Management	090601
Flight Operations	110601	Household Equipment	100504
Floriculture	010502	Housekeeping Management	100701
Fluid Mechanics (Engineering Mechanics)	081102	Housing	1005
Food and Nutrition	1003	Housing Planning	020902
Food Habits and Patterns	100304	Human Development and Family Studies	1006
Food Preparation	100314	Human Ecology	090704
Food-Production Technology	100305	Human Factors in Industry	081502
Food Service	100309	Human Information Processing	200403
Food-Service Management	100702	Human Relations	041103
Food Storage and Preservation	100310	Hydrology (Civil Engineering)	080703
Forest Biology	010902	Hygiene, Medical	090111
Forest Management and Administration	010901		
Forest Products and Wood Technology	010903	Ichthyology	150329
Forestry	0109	Industrial and Occupational Safety Services	210303
French	1210	Industrial Arts, Trades, and Technology	11
Functional Analysis	1605	Industrial Arts, Trades, and Technology,	
		Teaching of	070511
Genetics, General	150307	Industrial Engineering and Technology	0815
Geography	2203	Industrial-Health Administration	090705
Geology	1505	Industrial Psychology	200901
Geometrics	160604	Infectious Diseases	090113
Geometry and Topology	1606	Informal Logic	180501
Geomorphology	150501	Information and Database Systems	0605
German	1211	Information Communications	0406
Gerontology (Health Sciences)	090242	Information Communication Systems	040603
Gerontology (Home Economics)	100603	Institutional Housekeeping and Food-	
Gifted and Talented, Education of	070803	Service Management	1007

Insurance and Risk Management	0407	Marketing	0410
Interior Design	020103	Marketing Functions	041003
International Business	0408	Marketing Management	041004
International Economics	220214	Marketing of Products	041005
International Relations	220505	Marketing of Services	041006
Investments and Securities	040306	Marriage and Family	220605
Islam	180904	Materials Engineering and Technology	0819
Italian	1214	Mathematical and Statistical Biology	161107
		Mathematical and Statistical Psychology	161108
Japanese	1215	Mathematical Logic	160202
Journalism	0506	Mathematical Programming (Linear and	
Judaism	180905	Nonlinear)	161105
Juvenile Delinquency	220604	Mathematical Sciences	16
Juvenile Justice	130403	Mathematical Sciences, Teaching of	070516
		Mathematical Statistics	160803
Kinesiology	1902	Mathematics, General Perspectives	1601
		Mathematics of Business and Finance	161101
Labor and Manpower Economics	220211	Mathematics of Economics	161103
Labor-Management Relations	041104	Measure and Integration	160403
Landscape Architectural Design	020102	Mechanical Design	082006
Landscaping (Ornamental Horticulture)	010504	Mechanical Engineering and Technology	0820
Land Surveying and Subdivision	082601	Mechanics	150803
Language Analysis	120103	Medieval History	220452
Language, Linguistics, and Literature	12	Mediterranean History	220429
Language, Linguistics, and Literature,		Mental-Health Education	190507
Teaching of	070512	Mentally Handicapped, Education of	070806
Latin	1216	Metallurgical Engineering and Technology	0821
Latin American History	220427	Metaphysics	1806
Law	13	Meteorology	150202
Law Enforcement	210304	Methodology	071102
Learning Disabled, Education of	070805	Microbiology (Biology)	150311
Legal Bibliography	131502	Microbiology (Health-Care Sciences)	090114
Legal Skills	1315	Microprocessors	060404
Leisure and Recreation Planning	190703	Middle School Education Systems	070304
Leisure Studies	1907	Military History	1701
Libraries and Museums	14	Military Sciences	17
Libraries and Museums, Teaching	070514	Minority Enterprises	040501
Library Administration	140303	Minority Group History	220470
Library and Museum Services and		Missiology	181608
Functions	1408	Modern History	220453
Library and Museum User Groups	1409	Monetary and Fiscal Policy	040307
Library Science	1401	Monetary and Fiscal Theory and	
Life Insurance	040707	Institutions	220204
Life Sciences and Physical Sciences	15	Money and Banking	040308
Life Sciences and Physical Sciences,		Moral and Ethical Issues	181502
Teaching of	070515	Moral and Ethical Studies	1815
Linear and Multilinear Algebra	160306	Museology	1402
Linguistics (Diachronic and Synchronic)	1201	Music	0303
Literary Aesthetics and Appreciation	120202	Music in Education	030303
Literary Bibliography	120203	Music Studies	030302
Literary Criticism	120204	Music Studio and Performance	030301
Literary Studies	1202		
Literary Theories	120205	National Income	220205
Literature of the English Language	120307	Native American History	220471
Local and State History	220428	Native American Languages	1217
Logic and Philosophical Methodology	1805	Natural Resources, Renewable	0114
Logic, Sets, and Foundations	1602	Navigation	081802
		News Reporting and Writing	050608
Management	0409	Noise-Pollution Control	081302
Management Science	041202	Nonprint Materials	140709
Managerial Accounting	040111	Nonprint Media	050401
Manufacturing Engineering and		Norwegian	1218
Technology	0817	Nuclear Engineering and Technology	0823
Marine Biology	150310	Number Theory	160303
Marine Engineering and Naval		Numerical Analysis and Approximation	
Architecture	0818	Theory	1609

Numerical Computations	0606	Plant Pathology	150321
Nursing	090255	Plant Sciences	0106
Nutrition	100313	Political Behavior	220506
Nutrition Education (Health Education)	190508	Political History	220407
Nutrition Education (Home Economics)	100312	Political Parties and Public Opinion	220507
		Political Science and Government	2205
Oceanology	1506	Political Structures	220509
Office Occupations	070607	Political Theory	220510
Operating Systems	060806	Portuguese	1219
Operations Research (Business)	041203	Power and Energy	080907
Operations Research (Industrial		Power Systems	1103
Engineering)	081503	Pre-Elementary Education Systems	070301
Optics	150706	Print Media	0507
Ordinary Differential Equations	160406	Probability	1607
Organic Chemistry	150408	Product Service (Maintenance)	1104
Organizational Communication	051104	Professional Development	070708
Organizational Development and Behavior	040903	Programming Languages	0607
Organizational Psychology (Social)	200703	Programming Systems	0608
Organizational Theory and Behavior	210102	Property Insurance	040709
Oriental Philosophy	180405	Property Law	1309
Outdoor Recreation	0110	Property Management	041304
		Protective Services	210305
Paleontology	150504	Psychological Programs (Applied and	
Partial Differential Equations	160407	Professional)	2008
Pastoral Studies	1816	Psychological Sociology	220607
Performance Physiology	190203	Psychological Testing	200603
Personal and Family Finance	100206	Psychology	20
Personal Development	100604	Psychology in Economics, Industry, and	
Personnel Management and Administration	0411	Government	2009
Personnel Psychology	200902	Psychology of Adjustment	200505
Petroleum Engineering	0825	Psychology of Disadvantaged Persons	
Petroleum Exploration	082501	(Culturally or Physically Handicapped)	200507
Pharmaceutical Chemistry	090407	Psychology of Identifiable Sets (Women,	
Pharmaceutical Sciences	0904	Blacks, Others)	200508
Pharmaceutics	090408	Psychology of Learning	200406
Pharmacology	090118	Psychology of Personality	200509
Pharmacy Practices and Management	090411	Psychology of the Individual	2005
Phenomenology of Religion	1810	Psychology of Thinking and Problem	
Philosophical Anthropology	180605	Solving	200408
Philosophical Foundations	1808	Psychology, Teaching of	070520
Philosophy, Religion, and Theology	18	Psychometrics	2006
Photography	110504	Public Address	051107
Physical Anthropology	220106	Public Administration	2101
Physical Chemistry	150409	Public Administration and Social Services	21
Physical Education	1901	Public-Education Services and Functions	140803
Physical Education Administration	190106	Public Finance (Business)	040312
Physical Education Curriculum	190107	Public Finance (Finance)	220206
Physical Education, Health Education, and		Public Health	0907
Leisure	19	Public Policy and Natural Resources and	
Physical Education, Health Education, and		Environment	210111
Leisure, Teaching of	070519	Public Recreation	2105
Physical Education Instruction	190108	Public-Recreation Administration	210503
Physical Education Supervision	190109	Public Relations	0509
Physical Fitness	190510	Public Sanitation	210202
Physical Geography	220305	Public Works	2102
Physical Sciences, General	1508		
Physical Therapy	090305	Quantitative Methods (Business)	0412
Physics	1507	Quantitative Methods (Sociology)	220609
Physiology	090119	Quantum Physics	150708
Plane and Solid Geometry	160601		
Planning	0209	Radiation Control	082303
Plant Anatomy and Physiology	010601	Radiation Therapy	090307
Plant Genetics and Reproduction	010602	Radio	0510
Plant Insects and Control	010603	Radio and Public Policy	051001
Plant Management and Production	010604	Radiobiology (Basic Health-Care Sciences)	090121
Plant or Plant Products Selection and		Radio-Television Maintenance and Repair	110411
Evaluation	010607	Reading and Language Arts Programs	070610

Urban and Rural Economics	220216	Wildlife	0112
Urban Geography	220308	Wildlife Management	011202
Urban Sociology	220614	Word Processing	040208
		World History	220433
Vehicle Maintenance and Repair	110413	Writing, Critical and Persuasive	050602
Visual Arts	0305	Writing, Evaluative	050604
Visual Arts in Education	030503	Writing, Feature and In-Depth	050605
Visual-Arts Studies	030502	Writing for Radio	051004
Visual-Arts Studio and Production	030501	Writing for Television	051303
Visually Handicapped, Education of	070812	Writing the English Language	120310
Vocational-Technical Education Systems	070306		
		Yiddish	1227
Water and Sewage Control	081304		
Welding	110119	Zoology, General	150323
Welfare and Safety	041108		

INDEX TO SUBJECT–MATTER AREAS

Key to the Index

This index is based on the classification of educational subject-matter areas prepared by the National Center for Education Statistics (NCES). Listed in alphabetical order are twenty-two broad subject-matter areas, representing major academic disciplines, with more specific areas grouped under them in two levels of subordination. Each main index line has three elements:

- The NCES subject-area identification number, which appears at the left. (NCES numbers also appear in numerical order next to the names of courses in the "Institutions and Correspondence Courses Offered" section, so that the names of courses in an area can be quickly identified on an institution's page.)
- The name of the subject-matter area.
- The code number for the name of each institution offering one or more courses in the area, plus a code letter for each kind of course the institution offers in that area (E = Elementary, H = High School, C = College, G = Graduate, N = Noncredit).

Example:

NCES No.	Subject-Matter Area	Institutional Code No.
040101	Accounting Principles	1C, 2C, 11EHCN

To find the names of specific courses an institution offers in an area, make a note of the NCES number and institutional code number and identify the institution's name and page number in the Contents, where institutional code numbers and corresponding names are listed in numerical and alphabetical order. Or turn directly to the "Institutions and Correspondence Courses Offered" section, where code numbers and corresponding names are listed numerically and alphabetically at the beginning of institutional entries and—in dictionary fashion—at the top of pages.

(If you have difficulty locating a subject-matter area in this Index, refer first to the Alphabetical Listing of Subject-Matter Areas, which precedes the Index.)

01 AGRICULTURE AND RENEWABLE NATURAL RESOURCES

Agricultural Engineering is listed in the subject-matter area of Engineering and Engineering Technology, but Agricultural Technology is included here. Animal Sciences includes the general care of animals as factors of production. Agricultural Economics is included in this area, but the broad subject matter of Economics is included under Social Sciences and Social Studies. The elements within Plant Sciences are differentiated from similar elements in the area of Life Sciences and Physical Sciences by their emphasis on food and fiber production. Many of the elements listed here are closely related to those of Biology, and care should be exercised in the identification of basic units of instruction.

0101   Agricultural Economics   36C, 61C
010101   Agricultural Appraisal   6C
010102   Agricultural Credit and Finance   32C, 68C
010103   Agricultural Marketing   6C, 32C, 47C, 49C, 68C
010104   Agricultural Organizations   32C, 65CN
010106   Economic Development and International Trade   25C, 66C
010107   Farm and Ranch Management   32H, 41C, 68C
010199   Other Agricultural Economics   17C, 32C, 39C, 41C, 45C, 66C

0102   Agricultural Engineering (See 08—Engineering and Engineering Technology)

0103   Agricultural Technology
010301   Agricultural Design, Construction, and Maintenance   49C
010302   Agricultural Electrification   25C
010399   Other Agricultural Technology   14H, 50N

0104   Animal Sciences   22C
010402   Animal or Animal Products Selection and Evaluation   32C, 45C, 68C
010403   Animal Diseases, Parasites, and Insects   28N
010404   Animal Genetics and Reproduction   36C, 68C
010406   Animal Management and Production   6C, 17C, 25C, 26C, 39C, 53C, 61N, 66C, 68C
010407   Animal Nutrition   9CN, 25C, 45C, 66C, 68C, 69C
010499   Other Animal Sciences   35C, 47C, 49H, 65N

0105   Ornamental Horticulture   49C
010502   Floriculture   65N
010503   Greenhouse and Nursery   65N
010504   Landscaping   16N, 47C
010505   Turf Grass   69C
010599   Other Ornamental Horticulture   16H, 37H, 40C, 50H, 65N, 69C

0106   Plant Sciences   22C
010601   Plant Anatomy and Physiology   24C, 25C, 66C
010602   Plant Genetics and Reproduction   6C, 68C
010603   Plant Insects and Control   9CN, 40C, 66C, 69C
010604   Plant Management and Production   26C, 45C, 68C
010607   Plant or Plant Products Selection and Evaluation   25C, 45C
010699   Other Plant Sciences   26C, 32C, 36C, 39C, 71C

0107   Soil Sciences
010701   Soil Chemistry   25C, 68C
010702   Soil Classification   13C, 39C, 68C, 69C
010703   Soil Conservation and Land Use   45C
010704   Soil Fertility   32C

0108   Fisheries
010801   Fisheries Biology   68C

0109   Forestry   22C
010901   Forest Management and Administration   45C, 64C, 68C
010902   Forest Biology   65C, 66H
010903   Forest Products and Wood Technology   25C
010999   Other Forestry   40C, 61C, 65N

0110   Outdoor Recreation   68C

0112   Wildlife
011202   Wildlife Management   21C
011299   Other Wildlife   9C, 21C, 68C

0114   Renewable Natural Resources   35C, 36C, 47C, 57H

0199   Other Agriculture and Renewable Natural Resources   39C, 46CGN, 49H, 50H

02 ARCHITECTURE AND ENVIRONMENTAL DESIGN

Subject-matter elements in this area deal with the design of environments as well as the management of construction. Virtually all subject matter related to environmental planning has been included in this subject-matter area. Engineering theory and design involved in building and environmental systems are found in the area of Engineering and Engineering Technology. Elements relating to construction skills can be found in the subject-matter area of Industrial Arts, Trades, and Technology.

0201	**Environmental Design**	
020101	Architectural Design	6C, 27N
020102	Landscape Architectural Design	25C, 44N, 68C
020103	Interior Design	6HC, 37C, 38C
020199	Other Environmental Design	9C

0202	**Design and Planning Technology**	
020203	Site Analysis	44N
020299	Other Design and Planning Technology	26C, 38C

0204   **Communication in Architecture and Environmental Design**

020402	Architectural Drafting	65HN

0205	**Structural Technology**	
020502	Concrete Structures	65N
020599	Other Structural Technology	25N

0206	**Environmental Technology**	
020699	Other Environmental Technology	53C, 71C

0209	**Planning**	
020902	Housing Planning	17C
020906	Recreation-Resources Planning	44C

03   ARTS, VISUAL AND PERFORMING

Dance is listed in this area as an aesthetic art form. It is also listed in the area of Physical Education, Health Education, and Leisure, where the emphasis is on the physical activity. Film as an artistic medium is included in this area. The knowledge of Film for the transmission of messages is included in the subject-matter area of Communication. Arts Therapy in this subject-matter area should be differentiated from the formalized medical therapy that is included in the area of Health Care and Health Sciences.

0301   **Dance (See 1904—Dance)**

0302   **Film as Art (See 0503—Film as Communication)**

0303	**Music**	
030301	Music Studio and Performance	6C, 37C
030302	Music Studies	6H, 10C, 14C, 16H, 24C, 37HCN, 38C, 47C, 48C, 49C, 50H, 53C, 57C, 63C, 64C, 65HC, 66HC, 67C
030303	Music in Education	45C, 63C
030399	Other Music	4C, 16C, 17C, 27C, 33C, 35C, 37C, 46C, 48C, 50H, 53C, 66C, 69C

0304	**Theater Arts**	
030401	Theater Arts Studio and Performance	16C
030402	Theater Studies	3C, 8C, 18C, 25C, 27CN, 36C, 47C, 53C, 57C, 66C, 67C
030403	Theater in Education	6HC
030499	Other Theater Arts	8C, 15C, 17C, 18C, 27N, 36C, 43C, 47CN, 53C

0305	**Visual Arts** 35HN	
030501	Visual-Arts Studio and Production	16HC, 26C, 31C, 37HC, 61HN
030502	Visual-Arts Studies	6C, 16HC, 24C, 37C, 38H, 48C, 57H, 59H, 63C, 66HC, 67C, 68C
030503	Visual Arts in Education	38C
030599	Other Visual Arts	8C, 17H, 26N, 47C, 49H, 50C, 53C, 54C, 65HCN

0306	**Related Arts**	
030602	Related-Arts Studies	48C, 68C
030603	Related Arts and Aesthetic Education	6C, 37C
030699	Other Related Arts	65HC

0399   **Other Arts, Visual and Performing**   6C, 15C, 27C, 47C

04   BUSINESS

Subject matter that is a part of Distributive Education and Career Education Programs can be found in this area under Marketing. Also, selected subject matter in this classification is applicable to office occupations. Although the knowledge of Economics is an integral part of business, it is listed in the subject-matter area of Social Sciences and Social Studies and not here. The knowledge of the skills involved in many occupational programs is found in this area even though differences may exist in the form and substance of the subject matter as it is presented to students. This is particularly true for elements listed under Administrative and Office Services, such as Typewriting. The use of additional dimensions, such as type of program, can help to differentiate the subject matter where it is necessary to do so.

04   **Business**   61H

0401	**Accounting** 22C, 27C	
040101	Accounting Principles	2C, 3C, 8C, 13C, 14C, 16C, 17CN, 18C, 21C, 22C, 24C, 25HC, 26HC, 27C, 32C, 33C, 34C, 35C, 36C, 37HCN, 38H, 39C, 40C, 41C, 42C, 44C, 45HC, 46C, 47HC, 48C, 49C, 50HC, 51C, 52C, 53C, 54C, 55C, 57C, 58HC, 59HC, 60C, 63C, 65CN, 66C, 67C, 68C, 69C, 72C
040102	Accounting Systems	14H, 59C
040103	Auditing	17C, 24C, 26CN, 37C, 58C, 61C
040104	Bookkeeping	6H, 16H, 17H, 19H, 32H, 33HC, 35H, 36H, 41H, 49H, 57H, 60H, 61H, 62H, 65HN, 66H, 72C
040105	Controllership and Budgeting	13C
040106	Cost Accounting	13C, 16C, 17C, 18C, 21C, 24C, 25C, 33C, 37C, 38C, 42C, 45C, 54C, 57C, 58C, 61C, 65CN, 66C, 68C
040107	Data-Processing Accounting	58C
040108	General Accounting	4C, 6C, 57C, 58C, 61C
040109	Governmental and Institutional Accounting	6C, 13C, 16C, 26CN, 33C, 42C, 58C, 65N, 72C
040111	Managerial Accounting	4C, 8C, 17C, 24C, 27C, 32C, 34C, 38C, 41C, 44C, 49C, 50C, 63C, 65CN, 68C, 70C, 72C
040113	Recordkeeping	38C
040114	Tax Accounting	6H, 8C, 13C, 16C, 17C, 32C, 33C, 37C, 40C, 47C, 58C, 61C, 63C
040199	Other Accounting	6H, 16C, 29C, 32C, 37N, 48C, 60C

0402	**Administrative and Office Services** 22C, 61H	
040201	Administrative Procedures	6C, 17C, 34C, 36H, 40C, 45C, 48C, 58C, 61C, 68C
040203	Records Management	17C, 21C, 22C, 35C, 36HN, 41C, 54C, 61C, 66C
040205	Shorthand and Transcription	6HC, 16H, 17HC, 26C, 36H, 45HC, 47H, 50H, 57H, 58C, 59H, 60H, 63C, 65HN
040206	Specialized Secretarial Services	16HN, 21C, 26C, 43N, 48C, 50H
040207	Typewriting	6HC, 14EHC, 16H, 17HC, 19H, 36H, 45HC, 50HC, 57H, 59H, 60H, 61N, 63C, 66C
040208	Word Processing	40C
040299	Other Administrative and Office Services	10C, 15N, 16C, 17H, 21C, 26C, 38H, 43N, 49H, 50H

0403	**Banking and Finance** 6H	
040301	Business and Corporate Finance	4C, 17C, 21C, 24C, 27C, 33C, 40C, 43C, 45C, 48C, 51C, 54C, 57C, 58C, 60C, 61C, 62C, 63C, 66C, 68C, 70C
040302	Consumer Finance	16C, 18C, 26H, 27C, 38H, 47C, 57C, 63C, 65N

05 COMMUNICATION

Film as Communication in this subject-matter area is considered as a means of transmitting messages. In contrast, Film as Art in the area of Arts, Visual and Performing, is considered as an artistic medium. Journalism and Speech Communication are both found in this subject-matter area and not in the area of Language, Linguistics, and Literature with which they are closely related and often reported.

06   COMPUTER SCIENCE AND DATA PROCESSING

Most of the mathematical logic upon which computer systems are based is included in the subject-matter area of Mathematical Sciences. Knowledge of the engineering design and construction of computing equipment is found in the category of Electrical Engineering and Technology within the subject-matter area of Engineering and Engineering Technology. Knowledge about the ways in which computers and data-processing equipment are utilized can be classified under other subject-matter areas if the emphasis is on the application and not upon the computer or data-processing system.

07   EDUCATION

The subject matter in this area is concerned with the knowledge that is needed to teach and to otherwise carry out the process of education. Programs or other subject matter should not be reported from within this section. Only the knowledge that is needed to develop those programs or to teach the subject matter is presented here.

09   HEALTH CARE AND HEALTH SCIENCES

Under Basic Health-Care Sciences are those elements of knowledge that come from the Biological Sciences but whose emphasis is directed toward the care and treatment of humans and animals. General knowledge, not specific to the restoration or preservation of health, is included in the subject-matter area of Life Sciences and Physical Sciences. Where appropriate, cross-references are shown in this structure.

Clinical Health Sciences lists those elements of knowledge that are related to diseases, injuries, or deformities. The list is divided into five subjectively established categories: (1) knowledge related to body organs or localized parts of the body, (2) knowledge of disorders or general conditions of the body, (3) knowledge that is specific to an age group or type of patient, (4) knowledge of health care approaches that are not unique to areas of the body or type of patient but focus instead on the treatment itself, and (5) knowledge of special-purpose health care and health sciences.

Many of the elements in this subject-matter area can apply to either humans or animals.

11   **INDUSTRIAL ARTS, TRADES, AND TECHNOLOGY**

The elements in this subject-matter area can be used to record or report data in two distinct ways. One would be to consider knowledge or understanding about the elements that are listed. The second would be to consider the knowledge and skills that are related to the techniques and methods that the elements represent. For example, the subject-matter element of Carpentry may be used to code a basic unit of instruction that is designed to teach people about the trade. In another unit of instruction, Carpentry may involve teaching a student how to become a carpenter. Much of the subject matter of Industrial Arts falls under the first approach. Knowledge of the Trades and Technology falls under the second. The additional dimension of type of instructional program can further serve to differentiate the two.

Although there are many personal-service trades, those that are included in this subject-matter area are those that are commonly taught in educational agencies and institutions.

110699 Other Transportation   16C, 58C, 61C

1199   **Other Industrial Arts, Trades, and Technology**
17C, 46N, 47C, 50H, 53C, 72C

12   **LANGUAGE, LINGUISTICS, AND LITERATURE**

1201   **Linguistics (Diachronic and Synchronic)**

120101   Applied Linguistics   8C
120103   Language Analysis   9C, 34C, 38C, 58C, 65C, 69C
120199   Other Linguistics   16C, 64C

1202   **Literary Studies**

120201   Comparative Literature   4C, 10C, 16C, 24C, 25HC, 26C, 27C, 32C, 34C, 36HC, 38C, 45C, 47C, 57C, 58C, 60C, 65C, 66C, 68C
120202   Literary Aesthetics and Appreciation   18C, 24C, 25C, 27C, 37HC, 38C, 39C, 43C, 60C, 68C, 69C
120203   Literary Bibliography   58C
120204   Literary Criticism   16C, 25C, 32HC, 57C, 58C
120205   Literary Theories   58C
120299   Other Literary Studies   2C, 4C, 6N, 9C, 14HC, 18C, 33C, 39C, 41C, 43C, 47C, 48C, 49C, 50CN, 55C, 58C, 60HC, 63C, 64C, 68C, 69C, 71C

1203   **The Study and Uses of the English Language**   22C, 57H

120301   Dialects of the English Language   53C
120302   History of the English Language   3C, 32C, 37C, 48C, 52C, 57C, 61C, 62H, 65C
120303   English Language and Civilization   6H, 39H, 40C, 45C
120304   English Language and Contemporary Culture   16H, 38C, 39H, 46C
120305   English Language Structure and Grammar   3C, 6HC, 10HC, 11C, 13N, 14H, 15C, 16HCN, 17C, 19H, 25C, 26HN, 27HC, 32H, 33N, 35C, 36HC, 37HCN, 38H, 39HC, 40C, 41HC, 44C, 45H, 48C, 49H, 50HN, 53C, 54C, 57CN, 58C, 59HC, 60HC, 61HCN, 62H, 63C, 65HC, 66HC, 67C, 68C, 70C
120306   Listening Comprehension in English   6H
120307   English Language Literature   4C, 5C, 6HC, 8C, 10HC, 11C, 14HC, 15C, 16HC, 17C, 19H, 20C, 21H, 26HC, 27HC, 33HC, 34C, 35C, 36HC, 38H, 39HC, 40C, 41H, 42C, 43C, 44C, 45H, 46CN, 49HC, 50HC, 51C, 52C, 53C, 54C, 57C, 58C, 59HC, 60HC, 61HC, 62HC, 64C, 65HC, 66HC, 67C, 68C, 69C, 70C, 72C
120308   Reading in the English Language   6HC, 16HCN, 19H, 24C, 25C, 27H, 35CN, 36H, 37H, 38HC, 44N, 49H, 50H, 54C, 59H, 61HN, 65N, 68C, 71C
120309   Speaking the English Language   16C, 19N
120310   Writing the English Language   4C, 6HCN, 11C, 13CG, 14C, 15C, 16HC, 17CN, 18C, 24C, 25HC, 26C, 27C, 32C, 33C, 34C, 35HN, 36C, 37HCN, 38HC, 39C, 42C, 43C, 44C, 45CN, 47CN, 48C, 49C, 50HC, 52C, 53CN, 54C, 59HC, 60HC, 61HCN, 62HCN, 63C, 64C, 65HCN, 66C, 68C, 69C, 71C
120399   Other Study and Uses of the English Language   6HC, 9C, 13C, 14EH, 16HCN, 17HC, 19HN, 26C, 33C, 36HC, 37HC, 38CN, 44C, 45C, 46C, 49H, 50H, 51C, 52C, 58H, 60C, 61C, 64C, 65CN, 70C, 71C

1205   **Arabic**

120542   Modern Standard Arabic   65C

1207   **Chinese**   47C

120705   Chinese Language Structure and Grammar   6H
120709   Speaking the Chinese Language   37C

1208   **Danish**

120805   Danish Language Structure and Grammar   64C
120808   Reading the Danish Language   64C
120809   Speaking the Danish Language   64C

1209   **Finnish**   47C

120905   Finnish Language Structure and Grammar   64C
120908   Reading the Finnish Language   64C

1210   **French**   2C, 4C, 14HC, 16H, 18C, 19H, 21C, 26C, 27C, 33C, 35C, 42C, 45HC, 46CG, 47CN, 50H, 54C, 60H, 61HC

121003   French Language and Civilization   57C
121004   French Language and Contemporary Culture   58C
121005   French Language Structure and Grammar   4C, 6C, 8C, 36C, 40C, 44C, 49HC, 57HC, 59HC, 62C, 64C, 65HC, 66HC
121006   Listening Comprehension in the French Language   59C
121007   Literature of the French Language   2C, 4C, 8C, 42C, 57C, 59C, 65C
121008   Reading the French Language   8C, 17C, 36C, 44C, 49C, 57C, 64C, 65HN, 66C
121009   Speaking the French Language   8C, 37HC, 41HC, 53C
121010   Writing the French Language   4C, 8C, 35C, 36C, 57C, 65C
121099   Other Study and Uses of the French Language   8C, 17H, 27C, 43C, 51C, 65C

1211   **German**   14HC, 16H, 18C, 26C, 27C, 33H, 35C, 42C, 45HC, 46CG, 47CN, 50H, 54C, 61C

121102   History of the German Language   65C
121104   German Language and Contemporary Culture   58C
121105   German Language Structure and Grammar   6HC, 8C, 24C, 33C, 36C, 40C, 44C, 48C, 57C, 59HC, 60C, 62C, 64C, 65HC
121106   Listening Comprehension in the German Language   59C
121107   Literature of the German Language   6C, 53C, 57C, 64C, 65C
121108   Reading the German Language   17C, 36C, 37C, 44C, 57C, 62C, 64C, 65HN, 66C
121109   Speaking the German Language   17C, 37HC, 53C
121110   Writing the German Language   57C, 65C
121199   Other Study and Uses of the German Language   39C, 43C, 48N, 51C, 65N

1212   **Greek**   14C, 42C, 45C, 61N

121201   Dialects of the Greek Language (Synchronic and Diachronic)   59C
121205   Greek Language Structure and Grammar   59C
121207   Literature of the Greek Language   27C, 37C, 59C
121241   Classical Greek   18C, 24C, 47C, 57C, 62C, 65C
121243   New Testament Greek   18C, 57N, 62C, 65C
121299   Other Study and Uses of the Greek Language   57C, 59C

1213   **Hebrew**

121341   Classical Hebrew   6C, 57C, 64C, 65C
121342   Modern Hebrew   65C
121399   Other Study and Uses of the Hebrew Language   65C

1214   **Italian**   18C, 47C, 51C, 61C

121405   Italian Language Structure and Grammar   57C, 62C, 64C, 65C
121408   Reading the Italian Language   65N
121409   Speaking the Italian Language

1399   Other Law   47C, 49H

14   LIBRARIES AND MUSEUMS

The elements in this subject-matter area represent the substance of knowledge that has been determined to be appropriate to Libraries and Museums.

1401   Library Science   13C

140101   History of Libraries   18C
140199   Other Library Science   13CG, 18C, 24C, 25C, 47C, 48C, 52C, 61C, 63C

1402   Museology   41C

1403   Administration of Libraries and Museums

140303   Library Administration   66C
140306   Public-Library Administration   18C
140307   School-Library and Media-Center Administration   25C, 66C
140399   Other Administration of Libraries and Museums   18C

1404   Collection Management

140401   Cataloging of Collections   13C, 66C
140402   Classification of Collections   13C
140408   Selection and Acquisition of Collections   18C, 66C
140499   Other Collection Management   68C

1407   Materials for Libraries and Museums

140701   Archives   13C
140703   Bibliographies   13C
140709   Nonprint Materials   13C
140799   Other Materials for Libraries and Museums   13C, 18C, 68C

1408   Library and Museum Services and Functions

140803   Public Education Services and Functions   62C
140804   Reference and Retrieval   13C, 52C, 63C
140899   Other Library and Museum Services and Functions   63C

1409   Library and Museum User Groups

140902   Children Users   25C, 63C, 66C
140903   Adolescent Users   65H, 66C
140904   Adult Users   63C

1499   Other Libraries and Museums   16H

15   LIFE SCIENCES AND PHYSICAL SCIENCES

The arrangement of elements within the subject-matter category of Biology includes those that could be aggregated into Botany and Zoology as well. To have broken them out would have required another level of coding and two additional digits.

Many of the elements within Biology have been cross-referenced to identical titles in Health Care and Health Sciences. The related elements differ in that the subject matter of Health Care and Health Sciences emphasizes the restoration and preservation of health. Subject matter in Life Sciences and Physical Sciences is not as specific and can be related to a broad range of units of instruction.

15   Life Sciences and Physical Sciences   61H

1501   Astronomy   52C, 57C

150101   Cosmology   25C, 64C
150102   Solar Astronomy   16C, 35C, 39C, 47C, 48C, 58C
150103   Stellar Astronomy   16C, 17C, 25C, 39C, 47C, 62C, 66C

150199   Other Astronomy   14C, 15C, 16C, 17C, 21C, 37C, 44C, 45C, 59C, 60C, 63C

1502   Atmospheric Sciences

150201   Climatology   27C, 64C, 68C, 72C
150202   Meteorology   13C, 25C, 26C, 27C, 35C, 39C, 44C, 49C, 56C, 63C, 65C
150299   Other Atmospheric Sciences   27C

1503   Biology   14H, 17HC, 19H, 26H, 47C, 49H, 55C, 57H, 59H, 61H, 62H

150301   Biological Behavior   6H, 25C, 27C, 38H, 44C, 45C, 58H, 60C, 67C, 70C
150302   Cell Biology   6C, 62C, 65H, 68C
150303   Developmental Biology   3C, 62C, 65H, 70C
150304   Ecology   4C, 6HC, 8C, 40C, 47C, 50C, 63C, 66H, 67C, 68C
150306   Evolution   8C, 25C, 45C, 63C, 70C
150307   General Genetics   3C, 25C, 36C, 37C, 45C, 63C
150310   Marine Biology   58C
150311   Microbiology (See 090114—Microbiology)   6C, 8C, 42C, 45C
150316   General Botany   8C, 24C, 35C, 36C, 37C, 45C, 53C, 65C, 66C
150317   Bacteriology   36C
150321   Plant Pathology   35C
150323   General Zoology   24C, 37C, 45C, 51C
150324   Animal Anatomy   4C
150326   Animal Genetics   4C
150327   Entomology   37C, 50C, 68C
150329   Ichthyology   6C
150399   Other Biology   4C, 6C, 8C, 10C, 16HC, 17C, 24C, 27C, 32H, 33C, 36HC, 37HC, 43C, 44C, 45C, 47H, 48C, 50H, 51C, 60HC, 63C

1504   Chemistry   14H, 57C

150401   General Chemistry   4C, 6HC, 19H, 21C, 24C, 27C, 37C, 39C, 43C, 49H, 50H, 53C, 55C, 60H, 61C, 64C, 65C, 67C
150403   Biochemistry (See 090102—Biochemistry)   37C, 66C
150408   Organic Chemistry   4C, 24C, 25C, 27C, 34C, 37C, 57C
150409   Physical Chemistry   37C
150410   Surface Chemistry   37C
150499   Other Chemistry   48C, 52C, 71C

1505   Geology   4C, 14C, 26C, 35C

150501   Geomorphology   37C, 66C
150502   Hydrology (See 080703—Hydrology)
150504   Paleontology   6C
150599   Other Geology   4C, 6C, 16C, 17C, 25C, 26C, 32C, 39C, 43C, 47C, 49HC, 52C, 53C, 56C, 60C, 61C, 65C, 68C, 70C

1506   Oceanology   26C, 53C, 64C

1507   Physics   42C, 49H, 53C

150704   Electricity   17N, 49H
150706   Optics   27C
150708   Quantum Physics   37C
150799   Other Physics   6HC, 8C, 16HC, 17C, 24C, 25C, 26C, 27C, 32H, 33C, 37HC, 38H, 41C, 47C, 48C, 50HC, 58C, 63C, 65C

1508   General Physical Sciences   50H, 62H

150803   Mechanics   62C
150899   Other General Physical Sciences   3C, 6H, 8C, 16H, 17HC, 21C, 24C, 27C, 32H, 47H, 48C, 59H, 60C, 62C, 65H

1509   General Earth-Space Science   6H, 11C, 14C, 16H, 26H, 35H, 36C, 37H, 59H, 60C

19   PHYSICAL EDUCATION, HEALTH EDUCATION, AND LEISURE

Dance is listed both in Physical Education, Health Education, and Leisure and in Arts, Visual and Performing. As an art form, it is more concerned with aesthetics than with physical movement, although both factors are involved. In recording or reporting data about Dance, care should be taken to make clear distinctions as to which subject-matter area is represented.

Health Education deals with the knowledge that individuals use to maintain good health as members of society. Specific knowledge relating to the restoration and preservation of health is included in the subject-matter area of Health Care and Health Sciences.

Have You Seen These Other Publications from Peterson's Guides?

Who Offers Part-Time Degree Programs? The Most Complete Overview to Date of Part-Time Degree Opportunities—Daytime, Evening, Weekend, Summer, and External Degree Programs—Available from Accredited Colleges and Universities in the U.S.
Editorial Coordinator: Patricia Consolloy

The only handy reference that provides a complete overview of part-time degree opportunities in each state. Institutional profiles give a concise overview of the percentage of students in part-time degree programs, tuition figures, types of part-time options available, and which graduate units permit part-time study.

7" x 9¼", 350 pages
ISBN: 0-87866-121-2

Stock no. 1212
$6.95

Back to School: The College Guide for Adults
William C. Haponski, Ph.D., and Charles E. McCabe, M.B.A.

An essential guide for any adult who is starting school for the first time or contemplating a return to college. The authors discuss how to apply and get accepted, how to balance college with the demands of a job and family, learning good study habits and educational skills, and much more.

6" x 9", 256 pages
ISBN: 0-87866-197-2

Stock no. 1972
$7.95 paperback

Learning Vacations
Fourth Edition
Gerson G. Eisenberg

A guide to over 500 exciting, international, year-round educational vacations, including archaeological digs, arts and crafts, festivals, gourmet cooking, wilderness workshops, writing conferences, elderhostels, and more.

6" x 9", 273 pages
ISBN: 0-87866-175-1

Stock no. 1751
$7.95 paperback

Peterson's Annual Guide to Undergraduate Study
1983 Edition
Book Editor: Joan H. Hunter
Data Editor: Kim Kaye

The biggest college guide on the market—like three books in one! Contains data on two-year colleges, four-year colleges, majors. Lists over 3,300 colleges and gives information on financial aid, tuition and fees, ROTC, fraternities and sororities, enrollment, community facilities, and much more! Updated each year.

8½" x 11", 2,093 pages
ISBN: 0-87866-184-0

Stock no. 1840
$13.95 paperback

Peterson's Annual Guides to Graduate Study: Graduate and Professional Programs: An Overview
1983 Edition
Series Editor: Phyllis Marsteller

Covers the whole spectrum of U.S. and Canadian graduate programs in a single reliable volume. A special table correlates over 1,250 schools with the graduate and professional degrees they offer in any of 224 fields.

8½" x 11", 700 pages (approx.)
ISBN: 0-87866-185-9

Stock no. 1859
$13.95 paperback

SAT Success:
Peterson's Study Guide to English and Math Skills for College Entrance Examinations: SAT, ACT, and PSAT
Joan Davenport Carris and Michael R. Crystal

This brand-new step-by-step text is designed as an effective self-instruction aid to build both the skills and the confidence of students preparing for college entrance examinations. Quiz-filled verbal and math sections plus mock SATs as well as actual questions from recent SAT and ACT tests for practice.

8½" x 11", 380 pages
ISBN: 0-87866-208-1

Stock no. 2081
$8.95 paperback

Peterson's Guide to College Admissions: Getting into the College of Your Choice
Second Edition
R. Fred Zuker and Karen C. Hegener

This second edition takes students behind the scenes in the college admissions office and provides practical advice on how they can increase their chances of getting into the college of their choice.

8½" x 11", 310 pages
ISBN: 0-87866-122-0

Stock no. 1220
$8.95 paperback

National College Databank
Second Edition
Editor: Karen C. Hegener

This is the updated and expanded second edition of the innovative reference book that helps college-bound students zero in on the colleges that have special features and characteristics. It groups more than 2,700 colleges by hundreds of characteristics, from size to price range to special programs.

7" x 9¼", 950 pages
ISBN: 0-87866-165-4

Stock no. 1654
$8.95 paperback

The Competitive Colleges:
Who Are They? Where Are They? What Are They Like?
Second Edition
Compiled by the Editors of Peterson's Guides

The updated edition of the only book to determine college selectivity from objective data—and give the facts to prove it. This book provides a full page of comparative information on each school, including enrollment and faculty statistics, resources and special programs, student backgrounds, majors, sports, and much more.

7" x 9¼", 278 pages (approx.)
ISBN: 0-87866-210-3

Stock no. 2103
$7.95 paperback

After Scholarships, What? Creative Ways to Lower Your College Costs—and the Colleges That Offer Them
Editorial Coordinator: Patricia Consolloy

This campus-by-campus survey of expenses and cost-cutting options at 1,600 four-year colleges and universities gives college applicants and their families new ways to plan their college finances.

7" x 9¼", 386 pages
ISBN: 0-87866-129-8

Stock no. 1298
$8.00 paperback

Your Own Financial Aid Factory:
The Guide to Locating College Money
Robert Leider

This completely updated edition reflects all of the latest regulations of the federal government. It contains a section on calculating the difference between what college will cost and what families are expected to contribute; describes some 50,000 available scholarships, cooperative-education opportunities, and Pell Grants; and tells how to locate sources of student loans.

6" x 9", 190 pages
ISBN: 0-917760-29-8

Stock no. 0298
$6.95 paperback

Dollars for Scholars Student Aid Catalogs
A new series of books that list sources of financial aid for college students on a state-by-state basis, with complete descriptions and access information given for each source. Each catalog also contains a long section on sources of aid that is available nationally.

These catalogs are available at special discounts for bulk orders. Please contact Peterson's Guides at the address given below for complete details.

Dollars for Scholars Student Aid Catalog
Minnesota Edition
Marlys C. Johnson and Linda J. Thompson

8½" x 11", 200 pages (approx.)   Stock no. 1948
ISBN: 0-87866-194-8 $7.95 paperback

Dollars for Scholars Student Aid Catalog
New Hampshire Edition
Linda J. Thompson and Marlys C. Johnson

8½" x 11", 170 pages (approx.)   Stock no. 6193
ISBN: 0-87866-193-X $5.95 paperback

Architecture Schools in North America:
Members and Affiliates of the ACSA
Third Edition
Editors: Barbara C. Ready and Richard E. McCommons, AIA
Editorial Consultant: Gary P. Haney

This major reference guide contains the official architecture program descriptions of the 103 member schools and 30 affiliate schools of the Association of Collegiate Schools of Architecture, located throughout the United States and Canada.

8½" x 11", 285 pages   Stock no. 1778
ISBN: 0-87866-177-8 $11.95 paperback

Peterson's Guide to Undergraduate Engineering Study
David R. Reyes-Guerra and Alan M. Fischer

This comprehensive publication presents in-depth guidance plus all the detailed information necessary for students, parents, teachers, and counselors to compare 244 U.S. colleges that offer accredited bachelor's-level engineering programs (including computer science).

8½" x 11", 561 pages   Stock no. 1638
ISBN: 0-87866-163-8 $14.00 paperback

The American Film Institute Guide to College Courses in
Film and Television
Seventh Edition
Editor: Charles Granade Jr.
Associate Editor: Margaret G. Butt
Consulting Editor: Peter J. Bukalski,
      American Film Institute

A must for future cinematographers, audiovisual specialists, and media specialists, this guide contains the most up-to-date information available about the more than 7,600 courses in film and television offered by American colleges.

8½" x 11", 334 pages   Stock no. 1581
ISBN: 0-87866-158-1 $11.50 paperback

Jobs for English Majors and Other Smart People
John L. Munschauer

This book recognizes the realities of the job market for the generalist, the inexperienced, the career changer. The author offers down-to-earth advice about such common concerns as when to send and when not to send a résumé, how to identify alternative careers, and how to create a job when there is no advertised opening.

5½" x 8½", 180 pages   Stock no. 1441
ISBN: 0-87866-144-1 $6.95 paperback

Peterson's Guide to Engineering, Science, and Computer
Jobs 1983
Editor: Sandra Grundfest, Ed.D.

Acclaimed by faculty and placement advisers, this guide includes up-to-date information on over 1,200 manufacturing, research, consulting, and government organizations currently hiring technical graduates. In addition to focusing on the fast-growing high-technology job market, the book includes employers looking for business, liberal arts, and biology graduates. Updated annually.

8½" x 11", 787 pages (approx.)   Stock no. 2049
ISBN: 0-87866-204-9 $12.95 paperback

Where to Start: An Annotated Career-planning Bibliography
Third Edition
Madeline T. Rockcastle

Resources for career exploration, graduate study, and immediate employment in academic and professional areas. This book is published by Cornell University's Career Center and is updated yearly.

8½" x 11", 163 pages   Stock no. 1468
ISBN: 0-87866-146-8 $10.00 paperback

How to Order

These publications are available from all good booksellers, or you may order direct from **Peterson's Guides, Dept. 2, P.O. Box 3601, Princeton, New Jersey 08540.** Please note that prices are necessarily subject to change without notice.

- Enclose full payment for each book, plus postage and handling charges as follows:

Amount of Order	4th-Class Postage and Handling Charges
$1-$10	$1.25
$10.01-$20	$2.00
$20.01 +	$3.00

- For faster shipment via United Parcel Service (UPS), add $2.00 over and above the appropriate fourth-class book-rate charges listed.
- Bookstores and tax-exempt organizations should contact us for appropriate discounts.
- You may charge your order to VISA, MasterCard, or American Express. Minimum charge order: $15. Please include the name, account number, and validation and expiration dates for charge orders.
- New Jersey residents should add 5% sales tax to the cost of the books, excluding the postage and handling charge.
- Write for a free catalog describing all of our latest publications.